Modelling global change

Note to the reader from the UNU

Future Global Change and Modelling is an ongoing programme that aims to have the United Nations University serve as a forum on the megatrend of global change and structural transformation. This programme is a response to the need to evaluate recent changes in the perception and structure of the world's politics, economics, demography, technology, ecology, and ethics. Practitioners of futures research have, over the past few decades, developed an array of systematic and powerful methodologies in an effort to understand the range and probabilities of future global scenarios. The UNU brings together this international community of scholars to undertake futures studies of global change and incorporate a wide range of variables and methodologies to increase both the early warning and longer-term planning capacities of the UN system and policy makers in general.

This book is based on the first of a series of UNU conferences on Future Global Change and Modelling held in Tokyo in October 1991. Scholars and representatives from various UN agencies and leading research institutions from 17 countries discussed immediate and long-term world problems with simulation analysis by various model systems. Subsequent UNU conferences held under this programme include Arms Reduction: Economic Implications in the Post-Cold War Era, and Global Environment, Energy, and Economic Development.

Modelling global change

Edited by Lawrence R. Klein and
Fu-chen Lo

United Nations
University Press

TOKYO · NEW YORK · PARIS

United Nations University Press
The United Nations University, 53-70, Jingumae 5-chome,
Shibuya-ku, Tokyo 150, Japan
Tel: (03) 3499-2811 Fax: (03) 3406-7345
Telex: J25442 Cable: UNATUNIV TOKYO

UNU Office in North America
2 United Nations Plaza, Room DC2-1462-70, New York, NY 10017
Tel: (212) 963-6387 Fax: (212) 371-9454 Telex: 422311 UN UI

United Nations University Press is the publishing division of the United Nations University.

Typeset by Asco Trade Typesetting Limited, Hong Kong
Printed by Permanent Typesetting and Printing Co., Ltd., Hong Kong
Cover design by Kerkhoven Associates

UNUP-880
ISBN 92-808-0880-X
03500 P

Contents

Preface

The papers included in this volume were presented at the Tokyo Conference on "Global Change and Modelling," held in Tokyo from 29 to 31 October 1991. This conference was initiated together with the United Nations' Department of International Economic and Social Affairs and Soka University, under the United Nations University's programme on Future Global Change and Modelling, its first in an ongoing series of annual conferences designed to examine the megatrends of global change and help the United Nations in its efforts to respond to such trends.

The United Nations University, according to its Charter, is to devote its research to "pressing global problems of human survival, development, and welfare." Profound transformations in the perception and structure of world politics, economics, demography, technology, ecology, and ethics dictate that such change must be evaluated, and the necessary adjustments made. By publishing this volume, the UNU hopes to facilitate the promotion of awareness of global megatrends and response alternatives through global modelling and simulation studies.

In the closing years of the twentieth century, virtually all societies are wrestling with an acceleration and an intensification of change that are unparalleled in the course of human history. The end of the Cold War, as well as the increasing support for democratic, market-oriented, political and economic policies and solutions, are major factors that have spurred both the possibilities of global integration and the prospects for planned and targeted social change. Driving change, in addition to these factors, are continuing population growth and demographic changes, the globalization of science and technology, and a growing realization of the limitations of the global environment and resource base. The nations of the world are clearly moving towards the direction of increasing integration technologically, economically, and politically. The possibilities of global, regional, and national integration cutting across disparate social systems, ideologies, and cultures, present vast new opportunities for directing, shaping, and controlling future change in the world for the betterment of humankind.

Globalism is taking place through strong global integration and expansion of economic activities across national borders. The most recent global adjustment, however, has brought strong regionalism as well. The merger of the European Community and the European Free Trade Association, the emergence of NAFTA (North American Free Trade Agreement), and increased economic interdependence among the Asian Pacific nations reflect both trends. There is a possibility that this multi-polar development pattern will result in an uneven growth of the world economy in the coming decade.

On the other hand, the easing of East-West tension and the end of the Cold War offer great opportunities for disarmament and a growing convergence of views on effective approaches to economic and social development. In addition to the inclusion of the East European bloc into the world market system, the ending of the Cold War has given the superpowers the opportunity to release funds, or create a "peace dividend" that could be used for constructive purposes.

The development of technologies and their rate of dissemination and application are other determinants of future economic progress and global interdependence. Advances in micro-electronics, computers, telecommunications, new materials, biotechnologies and life sciences, and new energy sources have drastically transformed the global patterns of production, trade, management, and resource utilization. Because the rate of technological development is rising much more quickly in developed countries than in developing countries, the increasing technological gap will also become a prominent issue.

The changing ecological balance of our planet and its possible impact on the future of human prosperity has become one of the dominating challenges to the global future. The destruction of the world's environment continues at an alarming pace. Depletion of the ozone layer, global warming, transboundary air and water pollution, increasing desertification, and the losses of genetic diversity are some of the symptomatic threats to our global environment. Because these problems are not confined to individual countries, solutions will also require international cooperation.

In all of these areas we see a growing degree of global interdependence accompanying megatrends of change. Thus, there is an increasingly evident demand for models that incorporate a wide range of variables and methodologies in simulating global change in order to increase both the early warning and long-term planning capabilities of the UN system and policy makers generally.

Rather than a book on modelling methodology, this volume is an attempt to bring together large-scale global modelling groups and examine the applicability of their models and early warning systems in coping with the increasing interdependence and complexity of the world today. In doing so, the United Nations University hopes to identify new areas of collaboration and research in modelling activities in order to support policy initiatives to meet the challenges presented by current global trends.

Lawrence R. Klein
Fu-chen Lo

1

The modelling approach

Lawrence R. Klein

I. Some historical comments and methodological considerations

The United Nations constitute a global organization and their perspective on the world economy must transcend the interests of any single national state or restricted grouping of states. The model building approach to study of the world's economic problems does not constitute a unique way of facing the issues, but it is a fruitful way, and it is the purpose of this conference to carry model building as far as possible at the present time.

Within model building there are different approaches and multiple objectives; therefore it is useful now to take stock, see where we stand, and try to look forward, both substantively and methodologically.

The predecessor organization, The League of Nations, was confronted with the prolonged world slump of the interwar years and called on Jan Tinbergen to light the way for systematic study of the business cycle through the construction of a model – in that case a model of the United States. The League looked at alternative approaches, too, and Tinbergen's book on business cycles in the United

States was a companion effort to Gottfried Haberler's survey of business cycle theories.[1]

The League's effort, very advanced and forward looking for its time, more than a half-century ago, is noteworthy for two reasons:

1. A general macroeconomic survey approach was used as well as formal modelling.
2. Tinbergen hoped to be able to synthesize Haberler's survey analysis, which was not *national*, and to be able to gain some general insight for the good of the world.

Now the entire database is much enlarged and exists on a global scale, thanks to organizations like the United Nations and its counterpart international economic bodies, and there is no need to focus on the model of a single country. Also, there is no need to focus on one type of model or even one type of economic analysis. Those gathered here, in this meeting under the auspices of the United Nations University are, however, committed, one way or another, to the approach of consistent and systematic model building. Within the broad framework of formal mathematical and statistical model building, the attitude prevailing here is to let many flowers bloom and enjoy the bouquet scents.

It should be remarked that even in the days of the League of Nations economists had the idea of global modelling in mind, even though Tinbergen and Haberler did not stress that avenue of research.

One of Tinbergen's associates, J.J. Polak,[2] conceived the idea of international model building with both trade and domestic activity displayed separately, while Folke Hilgert's studies of the network of world trade at the League showed the layout of interrelatedness in the exchange of goods among nations.[3] His work was important for global modelling but not self-contained in the same sense as Polak's.

After the reconstruction of the world economy that was destroyed during World War II, it has been fully recognized that global growth accelerated during the rapid expansion period of the 1960s. At the same time, the issues concerned with interrelatedness of national economies became clear. Experience during this period showed that world economic progress depended on the smooth working of the interdependent transmission mechanism, both for short-run stability and for longer-run development.

The technique of modelling the international industrial structure was pioneered by Wassily Leontief and developed further by others for studying technical progress, arms control (reduction), environment, and other economic issues where the sector levels interacted with overall macroeconomic activity to affect global outcomes, particularly for the medium to long run. When the world economy was hit by supply-side shocks in both food and fuel, we had to turn to inter-industry analysis in order to understand the problem as fully as possible. In this conference we have the presentation by Faye Duchin, which extends and updates Wassily Leontief's early world models to make the input/output analyses of environmental problems.

Towards the end of the 1960s, Project LINK was conceived as a means for studying the international transmission mechanism, first at the short-run cyclical level and eventually at all levels – medium term (up to five years), longer run (up to 10 years), and beyond goods trade to services, capital flows, and exchange rates. The fall of the Bretton Woods Agreement on fixed parities and the changes in terms of trade *vis-à-vis* energy producers were early issues that the LINK system had to cope with, while putting into place, for the first time, a fundamental econometric structure.

Systems dynamics, based on the sensational studies of the Club of Rome, introduced another tool for model builders. In many respects, the models of systems dynamics were like the more conventional econometric models of LINK, but they tended to be more aggregative, based on simpler relationships, less data intensive, and longer run in character. They did not have to possess all these properties, but the early versions did. Also, they were interdisciplinary, yet less firmly grounded in tight economic theory.

The interdisciplinary nature of systems dynamic models led researchers into agronomy, demography, energy, environment, and many other fields. The rise of energy problems on a global scale in 1973–1974 (first oil shock), 1979–1980 (second oil shock), 1986 (oil price break), 1990–1991 (Gulf War) stimulated a great deal of modelling work for energy alone, not just is a modular component of a larger systems dynamic model. For the United States economy many energy scenarios from different models have been studied in the Energy Modelling Forum of Stanford University,[4] and the LINK system has often been used for oil pricing, embargoes, and other scenarios, even more recently for carbon taxes and other energy-related analyses.[5]

The model presented by Drs. H. Pitcher and J. Edmonds focuses on a particular environmental issue, namely, the emission of greenhouse gases, but the investigation of this problem is strongly related to energy analysis. A major source of greenhouse gas comes from energy use in connection with the internal combustion engine. They have built a model for their central problem, but they must deal with crude oil extraction, refining, fuel conversion to electric power, etc. In addition, they must go beyond strict energy modelling and deal with agriculture where greenhouse cause and effect plays a major role. Theirs is not a strictly econometric approach but has some aspects of that subject. From the policy side, carbon limitation through taxation is important, as in a purely econometric model, but their central problem of substance becomes menacing over a long period of time. Thus, they are not simply trying to look ahead to the start of the twenty-first century (year 2000+) but are aiming for an extrapolation horizon at year 2100. For such a long-term perspective, purely econometric estimates of relations in force during the last 25–50 years are clearly inadequate. Theirs is a truly challenging problem, and they do not shirk it only because of lack of a very long-term database; they tackle the problem as best they can but fully realize the limitations.

Another analysis of carbon reduction is examined in the paper by Drs. Piggott and Whalley. A distinctive feature of their analysis is that they use a Computable General Equilibrium model (CGE). There are interesting contrasts in the programme of this conference. On the one hand we have the purely econometric approach, which is data intensive; on the other hand, the large collection of sample data forms the basis for model estimation.

Simultaneously we have CGE models that exhibit market clearing throughout the economy and fulfilment of the marginal conditions of neoclassical economics. Where possible, the parameters of the model are statistically estimated from observable data, but this is generally not possible for a large part of the typical CGE model, so judgemental methods or simple ratio estimates are used where needed. This is the contrast with conventional econometric modelling.

The CGE approach does not lend itself well to probability statements based on statistical inference, but it can be checked against data, given enough time for simulation testing. It can also be tested for consistency with propositions from economic theory. An economy is rarely, if ever, in equilibrium, therefore the method is based on the assumption that the economy tends towards equilibrium, fluctuates about equilibrium, or that it is useful to know the economy's numerical properties in equilibrium. It is most useful as a tool for longer-run analysis because short-run movements of an economy are demonstrably not frequently near equilibrium conditions.

In some respects, CGE modelling can be said to provide a substitute for data, where extensive calibration is not possible. For present-day analyses of formerly socialist or communist economies it is frequently said that there is not statistical experience or databases for the analysis of the situation – either the prevailing situation or the target situation. It is, therefore, suggested that we turn to economic theory instead of to data for policy guidance and understanding of what is taking place. In this spirit, it would be natural to turn to CGE analysis to determine where the economy might be tending if market forces are given enough time to do their work.

The FUGI model is mainly like the LINK system in being an econometric model that is strongly based on sample data, but it is larger and has some characteristics like systems dynamic and CGE models. The EPA model is, in one sense, more restrictive in coverage than the LINK system but covers some international economic aspects in more detail – mainly the detail about the financial sector. In this respect, it resembles the Federal Reserve model.

It is used in the context of this conference to examine the impact of a cut in United States' budget deficits on the world economy. It is a well-executed analysis and reaches attractive conclusions about the effectiveness and need for international policy coordination. It also shows what are now consensus results on the fulfilment of the Marshall-Lerner conditions for most industrial countries and on the relative size of "own" versus cross-country multipliers for fiscal policy changes. This paper also looks at impulse relationships between fiscal changes in industrial countries and response in performance of developing countries, whether primary producers or newly industrializing countries.

The other models presented at this conference come under the heading of systems dynamic models and general simulation models, to some extent prepared in order to deal with particular problems.

II. Some problems of substance

While we are here to search for good techniques with which to analyse world problems, we are also deeply interested in the problems themselves, to see what can be done early on, to deal with vexing issues. In that respect, it should be noted that we do not have the luxury of a long waiting period for dealing with certain problems that are generated by fast moving world events. For the most part, we are taking a long view of global issues and can spend some time looking for the right methodology, but the reconstruction of Eastern Europe and the Soviet Union poses urgent problems, as do some of the current issues concerning arms control.

Some of the urgent and immediate problems are:

1. absorption of formerly centrally planned economies into the mainstream of global economics;
2. capital flows to finance investment needs for reconstruction, for third-world development, and for regular ongoing issues of development in the industrial countries;
3. policy coordination among the major economic powers, for global sterilization;
4. terms of North-South economic relations.

Longer-run problems to be considered are:

i. greenhouse and other environmental dangers of industrialization;
ii. technical progress;
iii. energy availability;
iv. arms reduction, arms trade, arms control of strategic weapons.

1. Economic reform in Eastern Europe and the Soviet Union

There has already been significant economic reform in China and entry into the main world economic organizations has already taken place. Economic reform has been modelled, and analytical studies of China are underway. It is to be expected that similar progress will occur in dealing with the countries of Eastern Europe. The reform process will take a long time to be completed, but the immediate problems of inflation, unemployment, and trade deficits are now visible and must be studied carefully with the help of quantitative methods, some of which were put to work in the Chinese case.

The Soviet Union has lagged behind both China and Eastern Europe in starting a significant reform process. Problems could get out of control at an early stage; that is why they are classified as urgent.

The modelling problem is inherently difficult. In China, some work experience was gained from the use of new databases that began in 1978, the starting date for economic reform. The old databases are of uncertain quality and refer to a different institutional framework. They are not useless but have limited value. The situation is not as bad in Eastern Europe and the Soviet Union as far as data are concerned, but they do have severe limitations. Some new data can be prepared from sampling surveys but a problem lies in the disorder associated with the reform process. The economic transition was more orderly in China. It will take a few years, at least, before the models for the Eastern European countries and the Soviet Union take definite shape.

To some extent CGE, input-output, and systems dynamic models, which have quite different data requirements may be used to good advantage.

2. Capital flows

There are large scale needs for financial capital in all parts of the world. The developing countries are, as ever, in need of funding for growth that will provide better living conditions, in some cases just to forestall famine. These needs are all the more urgent in areas that carry heavy debt burdens from 10 to 15 years ago. Other areas have been badly hurt by war. The transforming economies just mentioned above have extremely great funding needs in order to transform their economies. The rest of the world is always trying to grow and improve their lot and cannot be expected to channel all available resources to developing countries or to countries undergoing reform. All people together must try to save, improve productivity, and use investments wisely. In addition, receiving countries must be good hosts for incoming capital. They must do what they can to encourage and support the flow.

In an absolute sense, there is no such thing as capital shortage. Capital markets work efficiently and smoothly, more so than ever before in the global financial market place; so markets do clear. Capital supply equals capital demand, and the relevant markets adjust rather quickly to wipe out discrepancies, but the issue is – at what interest or yield rates? In this sense, creditor countries or investing countries have to try to be as generous as possible and to promote financial policies that are conducive to world growth. That means to try to keep interest rates low – certainly lower than they are now in major financial markets. These issues are addressed in the paper submitted by the EPA world model group.

Countries that are badly in need of capital infusion are now lowering the barriers to foreign investment, permitting majority ownership from abroad, restriction of earnings, convertibility of currency, joint ventures, and joining international organizations that have strict and formal rules of political-economic conduct.

In contrast to the proliferation of debt-burden scenarios that have been studied in the past, we are turning now to positive expansionary scenarios.

3. Policy coordination

In a sense creditor-debtor changes in attitudes, legal restraints, and market reform are all aspects of policy coordination, but the principal meaning of that expression in the present context refers to efforts (or lack thereof) among the leading industrial nations to coordinate their monetary, fiscal, and commercial policies among themselves. Coordination does not mean sameness of policies; it means the *dovetailing* of policies. At one time, it meant more prudent fiscal policy by the United States, offset by more liberal monetary policy. Simultaneously, there was a call for more liberal monetary *and* fiscal policy by Japan, Germany, and some other West European countries. Now, some of the West European countries have fallen into inflationary and other traps; so they must be more cautious. West Germany, in particular, assumed such a heavy burden in absorbing East Germany that it must restrain fiscal policy and, at best, try to refrain from being too tight on monetary policy.

In any event, policy coordination calls for constant vigilance for good forecasting of the global and domestic economy, together with the implementation of policies in concert with partner industrial nations to keep world economic conditions stable. The present recession in some major countries, together with a slowdown in others, has made it difficult for export marketing by countries who need to earn foreign exchange for growth and reform.

4. Terms of trade

Relative prices of heavily traded international commodities always fluctuate. These prices are of particular importance to primary producers among the developing countries. They are also of great importance in determining inflationary tendencies among industrial countries.

At the present time, prices of most major international raw materials are relatively low and unfavourable for primary producers who must cope with world inflation in importing finished goods for use in consumption or production. The terms of trade help to restrain world inflation but not to eliminate it. For a spell, after the invasion of Kuwait in 1990, oil exporters reaped a benefit on world markets, but oil prices have receded a great deal in 1991. Grains, fibres, tropical fruits, tropical beverages, metals, and other industrial materials are not at their high points now. Many have receded significantly. If the world economy shifts into more solid recovery, and if primary producers become more efficient, they stand to gain some fresh purchasing power through revival of export markets for primary commodities. The prices of these goods are capable of making wide swings on very short notice.

One way or another, the four short-run problems have been studied by model analysis in recent years, and some of the problems are being addressed at this UN Conference. They are all capable of simulation study through the various models assembled here.

It is useful, now, to look at some of the longer-range problems that can be studied in other simulations.

i. *Greenhouse and other environmental dangers*

Global warming through greenhouse gas emissions and other environmental hazards are now getting increasing attention. Many environmental problems are evident and deserve immediate attention through some study. Some are of immediate concern such as nuclear power plant failure, but others are best dealt with over a long time-span. Air, water, and land pollution can be met with taxation, subsidy, penalty, fees, etc. These are good subjects for medium- and long-term simulation. Traffic density, noise pollution, and congestion are best studied in special purpose models. Others are more speculative. A present topic of scientific and technological interest is global warming, mainly through the greenhouse effect. There are several different ways of modelling ozone depletion, one of the most common being through analysis of production of CO_2 emissions into the atmosphere, which calls for policy to curtail or regulate motor-car usage as well as other sources of the emissions.

The modelling of the emissions, though not overly simple, is relatively straightforward and understood. It is more difficult to attain good agreement on whether the greenhouse effect is inevitable or seriously devastating. Scientific opinion varies about this matter. That is no excuse for lack of study in order to be in a state of preparedness, but it does suggest that specific policy recommendations that are going to have a significant effect on global economic life should be treated with severe questioning. The National Academy of Sciences of the United States has, in a short span of time, sponsored studies of

Nuclear Winter, to warn about dangers of lowering earth's temperature and studies of global warming, and to warn about dangers of rising temperatures on earth. It is difficult to say which way things might go, and heavy investment in model-building efforts should not be undertaken until we are more certain where the problem lies. These uncertainties should not stand in the way of scenario analysis from models that are already available for the purpose, but they should lead us to keep the problem in proper perspective. The paper by Faye Duchin discusses the economics and technology of these issues. She skilfully combines economic and technical information to generate estimates of emissions to the year 2000, in different regions of the world.

ii. *Technical progress*

Scientific advances are always in the pipeline, coming from ongoing research. Sometimes they come from an organized, concerted effort but more normally from early professional efforts of scientists and technologists. These new ideas get translated, with a certain amount of delay, into economic *innovations*.

Input-output models that have access to engineering specifications, systems dynamic models with explicit technical change in specific industrial sectors, and econometric or CGE models with total factor productivity gains built into numerical production functions provide a basis for studying the effects of technical progress. This factor is important for improving economic efficiency and thereby holding back inflation. Environmental protection adds costs to the production of goods and services. A way of mitigating or overcoming these costs is through technical progress; and therefore we have an important ingredient for modelling. Even if most economic models are not very good at predicting the pace of technical progress, we are sure that it is present, and through simulation of alternatives we can take into account its effect on the economy.

iii. *Energy availability*

The treatment of energy in economic models is similar to the treatment of environmental protection and technical progress. It is mainly a long-run problem because there is an abundance of energy presently available. The question is whether availability will be ample in five or 10 years' time.

When oil prices rose, following the invasion of Kuwait, models were able to assess the inflationary and money-market effects right away. The overall recessionary impact became evident from the start. Models could not predict in advance that Saudi Arabia, Venezuela, and other producers could quickly make up for oil that was lost because of the conflict, but they could respond to immediate price rises on spot and futures markets, and these generated the recessionary movements.

It has been widely expected that oil prices would tend to rise about mid-decade (1990s). If the Americans and others continue to be profligate in energy consumption, it seems likely, on the basis of expert opinion, to expect pressure for another round of price rises by about 1995. This event can be studied quite well in the energy and more general economic models being used in this conference. Barring some major new discoveries and intensive exploitation of existing wells, we can look for concern with rising energy prices for about a decade, at least. Energy taxes, encouragement of conservation, development of fuel alternatives, and other policies can be looked at through model simulations. By now these are classical and tractable problems for running through model simulations, especially from the models of the global economy.

iv. *Arms reduction*

The initial announcements of the ending of the Cold War immediately stimulated thinking about a peace dividend. This was mainly based on the break-up of the Warsaw Pact (WTO) and even of the Soviet Union. The reduction of conventional forces in Europe (CFE) and the limitation of strategic arms (START) gave people confidence that a sizeable peace dividend could be generated by cutting back defence spending by the United States, the Soviet Union, other NATO and WTO countries together.

The surreptitious arming of Iraq, the invasion of Kuwait, the break-out of hostilities in Yugoslavia, and similar events changed the thinking about arms reduction and the ending of large deliveries of modern weapons to developing countries (from NATO countries, WTO countries, and two military superpowers). After a set-back of some months, the aim of defence cut-backs has taken hold again. There will be some reductions, a few have already occurred, but President Bush and other hawkish leaders have warned that an uncertain world environment requires that the United States defence budget, for example, should not be reduced beyond the modest proposals that have been made so far.

The peace dividend is very much alive, but lobbied against by members of the military-industrial complex. There will probably be some reduction because a Soviet threat is no longer possible. As much as \$40–\$60 billion per year can be cut from the United States defence budget. If this sum were appropriately matched by ability and willingness to cut back on a global basis, there could be a world peace dividend as large as \$200 billion per year, by the end of 1995 or 1996. This would be a major step by the United States and if followed in both the industrial and developing parts of the world, the capital shortfall could be significantly alleviated. Also, many countries could choose an economic trade-off between military and civilian capital outlays in such ways as to promote continuing peace and add to civilian output. This kind of choice will be available to all countries in the spectrum of development – from rich to poor, or advanced to developing.

Notes

1. J. Tinbergen, *Business Cycles in the United States of America, 1919–1932* (League of Nations, Geneva, 1939). G. Haberler, *Prosperity and Depression*, (League of Nations, Geneva, 1939).
2. J.J. Polak, "International Propagation of Business Cycles," *Review of Economic Studies* 6: 79–99 (February 1939).
3. Folke Hilgert, *The Network of World Trade* (League of Nations, Geneva, 1942).
4. Energy Modelling Forum, Working Group, "Macroeconomic Impacts of Energy Shocks: An Overview," Stanford, September 1984, in D.G. Hickman, H.G. Huntington, and J.A. Sweeney, *Macroeconomic Impacts of Energy Shocks* (North-Holland, Amsterdam, 1987).
5. Robert Kaufman and Peter Pauly, "Global Macroeconomic Effects of Carbon Taxes," (Boston University and University of Toronto, May 1991).

2

Project LINK: Past, present, and future

Bert G. Hickman and Kenneth G. Ruffing

Project LINK is at once a cooperative international research project and a forum for research on econometric methods and applications to the world economy. Its major accomplishment has been the development of a global model system which links together macroeconometric models for 79 countries or regions. The LINK model is used regularly to forecast the level and geographic distribution of world activity and trade and to analyse the impact of economic shocks or alternative policy scenarios on the international community.

Evolution of the LINK system: A capsule history[1]

The project was initiated in 1968 under the sponsorship of the Committee on Economic Stability and Growth of the US Social Science Research Council, acting at the suggestion of one of its members, Rudolf R. Rhomberg (International Monetary Fund), that it foster research on the international transmission mechanism. With the active involvement of committee members Robert A. Gordon (University of California at Berkeley), Bert G. Hickman (Stanford University), and Lawrence R. Klein (University of Pennsylvania), a small planning group was convened at Stanford University in July 1968 to launch the project. Included in the original system were models of Belgium (Jean Waelbroeck, Free University), Canada (John A. Sawyer, University of Toronto), West Germany (Wilhelm Krelle, Bonn University), Japan (Tsunehiko Watanabe, Kyoto University), the Netherlands (Petrus J. Verdoorn, Central Planning Bureau), the United Kingdom (R.J. Ball, London Business School) and the United States (Lawrence R. Klein). Professor Klein was named Project Co-ordinator and has been the intellectual and spiritual leader of LINK throughout its history.

The outcome of the initial planning meeting was a research strategy founded on four principles:

1. Each national model would be included in the form put forward by its resident econometric team, subject to group critique and the provision of necessary linkage elements.
2. The principal linkages would come initially through merchandise trade flows and prices, with services and capital flows to be added later.
3. Imports would be determined endogenously in each national model and exports would be allocated through a central trade matrix, with the world trade identity satisfied in the global solution.
4. The initial set of seven linked models would be expanded over time as model-building teams formed in other countries and joined the project. Group meetings would be held periodically to prepare forecasts, discuss research carried out by the various centres, and establish plans and priorities for future work.

This strategy has proved to be a prescient template for the successful evolution of the system. The first meeting of Project LINK was held in Hakone in September 1969 and the latest in Moscow in September 1991. The number of constituent models has increased elevenfold to 79. The system has grown not only in geographic detail but in the scope of endogenous international linkages, which now include interest and exchange rates in addition to trade flows and prices and will soon include invisibles in the current account and capital flows. Its size increased from 1,500 equations in 1972 to 3,000 in 1974, 5,000 in 1979, and 20,000 today.

National models

These fall into three principal groups: the developed market economies, the developing countries, and the centrally planned economies of Eastern Europe and the USSR. With regard to the first group, the number of indigenous industrialized country models increased from the original seven in 1969 to 11 in the early seventies (Ball 1973) and 13 in the mid-seventies (Waelbroeck 1976). By the mid-eighties all but four, and today all except two (Iceland and Ireland) of the OECD countries were represented by home-based models.

Project LINK was begun as a small system of existing developed-country models, with the primary objective of modelling the international transmission mechanism among the leading industrial countries. Even in the early years, however, the developing world was represented by simplified models built by the United Nations Conference on Trade and Development (UNCTAD), and there has been a steady expansion over LINK history in the geographic scope of third world modelling and the research agenda on third world problems and North-South interactions.

The UNCTAD models were initially simply reduced-form trade equations for 11 regional blocks, but in the early seventies these were replaced by structural macroeconomic models of Developing America, Developing Asia, Developing Middle East, and Developing Africa (Waelbroeck 1976, chapter 17). After the oil shock of 1973–1974, the UNCTAD regional models were disaggregated to distinguish between oil-importing and oil-exporting regions, and prices of primary commodities were endogenized to improve forecasts of worldwide inflation and the export earnings of the developing world (Glowacki and Ruffing 1979). During the early eighties, with advice from third world LINK participants, the research staffs at the United Nations and the Asian Development Bank, and Shinichi Ichimura, who had pioneered a sublinkage Pacific Basin model at Kyoto University, some 35 new models for individual developing countries were built for the system at LINK Central (University of Pennsylvania). One-third of these models have been replaced by newly constructed indigenous systems, in accord with standard LINK practice and models of seven African countries have been replaced by those built by the United Nations Department of International Economic and Social Affairs (Salvatore 1989).

The first-generation LINK system did not include countries of Eastern Europe, the USSR, or the socialist countries of Asia nor their contributions to world trade, owing to lack of experience with econometric models for these countries. A trade-flow model of the Council of Mutual Economic Assistance (CMEA) countries of Eastern Europe was built for LINK by UNCTAD in the early seventies, however, to be succeeded within a few years by macromodels of Bulgaria,

Czechoslovakia, the German Democratic Republic, Hungary, Poland, and Romania constructed by the staff of the Centre for Development Planning, Projections and Policies of the United Nations Secretariat (Costa and Menshikov 1979). The USSR was represented in LINK by a model developed in the United States by Wharton Econometric Forecasting Associates. A model of China was constructed for LINK by Lawrence J. Lau at Stanford University in the early eighties. During the mid-eighties, indigenous models of China, Hungary, and Poland were welcomed as LINK family members. In 1991, new models for Bulgaria, Czechoslovakia, the former German Democratic Republic, Romania and the USSR were constructed by Miroslav Gronicki representing the economic structure prevailing in those countries through 1989.

International linkages

Real trade flows were and remain the principal direct linkages among the constituent national models. The major research challenge in the early years was to show that an operational world model could be fabricated by linking the trade equations of national models. This was first demonstrated on the real side by development of the "Mini-LINK" algorithm in 1970–1971, which imposed the social-accounting requirement that the sum of imports predicted by the constituent models, given their predetermined variables and domestic activity levels, equals world trade. By 1972 the "Maxi-LINK" algorithm, which remains operational today, had been developed at LINK Central (Klein and van Peeterssen 1973). It improves on Mini-LINK by incorporating endogenous price adjustment as an equilibrating factor in world activity and trade and by ensuring the consistency of bilateral import and export flows in the world trade matrix.

This early work was closely related to existing techniques of (matrix) trade modelling, but with the important addition that by linking complete macroeconomic models through the trade model, Project LINK was in a position to deal directly with the transmittal of domestic disturbances abroad and with the effects of alternative policies on domestic and international activity.[2]

Modelling of exchange rates and capital flows became an increasingly important part of the LINK research programme following the breakdown of the Bretton Woods system in 1973 and the advent of floating exchange rates.[3] This work initially focused on providing endogenous explanations of the capital account and exchange rates in several of the constituent national models. Beginning in 1978, however, a series of submodels for exchange rate determination was introduced by LINK Central (Filatov and Klein 1981). The exchange rate submodel accepts inputs from the national models of selected market economies and feeds back exchange rates in an iterative procedure until convergence is achieved, playing a role analogous to that of the central trade matrix in accounting for trade flows.

Time horizon of the forecasts

In the early years of the Project forecasts and policy simulations were limited to the current year and one additional year, but as the system was expanded to include models of many developing countries interest in analysing medium-term macroeconomic issues deepened. During 1981, on an experimental basis, a 10-year projection was calculated at the request of the United Nations in the context of their work in elaborating an International Development Strategy for the decade of the 1980s. (Filatov et al. 1983). During 1982 the time horizon of simulations was routinely extended to five years. Beginning in 1991 a 10-year baseline projection has been made a regular feature of the Project. As should be obvious, it is only with respect to the two-year forecast that the LINK model might be appraised in terms of forecasting accuracy. The medium-term extensions are meant to provide a baseline "surprise-free" projection based on the assumptions of unchanged policy stances and minimal disturbances in international financial and commodity markets.

Project LINK as a cooperative research organization

Background

Project LINK is a cooperative, non-governmental, international research activity. The Project organizes two meetings a year at which 100 participants discuss both emerging world economic issues and LINK forecasts, as well as alternative scenarios analysing the impact on the forecasts of different economic policy assumptions or hypothetical market disturbances. The meetings also include technical sessions on econometric methodologies applicable to national or international modelling. From time to time special sessions or conferences are organized jointly with other international modelling groups.[4]

Following each LINK meeting, usually held in March and September, revised forecasts are prepared based on the discussions and mailed to project participants. In 1989 most of the central support functions of Project LINK were transferred from the University of Pennsylvania to the United Nations Department of International Economic and Social Affairs (DIESA). The Department has long been associated with Project LINK in econometric modelling and database management and regularly makes use of LINK forecasts in preparing United Nations reports on the short- and medium-term outlook for the world economy.

Organizational structure

An Executive Committee which oversees the general direction of Project LINK including decisions about new members, comprises Hickman (Chair), Klein, Peter Pauly (University of Toronto), representatives of DIESA and UNCTAD, and rotating co-opted members of the Project. It coordinates LINK-related research activities at participating national institutions and shares responsibility with the United Nations for organizing the biannual LINK conferences. The operations of the United Nations LINK Centre are supported by two academic centres, one at the University of Pennsylvania, headed by Klein, and another at the University of Toronto, directed by Pauly. The Project seeks support from research foundations, international agencies, and national banks and governments for specific research objectives.

A list of participating institutions that contribute constituent models to Project LINK, regularly undertake LINK-related research, or actively participate in the deliberations at LINK meetings is attached as Annex 1. Annex 2 provides information on the participating national models.

Theoretical structure of the LINK system

National models

The models of the developed market economies included in LINK are basically large disaggregated IS-LM systems of behavioural equations on the demand side and include supply structures featuring production and factor demand functions, labour supply equations,

Phillips-curve determination of wage rates, and mark-up pricing equations. Some incorporate considerable industry detail via input-output relationships. Some may be solved either with adaptive or rational expectations on key variables. Most are large models comprising 200 or more equations. Fourteen, including all of the seven largest industrial countries, are quarterly models, but at present the quarterly solutions are aggregated to annual values during the linkage process.

The models of developing countries also bear a family resemblance. In general, industrial output is supply-constrained by available capital stock and non-fuel imports, and agricultural production is also highlighted and may be treated in considerable detail. Consumption and investment are demand related and may also depend on import availability. The aggregate price level is usually a function of real money balances and foreign prices. The determination of export prices is discussed below.

The models for most of the countries of Eastern Europe, the USSR, and the socialist countries of Asia are based on the net material product social accounting scheme. They too emphasize the production process and supply constraints in the determination of aggregate economic activity. Production and investment functions include imports as explanatory variables and are disaggregated by industry, agriculture, and other major sectors. Wages are plan-determined and prices, which are also mostly fixed by government authorities, are a function of unit labour costs and import prices. Most of these models share the assumption that the "official economy" (socialized sector) is in a state of permanent disequilibrium. Notably, in the markets for consumption goods and investment goods produced in the socialized sector as well as in the labour market, demand exceeds supply in nearly all periods. Methods of disequilibrium econometrics are applied as described in Charemza and Gronicki (1988).

The specifications of the national models vary considerably in individual details, despite the general family resemblance within each of the three groups. No attempt is made to force a common mould on the indigenous models, on the basis of the guiding LINK philosophy that each modelling team knows its own country best. The necessary exceptions to this rule concern the need for each national model to include endogenous predictions of export prices and import quantities on a specified minimum level of disaggregation for the international trade linkages.

Trade linkages

A typical national model contains import demand functions and export price functions. Linkage of the national models through merchandise trade flows consists in solving the set of national models simultaneously, recognizing explicitly that one country's imports must be partner countries' exports, and that one country's import price must be a weighted average of the export prices of its supplying countries.

In the LINK model the explanation of real trade flows is decomposed into two stages.[5] First, the import-demand functions in the national models are used to explain their real imports. Given the imports of each country, the trade-share matrix is then used to derive the sum of the exports of each country to all of its trading partners.

The typical import equation in the ith national model is

$$m_i = m_i[y_i, (e_i \cdot pm/p)_i, z_i], \tag{1}$$

where m is real imports, y is real GDP or other domestic activity variable, p is the domestic price level and pm the import price index in the numeraire currency, which in the case of the LINK model is the US dollar, e is the exchange rate in local currency units per dollar, and z is a vector of other variables affecting imports, including lagged values of the dependent or independent variables. This is a structural demand function, homogenous in degree zero in prices and money incomes. Imports are assumed to be in infinitely elastic supply to country i, so that pm is exogenous to each country model. Exchange rate determination will be discussed below.

Now let the trade share matrix $[\alpha_{ij}]$ be defined as

$$\alpha_{ij} = x_{ij} \Big/ \sum_i x_{ij} = x_{ij}/m_j, \tag{2}$$

where x_{ij} is the constant-dollar exports from the ith country to the jth country and m_j is the total constant-dollar imports of the jth country. Thus, α_{ij}, is the share of the ith country's exports in the jth country's imports. Then the total export volume of the ith country is given by

$$x_i = \sum_j x_{ij} = \sum_j \alpha_{ij} m_j. \tag{3}$$

Similarly, the import price of the jth country is given by

$$pm_j = \sum_i \alpha_{ij} px_{ij}, \tag{4}$$

a weighted index of the export prices of its supplying countries. Note that:

$$pm_j = \sum_i \alpha_{ij} px_i \tag{4a}$$

if we assume there is no price discrimination in exports across markets.

For a predetermined share matrix $[\alpha_{ij}]$ and given m, the vector of imports into the national models, x, the corresponding vector of exports, is uniquely determined by equation (3). In particular, the sum of the x_i values is equal to the sum of the m_i values, and the total world trade identity is satisfied. Similarly, for a given px vector, pm is uniquely determined by equation (4) or (4a). To ensure consistency in the simultaneous solution of the national and trade models, any export demand or import price functions that may exist in individual stand-alone national models are suppressed in the solution algorithm. Instead, exports and import prices predicted with the share matrix are fed back to the national models. This will cause adjustments in the endogenous variables of the country models, including both imports and export prices. On the basis of this new information, the exports and import prices are updated again, using the trade share matrix. This process is continued until convergence is achieved.

Several routes exist by which changes in foreign prices can affect domestic prices and quantities in the LINK country models. (1) Import prices are direct arguments in the equations for the sectoral final demand deflators, with coefficients depending primarily on the import content of the goods in question and the degree to which the prices of domestically produced substitutes are affected by import competition. (2) In most of the models, import-led increases in consumer goods prices will induce additional wage increases and raise unit labour costs and prices generally. (3) Changes in the relative price of imported and domestic goods affect real imports and exports, trade balances, and domestic absorption at given income levels, with resulting multiplier effects on prices and incomes, in conformity with the elasticities approach to equilibration of payments imbalances. In accordance with the absorption approach to balance-of-payments adjustment and the Keynesian aggregate demand framework, real incomes and trade balances may also vary as a result of income-autonomous shifts in exports or imports, and import leakages may transmit income fluctuations abroad. In many of the models of developing countries and the formerly centrally planned economies, imports appear as arguments in aggregate supply equations.

A basic hypothesis originally maintained in Project LINK is that exports of goods are distinguishable by country of origin and are imperfect substitutes for one another and for domestic goods in any individual import market.[6] This implies that the real import shares α_{ij} will vary with changes in the relative prices of exports of the various supplying countries. Much early LINK research was therefore devoted to developing new approaches to the endogenous determination of trade shares and export demands as functions of changes in relative prices. The first approach was a modified version of a linear expenditure system by Klein and van Peeterssen which related the total nominal exports of each country to a weighted average of partner country nominal imports, with weights given by the known pre-forecast matrix of trade shares, and to the price of the exports of the country relative to a trade-weighted average of competitors' prices. In the second approach, Moriguchi modified the trade share matrix by relative price changes among export competitors and assumed the same elasticity of substitution of a particular exporting country across all import markets. These two approaches are compared in papers by Moriguchi (1973) and Klein et al. (1975). The third approach, co-authored by Hickman and Lau (1973), also explains changes in the market shares by relative price movements, but it assumes the same elasticity of substitution among all exporters in any country's import market, building on the theoretical model of a CES demand system by products distinguished by place of origin in Armington (1969).

In the LINK system merchandise trade is disaggregated into four classes with a separate share matrix for each: food and agricultural products (SITC 0 + 1), raw materials (SITC 2 + 4), fuel and lubricants (SITC 3), and manufactured products (SITC 5–9). The export predictions for the primary product groups 0 + 1, 2 + 4, and 3 have from the beginning been based on the "naive model" of constant *nominal* market shares, so that the real shares vary with relative export prices with an imposed elasticity of substitution of unity.

The Klein-van Peeterssen export demand function was the original method used for manufactured goods in Maxi-LINK solutions, in combination with an RAS adjustment to the previous year's trade share matrix to ensure that the identity

$$X = AM, \tag{5}$$

where $A = [\alpha_{ij}]$ and X and M are the vectors of the values of exports and imports respectively, is satisfied in the current period. This method was abandoned in the early eighties however, when the LINK system was greatly expanded by the addition of the 35 new models for developing countries and the data problems and computational burdens of re-estimating the LES export functions were judged to be greater than the likely benefits in terms of accuracy of the Maxi-LINK solutions. The current system is therefore solved with constant value share matrices for all trade categories.[7]

While this procedure was judged to be satisfactory over a time horizon as short as two years, it is clearly not satisfactory for projections over a longer period of time and work has now begun on estimating a new trade-share model. In the meantime a computer algorithm has been developed which accepts exogenous assumptions regarding changing trade shares of a subset of countries (e.g. fast growing exporters of manufactures, the countries in transition in Eastern Europe, and the USSR) and modifies all other trade shares proportionately so as to preserve consistency in the modified matrices.

The export prices determined in the national models drive the inflation rate of world exports in the linked system, just as trade quantities are driven by the real import demand functions in the national models. The prices of primary products are basically determined in the developing country models, with appropriate regard for external influences (Glowacki and Ruffing 1979). The unit value index of SITC category 3 is dominated by oil, which is assumed in the oil exporting developing countries to adjust proportionately to the price of exports of manufactures in the developed countries. Export unit values of non-oil exporting developing countries' areas dominate SITC categories $0 + 1$ and $2 + 4$ and are related to a set of commodity prices which in turn are determined by reduced-form equations dependent on commodity output and the growth and inflation rates of the developed market economies.[8]

The prices of manufactured exports (SITC 5–9) are largely determined in the developed country models by domestic cost factors and by import prices, so that they are dominated by local conditions in the various OECD nations.

Exchange rates

Monetary linkages are implemented directly for interest rates among some national models and through an exchange rate submodel for the major industrial countries. The exchange rate subsystem is based on a multi-country portfolio-balance asset market model with long-run exchange-rate expectations dependent on relative prices and current-account positions (Pauly and Petersen 1986). Reduced-form equations determine the bilateral dollar spot rates for Belgium, Canada, France, Germany, Italy, Japan, and the United Kingdom. The arguments for the spot rate include relative interest rates, relative consumer prices, and the current account positions. The United States is represented by an effective exchange rate index based on a trade-weighted average of the various bilateral rates.

Other linkages

Another feature of the LINK system is that any variable included in any national model may be used as an argument in any endogenous equation in any other model. In a single country model, these "foreign variables" are exogenous. After linkage, these will be determined endogenously in the Maxi-LINK simulation. For example, local currency/US dollar exchange rates are used directly in the German model (for 11 countries) and in the Canadian model (three countries). US interest rates are also used in computing interest payments on external debt for 34 developing country/regional models.

In the Canadian model, extensive use is made of variables generated by the US model as arguments in various equations, including US consumption of motor vehicles, real GNP, auto consumption deflator, GNP deflator, wholesale price index, index of hourly earnings and the Moody AAA corporate bond rating. The Canadian model also uses wholesale price indices from the German, Japan, and UK models.

The Japanese model also makes extensive use of US model variables, including real personal consumption expenditure, real GNP, personal consumption deflator, GNP deflator, producers' price index, export and import unit values and the US 10-year bond yield.

Dynamic properties of the LINK system

In this section we use recent simulations of the LINK system to illustrate the responses of economic activity at home and abroad to fiscal and monetary shocks in the G7 countries. Two simulations are evaluated for *unilateral* shocks originating in each of the seven countries. The baseline is provided by the LINK forecast for 1988–1992 dated 1 May 1988. The fiscal shock is represented by a sustained reduction of real government purchases equal to 1 per cent of baseline GNP in each year. The monetary shock is an increase in money stock by 2 per cent above the baseline level in 1988 and 4 per cent above baseline thereafter. The money stock is held constant in all countries during the fiscal shock and in all except the originating country during the monetary shock. These are fully linked simulations of the entire LINK model, so they reflect all external interactions, including those with countries and regions not separately reported in the tables.

These are not meant to be realistic policy scenarios, since they ignore real-world coordination of fiscal and monetary policy and real-world interaction among national policies, and since few governments would be expected to sustain once-for-all policy shifts over a five-year horizon irrespective of the outcome. Rather, they are designed to reveal model properties, to appraise these properties for consistency with mainline macroeconomic theory as exemplified by the standard IS-LM model with sticky prices, and in so far as possible, to attribute the similarities and differences among the models to specific structural features.

It must be emphasized that the simulation results reflect the structural properties partly of the individual country models and partly of the linkage subsystems built by LINK Central. When a Maxi-LINK simulation of the entire multi-country model is executed, certain variables that may be endogenous in each individual country model are overridden by solutions from the central trade model and the central exchange-rate model. In particular, exchange rates, import prices, and export volumes are determined by the central subsystems rather than by equations in the country models themselves.

Domestic responses to a contractionary fiscal shock

The own and cross-country responses of real income (GNP or GDP) to a reduction in government spending are shown in table 1. These are elasticity multipliers, expressed as percentage changes from the baseline solution.[9] The own multipliers appear on the main diagonal and will be discussed first. The interpretive comments are based on an examination of key endogenous variables in the complete model simulations, which cannot be reproduced here for lack of space.

Table 1 **International elasticity multipliers for real income: Negative fiscal shock**

Year	CA	FR	GE	IT	JA	UK	US	SUM6[a]
				Canada				
1988	−1.3	−0.0	−0.0	−0.0	−0.0	−0.0	−0.0	−0.0
1989	−1.7	−0.0	−0.0	−0.0	−0.0	−0.0	−0.1	−0.1
1990	−2.1	−0.1	−0.0	−0.0	−0.0	−0.0	−0.1	−0.2
1991	−2.2	−0.1	−0.1	−0.1	−0.0	0.0	−0.1	−0.4
1992	−1.9	−0.2	−0.1	−0.1	−0.0	0.0	−0.1	−0.5
				France				
1988	−0.0	−0.8	−0.1	−0.1	−0.0	−0.0	−0.0	−0.2
1989	−0.0	−0.8	−0.1	−0.1	−0.0	−0.0	−0.0	−0.2
1990	−0.0	−0.7	−0.1	−0.1	−0.0	−0.0	−0.0	−0.2
1991	−0.0	−0.8	−0.1	−0.1	−0.0	0.0	−0.0	−0.2
1992	−0.0	−0.9	−0.0	−0.1	−0.0	0.0	−0.0	−0.1
				Germany				
1988	−0.0	−0.0	−1.1	−0.0	−0.0	−0.0	−0.0	−0.0
1989	−0.0	−0.1	−1.5	−0.1	−0.0	−0.0	−0.0	−0.2
1990	−0.0	−0.1	−1.6	−0.1	−0.0	−0.0	−0.0	−0.2
1991	−0.0	−0.0	−1.4	−0.1	−0.0	−0.0	−0.0	−0.1
1992	−0.0	−0.0	−1.3	−0.1	−0.0	0.0	−0.0	−0.1
				Italy				
1988	−0.0	−0.1	−0.1	−1.1	−0.0	−0.0	−0.0	−0.2
1989	−0.0	−0.1	−0.1	−1.3	−0.0	−0.0	−0.0	−0.2
1990	−0.0	−0.1	−0.1	−1.4	−0.0	−0.0	−0.0	−0.2
1991	−0.0	−0.1	−0.1	−1.5	−0.0	0.0	−0.0	−0.2
1992	−0.0	−0.1	−0.1	−1.4	−0.0	0.0	−0.0	−0.2
				Japan				
1988	−0.0	−0.0	−0.0	−0.0	−1.2	−0.0	−0.0	−0.0
1989	−0.0	−0.0	−0.0	−0.0	−1.5	−0.0	−0.0	−0.0
1990	−0.1	−0.0	−0.0	−0.0	−1.5	−0.0	−0.0	−0.1
1991	−0.1	−0.0	−0.0	−0.0	−1.5	−0.0	−0.1	−0.2
1992	−0.1	−0.0	−0.0	−0.0	−1.5	0.0	−0.1	−0.2
				United Kingdom				
1988	−0.0	−0.0	−0.0	−0.0	−0.0	−1.0	−0.0	−0.0
1989	−0.0	−0.0	−0.1	−0.0	−0.0	−1.1	−0.0	−0.1
1990	−0.0	−0.0	−0.1	−0.1	−0.0	−1.1	−0.0	−0.2
1991	−0.0	−0.0	−0.1	−0.1	−0.0	−0.9	−0.0	−0.2
1992	−0.0	−0.0	−0.0	−0.1	−0.0	−0.7	−0.0	−0.1
				United States				
1988	−0.7	−0.1	−0.1	−0.1	−0.2	−0.1	−1.8	−1.3
1989	−1.2	−0.2	−0.3	−0.2	−0.3	−0.2	−1.6	−2.4
1990	−1.4	−0.2	−0.3	−0.3	−0.3	−0.1	−1.1	−2.6
1991	−1.6	−0.3	−0.3	−0.4	−0.3	0.1	−1.0	−2.8
1992	−1.7	−0.3	−0.3	−0.4	−0.3	0.2	−1.2	−2.8

a. The sum of the cross-multipliers in each row.

The income multipliers are universally negative as expected. For all countries except the United States, the impact multipliers range narrowly between –0.8 and –1.3. In these countries, the underlying components of private domestic expenditure decline almost universally, but offsetting increases of net exports mitigate the impact on income and limit its decline to approximately the amount of the autonomous reduction in public consumption expenditure. The response in the US model is not qualitatively different, but it is quantitatively stronger at –1.8.

With the exception of Canada and the United Kingdom, financial crowding in is relatively unimportant as a factor mitigating the income-induced declines in investment and income, since interest declines are small, owing to elastic LM curves in the models. (If the models were more monetarist in character, of course, their LM locuses would be steeper, interest rates would respond sharply to unaccommodated fiscal shocks, and crowding in or out would occur on a larger scale.) Nor is there an offsetting increase in competitiveness, such as would occur from exchange depreciation under high capital mobility and reduced interest rates. This is because, again with the exception of Canada, the induced decline in import demand increases the trade balance, dominating the fall in interest rates and appreciating the currency. Real export demand weakens from the appreciation in most of the models, as it should, but by much less than the income-induced reduction in real imports.

In the Canadian case, the interest reduction does cause a depreciation, partly because of the substantial magnitude of the interest decline and partly because the interest differential has a large weight in the Canadian equation of the LINK exchange-rate model. The resulting imported inflation in turn augments the depreciation by increasing the price differential affecting the spot rate.

The predominant finding of appreciation under a negative fiscal shock is a distinctive characteristic of the LINK system, not found in most multinational models (Hickman 1988), which give exclusive or relatively large weight to interest differentials in their exchange rate equations. The lack of consensus on exchange rate modelling, however, does not reflect itself in a similar disparity concerning the domestic price, income, and interest rate responses, apart from amplitude. If the currency appreciates under a negative shock, the effect is to augment the initial downshift of the IS locus. If it depreciates, the downshift will be mitigated but not reversed.

Consumer prices decline gradually as expected in most of the models, but they rise moderately in Canada and are virtually unchanged in Italy (table 2). In Canada, the rise occurs despite increasing unemployment and falling wages, owing to imported inflation.

According to the IS-LM paradigm with sticky prices, the unemployment resulting from a negative shock should set in motion gradual wage-price reductions, which tend to restore output to its previous level via induced increases in real money balances, which reduce interest rates (Keynes effect) and in real wealth, which affect consumption expenditures positively at a given income level (Pigou effect). A study of table 1 indicates that these equilibrating forces are at best slow and weak. After two or three years, real income does recover somewhat in the models for Germany, the United Kingdom and the United States, but these are still far short of the pre-shock level by the fifth year, whereas income shows no sign of recovering in the models for France, Italy, and Japan. In the case of Canada, there is a slight recovery in the fifth year, but it cannot be due to equilibrating price behaviour, since prices are rising throughout the simulation horizon (table 2). In short, there is nothing in these simulations to suggest a degree of downward price flexibility in any of the countries sufficient for complete recovery from a negative expenditure shock over a five-year span. The absence of stronger equilibrating forces in these models is due primarily to their combination of elastic LM locuses and elastic aggregate supply schedules. The former characteristic mitigates interest rate responses and financial crowding out, whereas the latter makes for slow and gradual wage-price reactions, and correspondingly slow and gradual changes in real money balances and wealth. The small interest responses are also insufficient to induce offsetting shifts in exchange rates and competitiveness within the portfolio-balance exchange-rate model. When account is taken of estimated elasticities and adjustment lags in money demand functions, labour-market Phillips curves, mark-up price equations, and labour productivity in the empirical models, the equilibrating process is substantially weakened and the "long run" may be long indeed.

International transmission of a fiscal shock

Let us turn now to the cross-multipliers for real income in table 1. Incomes abroad decline almost universally on impact, owing to induced declines in exports to the home country, and for most receiving countries the declines are permanent. As a rule they are also negligible or small, since the impact of a disturbance at home is spread

Table 2 **International elasticity multipliers for consumer prices: Negative fiscal shock**

Year	CA	FR	GE	IT	JA	UK	US	SUM6[a]
				Canada				
1988	0.1	0.0	−0.0	−0.0	0.0	−0.0	−0.0	0.0
1989	0.2	0.0	−0.0	−0.0	0.0	−0.0	−0.0	−0.0
1990	0.3	0.0	−0.0	−0.0	−0.0	−0.0	−0.0	−0.0
1991	0.4	0.0	−0.0	−0.0	−0.1	−0.1	−0.0	−0.2
1992	0.7	0.0	−0.0	−0.1	−0.1	−0.2	−0.1	−0.5
				France				
1988	−0.0	0.0	−0.0	−0.0	0.0	0.0	−0.0	−0.0
1989	−0.0	−0.1	−0.0	−0.0	0.0	−0.0	−0.0	−0.0
1990	−0.0	−0.3	−0.0	−0.0	−0.0	−0.1	−0.0	−0.1
1991	−0.0	−0.4	−0.0	−0.0	−0.0	−0.1	−0.0	−0.1
1992	−0.0	−0.6	−0.0	−0.1	−0.0	−0.1	−0.0	−0.2
				Germany				
1988	0.0	0.0	−0.0	−0.0	0.0	0.0	0.0	0.0
1989	−0.0	0.0	−0.1	−0.0	0.0	0.0	−0.0	0.0
1990	−0.0	0.0	−0.3	0.0	−0.0	−0.0	−0.0	−0.0
1991	−0.0	0.0	−0.6	0.0	−0.0	−0.0	−0.0	−0.0
1992	−0.0	0.0	−0.8	0.0	−0.0	−0.0	−0.0	−0.0
				Italy				
1988	−0.0	0.0	0.0	−0.0	0.0	0.0	0.0	0.0
1989	−0.0	0.0	0.0	−0.1	0.0	0.0	−0.0	0.0
1990	−0.0	−0.0	−0.0	−0.1	−0.0	−0.0	−0.0	−0.0
1991	−0.0	−0.0	−0.0	−0.1	−0.0	−0.1	−0.0	−0.1
1992	−0.0	−0.0	0.0	−0.2	−0.0	−0.1	−0.0	−0.1
				Japan				
1988	−0.0	0.0	−0.0	−0.0	−0.0	0.0	−0.0	−0.0
1989	−0.0	0.0	−0.0	−0.0	−0.2	−0.0	−0.0	−0.0
1990	−0.0	0.0	−0.0	−0.0	−0.5	−0.0	−0.0	−0.0
1991	−0.1	0.0	−0.0	−0.0	−0.7	−0.0	−0.0	−0.1
1992	−0.1	0.0	−0.0	−0.0	−0.9	−0.1	−0.0	−0.2
				United Kingdom				
1988	−0.0	0.0	0.0	−0.0	0.0	−0.5	0.0	0.0
1989	−0.0	0.0	0.0	−0.0	0.0	−0.1	−0.0	0.0
1990	−0.0	0.0	0.0	−0.0	−0.0	−0.5	−0.0	−0.0
1991	−0.0	0.0	−0.0	−0.0	−0.0	−1.4	−0.0	−0.0
1992	−0.0	−0.0	−0.0	−0.0	−0.0	−1.9	−0.0	−0.0
				United States				
1988	−0.3	0.0	0.0	−0.0	−0.0	0.1	0.0	−0.2
1989	−0.6	0.0	−0.0	−0.0	−0.1	0.0	−0.1	−0.7
1990	−0.6	0.0	−0.0	−0.0	−0.2	−0.2	−0.2	−1.0
1991	−0.6	0.0	−0.0	−0.1	−0.3	−0.5	−0.3	−1.5
1992	−0.3	0.0	−0.0	−0.1	−0.3	−0.6	−0.5	−1.3

a. The sum of the cross-multipliers in each row.

over many trading partners abroad.[10] A US disturbance does affect other countries moderately, however, owing to its huge size in the world economy and the larger amplitude of its domestic multiplier. The impact of a US shock is especially large in Canada, with its heavy dependence on US trade and its close integration with US financial markets, but a US fiscal contraction noticeably affects the individual continental European countries as well, though much less than own-shocks do.[11]

The sum of the cross-multipliers for the six countries in each row is shown in the last column of table 1. These are the unweighted sums of the percentage responses in each country to the external shock and may differ substantially from a multiplier calculated from the percentage increase in the aggregate GNP of the six countries. The unweighted sums are preferable for present purposes, however. An increase of 1 per cent in, say, Canadian GNP, is as important to that country as the same percentage increase in, say, the United States, is to it, even though world GNP will be increased by a much smaller percentage in the former instance than in the latter.

Apart from the United States, it is apparent that the total foreign impacts of external disturbances within this particular group of trading partners are small. The external impacts would be larger, of course, if induced changes in other countries or regions outside the G7 group were taken into account. Those for Japan, in particular, would be larger were the Asian-Pacific region included in the tables.

It is noteworthy that the countries affected by the US fiscal shock do not show the same income profiles as are found in the United States itself. Thus, with the exception of the United Kingdom, foreign incomes decline monotonically despite the upturn in US income. This is because the domestic recovery does not interrupt the contraction of US imports, owing to the continuing appreciation of the dollar. As a rule, prices also decline in the countries experiencing a negative external shock, although frequently by negligible amounts (table 2). This is true even for the Canadian shock, in which the price level rose in the home country. One implication of the Canadian case is that the response of prices in the foreign countries to the external shock depends more on the effects of induced changes in their exchange rates and export demands than on the price changes occurring in the home countries.

Since home-country currencies generally appreciated under the negative fiscal shock, the partner countries experienced imported depreciations. This effect was insufficient, however, to reverse the downward pressure on foreign price levels from reduced export demands. In the case of the Canadian fiscal shock, of course, home-country depreciation added to the downward pressure on prices abroad.

Domestic reactions to an expansionary monetary shock

For given prices, a monetary expansion in the IS-LM model will shift the LM curve rightward, increasing income and reducing the interest rate along the IS locus. Under the assumption of high capital mobility, the exchange rate will depreciate unambiguously as a capital outflow is induced by the decline in the interest rate. It will tend also to depreciate in portfolio-balance formulations such as used in LINK, since the interest rate falls, prices are inflated, and the current account also deteriorates from the income expansion and the J-curve effect.

Turning now to the simulation results, we find that income does rise as expected in all models (table 3). The range of responses is wider than for the fiscal shock, with the impact multipliers ranging from 0.1 in the UK to 1.7 in the US model. Also as expected, the expansion is led in most countries by fixed investment, stimulated initially by reduced interest rates and reinforced by accelerator effects. Net exports also increase owing to the currency depreciation (although a small initial increase in the United States is soon reversed by income-induced import growth). The induced investment booms are relatively more important in Canada, Italy, Japan, and the United States, whereas the increase in net exports strongly dominates the results for Germany and the United Kingdom.

The price level responds positively as expected to the monetary stimulus in all countries save France, where the consumption deflator declines gradually throughout the simulation horizon. This anomalous outcome for France occurs partly because of the depressing effects of induced productivity gains on unit labour costs and partly owing to the inclusion of interest costs in the pricing equation. A large reduction in interest rates under a monetary stimulus directly reduces prices, which in turn induces wage declines through indexation, notwithstanding tightening labour markets.

With regard to the exchange rate, it depreciates as predicted in all the models, but in the case of the US shock, a strong import response

Table 3 **International elasticity multipliers for real income: Positive monetary shock**

Year	CA	FR	GE	IT	JA	UK	US	SUM6[a]
				Canada				
1988	0.7	−0.0	−0.0	0.0	−0.0	−0.0	−0.0	−0.0
1989	1.3	−0.0	−0.0	0.0	−0.0	0.0	−0.0	−0.0
1990	1.1	−0.1	−0.0	0.0	0.0	0.0	−0.0	−0.1
1991	0.9	−0.0	−0.0	0.0	0.0	0.0	−0.0	−0.0
1992	0.8	−0.0	0.1	0.0	0.0	0.0	−0.0	0.1
				France				
1988	−0.0	0.1	−0.0	0.0	−0.0	0.0	−0.0	−0.0
1989	−0.0	0.2	−0.0	0.0	−0.0	0.0	−0.0	−0.0
1990	−0.0	0.3	−0.0	0.0	−0.0	0.0	−0.0	−0.0
1991	−0.0	0.4	−0.0	−0.0	0.0	0.0	−0.0	−0.0
1992	−0.0	0.4	−0.0	−0.0	0.0	0.0	−0.0	−0.0
				Germany				
1988	−0.0	−0.0	0.4	−0.0	−0.0	0.0	−0.0	−0.0
1989	−0.0	−0.1	1.0	−0.1	−0.1	0.0	−0.0	−0.3
1990	−0.0	−0.1	0.8	−0.1	−0.0	0.0	−0.0	−0.2
1991	−0.0	−0.1	0.5	−0.1	−0.0	0.1	−0.0	−0.1
1992	−0.0	−0.1	0.5	−0.1	−0.0	0.1	−0.0	−0.1
				Italy				
1988	0.0	0.0	0.0	0.6	−0.0	0.0	0.0	0.0
1989	0.0	0.0	0.0	1.2	−0.0	0.0	0.0	0.0
1990	0.0	0.0	0.0	1.4	−0.0	0.0	0.0	0.0
1991	0.0	0.0	0.0	1.5	0.0	0.0	0.0	0.0
1992	0.0	0.0	0.0	1.4	0.0	0.0	0.0	0.0
				Japan				
1988	0.0	0.0	0.0	0.0	0.3	0.0	0.0	0.0
1989	0.0	−0.0	−0.0	0.0	0.5	0.0	0.0	0.0
1990	0.0	−0.0	−0.0	−0.0	0.5	−0.0	−0.0	−0.0
1991	−0.0	−0.0	−0.0	−0.0	0.4	−0.0	−0.0	−0.0
1992	−0.0	−0.0	−0.0	−0.0	0.4	0.0	−0.0	−0.0
				United Kingdom				
1988	−0.0	−0.0	−0.0	−0.0	−0.0	0.2	−0.0	−0.0
1989	−0.0	−0.0	−0.0	−0.0	−0.0	0.4	−0.0	−0.0
1990	−0.0	−0.1	−0.1	−0.1	−0.0	−0.2	−0.0	−0.3
1991	−0.0	−0.1	−0.1	−0.1	−0.0	−0.8	−0.1	−0.4
1992	−0.1	−0.1	−0.1	−0.1	−0.0	−1.1	−0.1	−0.5
				United States				
1988	0.3	0.0	0.1	0.0	0.1	0.1	1.7	0.6
1989	1.6	0.2	0.3	0.2	0.3	0.3	4.4	2.9
1990	2.5	0.4	0.6	0.5	0.6	0.3	3.5	4.9
1991	2.7	0.6	0.6	0.7	0.7	0.0	1.8	5.3
1992	3.1	0.8	0.8	0.8	1.1	−0.1	1.4	6.5

a. The sum of the cross-multipliers in each row.

Table 4 **International elasticity multipliers for consumer prices: Positive monetary shock**

Year	CA	FR	GE	IT	JA	UK	US	SUM6[a]
				Canada				
1988	0.1	0.0	−0.0	−0.0	−0.0	−0.0	−0.0	−0.0
1989	1.0	−0.0	−0.0	−0.0	−0.0	−0.0	−0.0	−0.0
1990	2.2	−0.0	−0.0	−0.0	−0.0	−0.1	−0.0	−0.1
1991	3.2	−0.0	−0.0	−0.0	−0.0	−0.1	−0.0	−0.1
1992	4.1	−0.0	−0.1	−0.0	−0.0	−0.1	−0.0	−0.1
				France				
1988	0.0	−0.0	−0.0	−0.0	0.0	−0.0	−0.0	−0.0
1989	−0.0	−0.0	−0.0	−0.0	0.0	−0.0	−0.0	−0.0
1990	−0.0	−0.2	−0.0	−0.0	0.0	−0.0	−0.0	−0.0
1991	−0.0	−0.3	−0.0	−0.0	0.0	−0.0	−0.0	−0.0
1992	−0.0	−0.5	−0.0	−0.1	−0.0	−0.0	−0.0	−0.1
				Germany				
1988	−0.0	−0.0	0.1	−0.1	0.0	−0.0	−0.0	−0.0
1989	−0.1	−0.0	0.5	−0.2	−0.0	−0.2	−0.0	−0.5
1990	−0.1	−0.0	0.7	−0.1	−0.0	−0.3	−0.0	−0.5
1991	−0.1	−0.0	0.9	−0.1	−0.0	−0.3	−0.0	−0.5
1992	−0.0	−0.0	1.0	−0.2	−0.0	−0.2	−0.0	−0.4
				Italy				
1988	0.0	−0.0	0.0	0.3	0.0	−0.0	−0.0	0.0
1989	0.0	−0.0	−0.0	0.5	0.0	−0.0	−0.0	−0.0
1990	0.0	−0.0	−0.0	0.5	0.0	−0.0	−0.0	−0.0
1991	0.0	−0.0	−0.0	0.5	0.0	−0.0	0.0	0.0
1992	0.0	−0.0	−0.0	0.5	0.0	0.0	0.0	0.0
				Japan				
1988	0.0	0.0	0.0	0.0	0.1	0.0	0.0	0.0
1989	0.0	0.0	0.0	−0.0	0.4	0.0	0.0	0.0
1990	−0.0	0.0	−0.0	−0.0	0.7	0.0	0.0	0.0
1991	−0.0	0.0	−0.0	−0.0	0.9	−0.0	−0.0	−0.0
1992	−0.0	0.0	−0.0	−0.0	0.9	−0.0	−0.0	−0.0
				United Kingdom				
1988	−0.0	−0.0	−0.0	−0.0	0.0	0.2	−0.0	−0.0
1989	−0.0	−0.0	−0.0	−0.0	0.0	1.3	−0.0	−0.0
1990	−0.0	−0.0	−0.0	−0.0	−0.0	3.1	−0.0	−0.0
1991	−0.0	0.0	−0.0	−0.0	−0.0	5.3	−0.0	−0.0
1992	−0.0	0.0	0.0	−0.0	−0.0	6.0	−0.0	−0.0
				United States				
1988	0.2	−0.0	−0.0	0.0	0.0	−0.0	0.0	0.2
1989	0.7	−0.0	0.0	0.1	0.1	−0.1	0.4	0.8
1990	1.3	−0.0	0.0	0.1	0.3	0.1	1.1	1.8
1991	1.5	−0.1	0.1	0.2	0.4	0.6	1.6	2.7
1992	1.4	−0.1	0.1	0.3	0.6	1.1	2.0	3.4

a. The sum of the cross-multipliers in each row.

to income growth reduces the trade balance despite the increase in competitiveness.

The domestic response of the models over the entire simulation span is only partly consistent with theoretical predictions that reduced unemployment will induce wage-price increases and depress income through the Keynes and Pigou effects. The exchange rate should rebound as interest rates rise during the equilibrating process, eroding the earlier gain in competitiveness. The process should stop when real income has returned to the baseline level, and the price level has risen in proportion to the exogenous increase in the money stock to restore real balances and the interest rate to their original levels.

There are distinct signs of an equilibrating process over the five-year span in four of the models. Income peaks in the second year for Canada, Germany, the United Kingdom, and the United States, and the subsequent contractions are accompanied by rising interest rates as predicted by the prototype model. The equilibrating process appears to be working with a long lag in the Italian model, with interest rates rising after the second year and income falling slightly in the fifth. There is, however, no sign of equilibration in the models for France and Japan.

As for prices, they generally fall far short of matching the 4 per cent increase in nominal money stock in most models. Prices increase by half as much as the money supply in the United States, by one-fourth as much in Germany and Japan, and by one-eighth as much in Italy. Prices increase as much as money does in the Canadian model, but without restoring income to its pre-shock level. In the case of the United Kingdom, the price level actually overshoots the monetary expansion by two percentage points, and real income falls well below baseline in the process. Finally, as already noted, the price level declines monotonically in the French simulation.

International transmission of the monetary shock

According to the IS-LM model, real income and the price level should rise and the currency and interest rate should fall in the home country when it undergoes a monetary expansion, as borne out by the simulation results in table 3. The rise in home-country incomes will increase their demands for foreign goods, whereas their currencies will depreciate, tending to reduce their imports and increase their exports. The foreign IS curves, and hence foreign incomes, may therefore shift in either direction, according to the strength of these opposing forces.

It is apparent from table 3 that the cross-multipliers can be either positive or negative as expected. Again, the cross-multipliers are generally small except for the US shock. Negative foreign reactions are preponderant for shocks originating in Canada, France, Germany, and the United Kingdom, and in the later years in Japan, because net exports rise in those countries owing to their induced depreciations. Positive cross-multipliers are virtually universal for a US shock, however, since the income-induced increase in home-country import demand far outweighs the gain in US competitiveness from dollar depreciation. Just as under the fiscal shock, the income cross-multipliers follow the path of US imports rather than US income.

By and large the cross-multipliers for prices are negative except under the US shock. The same induced increases in net exports which depress incomes abroad also reduce prices abroad from the demand side, and are sometimes reinforced by induced foreign appreciations working in the same direction from the supply side. In contrast, the US shock induces export-led expansions abroad, which raises prices despite the accompanying foreign appreciations.

Summary

As a group, the domestic short-run responses of the country models to fiscal and monetary shocks are largely as predicted by theory. In the case of a negative fiscal shock, however, the G7 models either do not equilibrate or they exhibit only an incomplete recovery within five years. The equilibrating process is stronger under the monetary shock, with income peaking in the second year for Canada, Germany, the United Kingdom and the United States, the third year for Japan, and the fourth for Italy.

Although a US shock has moderate impacts abroad, shocks originating in the European countries, Canada, or Japan do not impinge heavily on the other nations in this group of large industrial economies, as evidenced by the low values of the cross-multipliers in the simulations. A negative fiscal shock depresses income and prices in the other countries at least slightly, however, whereas the impact can go in either direction under a positive monetary shock.

Scenario analyses with the LINK system

Historical examples

Simulation studies of the international transmission mechanism, control theory applications to exchange rate determination, and numerous scenarios on the effects of international disturbances and on international policies and policy coordination have been a staple of LINK research since its inception. Several of these have been undertaken mainly for model analytical purposes to elucidate the system properties of the highly non-linear LINK system. Table 5 simply lists a number of these in chronological order. They are more fully described, together with references, in Hickman (1991).

Many more scenarios have been undertaken in order to analyse contemporary disturbances or as a contribution to contemporary discussions of appropriate national or international policies. Some of these have been carried out on numerous occasions, e.g. oil-price shocks, coordinated fiscal and/or monetary policy, etc., and others less frequently. Table 6 lists most of these. Those prepared from 1974 to 1986 are described in Hickman (1991). Those prepared in 1990 and 1991 are described in United Nations Department of International Economic and Social Affairs (1990 and 1991a).

For seven recently calculated scenarios, some of the major impacts are displayed in schematic form in table 7. In each case the results are presented as percentage deviations from baseline, where the baseline was meant to be the most probable forecast for the world economy, given actual or announced policy intentions and assuming no dis-

Table 5 **Illustrations of analytical simulations with the LINK model**

Year	Simulation
1974	Differential responses of individual countries to exchange rate shocks with and without international linkages
1974	Amplification effects of synchronized real (expenditure) and nominal (wage) shocks in the various country models in linked mode
1974	Matrix multipliers for own- and partner-country responses for independent expenditure shocks in 11 of the national models
1977	Matrix multipliers for own- and partner-country responses for independent wage shocks in nine of the national models
1984	Wage and price responses to demand (fiscal) and supply (oil) shocks
1986	Comparative simulations of the effects of fiscal and monetary shocks originating in both US and OECD for 12 multi-country models

Table 6 **Scenario analyses of contemporary issues**

Year	Type of scenario
1974	Higher import absorption by Middle East oil exporting countries
1974	Inventory recessions in the US, UK, Italy
1974, 1978, 1987	Higher commodity export prices for developing countries
1974	Sensitivity of the world inflation rate to alternative patterns for the price of crude oil
1974	Effects of the second, post-Smithsonian wave of currency re-alignments in early 1973
1977	Coordinated economic policies: various combinations of fiscal stimulus by Japan, Germany, and the US alone and in combination with exchange rate re-evaluations
1977	Fiscal stimulus in six or seven countries with and without revaluation of the big three currencies
1978, 1979, 1983, 1984, 1987, 1988, 1990, 1991	Hypothetical increases/decreases in oil prices
1978	Worldwide grain shortage
1979, 1985	Protectionism
1981, 1987, 1988	Coordinated monetary policies with and without alternative fiscal policies
1982, 1983, 1990	Medium-term simulation of industrial policy and increases in development assistance
1984	Stabilizing exchange rates through coordinated monetary policies by Japan, Germany, and the US: an application of control theory to the Maxi LINK system
1984	Increase in gasoline prices
1984	Alternative fiscal and monetary policy responses to the base-case oil shock
1984	Unemployment prospects in the OECD area
1984	World recovery strategies and growth in developing countries
1987	Appreciation of other OECD currencies and Korea and Taiwan *vis-à-vis* US dollar
1988	Easier US monetary policy alone and accompanied by fiscal stimulus in Japan, Germany, Italy, and the UK
1988	Interest rate reductions in US and other OECD countries to offset fiscal tightening
1988	No fiscal tightening leading to interest rate increases
1989	Debt relief scenarios
1989	Changes in interest rate differential
1989	US excise tax rates on gasoline increased in phases over four years
1990	Increase in net transfers to economies in transition in Eastern Europe and USSR
1990	Reduced military spending in NATO and /or in USSR with and without compensation policies
1991	Net transfers to Eastern Europe and USSR combined with defence cuts and monetary stimulus

Table 7 **LINK model scenario analyses (impact expressed in percentage deviation from baseline in years indicated)**

Scenarios	GDP in world	GDP in developed market economies	GDP in developing countries	GDP in countries of Eastern Europe	GDP in USSR	World trade volume	Inflation in developed market economies	Unemployment in developed market economies
After 1, 3, 5 yrs								
A. Increase net transfers to developing countries	0.1	0.1	0.7	0.0	0.0	0.2	0.0	0.0
	0.4	0.3	2.3	0.0	0.0	0.8	0.0	−0.1
	0.6	0.4	3.2	0.0	0.0	1.1	0.1	−0.2
B. Increase net transfers to Eastern Europe	0.0	0.0	0.0	0.0	0.0	0.2	0.0	0.2
	0.4	0.2	0.1	1.5	1.6	0.7	0.0	−0.1
	0.7	0.5	0.2	3.3	2.3	1.4	0.1	−0.2
C. Reduce military spending in industrial countries	−0.1	−0.1	0.0	0.0	0.0	−0.1	0.0	0.1
	−0.3	−0.5	−0.1	0.0	0.0	−0.5	−0.1	0.3
	−0.7	−0.9	−0.2	0.0	0.0	−1.1	−0.1	0.4
D. Reduce interest rates in G7	0.3	0.4	0.1	0.0	0.0	0.3	0.0	−0.4
	1.1	1.5	0.3	0.0	0.0	1.5	0.1	−0.5
	1.3	1.8	0.4	0.0	0.0	2.1	0.2	−0.5
E. Composite	−0.1	−0.1	0.0	0.5	−0.1	0.2	0.0	0.1
	0.5	0.2	0.1	3.9	2.9	1.2	0.0	0.0
	0.7	0.0	0.1	4.9	7.5	1.0	0.1	0.2
After 2 yrs								
F. Oil price increase of $10 per barrel	−0.4	−0.4	−0.3	0.0	0.0	−0.6	0.6	0.1
G. Oil price decrease of $5 per barrel	0.2	0.2	0.3	0.0	0.0	0.3	−0.2	−0.1

Scenario A: Additional net transfers to developing countries of $6 billion in first year increasing to $30 billion in fourth year (March 1990).

Scenario B: Additional net transfers to Eastern Europe (including the former GDP) of $8 billion in first year increasing to $34 billion in fifth year (March 1990).

Scenario C: Military spending in six large industrial countries reduced cumulatively by 5 per cent over five years with no offsetting policy measures (March 1990).

Scenario D: Permanent interest rate reduction of 100 basis points in G7 countries beginning in base year (October 1991).

Scenario E: This composite scenario assumes additional net transfers to Eastern Europe (excluding the former GDR) and the USSR of $9 billion in the base year rising to $48 billion by year five; the transfers are assumed to be financed by cumulative savings from defence cuts among the G7 industrial countries of about $1,000 billion in current prices over the decade compared with the baseline; in the USSR permanent defence cuts of 6 billion roubles are assumed in the first year and sustained; since the defence cuts over-finance the transfers, interest rates are reduced by 50 basis points in Japan and by 100 basis points in other G7 countries (December 1991).

Scenario F: Oil prices increased by $11 per barrel from $30 per barrel to $40 per barrel, simulating one possible outcome of the 1990 Gulf crisis (November 1990).

Scenario G: Oil prices decreased by $5 per barrel from $30, simulating uncertainty in the aftermath of the Gulf War (March 1991).

turbances in commodity or financial markets. In many cases, scenario design meant the introduction of appropriate constant adjustments for several variables in many separate models. This procedure may be illustrated by describing in some detail scenario E listed in the table.

A composite scenario of reduced military spending with increased capital flows to Eastern Europe and the USSR

In this scenario, net transfers were assumed to increase imports in a group of five Eastern European countries (Bulgaria, Czechoslovakia, Hungary, Poland, and Romania) and in the USSR by $9 billion (all dollars are US dollars) in 1991 and $33 billion in 1992 rising to $48 billion in current prices by 1995 with the USSR accounting for slightly less than 50 per cent of the total. It was further assumed that military spending in the USSR would be reduced by 6 billion roubles at 1982 prices and held at this lower level throughout the simulation period. Savings from the defence spending cuts and additional import capacity were assumed to lead to increases in investment by amounts greater than the increase in imports.

Financial transfers to the reforming countries were assumed to be financed by defence spending cuts in the G7 industrial countries totaling $26 billion in current prices in 1991 and rising to $113 billion in 1995 as compared with the baseline. In the calculations the G7 reductions expressed in percentage terms were 4 per cent per year over four years and 2 per cent per year thereafter. This is the equivalent of cumulative cuts of 3 per cent per year if sustained over 10 years, or about $1,000 billion in cumulative savings at current prices.

This is much more than required to finance the transfers mentioned above. In fact, the savings could finance an additional $25 billion of transfers to developing countries or increases in non-military domestic spending, or could permit the monetary authorities in most of the G7 industrial countries to reduce interest rates by 100 basis points. This last option was the one implemented in this composite scenario. The results of the composite scenario are shown in table 7 as scenario E.

The impact of the composite scenario on output is significant in the countries of Eastern Europe and the USSR. By the fifth year, output in the five countries of Eastern Europe would be about 5 per cent higher than in the baseline scenario, and their trend rate of growth about 1 per cent higher on an annual basis. Because of the defence expenditure reductions assumed in the case of the USSR, financial transfers of roughly similar size to those assumed for Eastern Europe result in an initial small reduction in the level of output in the base year, but a cumulative increase in output by about 7.5 per cent in year five as compared with the baseline. In this scenario world trade is increased by 1 per cent and this results in small positive feedbacks to GDP in developing countries. Since the other elements of fiscal and monetary policy described above were designed to offset one another, the net impact on GDP in developed market countries is negligible, and the impact on inflation and unemployment is nil.

Limitations of scenario analysis

As explained elsewhere in the paper, the propagation of domestic shocks operates primarily by their effects on real import demand or export prices. Since trade in services, including direct investment income and interest income are not comprehensively linked, there are still significant leakages, which result in some underestimation of the impact of most scenarios.

Shocks affect the trend rate of growth of GDP if they result in a shift from consumption to investment in those models where capacity utilization is a constraint on GDP. A similar effect operates in models constrained by import capacity if the shocks ease the constraint. Investment is also affected by interest rates, which in many models are affected by changes in budget deficits. In so far as scenarios, such as military spending reductions or changes in the composition of trade, have macroeconomic consequences such as those just mentioned, LINK simulations, of course, do reflect them. However, the dynamic efficiency gains of reallocating spending among producing sectors, presumably from less to more remunerative activities, are largely absent. This can be remedied in an ad hoc way only by making use of results from other quantitative exercises relating to increases in investment or its reallocation and imposing these on the LINK models where appropriate.

Future scenario analysis

Among the planned future scenarios the following are included:
- Expansion of the trade model in LINK to include a number of separate categories of manufactured exports, reflecting different market conditions (automobiles, textiles) and differing degrees of

dynamism (computers, telecommunication equipment, and semiconductors), will make it possible to explore more readily the impact of the Uruguay Round and various free-trade arrangements presently being negotiated around the world.

- Combining LINK macroeconomic projections with physical models of pollution processes, a global input-output model, or both, will also help to evaluate the macroeconomic impacts of various sets of policy measures aimed at reducing global warming or mitigating other types of environmental degradation.
- As significant disarmament becomes a more realistic policy option, more careful analyses of its macroeconomic consequences will be undertaken in conjunction with studies of the structural impact of sharp reductions in military budgets.

Current LINK modelling research

Linkage mechanisms

Merchandise trade

A major research project on the determinants of trade shares is presently underway under the direction of Peter Pauly at the University of Toronto in collaboration with the United Nations. The new trade model will have four categories of primary and semi-processed goods and nine categories of manufactures, chosen in such a way as to approximate industry disaggregation and thus to lend itself more readily to the discussion of trade policy issues. While the new trade model will continue to use an equilibrium trade model (ETM) approach to the manufacturing sector, a commodity market approach emphasizing supply factors will be used for the four primary commodity sectors. A special case of this approach is the treatment of the world oil market discussed below.

Another innovation will be to replace the unit values used in standard ETM models with national factor-cost determinants and variables representing mark-up behaviour, for a given category of exports, i.e.

$$VX_{i,j} = f(Z_i, Z_j, FC_j, VM_j), \qquad (6)$$

where $VX_{i,j}$ is the value of exports from country i to country j; Z is a vector of mark-up behaviour; FC_j is an appropriate aggregator function for foreign factor cost elements, and VM_j is the value of imports by country j. The functional forms will be analogous to standard versions of an Armington (1969) ETM.

This approach will obviate the need to use unit values as proxies for export price indices. The problems of using unit values are well known. They are subject to large measurement errors, and are distorted further by shifts in the composition of trade at the item level. Moreover, competitiveness issues are analysed more easily in terms of unit-cost factors (wages, productivity, structure of indirect taxation and subsidies, levels of effective protection, etc.) and the translation of these factors into unit values is not immediately apparent.

A major part of the theoretical research will be the search for alternative specification of trade allocation models under explicit imperfect competition. Early attempts can be found in the literature on computable general equilibrium models (CGE). The basic complication of these models is that they require specific assumptions about strategic behaviour and market participants and possible market entry/exit restrictions. In any case, the major distinction between these models and traditional ETMs is the explicit modelling of market-specific mark-up behaviour reflecting the strategic environment.

Services trade and transfer payments

The present LINK system lacks a mechanism for capturing the international transmission of economic disturbances through the flows of trade in services and other invisibles in the current account of the balance of payments. It also fails to impose a check for global consistency on these balance of payments items similar to that imposed on merchandise trade. This is a serious omission since services and transfer credits amount to about 25 per cent of the value of merchandise exports f.o.b. A research project presently underway at the United Nations aims to develop a services and transfer payments model. A data set consisting of IMF data with gaps filled by estimates provided by DIESA and UNCTAD research staff has nearly been completed for four financial categories (investment income, interest income, private unrequited transfers, and official unrequited transfers) and four non-financial categories (shipping services, tourism, other factor services, and other commercial services). For the non-financial categories and for private unrequited transfers (which include workers' remittances) behaviour, equations of the demand for services (debits) will be estimated. Investment-income and interest-income debits will be financial-accounting identities, and official unrequited transfers will be an exogenous policy variable.

A typical equation estimated by single-stage least squares will be of the log–log type using the following explanatory variables, as appropriate: for shipping services, export and import volumes and freight rates; for tourism, own GDP, relative consumer-price indices, and exchange rates; for private unrequited transfers, other factor services and other commercial services, own GDP.

The sum of debit entries for all countries and regions in each category would constitute total world demand. In a second phase trends in the shares of each country/regional contribution to world supply (allowing for the global discrepancy between debits and credits in the reported data) will be analysed and a model estimated explaining changes in shares in world supply over time. By necessity this "world pool" approach will be used instead of a bilateral shares approach because of the lack of sufficiently comprehensive data.

Exchange rates

The approach to exchange rate modelling in LINK assumes that short-term interest rates are determined by monetary policy. Interest rate differentials, in turn, together with other factors such as relative inflation rates and current-account balances scaled by GDP, determine changes in exchange rates. A new exchange-rate model is presently being estimated by Peter Pauly at the University of Toronto to take into account the emergence of the European Monetary System (EMS).

The new model will utilize a two-stage, recursive procedure. In the first stage, reduced-form equations derived from a multi-country portfolio-balance asset-market model will determine the bilateral dollar-spot rates for Germany and Japan. In the second stage, bilateral Deutsche Mark spot rates will be determined for the EMS countries using similar equations, but constrained by the upper and lower EMS bounds for each currency.

World oil market

As mentioned above, trade in primary commodities should be modelled with supply and demand equations appropriately linked to the constituent macroeconomic models of LINK. A model of the world oil market by Robert Kaufmann (Kaufmann 1990), which meets this criterion, has recently been developed and will soon be formally incorporated in the LINK world model.

The model is driven by net oil demand (SITC 3) calculated in the LINK world simulation. Production equations for nine non-OPEC regions are estimated explaining deviations from a Hubbert logistic curve fitted to cumulative production data to represent the production cycle of a non-renewable resource. Deviations are explained by OLS regression equations, which include as arguments the ratio of reserves to production, the relative prices of oil and natural gas, and estimates of shut-in capacity. OPEC production is calculated as the difference between world oil demand and non-OPEC sources of liquid fuels. (In this identity, net exports of the formerly centrally planned economies and natural gas liquids are exogenous.) Finally, oil prices are determined in an equation which includes as arguments OPEC capacity, the capacity utilization rate, the share of world oil demand supplied by OPEC crude, OECD stocks (exogenous), OECD share in supplying world oil demand, and a dummy variable reflecting the strategic behaviour of OPEC. This variable allows for a switch between two regimes: one in which OPEC is assumed to defend a target price and another in which OPEC is assumed to abandon production quotas or target prices.

Feedback effects from prices to demand in the LINK macroeconomic models will impose consistency on the demand and supply projections, but no explicit links between the supply projections and aggregate output in the macroeconomic models are contemplated at present.

Capital flow modelling

The modelling of capital flows for Project LINK has long formed part of the research agenda. For medium-term forecasts or policy simulations, the pattern of current account imbalances needs to be assessed for plausibility against the magnitude, source, and type of capital flows that would be necessary to finance them. Also, isolating the short-term component in international capital flows could lead to further refinements in the modelling of exchange-rate determination.

In order to prepare a database for this and related work, the Institute of Social Studies at the Hague and the United Nations began collaborating on a research project in 1990 (de Jong et al. 1991). This project aims at the construction of a series (1985–1988) of international financial flow matrices for a pre-defined classification of 23 countries and country groups. The matrices distinguish among the following six categories of capital flows or balancing items based on the balance of payments statistics of the International Monetary Fund: equities and direct investment; long-term and short-term debt creating capital flows; changes in reserve positions; and errors and omissions. For developing countries and Eastern Europe (nine groups) a further breakdown is given for long-term external liabilities (eight categories): bilateral and multilateral official flows; distinguishing concessional from non-concessional loans; private bank loans and suppliers' credits; distinguishing publicly guaranteed from non-guaranteed. For the developing countries, such distinctions are highly policy relevant given the fact that these represent different capital market segments with different supply conditions.

The matrices are designed as part of the broader framework of world accounting matrices (WAM), which impose consistent accounting relations among trade flows, investment and savings, and acquisition of external financial assets and liabilities. The financial flow matrices constructed in this research effort were checked for consistency with the savings-investment and current account balances for each group. Since the matrices are compiled with data emanating from various sources, reconciliation of discrepancies is necessary. For 1985 the matrices were balanced by application of the Stone/Byron balancing method (Stone 1977; Byron 1978; Barker et al. 1984).

Future work envisaged by this project include (i) completion of the balanced flow-of-funds matrices for 1986–1988; (ii) inclusion of fully specified current account blocks (1985–1988) for reassessment of reference totals and reconciliation procedures; (iii) additional data collection to fill the most important data gaps and (iv) investigation of the links between stock and flow data leading to asset and liability revaluations for all types of capital transactions.

National models

Following the historical economic and political changes in Eastern Europe and the USSR, national modelling centres in Czechoslovakia, Romania, and the USSR have joined LINK and are actively constructing new models intended to reflect the shift to greater reliance on market clearing prices. The team at the University of Hamburg is re-estimating its model of the Federal Republic of Germany to include the five new *Länder* that constituted the former German Democratic Republic.

Nearly all of the modelling centres providing models of developed market economies are continually re-estimating their models. New models have been received or been promised soon for the following additional countries: Australia, Canada, Denmark, Italy, New Zealand, Netherlands, Norway, Spain, South Africa, and the United

Kingdom. They will be installed in the course of 1992. A number of the new generation of models include forward-looking expectations in their monetary sectors. The UK model, which had included "model-consistent" expectations, will not include this specification in the new version, experience having been somewhat disappointing, but will use instead a specification for forward-looking expectations based on learning from past experience.

Among the developing country modelling centres, new models are expected shortly for Argentina, Brazil, India, Indonesia, Kenya, Malaysia, Mexico, Peru, the Philippines, Tunisia, Turkey, Uruguay, and Venezuela.

The future of Project LINK

Extracting more information from the system

As mentioned earlier, many of the LINK models including all of the G7 countries are quarterly, yet linkage has been annual. Consequently, the short-term forecasting potential of the system has been under-utilized. Recently it has become possible to extract efficiently quarterly trade data, which can be used to impose seasonal adjustments on the trade matrices, from the United Nations Statistical Office for most of the countries represented by quarterly models in LINK. Adaptation of the LINK computational algorithm to produce linked quarterly solutions for the major industrial countries is not expected to pose any serious problems. This should enable LINK to begin producing linked quarterly forecasts for these countries over a two-year time horizon in 1992 alongside the 10-year annual baseline projections.

Concomitantly with introducing more detailed trade categories into the system, the database is being expanded to provide for an additional 26 developing countries and regions, principally in sub-Saharan Africa, Central America, and the Caribbean. Efforts are now underway to identify potential modelling centres in many of these countries as well as sources of financial support for national modelling work. Over a period of perhaps five years the system will thus be expanded to 105 countries and subregions.

Improving the usefulness of the system to Project participants

Until recently the principal benefits to Project participants have been limited to those derived from the participation in the semi-annual meetings, as discussed earlier, and to the LINK projections of world market variables, such as prices, exchange rates, interest rates, world trade growth, etc., which some participants use as a source of values for exogenous variables used in the stand-alone national models. Due to advances in telecommunication technology and the addition of an external user interface to the LINK computer software, it has now become possible for Project participants to establish on-line access to the system from their national modelling centres. Experimental policy simulations using the LINK model at UN headquarters in New York or simply browsing through the current LINK baseline projections have been carried out from Buenos Aires, Geneva, Kitakyushu, Moscow, Philadelphia, Santiago, and Toronto.

In the near future an additional feature will be added to the external user interface, which will allow alternative national models to be included in Maxi-LINK simulations. These developments are expected to lead to increased use of the LINK world model by the national modelling centres and international organizations participating in Project LINK for model-based policy analysis.

Improving the computer environment

The size and complexity of the LINK system has required the use of large mainframe computers from the outset, with continuous efforts to improve the efficiency of large-scale simulation. These efforts have been successful but have come at the cost of efficiency and flexibility in database management and in graphical presentation. A project is presently underway at the United Nations to develop an interface between the mainframe and the personal computer environment where software for graphics and desktop publishing will be used for the presentation of LINK outputs.

Organizational changes

The expansion of the Project both in terms of the number of participants at the meetings and in terms of the number of economies whose economic prospects are discussed may lead to the organization of several meetings per year, each with a differing focus. An annual meeting might be held to discuss world issues and the economic policies and prospects in the major industrial countries with less comprehensive attention being paid to regional issues. Another meeting might be held in a major world region where the emphasis would be on the policy issues and economic prospects for the countries of the region with a compressed discussion of the situation elsewhere. Still another meeting might concentrate exclusively on the technical concerns of the active economic policy modellers participating in the Project.

In its third decade this unique international research project is not likely to exhaust its potential to provide insights into the international transmission process and serve as a useful tool of analysis for those engaged in the study of national policy options in an interdependent world.

Notes

1. The history of Project LINK is documented more thoroughly in Hickman (1991).
2. See Hickman (1991) for a discussion of antecedents to the LINK approach in the work of J.J. Polak, Lloyd A. Metzler, Ragnar Frisch, and Rudolf R. Rhomberg.
3. See Hickman (1983a) for details.
4. Examples include a special session on capital flows and exchange rates at the Bundesbank (Klein and Krelle 1983), another session on comparative simulations of oil-price reductions and development assistance jointly with the FUGI-ESCAP and Tsukuba-FAIS modelling groups (Bollino et al. 1984), a conference on exchange rates at a joint meeting at the Bank of Japan, published in the *European Economic Review*, February 1986, and a conference on the foreign debt problem co-sponsored with the Federal Reserve Bank of San Francisco (Hickman 1984).
5. See the papers by Rhomberg, Hickman, and Waelbroeck in Ball (1973) on the theoretical structure and methodology of linkage through a trade-share model.
6. For empirical evidence on this point, see Kravis and Lipsey (1977) and Dornbusch and Krugman (1976).
7. Estimates of the elasticity of substitution in the Hickman-Lau framework for the SITC 5–9 category in 12 developed countries during 1960/71 averaged 0.59 in the short run and 1.37 in the long run, providing some support for a simplifying assumption of unity as a reasonable approximation (Gana et al. 1979, Appendix II).
8. In the seventies a set of 23 commodity models was integrated into the LINK system. The augmented system was known as COMLINK and featured structural models of the world commodity markets, in recognition of the fact that these markets for relatively homogenous products are not strongly localized in individual countries in the manner of manufactured products. See Adams (1979) for a description of the commodity models and for simulations of the complete COMLINK system. Unfortunately it has not been possible to maintain the structural commodity models, but the simpler reduced-form models described in Glowacki and Ruffing (1979) and maintained in UNCTAD have functioned reasonably well and are particularly useful in incorporating expert opinion regarding the future evolution of commodity prices.
9. Elasticity own and cross-multipliers measure the ratio of the percentage response of an endogenous variable at home or abroad to a given exogenous percentage change in income at home – in the present case, to a decrease in government expenditure equalling 1 per cent of GDP or GNP along the baseline path.
10. This finding of generally small cross-multipliers has been true of LINK simulations from the time of the first experiments in the early seventies (Hickman 1974).
11. The magnitudes of the various cross-multipliers from a unilateral shock depend in general

on (1) the size of the domestic income and import multipliers in the originating country, (2) the importance of the originating country in world trade and the geographic distribution of its trading partners, and (3) the internal response mechanisms of the receiving countries to external shocks. See Hickman (1983; 1988) for analytical decompositions of the impulse and response components of international income and price multipliers respectively in LINK alone and in a set of 12 multinational models including LINK.

Annex 1: Participants[1]

National and regional centres

* Serfina, SA (ARGENTINA)
* National Institute of Economic and Industry Research (AUSTRALIA)
University of Melbourne (AUSTRALIA)
* Institute for Advanced Studies (AUSTRIA)
* Free University of Brussels (BELGIUM)
* Institute for Economic and Social Planning/Institute for Survey Analyses; IPEA/INPES (BRAZIL)
Canadian Department of Finance (CANADA)
Economic Council of Canada (CANADA)
* University of Toronto (CANADA)
* Center for Research on Economics and Planning (CHILE)
* State Economic Information Centre (CHINA, PEOPLE'S REPUBLIC)
* Statistics Denmark (DENMARK)
* Bank of Finland, Research Department (FINLAND)
Banque de France (FRANCE)
* National Institute of Statistics and Economic Studies: INSEE (FRANCE)
University of Paris-Nanterre (FRANCE)
* University of Hamburg (GERMANY, FEDERAL REPUBLIC)
Bank of Greece (GREECE)
* Center of Planning and Economic Research (GREECE)
* The Chinese University of Hong Kong (HONG KONG)
* Budapest University of Economics (HUNGARY)
* Delhi School of Economics (INDIA)
Bank of Indonesia (INDONESIA)
* Central Bank of Ireland (IRELAND)
* Economic Models Ltd (ISRAEL)
Bank of Italy (ITALY)
* Prometeia Associates/University of Bologna (ITALY)
Bank of Japan (JAPAN)
Economic Planning Agency (JAPAN)
International University of Japan (JAPAN)
* Osaka University (JAPAN)
Soka University, Tokyo (JAPAN)
* Korean Development Institute (REPUBLIC OF KOREA)
* Central Planning Bureau (THE NETHERLANDS)

* Reserve Bank of New Zealand (NEW ZEALAND)
* University of Ibadan (NIGERIA)
* Bank of Norway (NORWAY)
* Central Bureau of Statistics (NORWAY)
* Pakistan Institute of Development Economics (PAKISTAN)
* National Economic and Development Authority (PHILIPPINES)
* Philippines Institute of Development and Statistics (PHILIPPINES)
* University of Lodz (POLAND)
* University of Portugal (PORTUGAL)
  National University of Singapore (SINGAPORE)
* University of Pretoria (SOUTH AFRICA, REPUBLIC)
* Autonomous University of Madrid (SPAIN)
* University of Göteborg (SWEDEN)
* University of Lausanne (SWITZERLAND)
* Institute of Economics (TAIWAN, PROVINCE OF CHINA)
* Thailand Development Research Institute (THAILAND)
  Bogazici University (TURKEY)
* Central Bank of Turkey (TURKEY)
  State Institute of Statistics (TURKEY)
* London Business School (UNITED KINGDOM)
  Academy of Sciences: Central Economic and Mathematical Institute (USSR)
  Ministry of Foreign Affairs (USSR)
  State Planning Office (USSR)
  East-West Center (UNITED STATES)
  Iowa State University (UNITED STATES)
* Stanford University (UNITED STATES)
  United States Department of Agriculture (UNITED STATES)
  United States Department of State (UNITED STATES)
  United States Federal Reserve Board (UNITED STATES)
* University of Pennsylvania (UNITED STATES)
* Wharton Econometrics Forecasting Associates Group (UNITED STATES)
* Metro Economica (VENEZUELA)
* Zagreb Economic Institute (YUGOSLAVIA)

International organizations

  Asian Development Bank
  Commission of the European Communities
  Food and Agricultural Organization
  International Monetary Fund
  Organization for Economic Co-operation and Development
* Secretariat of the Andean Group
* United Nations Conference on Trade and Development
* United Nations Department of International Economic and Social Affairs
  United Nations Economic Commission for Africa
  United Nations Economc Commission for Europe
* United Nations Economic and Social Commission for Asia and the Pacific

* United Nations Economic and Social Commission for Latin America and the Caribbean
United Nations Industrial Development Organization
World Bank

Note

1. Active participating institutions are those that contribute to the constituent models of Project LINK (denoted by an asterisk), regularly undertake LINK-related research, or actively participate in the deliberation of the meetings.

Annex 2

Table A1 **The LINK network: National models and participating institutions**

Row no. in trade matrix	Country	Periodicity/ model size		Participating institution	Affiliation
1	Canada	Q	large	University of Toronto	non-profit/ academic
2	France	Q	very large	National Institute of Statistics and Economic Studies (Paris)	government agency
3	Federal Republic of Germany	Q	large	University of Hamburg	academic
4	Italy	Q	large	University of Bologna	commercial/ academic
5	Japan	Q	large	Osaka University	academic
6	United Kingdom	Q	large	London Business School	commercial/ academic
7	United States	Q	very large	Wharton Econometric Forecasting Associates/ University of Pennsylvania (Philadelphia)	commercial/ academic
8	Austria	A	large	Institute of Advanced Studies (Vienna)	academic/ government
9	Belgium/ Luxembourg	A	large	Free University of Brussels	academic
10	Denmark	A	very large	Denmark Statistical Office (Copenhagen)	government
11	Finland	Q	medium	Bank of Finland (Helsinki)	government
12	Netherlands	Q	large	Central Planning Bureau (Hague)	government

Table A1 **(cont.)**

Row no. in trade matrix	Country	Periodicity/ model size	Participating institution	Affiliation
13	Norway	A large	Central Statistical Office (Oslo)	government
14	Sweden	A large	University of Göteborg	academic
15	Switzerland	A medium	University of Lausanne/ Institute of Applied Macroeconomics	academic
16	Australia	Q medium	Treasury/National Institute for Economic and Industry Research (Melbourne)	government
17	Greece	A medium	Center of Planning and Economic Research (Athens)	government
19	Ireland	A medium	Central Bank of Ireland (Dublin)	government
20	New Zealand	Q medium	Reserve Bank of New Zealand (Wellington)	government
21	Portugal	A small	Universidade Portucalense (Porto)	academic
22	Spain	A medium	Autonomous University of Madrid	academic
18, 24, 25	Turkey,* Iceland, Yugoslavia*	A small	University of Pennsylvania	academic
23, 26, 27	South Africa* Israel,* Cyprus/Malta	A very small	University of Pennsylvania	academic
28	Argentina*	A small	University of Pennsylvania	academic
29	Brazil	A medium	Institute for Economic and Social Planning/Institute for Survey Analysis (Rio de Janeiro)	government
30	Chile	A medium	Center for Research on Economics and Planning (Santiago)	non-profit
31, 32, 34, 36	Bolivia, Colombia, Ecuador, Peru	A small	Acuerdo de Cartagena (Lima)	inter-governmental
33	Mexico	A large	Center for Economic Research on Mexico (CIEMEX-WEFA) (Philadelphia)	commercial

Table A1 **(cont.)**

Row no. in trade matrix	Country	Periodicity/ model size	Participating institution	Affiliation
35	Venezuela	A medium	Metro Economica (Caracas)	commercial
37, 38	Paraguay, Uruguay	A small	University of Pennsylvania	academic
39	Caribbean and Central America[a]	A small regional model	University of Pennsylvania	academic
40, 42	Algeria, Libya	A small	University of Pennsylvania	academic
41	Gabon	A small	Department of International Economic and Social Affairs, United Nations (New York)	international
43	Nigeria	A large	University of Ibadan	academic
44	Egypt	A small	University of Pennsylvania	academic
45	Morocco	A small	Department of International Economic and Social Affairs, United Nations (New York)	international
46	Tunisia	A small	Department of International Economic and Social Affairs, United Nations (New York)	international
47	Sudan	A small	Department of International Economic and Social Affairs, United Nations (New York)	international
48	Ghana	A small	Department of International Economic and Social Affairs, United Nations (New York)	international
49	Kenya	A small	Department of International Economic and Social Affairs, United Nations (New York)	international
50	Ethiopia	A small	Department of International Economic and Social Affairs, United Nations (New York)	international
51	Other Africa[b]	A small regional model	University of Pennsylvania	academic

Table A1 **(cont.)**

Row no. in trade matrix	Country	Periodicity/ model size		Participating institution	Affiliation
52	Africa least developed[c]	A	small regional model	University of Pennsylvania	academic
53, 54, 55, 56	Iran, Iraq, Kuwait, Saudi Arabia	A	small	University of Pennsylvania	academic
57	Other West Asia oil exporters[d]	A	small regional model	University of Pennsylvania	academic
58	Other West Asia non-oil exporters[e]	A	small regional model	University of Pennsylvania	academic
59	Indonesia*	A	small	University of Pennsylvania	academic
61	Hong Kong	A	small	Chinese University of Hong Kong	academic
62	India	A	medium	Delhi School of Economics (Delhi)	academic
65	Pakistan	A	medium	Pakistan Institute for Development Economics (Islamabad)	
66	Philippines	A	medium	National Economic and Development Authority (Manila)	government
64, 67	Malaysia,* Singapore*	A	medium	Economic and Social Commission for Asia and the Pacific United Nations (Bangkok)	international
68	Thailand	A	medium	Economic and Social Commission for Asia and the Pacific United Nations (Bangkok)	international
60	Taiwan Province	A	medium	Academica Sinica (Taipei)	academic
69	Other South East Asia[f]	A	small regional model	University of Pennsylvania	academic
63	Republic of Korea	Q	medium	Korean Development Institute (Seoul)	government
70	South East Asia least developed[g]	A	small regional model	University of Pennsylvania	academic
71	Bulgaria	A	small	University of Pennsylvania	academic

Table A1 **(cont.)**

Row no. in trade matrix	Country	Periodicity/ model size		Participating institution	Affiliation
72	Czechoslovakia	A	small	University of Pennsylvania	academic
73	German Democratic Republic	A	small	University of Pennsylvania	academic
74	Hungary	A	large	Institute of Market Research (Budapest)	academic
75	Poland	A	very large	University of Lodz	academic
76	Romania	A	small	University of Pennsylvania	academic
	USSR*	A	medium	University of Pennsylvania	77 government
78	China	A	small	State Economic Information Center (Beijing)	academic
79	Other Asian centrally planned regional model[h]	A	small	University of Pennsylvania	academic

Note: Q, Quarterly; A, Annual; very large, more than 1,000 variables; large 350 to 1,000 variables; medium, 200–350 variables; small, less than 200 variables; asterisk indicates that a good model exists in a national modelling centre which may be ready to join soon; countries in italics are countries for which medium-size models have been built by the United Nations Department of International Economic and Social Affairs (see *b*, *c* below).

a. Antigua, Bahamas, Barbados, Bermuda, Belize, British Virgin Islands, Costa Rica, Cuba, Dominican Republic, El Salvador, French Guiana, Guadelope, Guatemala, Guyana, Honduras, Jamaica, Martinique, Netherlands Antilles, Nicaragua, Panama, Surinam, Trinidad and Tobago, Virgin Islands

b. Angola, *Cameroon*, Congo, *Ivory Coast*, Liberia, *Madagascar*, Mauritania, Mauritius, Mozambique, Reunion, *Senegal*, Seychelles, *Sierra Leone*, Togo, *Zaire*, *Zambia*, *Zimbabwe*

c. Benin, Botswana, Burkina Faso, Burundi, Central African Republic, Chad, Gambia, Malawi, Mali, Niger, *Somalia*, *Uganda*, *United Republic of Tanzania*

d. Bahrain, Oman, Qatar, United Arab Emirates

e. Cyprus, Jordan, Lebanon, Syria, Yemen

f. Brunei, Burma, Fiji, Macao, Papua-New Guinea, Sri Lanka

g. Afghanistan, Bangladesh, Lao People's Democratic Republic, Nepal, Western Samoa

h. Democratic People's Republic of Korea, Mongolia, Viet Nam

References and bibliography on Project LINK

Adams, F. Gerard. 1978. "Primary Commodity Markets in a World Model System." In: F. Gerard Adams and Sonia A. Klein, eds. *Stabilizing World Commodity Markets*. Lexington: Lexington Books.

—— 1979. "Integrating Commodity Models into LINK. In: John A. Sawyer, ed. *Modelling the International Transmission Mechanism.* Amsterdam: North-Holland, pp. 273–294.

Armington, Paul S. 1969. "A Theory of Demand for Products Distinguished by Place of Production." *Staff Papers: Vol. 16*. Washington, D.C.: International Monetary Fund, pp. 159–178.

Ball, R.J., ed. 1973. *The International Linkage of National Economic Models.* Amsterdam: North-Holland.

Barker, T., F. Van der Ploez, and M. Weale. 1984. "A Balanced System of National Accounts for the United Kingdom." *Review of Income and Wealth* 30(4): 461–479.

Beaumont, Paul, Ingmar Prucha, and Victor Filatov. 1979. "Performance of the LINK System: 1970 versus 1975 Base Year Trade Share Matrix." *Empirical Economics* 4: 11–42.

Bollino, C. Andrea, and Lawrence R. Klein. 1984. "World Recovery Strategies in the 80's: Is World Recovery Synonymous to LDC Recovery?" *Journal of Policy Modeling* 6(2): 175–207.

Bollino, C. Andrea, Akira Onishi, Peter Pauly, Christian E. Petersen, and Shuntaro Shishido. 1984. "Global Impact of Oil Price Reductions and Official Development Assistance: Medium-Term Comparative Simulations with Alternative Global Econometric Models." *The Developing Economies* 22: 3–26.

Bollino, C. Andrea, Peter Pauly, and Christian E. Petersen. 1983. "National and International Aspects of the EMF7 Scenarios: Results from Project LINK." *EMF 7.13*. Energy Modeling Forum, Stanford University, December.

Byron, R. 1978. "The Estimation of Large Social Accounting Matrices." *Journal of the Royal Statistical Society*. Series A, 141(3): 359–367.

Charemza, W., and M. Gronicki. 1988. *Disequilibrium Analysis of Centrally-planned Economies: The Case of Poland.* Amsterdam: North-Holland.

Costa, Antonio M., and Stanislav M. Menshikov. 1979. "Short-term Forecasting Models for the Centrally-planned Economies of Eastern Europe." In: John A. Sawyer, ed. *Modeling the International Transmission Mechanism.* Amsterdam: North-Holland, pp. 163–202.

de Jong, Niek, Rob Vos, and Tjeerd Jellema. 1991. Financial Flows in a World Accounting Framework. The Hague: Institute of Social Studies. Mimeo.

Dornbusch, Rudiger, and Paul Krugman. 1976. "Flexible Exchange Rates in the Short Run." *Brookings Papers on Economic Activity*, 537–584.

Filatov, Victor, and Lawrence R. Klein. 1981. A Quick LINK Short Run Exchange Rate Model. Paper presented at Project LINK meeting, La Hulpe, Belgium, September.

Filatov, Victor, Bert G. Hickman, and Lawrence R. Klein. 1983. "Long-term Simulations with the Project LINK System, 1978–1985." In: Bert G. Hickman, ed. *Global International Economic Models*. Amsterdam: North-Holland, pp. 29–52.

Frisch, Ragnar. 1947. "On the Need for Forecasting a Multilateral Balance of Payments." *American Economic Review*, September, pp. 535–551.

Gana, Jorge L., Bert G. Hickman, Lawrence J. Lau, and Laurence R. Jacobson. 1979. "Alternative Approaches to the Linkage of National Economic Models." In: John A Sawyer, ed. *Modelling the International Transmission Mechanism.* Amsterdam: North-Holland, pp. 9–44.

Glowacki, J., and K.G. Ruffing. 1979. "Developing Countries in Project LINK." In:

John A. Sawyer, ed. *Modelling the International Transmission Mechanism*. Amsterdam: North-Holland, pp. 203–18.

Helliwell, John F. 1978. Discussion of "Disturbances to the International Economy." In: Robert M. Solow, ed. *After the Phillips Curve: Persistence of High Inflation and High Unemployment*. Boston: Federal Reserve Bank of Boston.

Hickman, Bert G. 1974. "International Transmission of Economic Fluctuations and Inflation." In: Albert Ando, Richard Herring and Richard Marston, eds. *International Aspects of Stabilization Policies*. Boston: Federal Reserve Bank of Boston, pp. 201–231.

—— 1975. "Project LINK in 1972: Retrospect and Prospect." In: G.A. Renton, ed. *Modelling the Economy*. London: Heinenmann.

—— 1983a. "Exchange Rates in Project LINK." In: Paul DeGrauwe and Theo Peeters, eds. *Exchange Rates in Multicountry Econometric Models*. London: Macmillan, pp. 103–133.

—— 1988a. "The U.S. Economy and the International Transmission Mechanism." In: Ralph C. Bryant, Dale W. Henderson, Gerald Holtham, Peter Hooper and Steven A. Symansky, eds. *Empirical Macroeconomics for Interdependent Economies*. Washington, D.C.: The Brookings Institution, pp. 92–130.

——, ed. 1983b. *Global International Economic Models*. Amsterdam: North-Holland.

——, ed. 1984. *International Monetary Stabilization and the Foreign Debt Problem*. San Francisco: Federal Reserve Bank of San Francisco.

—— 1988b. "The U.S. Economy and the International Transmission Mechanism." In: Ralph C. Bryant, Dale W. Henderson, Gerald Holtham, Peter Hooper, and Steven A. Symansky, eds. *Empirical Macroeconomics for Interdependent Economies*. Washington, D.C.: The Brookings Institution, pp. 92–130.

—— 1991. "Project LINK and Multi-country Modelling." In: Ronald G. Bodkin, Lawrence R. Klein, and Kanta Marwah, eds. *A History of Macroeconometric Model-Building*. Aldershot, England: Edward Elgar, pp. 482–506.

Hickman, Bert G., and Victor Filatov. 1983. "A Decomposition of International Income Multipliers." In: F. Gerard Adams and Bert G. Hickman, eds. *Global Econometrics: Essays in Honor of Lawrence R. Klein*. Cambridge, Massachusetts: MIT Press, pp. 340–67.

Hickman, Bert G., and Lawrence R. Klein. 1979. "A Decade of Research by Project LINK." *Social Science Research Council Items* 33(3/4): 49–56.

—— 1984. "Wage-Price Behavior in the National Models of Project LINK." *American Economic Review, Papers and Proceedings*, May, pp. 150–154.

—— 1985. "Recent Developments in Project LINK." *Social Science Research Council Items* 39(1/2): 7–11.

—— 1989. "Project LINK at 20." *Social Science Research Council Items* 43(1): 4–6.

Hickman, Bert G., and Lawrence J. Lau. 1973. "Elasticities of Substitution and Export Demand in a World Trade Model." *European Economic Review* 4: 347–380.

Hickman, Bert G., and Stefan Schleicher. 1978. "The Interdependence of National Economies and the Synchronization of Economic Fluctuations: Evidence from the LINK Project." *Weltwirtschaftsliches Archiv* 114(4): 642–708.

Johnson, Keith N. 1979. Balance of Payments Equilibrium and Equilibrating Exchange Rates in a World Economic Model. Ph.D. dissertation, University of Pennsylvania.

Johnson, Keith N., and Lawrence R. Klein. 1974a. "LINK Model Simulations of International Trade: An Evaluation of the Effects of Currency Realignment." Papers and Proceedings, *Journal of Finance* 29: 617–630.

—— 1974b. "Stability in the International Economy: The LINK Experience." In: Albert Ando, Richard Herring and Richard Marston, eds. *International Aspect of Stabilization Policies*. Boston: Federal Reserve Bank of Boston, pp. 147–88.

Kaufmann, Robert K. 1990. A Model of the World Oil Market for Project LINK. Department of Geography and Center for Energy and Environmental Studies, Boston University. Mimeo.

Klein, Lawrence R. 1973. "Project LINK: Entering a New Phase." *Social Science Research Council Items* 27(2): 13–16.

—— 1978. "Disturbances to the International Economy." In: Robert M. Solow, ed. *After the Phillips Curve: Persistence of High Inflation and High Unemployment*. Boston: Federal Reserve Bank of Boston.

—— 1985. "Empirical Aspects of Protectionism: LINK Results." *Journal of Policy Modeling* 7(1).

Klein, Lawrence R., C. Andrea Bollino, and Shahrokh Fardoust. 1982. "Industrial Policy in the World Economy: Medium Term Simulations." *Journal of Policy Modeling* 4(2): 175–189.

Klein, Lawrence R., Shahrokh Fardoust, and Victor Filatov. 1981. "Purchasing Power Parity in Medium Term Simulation of the World Economy." *Scandinavian Journal of Economics* 4: 479–496.

Klein, Lawrence R., and Wilhelm Krelle, eds. 1983. *Capital Flows and Exchange Rate Determination*. Zeitschrift für Nationalökonomie, Supplementum 3. Vienna and New York: Springer-Verlag.

Klein, Lawrence R., Chikashi Moriguchi, and Alain van Peeterssen. 1972. "NEP in the World Economy: Simulation of the International Transmission Mechanism." Project LINK Working Paper 2.

—— 1975. "The LINK Model of World Trade with Applications to 1972–73." In: Peter Kenen, ed. *International Trade and Finance*. New York: Cambridge University Press.

Klein, Lawrence R., M. Politi, and Vincent Su. 1978. Scenario of a World Wide Grain Shortage. LINK memorandum, July.

Klein, Lawrence R., Richard Simes, and Pascal Voisin. 1981. "Coordinated Monetary Policy and the World Economy." *Prévision et Analyse Économique* 2(3): 75–105.

Klein, Lawrence R., and Vincent Su. 1979. "Protectionism: An Analysis from Project LINK." *Journal of Policy Modeling* 1: 5–35.

Klein, Lawrence A., and Alain van Peeterssen. 1973. "Forecasting World Trade Within Project LINK." In: R.J. Ball, ed. *The International Linkage of National Economic Models*. Amsterdam: North-Holland, pp. 429–63.

Kravis, Irving B., and Robert E. Lipsey. 1977. "Export Prices and the Transmission of Inflation." *American Economic Review: Papers and Proceedings*, May, pp. 155–173.

Metzler, Lloyd A. 1941. "Underemployment Equilibrium in International Trade." *Econometrica* 10: 97–112.

—— 1950. "A Multiple-Region Theory of Income and Trade." *Econometrica* 18: 329–354.

Moriguchi, Chikashi. 1973. "Forecasting and Simulating the World Economy." *American Economic Review: Papers and Proceedings*, May, pp. 402–409.

Pauly, Peter. 1984. "Unemployment Prospects for the OECD Area: Alternative Scenarios with the LINK System." In: *Forecasting Models and the Employment Problem*. Geneva: International Labor Organization.

Pauly, Peter, and Peter Hooper. 1984. "Impact of an Oil Price Shock on the U.S. Economy: International Repercussions." Federal Reserve Board, International Finance Discussion Paper 262. Washington: Federal Reserve Board.

Pauly, Peter, and Christian E. Petersen. 1986. "Exchange Rate Responses in the LINK System." *European Economic Review* 30(1): 149–170.

Petersen, Christian E. 1985. *Simnew User's Guide*. Project LINK, University of Pennsylvania.

—— 1988. Dynamic Bilateral Tariff Games: An Econometric Analysis. Ph.D. dissertation, University of Pennsylvania.

Polak, J.J. 1953. *An International Economic System*. Chicago: University of Chicago Press.

Polak, Jacques J., and Rudolf R. Rhomberg. 1962. "Economic Instability in an International Setting." *American Economic Review: Papers and Proceedings*, May. Reprinted with model appendix added in Robert A. Gordon and Lawrence R. Klein, eds. *Readings in Business Cycles*. Homewood, Illinois: Richard D. Irwin.

Salvatore, Dominick, ed. 1989. *African Development Prospects: A Policy Modeling Approach*. New York: Taylor & Francis, New York Inc.

Sawyer, John A., ed. 1979. *Modelling the International Transmission Mechanism*. Amsterdam: North-Holland.

Stone, R. 1977. "Foreword." In: G. Pyatt, A. Ros et al. *Social Accounting for Development Planning with Special Reference to Sri Lanka*. Cambridge: Cambridge University Press.

United Nations Department of International Economic and Social Affairs. 1990. Report on the Meeting of the Expert Group on Short- and Medium-Term Projection of the World Economy (Project LINK), New York, 7–9 March 1990: Occasional Paper No. 2. Mimeo.

—— 1991. Report on the Meeting of the Expert Group on Short-and-Medium Term Projections of the World Economy (Project LINK), Manila, 5–9 November 1990. Occasional Paper No. 3. Mimeo.

—— 1991b. Report on the Meeting of the Expert Group on Short-and-Medium Term Projections of the World Economy (Project LINK), New York, 6–8 March 1991. Occasional Paper No. 4. Mimeo.

Waelbroeck, Jean L., ed. 1976. *The Models of Project LINK*. Amsterdam: North-Holland.

Comments on chapter 2

1. Ralph C. Bryant

It was a pleasure to participate in this international conference and to comment on the paper by Bert Hickman and Ken Ruffing. The paper provides a skilful overview of Project LINK, including a survey of its history, its major substantive contributions, and its plans for the future.[1]

Project LINK is an important international research effort and has many achievements to its credit. Some seminal empirical contributions to the analysis of economic interdependence preceded the launching of LINK in the late 1960s. I am thinking in particular of the work of Frisch (1947), Metzler (1950), Polak (1953), Polak and Rhomberg (1962), and Rhomberg and Boissoneault (1964). Yet LINK was the first truly multinational collaborative effort and the first time an articulate vision was given of the need to devote major resources to empirical, multi-country modelling. It is easy for observers today to take a global analytical perspective. It was not so in the late 1960s. One must understand the intellectual and policy climate in the 1960s to have an adequate appreciation of the farsighted leadership manifested by the originators of the LINK project.

LINK has remained the multi-country modelling effort with the largest scale and highest ambitions. Many individuals have played important roles. It is none the less apt to single out in particular the catalytic intellectual influence of the chairman of our session today, Lawrence Klein. Klein and the key colleagues in LINK whom he has helped to bring together have inspired many of the rest of us in the economics profession to follow in their pioneering footsteps.

In my comments on the Hickman-Ruffing paper, I will say a few things trying to put LINK into perspective with other current strands of empirical multi-country research. I will focus on differences in strategies that have been followed as researchers try to make progress in constructing macroeconometric models of the global economy. Then I shall comment on the properties of today's LINK model, as discussed in the section of the Hickman-Ruffing paper on "dynamic properties." Finally, I shall add a few remarks about future research priorities.

Alternative modelling strategies

The research strategy that has guided LINK from its inception has several key characteristics. First, the project has emphasized disaggregated geographical detail. Nation states – lots of them! – are the relevant political entities in the world. Accordingly, LINK has presumed that separate national models will be required for the individual nations. Secondly, LINK has relied on a network of modellers who have developed national models for the individual countries. The presumption has been that the national modelling groups have a rich institutional knowledge of their own particular nation and its economic differences from other nations, and therefore, are most qualified to construct and maintain a model for that nation. Thirdly, because financial interactions among countries through exchange rates, interest rates, and capital flows are difficult to model, LINK researchers concentrated initially on merchandise trade flows and prices. The presumption has been that the financial and service components of international transactions would be included later on.

I think of this LINK strategy as quintessentially a "bottom-up" approach to global modelling. One starts with the individual geographical pieces of the world economy, as defined by the political map. Although the models for these individual pieces are heterogeneous, differing significantly from each other in the conceptual way they have been built, the pieces are assembled into a global model through a centralized linkage mechanism. The bottom-up strategy assumes the individual country researchers will continue to keep working to improve the national models, even while the project leaders operate the linked system as a global entity.

Another approach to global modelling which I shall label a "top-down" strategy sharply limits the amount of geographical desegregation at the outset, thereby permitting the model to be relatively small. (Later states of such a strategy plan call for further disaggregation in additional discrete steps, but these later steps are taken only after working out key problems encountered at the higher levels of aggregation. A top-down strategy uses a common theoretical structure for all regional blocks of the model, at least initially, and similarly tries to develop databases for the regions that are as conceptually comparable as possible. It gives highest priority in the design of the overall model, and in the design of each regional block, to the channels of interactions among the regions, thereby making the interdependence aspects the central motivating force behind the model's construction. Given the common theoretical approach to each regional block, a top-down strategy permits behavioural parameters to differ across the regional blocks only where it can be shown that cross-region differences are identifiable and important (e.g., are statistically significant in estimation). Another characteristic of a top-down strategy is the high premium it places on analytical transparency in understanding the model's results and, correspondingly, a willingness to trade off realistic modelling of details to achieve that transparency.

My characterizations here of bottom-up and top-down strategies are of course oversimplified. One might think of the two alternatives as opposite ends of a spectrum, useful as contrasting benchmarks when describing actual models. The ultimate objectives of the bottom-up and top-down strategies are essentially the same. And eventually, the two strategies should converge toward a shared empirical knowledge about how the world economy actually functions. The differences between the two approaches pertain to the shorter run, when knowledge is still very imperfect and uncertain.

In recent years, a variety of multi-country empirical models other than Project LINK have been built to study macroeconomic interactions among national economies. It may be helpful to identify some of these other efforts, particularly with respect to their adoption of bottom-up or top-down strategies, as a way of viewing LINK within a broader perspective. Accordingly, I offer the following rough classification of multi-country modelling efforts.[2]

Comprehensive models based on a bottom-up approach include LINK itself, the MIMOSA model in France (CEPII/OFCE 1990), the FUGI global model (Onishi, this volume), and also the GLOBUS model (Bremer 1987). Among a group of medium to large models that have elements of both the bottom-up and top-down strategies in their construction are the OECD Interlink model (Richardson 1988), the world model of the Japanese Economic Planning Agency (Economic Research Institute of EPA 1991), the GEM model of the London Business School and the National Institute of Economic and Social Research (Wren-Lewis and Barrell 1988), and the QUEST model of the staff of the European Commission in Brussels (Brandsma et al. 1991). One might also place in this category the modelling effort underway at the International Economics Department at the World Bank under the direction of Paul Armington. Moving along the spectrum further, one encounters medium-size multi-country models built primarily with a top-down strategy; the main example that comes to mind is the MCM model at the Federal Reserve Board (Stevens et al. 1984; Edison et al. 1987).[3] Finally, by moving still further along the spectrum, one comes to smaller models explicitly designed from the perspective of the top-down strategy. These include the MULTIMOD model of the IMF Research Department (the successor to the earlier MINIMOD; see Haas and Masson 1986 and Masson et al. 1988; 1990), the Canadian cousin of MULTIMOD known as INTERMOD (Helliwell et al. 1990; Meredith 1989), the model built by John Taylor for the G7 countries (Taylor 1988; 1989), the MSG model built by Warwick McKibbin and Jeffrey Sachs and now being extended by McKibbin (McKibbin and Sachs 1991), the model built at the University of Liverpool by Patrick Minford et al. (1985; 1988), and the MX3 model built at the Federal Reserve Board by Joseph Gagnon (1991).

It is my personal view that the economics profession will be better off, now and in the foreseeable future, if the bottom-up and top-down approaches to multi-country modelling are both pursued actively. And it would be easier for me here, and probably more diplomatic, not to try to say more about the relative merits of the two strategies. However, that course would also be a bit cowardly and would fail to provide a stimulus for constructive dialogue. Accordingly, I shall share with you my opinion that the top-down approach has a better chance than the bottom-up approach of making rapid progress in the short run.

The basis for my opinion is the great importance, in the current stage of research on the global economy, of analytical transparency. Especially when uncertainty about a subject is pervasive, the profession should value analyses that can be readily and clearly understood. Such analytical transparency is much easier to attain in smaller, top-down models than in large, bottom-up models.

A reliance on the heterogeneous modelling practices of a variety of country experts, as in LINK, means that the resulting global model is extremely complex and not analytically transparent. The large amount of geographical detail in a bottom-up model interacts with the heterogeneity of diverse modelling practices, reducing still further the ability of researchers to understand clearly the systemic behaviour of the global model. Unfortunately, the trade-off seems very steep: to obtain the individualized national modelling by country experts and the disaggregated geographical detail, it appears to be necessary to sacrifice a great deal of analytical transparency. All things considered, it is more likely, I believe, that key theoretical issues will get priority attention in a top-down strategy.

Dynamic properties of LINK simulations

The generalization I have just made seems to me born out when one examines closely the dynamic properties of the LINK system, as summarized in the Hickman-Ruffing paper. Some aspects of the simulation results strike me as puzzling and problematic. I fear these results may be symptomatic of deeper specification problems.

Consider first the effects of a fiscal contraction (tables 1 and 2 in the paper and the associated discussion). What do we expect on theoretical grounds? A fiscal contraction should result in a fall (relative to baseline) in own-country output, incomes, and prices. Home interest rates should fall, and with a lag should begin to cause "crowding in" (the negative income effects of the government-spending reduction being partly offset by increases in other spending induced by the lower interest rates and prices). The direction of movement of the exchange value of the own country's currency is ambiguous in expository theoretical models. It depends on, among other things, the degree of substitutability between assets denominated in the home and foreign currencies; the greater the degree of substitutability, the more likely is the home currency to depreciate after a fiscal contraction. With increasingly integrated world financial markets, the depreciation outcome is increasingly likely. Because of income/absorption effects, home imports should fall as home incomes fall, improving the trade and current account balances. Expenditure-switching effects, assuming the home currency depreciates, also tend to improve the initiating country's external balance. Stated another way, the depreciation of the home currency also begins to induce home crowding-in effects that reinforce the crowding in due to declines in home interest rates. Transmission of the fiscal contraction to the rest of the world should be "positive" (foreign outputs and price levels should also fall relative to baseline). Foreign interest rates fall, and weaker though significant crowding-in effects should also be observed in foreign countries.

In the great majority of other empirical multi-country models, interest-rate declines and crowding-in effects are quantitatively important, with the effects becoming progressively more important through time. Recent model comparison exercises, moreover, have shown that the great majority of multi-country empirical models now report own-currency depreciation after a fiscal contraction.[4] On these crowding-in effects (or crowding out for fiscal expansions), the LINK system is rather far out of line with other models. Interest rates hardly move at all, and fiscal contractions lead to own-country currency appreciations rather than depreciations (with the exception of Canada). Because the LINK system has little own-country crowding in, crowding-in effects in foreign countries are also very small – unlike in most other models. (The LINK system does show, as do other models, positive international transmission of the fiscal contraction to foreign countries' outputs.)

The Canadian model in LINK, which the authors discuss, seems unusually far out of line with what other models tend to say about fiscal actions or expenditure shocks in Canada. Prices monotonically *increase* in Canada (see the paper's table 2). Hickman-Ruffing attribute this unusual price behaviour to the (atypical in LINK) depreciation of the own currency. But in virtually all the other multi-country models, home currencies depreciate after a fiscal contraction while price levels progressively fall *below* baseline).

It is conceivable, of course, that the LINK system's conclusions about own-country appreciations and very weak crowding in after a fiscal contraction are correct while all the other models' conclusions are qualitatively misleading. But in my opinion the opposite is much more likely. I conjecture that these properties of the LINK system should be attributed to specification problems that have not yet been identified (the issue of analytical transparency!) and that real-world behaviour is closer to that shown in the other models.

Consider next the effects of monetary expansion (a persisting increase in the level of the money stock – tables 3 and 4 in the paper). Theoretical models lead us to expect home interest rates to fall, the home currency to depreciate, and home output and prices to rise. Over the medium and longer run, the rise in home output is expected to be partially if not wholly reversed; prices will continue to rise until fully adjusted to the increase in money. The direction of movement for the home trade and current account balances is theoretically and empirically ambiguous; income/absorption effects raise imports and tend to worsen the external balance, whereas expenditure-switching effects (because of the home currency depreciation) tend to improve the external balance. Since the net effects of a home monetary expansion on the home current account are small, the spillover effects on foreign countries' outputs may also be small (international transmission may be either negative or positive in expository theoretical models).

As stated by Hickman-Ruffing, the LINK system exhibits many of the theoretically expected effects. In several respects, however, the simulations differ qualitatively from those obtained in many other multi-country models. In particular, LINK appears to show less own-country reversal of the output increases in the medium and longer run. In table 3, for example, home output shows hardly any reversal even by the fifth year for French, Italian, and Japanese monetary expansions, while the amount of the longer-run reversal seems small (relative to other models) for Canadian, German, and US monetary expansions. (A UK monetary expansion is the exception; by the fourth year, that expansion has pushed UK output well below baseline, with the amount of the decline still increasing in the fifth year.) I am also puzzled by the relatively large size of cross-border transmission effects to foreign output from US monetary actions (bottom panel of table 3).

Table 4 exhibits a great heterogeneity of price level effects. An increase of 4 per cent in the home money stock leads by the fifth year to increases in home consumer prices of only 1 per cent or less in Germany, Italy, and Japan, to only 2 per cent in the United States, 4.1 per cent in Canada, and fully 6 per cent in the United Kingdom. The results for France are troublesome (as the paper acknowledges) and unbelievable: prices in France *fall* after a monetary expansion, and keep falling monotonically through the fifth year.

In general, several of the LINK national models seem not to capture adequately the price effects of monetary policy actions. As presumptive evidence for this conjecture, consider the simulation results reported in table 7 for a permanent reduction of 100 basis points in interest rates in all G7 countries (scenario D). By the third year, there appears to be only a 0.1 per cent increase in the inflation rate for the developed market economies, and only 0.2 per cent by the fifth year. Those figures seem to me implausibly low; they cast significant doubt on the credibility of LINK monetary policy simulations.

I want to make one other comment on the discussion of the LINK simulations in the paper that is largely semantic, but I believe none the less important. When writing about the cross-border transmission of both the fiscal and monetary actions, Hickman-Ruffing describe the transmission effects as "negligible or small' except for US policy actions. They stress that "this finding of generally small cross-multipliers has been true of LINK simulations from the time of the first experiments in the early 1970s." When reading such statements, one must be careful to reflect on the perspective taken and to interpret "small" properly. The statements are potentially misleading.

It is self evident that GDPs or money stocks or for that matter the populations of Italy or Germany are considerably smaller than the GDP or the money stock or the population in the United States. Hence a fiscal action of 1 per cent of own-country GDP taken by Italy or Germany will of course have smaller effects on foreign countries than will a fiscal action equivalent to 1 per cent of own GDP taken by the United States. It is scarcely surprising that policy actions in big countries have "larger" consequences abroad, measured as a percentage of the foreign economies, than policy actions taken by small countries. The Hickman-Ruffing statements about the "small" cross-border effects of other countries' policy actions relative to those of the United States should be interpreted to mean nothing more than that.

One could ask a different and also interesting question: do own-country policy actions or non-policy shocks spill over into the rest of the world "more powerfully" from country X than from country Y? To answer that question, it could be illuminating to calibrate the shocks to be of equivalent absolute size rather than scaling the shocks to be proportional to the size of the economies. (For example, one might postulate, for both country X and country Y, a shock to expenditure equal to $1 billion and ask about the absolute sizes of the cross-border consequences in both countries.) Judged from this alternative perspective, it would *not* be true that the cross-border consequences of policy actions taken by non-US countries were negligible or small relative to US actions. For a number of economies more open than the United States, cross-border transmission effects are indeed *more* powerful, adjusted for the size of the shock, than those emanating from the United States.

How sizeable does a cross-border transmission effect have to be before we should cease labelling it as "small"? For my taste, if more than, say, a fifth of the total (absolute) effects should fall on foreign rather than own-country key variables, the cross-border effects deserve to be labelled as something other than small. Judged by this rough standard, moreover, the spillover effects of many types of policy actions and non-policy shocks, for a majority of the world's countries, are non-small.

Future research

Toward the end of the Hickman-Ruffing paper, the authors indicate some main avenues envisaged by LINK participants for their current and future research. The priority projects include research on the determinants of trade shares (by Peter Pauly and UN staff); on services trade and transfer payments (UN staff); on a new approach to exchange-rate modelling in LINK, in part to better capture the behaviour within the European Monetary System (Peter Pauly at the University of Toronto); on a model of the world oil market (Robert Kaufmann); and on improvement of the database for the modelling of international capital flows (Institute of Social Studies at the Hague and UN staff).

My own list of research priorities for the next steps in developing empirical multi-country models overlaps partially with the areas identified in the Hickman-Ruffing paper. I particularly want to endorse the need for improved modelling of exchange rates (and hence of interest rates, capital flows, and domestic financial sectors more generally). Virtually all the multi-country modelling groups acknowledge that their existing treatments of exchange-rate determination are deficient.

I want also to identify four other areas that deserve priority attention. The first of these is the manner in which multi-country models specify the behaviour of national fiscal and monetary authorities. To put the matter in technical jargon, modelling groups presently employ a wide variety of alternative "closure rules" for fiscal and monetary policies. We need to pay closer attention to the internal consistency and theoretical plausibility of these heterogeneous specifications (and of course their effects on key macroeconomic variables). In order to evaluate any particular model *vis-à-vis* other models, moreover, we need to reach more of a consensus on the way to standardize specifications. As more has been learned about the simulation properties of empirical models, and in particular those making use of model-consistent expectations, evidence has accumulated that different specifications for tax-rate or government-expenditure reaction functions can lead to significant differences in simulation results. An analogous point applies to alternative specifications for the behaviour of monetary policy. Without greater standardization of the reaction functions specified for fiscal and monetary policies, it may be impossible to diagnose the many other causes of differences in simulation results across models.

More generally – not just with respect to the modelling of fiscal and monetary policies – modelling efforts need to pay more careful attention to the long-run, stationary-state properties of the models. The problems inherent in many of the existing models are readily apparent when we try to use the models to carry out medium- or longer-run "what if" simulations. But these problems about long-run properties may even have substantial importance, I conjecture, for the abilities of the models to generate adequate forecasts or policy simulations for the shorter run.

A second area for priority research is the development of innovative model specifications that permit the taking into account of rapid "structural change." This issue is especially important for how we treat Eastern Europe and the former Soviet Union. Ways must be found to incorporate representations of these formerly centrally-planned regions into global models even as the countries attempt rapid transition to mixed, more market-oriented structures. But we face several other important instances of structural-change problems. For example, how should we be capturing, in the modelling of financial sectors, the rapid advances in communications and information technology? How should the models treat secular changes in "velocity" in money-demand and asset-demand equations? Improved ways need to be found to allow for increases in the cross-currency substitutability of assets in the modelling of exchange rates, interest rates, and capital flows.

A third research area, which I believe has been relatively neglected within Project LINK, is the treatment of expectations. The profession generally, and empirical modellers in particular, need to continue efforts to refine the way we incorporate forward-looking behaviour and learning into our analyses. Backward-looking, adaptive treatments of expectations are plainly not adequate. Use of the assumption of model-consistent (rational) expectations, while an important innovation, also seems to me inadequate. We need innovative halfway houses between these extremes.[5]

Finally, I would single out as a continuing priority the need for refinements in the way that multi-country models treat the interactions between industrial and developing countries. Project LINK has long been a leader in the incorporation of developing countries into a linked global model. However, its bottom-up strategy has not consistently led to innovations in the systemic treatment of the external debts, interest rates, and exchange rates of the developing countries. No doubt there also remains ample room for refinements in the way that global models incorporate commodity prices and the underlying forces of supply and demand for commodities.

For each of these additional research areas I have identified, I believe the short-run prospects for progress are somewhat better for modelling efforts that follow top-down rather than bottom-up strategies.

Final remark

In these comments on the Hickman-Ruffing paper, I have said some critical as well as favourable things about Project LINK. I want to conclude on a supportive note. The enterprise on which LINK and other research groups are engaged is a vitally important one. The world community badly needs a better analytical understanding of how the global economy functions. Notwithstanding LINK's weaker and problematic aspects as an ongoing model, the project deserves intellectual and financial support. As the authors of the paper observe in their concluding sentence, an observation with which I concur, LINK has by no means exhausted its potential. May it be still more successful during the 1990s in contributing to our analytical understanding of global economic interdependence.

Notes

1. The paper updates earlier surveys, such as Hickman (1991).
2. For brevity, my list of models does not include commercial multi-country models (e.g., DRI and WEFA international models built in the United States, the Nikkei and Nomura Research world models operated in Japan, and the Oxford Economic Forecasting world model in the United Kingdom). Nor does it include modelling efforts making predominant use of

input-output or computable general equilibrium techniques; both input-output and CGE models are well represented in this conference volume.

3. Another example would be the MPS model of the Federal Reserve Board. Although this model was originally constructed as a model of the US domestic economy, in recent years it has incorporated a rudimentary and aggregative representation of the rest of the world (Brayton and Mauskopf 1987).
4. The Brookings Institution and several other organizations have sponsored in recent years a series of model comparison and evaluation exercises, an international collaboration much in the spirit of Project LINK. See Bryant, Henderson et al. (1988); Bryant, Holtham, and Hooper (1988); Hooper et al. (1990); Bryant, Currie et al. (1989). Bryant, Helliwell, and Hooper (1989) provide an analytical overview.
5. A recent example of efforts to explore a treatment of expectations intermediate between the adaptive and consistent model extremes, applied to the problem of modelling inflation with the IMF's MIULTIMOD, may be found in Chadha et al. (1991).

References

Brandsma, Andries, Juul op de Beke, Liam O'Sullivan, and Werner Roger. 1991. "Quest: A Macroeconomic Model for the Countries of the European Community as Part of the Whole Economy." *European Economy* 47, March.

Brayton, Flint, and Eileen Mauskopf. 1987. "Structure and Uses of the MPS Quarterly Econometric Model of the United States." *Federal Reserve Bulletin*, February, pp. 93–109.

Bremer, Stuart A. 1987. *The Globus Model: Computer Simulation of Worldwide Political and Economic Developments*. Germany: Frankfurt Campus Verlag and Boulder, Colo.: Westview Press.

Bryant, Ralph C., David Currie, Jacob A. Frenkel, Paul R. Masson, and Richard Portes, eds. 1989. *Macroeconomic Policies in an Interdependent World*. Washington, D.C.: International Monetary Fund, Brookings Institution, Centre for Economic Policy Research, September.

Bryant, Ralph C., John F. Helliwell, and Peter Hooper. 1989. "Domestic and Cross-Border Consequences of U.S. Macroeconomic Policies." In: Bryant, Currie et al., eds. *Macroeconomic Policies in an Interdependent World*. Washington, D.C.: International Monetary Fund, Brookings Institution, Centre for Economic Policy Research, September. Unabridged version available as Brookings Discussion Paper in International Economics No. 68, Washington, D.C.: Brookings Institution, January.

Bryant, Ralph C., Dale W. Henderson, Gerald Holtham, Peter Hooper, and Steven A. Symansky, eds. 1988. *Empirical Macroeconomics for Interdependent Economies*. Washington, D.C.: Brookings Institution.

Bryant, Ralph C., Gerald Holtham, and Peter Hooper. 1988. *External Deficits and the Dollar: The Pit and the Pendulum*. Washington, D.C.: Brookings Institution.

CEPII/OFCE (Centre d'Études Prospectives et d'Informations Internationales and Observatoire Français des Connunctures Économicques). 1990. MIMOSA: A Model of the World Economy. CEPII Working Paper 90-02, May.

Chada, Bankim, Paul Masson, and Guy Meredith. 1991. Models of Inflation and the Costs of Disinflation. International Monetary Fund, Research Department Working Paper, October.

Economic Research Institute, Economic Planning Agency, Government of Japan. 1991. *EPA World Economic Model: Vol. I. Model Structure; Vol. II. Multipliers.* January 1991 version. Tokyo: Economic Planning Agency.

Edison, Hali J., Jaime R. Marquez, and Ralph W. Tryon. 1987. "The Structure and Properties of the Federal Reserve Board Multi-country Model." *Economic Modeling* 4, April.

Frisch, Ragnar. 1947. "On the Need for Forecasting a Multilateral Balance of Payments." *American Economic Review* 37: 535–551.

Gagnon, Joseph E. 1991. "A Forward-looking Multi-country Model for Policy Analysis: MX3," *Economic and Financial Computing* 1: 311–361.

Haas, Richard, and Paul Masson. 1986. "MINIMOD: Specification and Simulation Results." *IMF Staff Papers* 33, December.

Helliwell, John F., Jon Cockerline, and Robert Lafrance. 1990. "Multi-country Modeling of Financial Markets." In: Peter Hooper et al., eds., *Financial Sectors in Open Economies: Empirical Analysis and Policy Issues.* Washington, D.C.: Board of Governors of the Federal Reserve System.

Helliwell, John F., Guy Meredith, Philip Bagnoli, and Yves Durand. 1990. "INTERMOD 1.1: A G-7 Version of the IMF's MULTIMOD." *Economic Modeling* 7, January, pp. 3–62.

Hickman, Bert G. 1991. "Project LINK and Multi-country Modeling." In: R.G. Bodkin, L.R. Klein, and K. Marwah, eds. *A History of Macro-Econometric Model-Building.* Aldershot, England: Edward Elgar.

Hooper, Peter et al., eds. 1990. *Financial Sectors in Open Economies: Empirical Analysis and Policy Issues.* Washington, D.C.: Board of Governors of the Federal Reserve System.

Masson, Paul R., Steven Symansky, Richard Haas, and Michael Dooley. 1988. "MULTIMOD: A Multi-Region Econometric Model." In *Staff Studies for the World Economic Outlook.* Research Department of the International Monetary Fund, July, pp. 50–104.

McKibbin, Warwick J., and Jeffrey D. Sachs. 1991. *Global Linkages: Macroeconomic Interdependence and Cooperation in the World Economy.* Washington, D.C.: Brookings Institution.

Meredith, Guy. 1989. "Model Specification and Simulation Properties." *Working Paper No. 89-7.* Ottawa: Working Group on International Macroeconomics, Department of Finance.

Metzler, Lloyd A. 1950. "A Multi-Region Theory of Income and Trade." *Econometrica* 18: 329–354.

Minford, Patrick. 1985. "The Effects of American Policies – New Classical Interpretation." In: Willem H. Buiter and Richard C. Marston, eds. *International Economic Policy Coordination.* Cambridge, England: Cambridge University Press for the Centre for Economic Policy Research.

Minford, Patrick, P.-R. Agenor, and E. Nowell. 1986. "A New Classical Macro-econometric Model of the World Economy." *Economic Modeling* 3: 154–176.

Polak, Jacques J. 1953. *An International Economic System.* Chicago: University of Chicago Press.

Polak, J.J., and Rudolph R. Rhomberg. 1962. "Economic Instability in an International Setting." Reprinted in R.A. Gordon and L.R. Klein, eds. *Readings in Business Cycle Theory.* Homewood, Ill.: Irwin.

Rhomberg, Rudolph R., and Lorette Boissoneault. 1964. "Effects of Income and Price Changes on the U.S. Balance of Payments." *IMF Staff Papers* 11, 59–124.
Richardson, Pete. 1988. "The Structure and Simulation Properties of OECD's Interlink Model." *OECD Economic Studies* 10, Spring.
Stevens, Guy, Richard Berner, Peter Clark, Ernesto Herrandez-Cata, Howard Howe, and Sung Kwack. 1984. *The U.S. Economy in an International World: A Multi-country Model.* Washington, D.C.: Board of Governors of the Federal Reserve System.
Taylor, John B. 1988. "The Treatment of Expectations in Large Multi-country Econometric Models." In: Bryant, Henderson, Holtham, eds. *Empirical Macroeconomics for Interdependent Economies.* Washington, D.C.: Brookings Institution.
—— 1989. "Policy Analysis with a Multi-country Model." In Bryant, Currie et al. eds. *Macroeconomic Policies in an Interdependent World.* Washington, D.C.: International Monetary Fund, Brookings Institution, Centre for Economic Policy Research, September.
Wren-Lewis, Simon, and Ray Barrell. 1988. GEM Model Manual: A Description and Equation Listing of the National Institute's Global Econometric Model. Preliminary mimeo version, January.

2. Valery L. Makarov

The world economy becomes more and more interdependent; it behaves more and more as a unitarian organism. This overall interdependence has a great impact on individual countries, especially on their economies. It increases the role and responsibility of international organizations in controlling and managing so-called global issues that are of very wide scope. There are those that have to be carefully analysed since these are more sensitive and actually present. Linkages between countries can be so complicated and sophisticated that it is impossible to understand and predict consequences without using different modelling tools. For example, a global issue arose recently regarding maintenance and increase of the general level of security of investment in the economy of an individual country (the Chernobyl case, nuclear disarmament and conversion, etc.). Needless to say, a number of consequences related to the collapse of the so-called World Socialist system (states with centrally planned economies) have to be analysed carefully. The general impact of the event on the world economy is not as clear as we may think.

Project LINK is a remarkable example of an analytical tool for the global issues investigation. Unquestionably, it is an exceptional international organization with representatives from over 80 countries. It is well balanced in relation to keeping unchangeable basic principles and structures and adaptive to a developing process that enhances the incorporated models.

The Project, based on individual country models, was always built by national teams following LINK standards. This principle gives the necessary flexibility for providing various schemes of interrelation among the countries.

It is interesting to note some externalities related to Project LINK as an international activity. It has an impact itself of integration among so-called instrumental economists. It initiates a learning process, a process of adjustment in preparing statistical data, using computer software, working out standards in simulations, the production of scenarios, etc.

Let me be more specific. There are numerous types of linkages among countries. Some of them are as follows:

- trade flows of goods;
- flows of capital, exchange rates;
- technology transfers, intellectual property rights issues;
- migration of the labour force;
- pollution, environmental issues;
- information flows; and
- externalities issues.

The first two types are explored in various ways in Project LINK.

Trade flows

This functions as a nice scheme for adjustment of trade flows and prices, based on the following assumptions: import of an individual country depends on GDP (or similar variable), exchange rate of domestic currency and the dollar, domestic price level, and import price index. Export of an individual country is defined as the sum of imports of all countries from the country, which is calculated by using a matrix of trade shares. The import price of an individual country is equal to the weighted index of the export prices of its supplying countries. So, if one has the given matrix of trade shares, the vector of imports, and the vector of all export prices, it is possible to define vectors of exports and import prices. The circle get closed and one can repeat the procedure until convergence is achieved.

The scheme is "homogeneous" and thanks to that is a simpler, workable, and consistent economic theory. But the present economic world is unfortunately not so homogeneous. Trade relations among former socialist countries and among former Soviet republics are not satisfactory to the named assumptions. Conditions of trade inside former CMEA and the former Soviet Union are different in comparison with conditions for trade with OECD or third world countries. For example, non-convertibility of domestic currency affects major dependence of import from the West on export to the West. A national debt is a crucial variable. So, a possible way is to work out a more appropriate scheme that simulates trade relations between former socialist countries and former Soviet republics.

I do agree with Professor Klein's suggestion for using the CGE (Computable General Equilibrium) model to analyse the reforming process in former socialist countries, especially because the CGE approach requires less statistical data. But at the same time I think that it is important to apply the LINK-type approach to former Soviet Socialist republics. Three of these republics (Baltic) have now become fully independent states. Many of the others are on the way to being fully independent. There are several specific problems related to an economic alliance of the former Soviet republics. How can adjustment process of setting trade prices be organized? What will happen if national currencies instead of the rouble are introduced in all or in some of these states? In some of the states two currencies will operate. For example, in Ukraine there is a plan to introduce universal coupons that can be used many times. So the coupons are similar to the standard currency. At the same time one has to pay roubles when using coupons. Analogous plans were discussed in Russia. So the problem of numerous exchange rates arises. Coming back to the adjustment process of trade flows and prices I can suggest a simple scheme for the former Soviet republics.

Starting from imports of Western countries to the USS (Union of Sovereign States – new name for the former USSR) one can define the exports of the USS. It corrects the iterating process and makes it more realistic.

Capital flows

These are an important part of linkages among countries in a modern world. Relating to the former Soviet Union, we see much activity in establishing joint ventures in different industries. In the Hickman-Ruffing paper a composite scenario of reduced military spending with increased capital flows to Eastern Europe and the USSR is presented. My comment, related to that, is the following. It is doubtful that import capacities will increase as was assumed in the scenario. But it is necessary to take into account the balance of payments. The USS has a relatively big foreign debt and the amount of import depends very much on the credit policy of Western banks. On the other hand, this kind of scenario is realistic. For example, if the "Big Seven" make a decision to increase the Russia's share of world market nuclear products, then Russian exports and imports immediately increase as well.

Related to the other types of links among countries, I would like to pay attention to the nice feature in the LINK system: the opportunity to use a variable of a national model as an argument in any endogenous equation in any other model. It means that specific variables in a Russian model, like a share of an alternative sector in GDP or a level of poverty or some parameter of instability can be put into any other model as an endogenous variable. This provides the possibility of an assessment of different policies for influencing economic and political situations in the former Soviet Union.

3. Chikashi Moriguchi

First, I should like to mention a potential research aspect of the multi-country econometric model. It should be noted that an interesting field of linking national models is to link them not only through macroeconomic trade relations, but also through industry sectoral trade relations. Intra-industry trade relations in some of the major manufacturing industries are commonplace. Professor Kinoshita of Nagoya University did pioneering work in this field. He dealt with the international linkage of auto, steel, and textile industries and tried to measure impacts of protectionism. I think his work should be mentioned in the survey.

Now I should like to proceed to discuss the Project LINK world model. It has made a great contribution to the econometric modelling clear. There seems to be a tendency that the magnitude of observed international repercussions produced by the system to any given shocks are rather significantly smaller than what has been anticipated by theoretical insights.

Estimated impact and dynamic multipliers (whether they are measured in terms of elasticity or not) are small in the cases of France and some other countries (a diagonal, within-in country effect). Off-diagonal multipliers, which reflect international repercussions, are so small that the so-called "Locomotive Thesis" in the arena of international policy coordination loses its own steam from the lack of positive support from quantitative research.

I should like to present some of the reasons why this is so, and how we can possibly overcome this obstacle.

1. Some country models show small magnitude of direct impact multipliers (diagonal) and there are reasons why this is so. In the case of France (the INSEE model of the French economy) entrepreneurial activities of firms in business with fixed investments do not exist due to the fact that major industries are nationalized and are treated as an "exogenous" factor in the model. In addition, consumption behaviours are modelled in the way in which various socio-economic and demographic factors are dealt with in detail, weakening the direct income-consumption relation.

2. In the contemporary world, where "managed trade" prevails significantly, the seemingly free-trade submodel of national economic models tends to underestimate the basic income and price elasticities of trading behaviour, giving a set of small off-diagonal multiplier effects.

3. In addition to these, I should like to point out that one of the major international links in the world economic system is not well treated in the world model. That is the service industry sector. Due to a lack of appropriate statistical data for the bilateral flow of freight, insurance, investment income, and tourism, this growing sector of the world economy is only partly endogenized in contemporary world models, including the LINK world model. Japan's demand for overseas tourism is the fastest growing element in private sector demand. Income elasticity of demand as well as price elasticity is high, and potential international repercussions throughout this sector are entirely neglected by the world model. The Japanese model produces an impact effect of overseas tourism to a given income or price shock, but it is not distributed to other countries' national models as increments of their service exports. The present international linkage system deals with commodity trade.

Dr. Bryant made some critical points on the contemporary multicountry models which follow the "bottom-up" method of model-building, the present-day method that absorbs whatever national models are built up and preferred by country model builders. I think that most of his points are legitimate for the above stated reasons. However, my points also offer some possibility of improvement in the future. Endogenizing efforts on services trade will be the single most important matter, but it is important as well that the "top" which is the central link in the case of the LINK model, grasps the intrinsic nature of individual national economic models.

3

Global demand for capital, the rate of interest, and world models

Paul S. Armington

Summary

The Development Community expects exceptional global demand for capital of about $100 billion (US dollars) per year for the next 10 years. A state-of-the-art structural model, used to calibrate a basic IS-LM framework applied at the global level of aggregation, shows that this exceptional demand is likely to raise the global real rate of interest by about 160 basis points in the medium term. For the developing countries, such an increase in interest would nullify within three years the benefit to them of the upward shift in demand. The reduction of developing-country growth stemming from the rise of the interest rate itself would be about 0.4 per cent per annum in the medium term. Single-equation estimation of the global interest rate corroborates the structural model and its calibration. This equation may be usefully applied in large global systems that link national models through an integrated international capital market.

Introduction

High global demands for capital over the coming decade and beyond are widely expected. The oft-cited elements in this picture are the rebuilding of the Eastern *Länder* of Germany and of war-torn areas of the oil-rich Middle East; remodelling the infrastructure of Taiwan and other NIEs; plus potentially large replacement of the deteriorating public infrastructure in the United States and some other industrial countries. These *ex ante* demands will be effective – i.e., will actually move economic variables like capital flows and interest rates – because the creditworthiness of the borrowers is not in doubt. In addition, the catch-up of Eastern Europe and the Soviet Union, as well as the rebuilding of developing countries where debt has caused decay in the eighties, represent potentially large calls on the world capital market. Creditworthiness will determine the effective size of these calls. Finally, of course, the price tag on any credible global effort to begin protecting the environment, reversing the erosion of the "Global Commons," is bound to be large.

The total exceptional global demand for capital cannot be appraised with any precision, of course, but it is certainly large. One tally made in the World Bank earlier this year [1991] suggested a total effective demand of $1 trillion over the next 10 years, or some $100 billion per year. This would be *in addition* to the business-as-usual scale of investment that we would expect and project on the basis of trend growth in world output and the kinds of normal relationships found in global models.

We do not see any comparably strong reasons for expecting exceptionally high levels of global (*ex ante*) savings. The hope of government action to reduce fiscal deficits in the OECD countries is the main favourable factor on the savings side; however, were these hopes to become certainties, a partly-offsetting fall in private savings rates could be expected (according to "Ricardian equivalence" theory). In the OECD area, and hence in the world aggregates, too, it is investment that drives savings, not the other way around.

The question raised in this note, therefore, is how big an effect on world (real) interest rates should we expect to result from (each) $100 billion of additional effective demand for capital, at the global level of aggregation and at the present scale of the world economy (if it is not matched by a comparable shift in desired savings). We then draw the implications of our answer for growth in the developing countries.

The basic framework

The basic framework of analysis that is suitable for addressing this question is the familiar IS-LM model. Here, savings (S) is global *pri-*

vate savings, while, correspondingly, investment (gross of depreciation) includes the public-sector deficit (+). All flows and stocks are measured in constant 1991 dollars. The rate of interest (r) is conceived as a global representative or average short-term rate, and is adjusted for expected inflation. The relationships are posited to be locally linear around the present equilibrium level of world income or GDP (Y). Signs are consistent with positive expected values for all parameters. Constant terms are unnecessary and are omitted. This framework will only be used here to assess the effects of a sustained real shift – an increase (ΔZ) of \$100 billion per annum, lasting for several years, in the desired level of global real investment (including the public-sector deficit). The global real money supply (M) is assumed to accommodate this shift, i.e., respond positively to any increase in r that the shift induces, to a certain extent f, as shown in the "policy rule for stabilization."

Desired investment:

$$I = -ar + Z, \tag{1}$$

where Z, depending on private expectations and on fiscal policy, is assumed to be exogenous

Desired private savings:

$$S = br + cY \tag{2}$$

Demand for money:

$$L = dY - er \tag{3}$$

Policy rule for stabilization:

$$M = fr \tag{4}$$

Equilibrium conditions

$I = S$:

$$r = -\frac{c}{a+b}Y + \frac{1}{a+b}Z \tag{5}$$

$L = M$:

$$r = \frac{d}{e+f} Y \tag{6}$$

Equilibrium income:

$$\Delta Y = \Delta Z \bigg/ \left[\frac{(a+b)d}{e+f} + c \right] \tag{7}$$

Equilibrium interest rate:

$$\Delta r = \Delta Z \bigg/ \left[(a+b) + \frac{c}{d}(e+f) \right]. \tag{8}$$

From equation (8) it follows that an *additional* demand for capital of \$100 billion ($\Delta Z = 100$) raises the world real interest rate (in basis points) by the *reciprocal* of the function $a + b + (c/d)(e+f)$. Since all parameters in this function are expected to be positive, the change in r is unambiguously expected to be upward. The *extent* of the rise will be *more*:

- if the derivatives of investment and savings with respect to the interest rate (a and b) are small;
- if the marginal propensity to save (in all forms of private wealth accumulation) is a small multiple of the marginal propensity to demand money balances (i.e., if c/d is small);
- if the stabilizing feedback through the excess demand for money is small – i.e., if the function $e+f$ is small.

Note that if monetary policy were targeted on fixing the level of Y (in this case, preventing it from rising), only a and b (determining the slope of the IS curve) would be relevant. In this case the number we seek would be inferable directly from differentiating the $I = S$ equilibrium condition, with Y constant. However, realistically speaking, central banks do not react this way. Thus, the rise in the interest rate cannot be obtained simply by inverting the savings and investment functions, as is being incorrectly done in some current assessments of capital shortage.[1] In short, we must not overlook the "LM" side of the analysis.

Calibrating the effect of additional investment demand on the interest rate and on income

This basic framework is embedded in most operational models of the world economy. These models differ in the specific ways they handle the I, S, L, and M functions. In realistic models the derivatives *a* through *f* will not generally be constants but rather complex functions of many variables, including expectations. While it will not generally be possible to derive these functions analytically (especially in large, forward-looking models), full-model simulations can be used to evaluate these derivatives with respect to any particular interval of time, and hence to derive the coefficients of ΔZ in equations (7) and (8) for this interval. In this section we illustrate such a calculation for 1991–1993.

For this exercise we have chosen the McKibbin-Sachs Global (MSG) model.[2] This model has rigorously specified long-run restrictions on stocks and flows. Moreover, it solves for the real rate of interest under model-consistent expectations about inflation, exchange rates, and asset prices, and builds this price information into the structure of demand and supply for goods and assets. Hence, changes in flows that imply future disequilibria in stocks cause prices such as exchange rates to change in anticipatory fashion. The model features integrated capital markets in money, bonds, and equities, equalizing long-run expected rates of return on comparable assets across the major countries after due allowance for expected exchange rates and inflation rates. Hence, following some given disturbance, real interest rates of the major countries tend to converge over time, as expected changes in exchange rates diminish in importance.

Because the international capital markets are well integrated, a \$100 billion increase in Z will affect the *average* real rate of interest in the core group of countries (say, the G3: Japan, Germany, and the United States) in much the same way no matter where it occurs. In the present illustration we assume a sustained rise of \$100 billion in US government spending, beginning in 1991. More precisely, the shift is specified as a constant percentage of US present and future (baseline) GNP, amounting to \$100 billion in 1991. The shift is "sustained" in the sense that it continues through the nineties, but it is not literally permanent since the MSG includes restrictions on government debt at a given horizon, several decades out. We compute the effects of such a shift, year by year, on real short-term (1-year) interest rates of the United States, Japan, and Germany. While

Table 1 **Effects on real short-term rates of a sustained increase of $100bn per annum in US government spending, beginning in 1991 (in basis points above baseline)**

	1991	1992	1993
With money supplies unchanged			
United States	210	180	192
Japan	11	153	196
Germany	44	127	169
Simple average	88	153	186
With US money supply set to keep US GNP unchanged			
United States	456	348	244
Japan	61	213	221
Germany	80	183	202
Simple average	192	248	222

Source: McKibbin-Sachs Global model.

the model also solves for long-term (10-year) rates, the short rates are closer to the opportunity cost of money that satisfies $L = M$. The time horizon for averaging the (short-term) interest-rate effects is somewhat arbitrary: in the tables below, we focus on the first three years, where most of the changes in rates are concentrated. However, the interest-rate effects continue to drift upward after three years, as public-sector debt accumulates.

The model solution with the expenditure shift and no changes in money supplies yields an estimate of the reciprocal of $a + b + (c/d)e$. That is, our accommodation parameter f is taken to be zero in this case. The results are in the top half of table 1, for the individual countries. Using a simple average of the G3 rates to represent the "global" interest rate, we summarize the results "with no monetary accommodation" in the first column of table 2. Note that the upward effect on the G3 increases over time, as public debt increases and as the effects on non-US rates tend to converge toward the initially high US effects. During the first three years on average, $a + b + (c/d)e = 0.70$, and the effect on the G3 average interest rate is its reciprocal, 1.42.

If the same total shift of $100 billion were distributed over the three centres – say United States 40, Japan 30, and Germany 30 – the effect on the G3 average interest rate would be much the same: 1.38 during the first three years on average. Of course, the results for each

Table 2 **Summary of effects on the average G3 short-term rate of interest of a sustained increase of $100bn per annum in US government spending (in basis points above baseline)**

Average rise	With no monetary accommodation	With reasonable monetary accommodation
Year 1	88	57
Years 1 and 2	121	84
Years 1, 2, and 3	142	105
Year 3	186	159

Source: McKibbin-Sachs Global model and author's calculations.

of the national interest rates (and for the exchange rates) are quite different, comparing these two simulations.

Going back to the case where the total shift occurs in the United States, can we quantify the different parameters of the basic framework, a to f?

The slope of the $I = S$ curve, or $1/(a + b)$, can be obtained by combining the US expenditure shift with a sufficiently-large contraction of the US money supply to prevent output from rising. The ratio of the resulting change in interest rate to the size of the given shift in expenditures is an estimate of $1/(a + b)$. The results are in the bottom half of table 1. During the first three years on average, this slope is estimated to be about 220 basis points per $100 billion. That is, $a + b$ is about 0.45 (reciprocal of 2.20).

Monetary adjustment contributes the remaining 0.25 (0.70–0.45). That is, $(c/d)e = 0.25$. How big are these parameters? If a change in income does not change the desired ratio of global saving to real money balances, the ratio of the *marginal* propensities, (c/d), would be about the same as the ratio of the *average* propensities, which appears to be about 5 worldwide (for M2). This would imply, in turn, that e is 0.05. A rise of 100 basis points in the world interest rate lowers the global demand for money balances by $5 billion. If we use a marginal propensity to save (private saving out of disposable income) of 0.20, then c is 0.20, and d can be put at 0.04.

Finally, how big is f? What is the accommodating rise in money supply normally occasioned by a rise of 100 basis points? If public and private reactions make the same absolute contribution to the stabilizing feedback function $(e + f)$, then $f = e = 0.05$. If this is a reasonable degree of monetary accommodation, we can now answer the original question. For 1991–1993 on average, the function $a+b+(c/d)(e+f)$ is estimated to be 0.95, and its reciprocal is thus 1.05.

Thus,

$$\Delta r = 1.05\Delta Z, \tag{8a}$$

for the first three years on average – the "short run."

In other words, a sustained additional demand (by government) for capital of $100 billion will add an estimated 105 basis points to the world real short-term rate of interest during 1991–1993, assuming reasonable monetary accommodation (table 2, second column). During the first year only, the increase would be about 60 basis points, but this result is sensitive to the weights used in aggregating the G3. By the third year, when G3 rates have approximately converged, the global result is 160 basis points. This figure can be taken to represent the medium-term effect:

$$\Delta r \cong 1.60\Delta Z \tag{8b}$$

in the medium term.

Given these estimates of the structural parameters ($a+b=0.45$, $c=0.20$, $d=0.04$, and e and $f=0.05$ each), the effect of a change in Z on world GDP (Y) can be calculated from equation (7). The bracketed function in (7) is 0.38. Thus, a $100 billion increase in Z yields a one-time increase in Y of about $260 billion, which is about 1 per cent of present world GDP (some $25 trillion at 1991 prices and exchange rates). This is a useful relationship for evaluating the effects of a change in Z on growth in developing countries, to which we now turn.

Implications for growth in developing countries

The *level* of real world interest rates affects the *growth rates* of developing countries in the medium-term because it affects their sustainable investment ratios and hence their trend growth rates of output, for given levels of dynamic efficiency (usually measured by their incremental capital-output ratios). This relationship is strongest for countries that:

- are highly indebted;
- will actually meet their debt-service obligations;

- lack access to additional external financial assistance;
- lack scope for compressing consumption or for increasing efficiency in the use of capital;
- encounter high costs (e.g., because of supply rigidities, lack of market mechanisms, or weak government) of mobilizing domestic resources to pay external creditors.

Unfortunately, these factors characterize many of the low- and middle-income ("developing") countries that borrowed heavily in the years after the oil crisis of 1973 and that were then forced to compress their domestic absorption severely in the "debt crisis" of the 1980s. An aggregation of country-by-country assessments, using the projections models developed in the World Bank, indicates that, for developing countries in the aggregate, a sustained 160 basis-point rise in world real short-term interest rates would reduce their medium-term growth rate by about four-tenths of a percentage point *per annum*. This is a significant cost to them, especially as the loss keeps mounting up over time. It would soon swamp the static efficiency gains of almost any one-shot improvement in the allocation of their resources, or of any small, one-time increase in the demand for their exports.

In particular, as already noted, a sustained shift in Z of $100 billion would raise the *level* of world GDP by an estimated 1 per cent, but there is no presumption that it would raise the sustainable *growth rate* of world GDP. Suppose that developing countries' own output fully participated in this rise, i.e., increased by 1 per cent. Using the medium-term interest rate effect (160 basis points), we calculate that this whole gain would be eroded away in two to three years ($1.0/0.4 = 2.5$). After about three years the developing countries would be worse off, owing to the shift in Z, unless this shift raises the sustainable growth rate of the world economy. This last condition is clearly crucial to the long-run "bottom line" for the developing countries. Unfortunately, the IS-LM framework is not suited to investigating this growth issue, and this problem is not pursued further in this paper.

In sum, the issue of "global savings shortage," as seen from the standpoint of the developing countries, is that of how to shift the global savings rate upward so that the potential benefits to them of more global spending are not soon eroded away through higher global interest rates. Thus, the developing countries have a special interest in OECD policies that could shift savings upward over the coming decade. The present debate covers policies toward the taxation of capital income of households, the subsidization of business investment, and the levels of government consumption, including military spending.[3]

Single-equation estimation of the global interest rate

For purposes of forecasting, especially using LINK-type models, it will be efficient to model the global real rate of interest by a reduced-form equation like (8), above; each national real rate could then be linked to the global real rate through a dynamic adjustment process that allows for differences in the degree of market integration and in national risk premiums. Estimating the reduced form also provides some check on our calibration of the IS-LM structure.

To get an estimatable equation for the global interest rate, one should assume that the coefficient of Z in equation (8), say X, varies over time. Thus, differentiating equation (8), we get $dr = XdZ + ZdX$. To allow for the upward trend in Z, we normalize the trendy arguments by Z, giving: $dr = X\dot{Z} + dX$, where $\dot{Z}$ is the rate of change of Z, i.e., the rate of change of the exogenous parts of private investment and of the budget deficit. How, then, to measure $\dot{Z}$ and dX?

A good indicator of $\dot{Z}$ may be the lagged rate of change in global equity prices, as argued in Barro and Sala-i-Martin (1990).[4] But unless the model in question is going to forecast the stock market at least as well as the rate of interest, a broader indicator of $\dot{Z}$ will be needed. Instead, the (not-lagged) growth rate of world output works well statistically, according to a study in progress in the World Bank.[5] Needless to say, this estimation cannot identify the components of X well enough to confirm or deny the estimates of the structural parameters in the underlying IS-LM system; for this, there is no alternative to the use of appropriate structural models. But it is possible to check the consistency of the estimated coefficient of world GDP growth with the calibrated IS-LM structure.

The term dX represents the shifts in the structural parameters that have occurred over the period of observation, which in our study starts in the mid 1960s. It uses a *global* database (developed in the International Economics Department of the World Bank), not a subset of countries to somehow represent the world.

We find, confirming Barro, that the price of oil was an important factor shifting X: higher oil prices meant higher real interest rates (*ceteris paribus*). We cannot tell why. It may have worked through lowering the marginal savings rate, as Barro proposes, or it could have worked through increasing the propensity to hold real money balances, or through lowering the interest elasticities of demand for investment, savings, or money, or through inducing the central banks to be less accommodating. All these explanations are plausible and consistent with the empirical results and with the definition of X.

In addition, there is evidence that the degree of accommodation (f) varied over the period of observation for reasons not connected to the price of oil. This evidence is that the lagged growth of G5 money (a plausible indicator of f) has an estimated negative effect on r.

The global interest rate is found to be directly related to the endogenous component of the public sector's balance on current account, or net public saving. This variable is estimated as $ln\,(1+CAB/GDP)$, where CAB is the global public sector's total net receipts from goods, factor and non-factor services, and transfers, and where GDP is world GDP, both in current US dollars. (The negative of CAB is the world's public sector borrowing requirement.) The relationship between this variable and r is plotted in the following chart. The direct relationship is obvious from the picture, with the period 1981–1983 being highly exceptional. For the world as a whole, net private savings *plus* net public saving *equals* zero *ex post* (apart from measurement error). Thus, it should not be surprising if the private sector's marginal propensity to save, c, moves inversely with the net

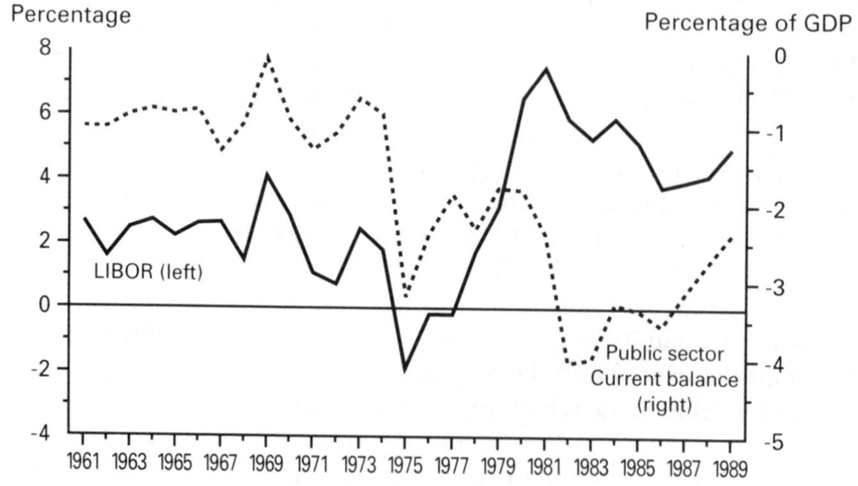

Fig. 1 **Real LIBOR and world public current balance**

```
DADIR2
Ordinary Least Squares
ANNUAL data for   28 periods from 1962 to 1989
Date:  7 OCT 1991

log((1+(r/100)))

  =    0.96657 * log((1+(r/100)))[-1] + 1.18779 * lgfr_gdp
       (7.97739)                         (3.78395)

     + 0.90301 * dlog(y) + 0.02289 * log(op/uspgdp)
       (4.20382)            (5.39951)

     - 0.25832 * log(m.1) + 0.02578
       (2.35626)             (1.58408)

Sum Sq       0.0022   Std Err     0.0100   LHS Mean    0.0291
R Sq         0.8204   R Bar Sq    0.7795   F  5, 22   20.0950
D.W.( 1)     2.2527   D.W.( 2)    1.6893
H           -1.0717
```

DATE	ACTUAL	FITTED
1962	1.53	2.53
1963	2.45	1.16
1964	2.69	4.14
1965	2.18	2.77
1966	2.59	2.53
1967	2.62	1.34
1968	1.35	2.06
1969	4.14	2.93
1970	2.82	3.66
1971	1.01	1.45
1972	0.65	0.02
1973	2.44	1.46
1974	1.76	2.98
1975	-1.96	-0.51
1976	-0.21	-0.26
1977	-0.28	1.30
1978	1.73	1.10
1979	3.08	2.66
1980	6.53	5.00
1981	7.50	7.36
1982	5.80	4.87
1983	5.20	5.31
1984	5.90	6.03
1985	5.10	6.40
1986	3.70	3.25
1987	3.90	3.50
1988	4.10	3.69
1989	5.00	4.48

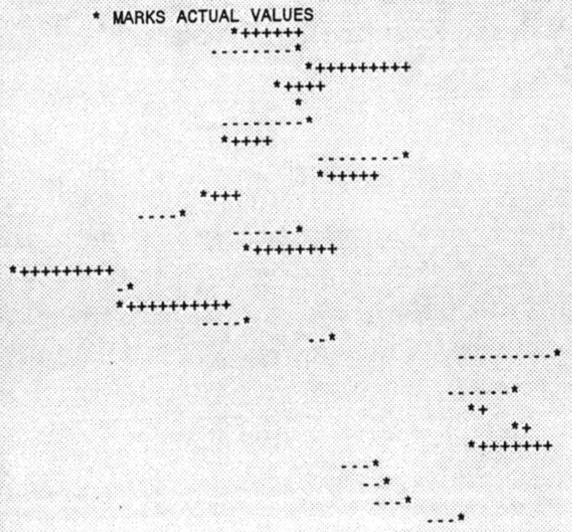

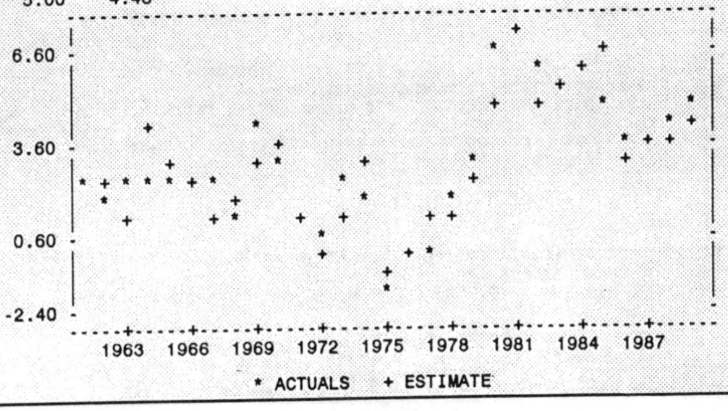

Fig. 2 **DADIR2 (ordinary least square regression statistics)**

public-sector surplus. When the former is high, as in global recession, private *ex ante* demand for financial claims is high, and real interest rates are low. Then also, tautologically, the *ex post* public sector savings rate is low. Aggressive reduction of tax rates, as in the 1981 US

```
                        Chow Tests for Structural Stability
                        -----------------------------------
DADIR2
Ordinary Least Squares
ANNUAL data for   28 periods from 1962 to 1989
Date:  7 OCT 1991

log((1+(r/100)))

  =    0.96657 * log((1+(r/100)))[-1] + 1.18779 * lgfr_gdp
      (7.97739)                        (3.78395)

     + 0.90301 * dlog(y) + 0.02289 * log(op/uspgdp)
      (4.20382)           (5.39951)

     - 0.25832 * log(m.1) + 0.02578
      (2.35626)            (1.58408)

Sum Sq      0.0022   Std Err     0.0100   LHS Mean    0.0291
R Sq        0.8204   R Bar Sq    0.7795   F  5, 22   20.0950
D.W.( 1)    2.2527   D.W.( 2)    1.6893
H          -1.0717
-------------------------------------------------------------------

                        H0:  b0 = b1 = b2 = B
                        ---------------------
                        H1:  b0 ne b1 ne`b2

                     reject if  F        >  F          (critical value)
                                 r1,r2       r1,r2,p

** Chow test of stability for break after  1970
      19 observations from end of sample   ----
   F(    9  13 ):       1.2261       ( based on two regressions )

                 F     1.2261  <  F      4.19  (critical value)
                  9,13              9,13,0.99

        cannot reject null hypothesis at 1 percent level ....

** Chow test of stability for break after  1973
      16 observations from end of sample   ----
   F(    6  16 ):       2.0255       ( based on three regressions )

                 F     2.0255 <  F      4.20  (critical value)
                  6,16             6,16,0.99

        cannot reject null hypothesis at 1 percent level ...

** Chow test of stability for break after  1980
      9 observations from end of sample   ----
   F(    9  13 ):       0.4329       ( based on two regressions )

                 F     0.4329 <  F      4.19  (critical value)
                  9,13             9,13,0.99

        cannot reject hull hypothesis at 1 percent level ...

** Chow test of stability for break after  1985
      4 observations from end of sample   ----
   F(    4  18 ):       0.2500       ( based on two regressions )

                 F     0.2500 <  F      4.58
                  4,18             4,18,0.99

        cannot reject hull hypothesis at 1 percent level ...
```

Fig. 3 **DADIR2 (Chow tests for structural stability)**

tax cut, only disturbed this relationship temporarily. Thus, high public-sector deficits or, more precisely, the *endogenous components* of these deficits (which normally dominate the variance of the series) and low real interest rates normally go together. In 1991, for exam-

DYNAMIC SIMULATIONS

SIMULATION 1970-89
Number of equations predicted 1

	ACTUALS	FORECAST	A-F
1970	2.82	3.66	-0.84
1971	1.01	2.24	-1.23
1972	0.65	1.19	-0.55
1973	2.44	1.99	0.45
1974	1.76	2.54	-0.77
1975	-1.96	0.22	-2.18
1976	-0.21	1.89	-2.10
1977	-0.28	3.36	-3.64
1978	1.73	4.67	-2.94
1979	3.08	5.53	-2.44
1980	6.53	7.41	-0.88
1981	7.50	8.22	-0.72
1982	5.80	5.54	0.26
1983	5.20	5.06	0.14
1984	5.90	5.90	-0.00
1985	5.10	6.40	-1.30
1986	3.70	4.49	-0.79
1987	3.90	4.25	-0.35
1988	4.10	4.03	0.07
1989	5.00	4.41	0.59

(R.A-DADIR2.FORECAST)
ANNUAL Data for 20 periods from 1970 to 1989
Mean -0.96 Standard deviation 1.17
Maximum 0.59 in 1989
Minimum -3.64 in 1977

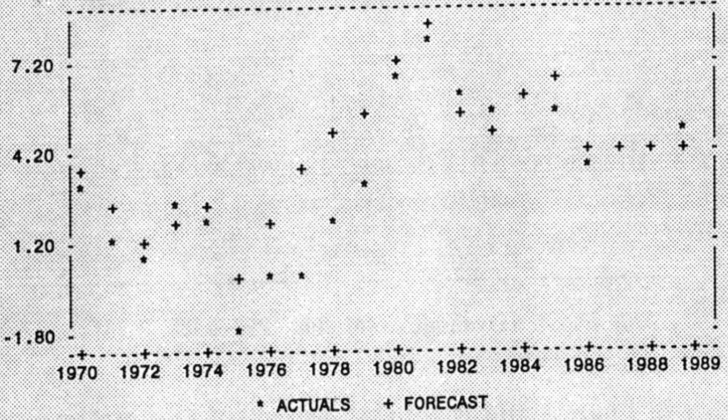

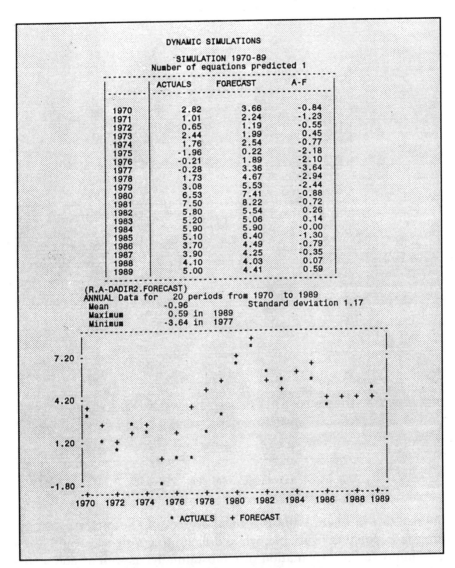

Fig. 4 **Dynamic simulation 1970–1989**

ple, both are manifestations of the downturn in private demand, or of the increase in the rate of private saving. By mid-1991, G5 real LIBOR was down to 3.5 per cent, from 5 per cent in 1989.

This study has not yet taken into account variations in the net tax treatment of corporate income (depreciation allowances, profit tax rates, business deductions). Easier tax treatment of business reduces

SIMULATION 1970-80
Number of equations predicted 1

	ACTUALS	FORECAST	A-F
1970	2.82	3.66	-0.84
1971	1.01	2.24	-1.23
1972	0.65	1.19	-0.55
1973	2.44	1.99	0.45
1974	1.76	2.54	-0.77
1975	-1.96	0.22	-2.18
1976	-0.21	1.89	-2.10
1977	-0.28	3.36	-3.64
1978	1.73	4.67	-2.94
1979	3.08	5.53	-2.44
1980	6.53	7.41	-0.88

(R.A-DADIR2.FORECAST)
ANNUAL Data for 11 periods from 1970 to 1980
Mean -1.56 Standard deviation 1.20
Maximum 0.45 in 1973
Minimum -3.64 in 1977

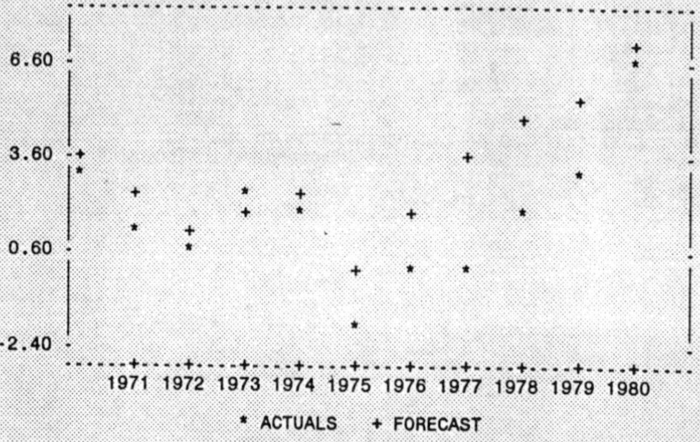

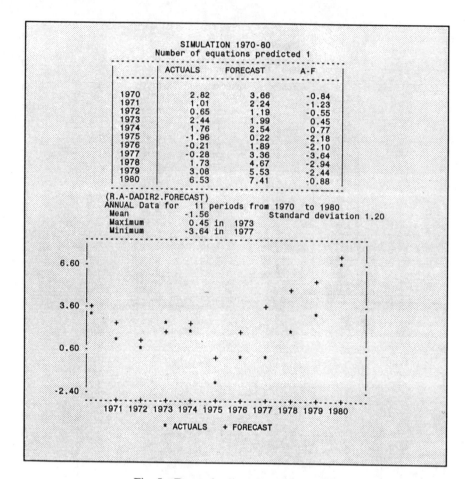

Fig. 5 **Dynamic simulation 1970–1980**

the net cost of finance and is thus an aspect of parameter *a*. An appropriate global tax variable, while difficult to construct, would probably improve the explanation of *r* substantially, as well as add a specific fiscal instrument for use in policy analysis.

Results of the present estimation are summarized in the following page of analysis. It reports an OLS regression of *r* (in log form) on its unrestricted lagged level, the change in logarithm of world real GDP, the log level of the real price of oil, the lagged rate of change in M2 of the G5 countries as a group (this variable is labelled *m.1*), and the normalized global government CAB (labelled *lgfr – gdp*).

The interest rate *r* is constructed as the average (using shares in the

SIMULATION 1973-85
Number of equations predicted 1

	ACTUALS	FORECAST	A-F
1973	2.44	1.46	0.98
1974	1.76	2.02	-0.26
1975	-1.96	-0.27	-1.70
1976	-0.21	1.41	-1.62
1977	-0.28	2.89	-3.17
1978	1.73	4.21	-2.48
1979	3.08	5.08	-1.99
1980	6.53	6.96	-0.43
1981	7.50	7.79	-0.29
1982	5.80	5.14	0.66
1983	5.20	4.67	0.53
1984	5.90	5.52	0.38
1985	5.10	6.03	-0.93

(R.A-DADIR2.FORECAST)
ANNUAL Data for 13 periods from 1973 to 1985
Mean -0.79 Standard deviation 1.31
Maximum 0.98 in 1973
Minimum -3.17 in 1977

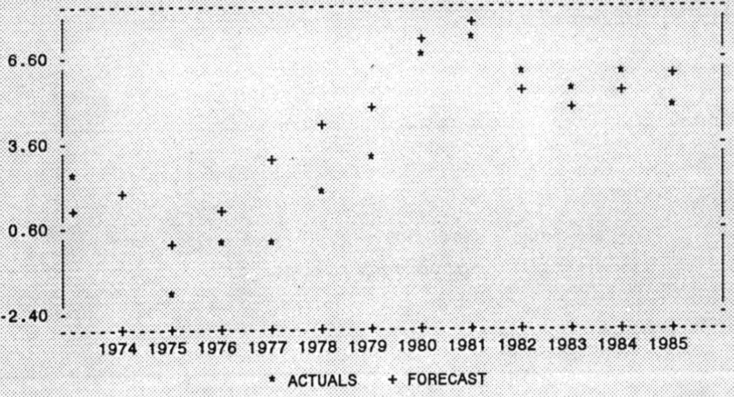

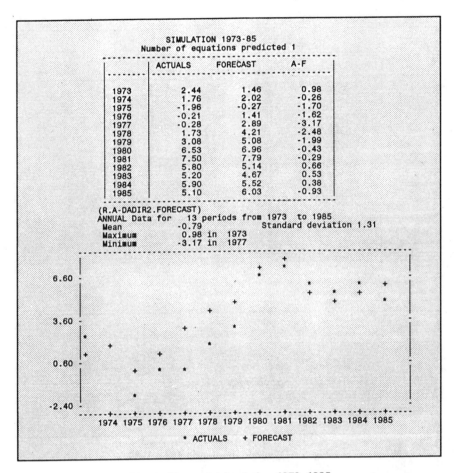

Fig. 6 **Dynamic simulation 1973–1985**

SDR basket as weights) of six-month LIBOR rates of the G5 (G3 plus France and the United Kingdom), deflated by respective actual rates of change in GNP deflators. Any differences between actual inflation and expected inflation will thus show up as noise in this series. The statistics of fit could probably be improved if expected inflation rates were computed from rolling autoregressive forecasts.

Note that the coefficient on the lagged dependent variable is about 1; that is, the equation is explaining the change in the interest rate. The coefficient of 0.9 on $d\ log(y)$ implies that, for every percentage point by which global growth exceeds trend, the world interest rate rises by 90 basis points. This seems broadly consistent with the cali-

SIMULATION 1981-89
Number of equations predicted 1

	ACTUALS	FORECAST	A-F
1981	7.50	7.36	0.14
1982	5.80	4.74	1.06
1983	5.20	4.29	0.91
1984	5.90	5.15	0.75
1985	5.10	5.67	-0.57
1986	3.70	3.79	-0.09
1987	3.90	3.58	0.32
1988	4.10	3.38	0.72
1989	5.00	3.78	1.22

(R.A-DADIR2.FORECAST)
ANNUAL Data for 9 periods from 1981 to 1989
Mean 0.50 Standard deviation 0.59
Maximum 1.22 in 1989
Minimum -0.57 in 1985

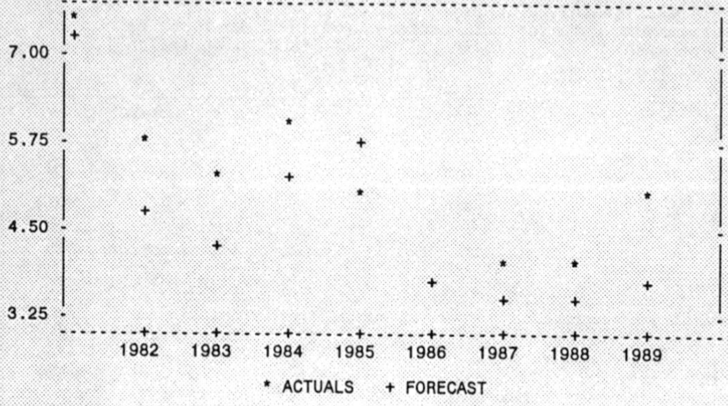

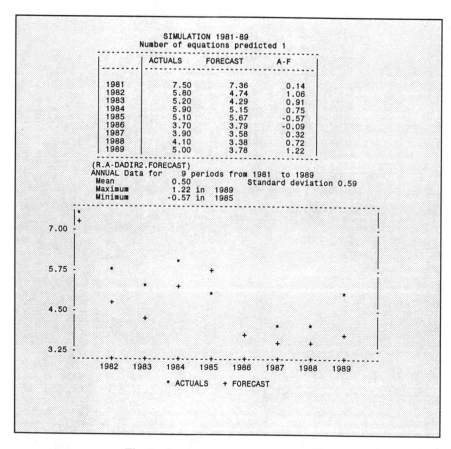

Fig. 7 **Dynamic simulation 1981–1989**

bration of the structural model. We noted earlier that a $100 billion increase in Z should raise world income by about 1 per cent and the world real short-term interest rate by some 80–90 basis points during the first couple of years (table 2). Thus, the regression results seem consistent with the hypothesis that the observed variations in both r and Y are being generated by Z and the structural model, approximately as we have calibrated it.

Overall, the regression statistics are quite respectable. The within-simple static and dynamic simulations and Chow tests are shown below, and they seem generally encouraging (see the following figures).

In sum, the structural parameters of our basic IS-LM framework have varied over the past 25 years. Using a single-equation approach

SIMULATION 1985-89
Number of equations predicted 1

	ACTUALS	FORECAST	A-F
1985	5.10	6.40	-1.30
1986	3.70	4.48	-0.78
1987	3.90	4.25	-0.35
1988	4.10	4.03	0.07
1989	5.00	4.41	0.59

(R.A-DADIR2.FORECAST)
ANNUAL Data for 5 periods from 1985 to 1989
Mean -0.35 Standard deviation 0.73
Maximum 0.59 in 1989
Minimum -1.30 in 1985

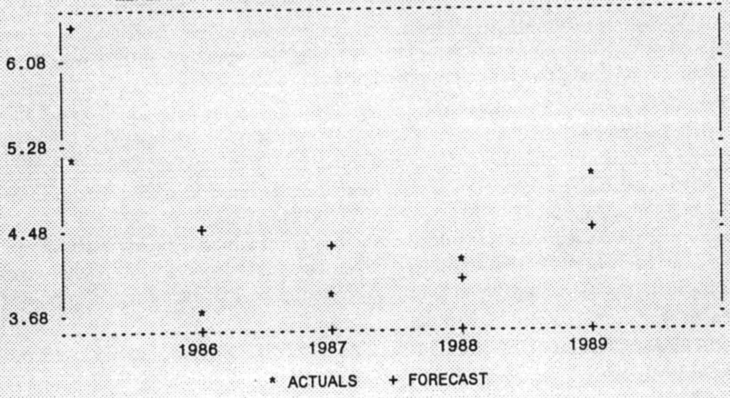

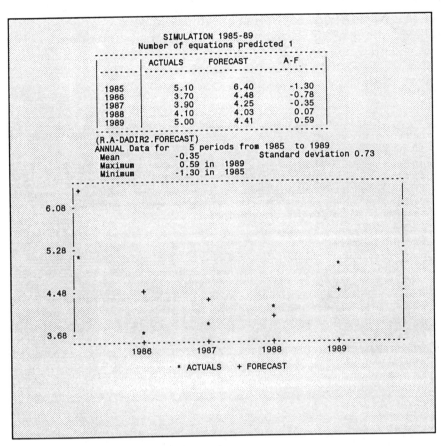

Fig. 8 **Dynamic simulation 1985–1989**

to estimating the reduced form, we find that movements in the overall coefficient of *Z* can be explained well, while *Z* itself can be proxied by growth of the world economy. This yields a quite respectable equation for explaining and forecasting the world real rate of interest. One key to better forecasts of the global real interest rate will be better forecasts of global private savings, which normally drive the net savings of the world's public sector.

This equation opens up an elementary way to link national models financially, by linking national interest rates to the global rate, which is solved in the "linkage bloc" of the system by bringing together all the relevant national prices and quantities from solutions of the national models. This is the research strategy presently being followed in the World Bank, in closing its global economic model, BANK-GEM.[6] Simulations of the model with this financial closure will be documented shortly.

Notes

1. See, for example, Susan M. Collins and Dani Rodrik, "Eastern Europe and the Soviet Union in the World Economy," *Policy Analyses in International Economics* 32, 1991 (Institute for International Economics, May, chs. 3 and 4).
2. The MSG model is documented in Warwick J. McKibbin and Jeffrey D. Sachs, *Global Linkages: Macroeconomic Interdependence and Cooperation in the World Economy* (The Brookings Institute, Washington, D.C.). Thanks are due to Mr. McKibbin for access to his model and for advice, and to Mr. Menahem Prywes for expert use of this system.
3. For example, Working Party 1 of the OECD's Economic Policy Committee discussed at their October 1991 meeting the Secretariat paper, "The Future of Capital Income Taxation in a Liberalized Financial Environment," (ESD/CPE/WP1(91)7). The paper emphasized asymmetries in the incentives that OECD policies give to savings and investment.
4. R.J. Barro, and X. Sala-i-Martin, *World Real Interest Rates and Investment*, 1990 (NBER Macroeconomics Annual 1990, MIT Press, Cambridge, Mass.)
5. A memorandum on regression results to date may be obtained from Mick Riordan, "Further Progress in Real LIBOR Regressions," 2 October 1991, International Economic Analysis and Prospects Division, the World Bank. The econometric work for this section of the present paper was prepared by Mr. Riordan.
6. Current documentation of this model is available in Petersen et al., "BANK-GEM: A World Bank Global Economic Model," 1991 (International Economics Department, mimeo, September).

Rejoinder

Paul S. Armington

Dr. de Souza raised the issue of uneven growth among major groups of countries and related it to the continuing debt problem and global capital shortage.[1] Dr. Klein identified this problem as one of high interest rates, stemming from high demands for capital and from lagging savings rates. The question I want to raise is: what use are models for addressing this problem? And what directions should model-based research take in order to help policy makers deal better with the issue of high interest rates in the future?

Is there a problem of capital shortage? Some say no. (G5 real LIBOR will average about 3.5 in 1991, down from 5 per cent in the 1980s. This spring WP1 of OECD held a meeting; a variety of views were expressed, from Japan at one extreme to Ireland at the other. In the World Bank, planning assumptions for 10 years ahead have shifted over the last few years, from the 2–3 per cent range (of real LIBOR) to the 3–4 per cent range. What used to be our *downside* LDC growth scenario for *r* is now our baseline. Why? The main reason is loss of faith that fiscal deficits will be corrected, implying permanently higher debt ratios for high-income countries as a group.

It appears that the shift in fiscal/monetary mix around 1979/81 was important. At this time there was a dramatic shift in the otherwise tightly correlated series for G5 real LIBOR and the global public sector's CAB/GNP ratio. This shift was caused by a change in the "fiscal-monetary mix," featuring the monetarist revolution of Paul Volcker and the supply-side revolution of Arthur Laffer and friends. In my view, if this mix were reversed, the two lines would cross over again, and we would get real LIBOR averaging in the 2–3 per cent range again. But hopes of this happening have been waning. Note present Consensus Forecasts of long-term real interest rates.

Do the existing global models support the idea that fiscal expansion in the United States, with non-accommodating monetary policy, would raise interest rates? Conversely, would savings from, say, military cuts of $150 billion per year (mentioned by Dr. de Souza) have a big downward effect on real interest rates? Yes.

1. See the Hickman paper in this volume, chapter 1. Simulations imply an almost 200 basis points rise per $100 billion rise in US government spending, for constant nominal money supply. (Real MS may be shrinking if near full employment, as the price level rises.)

2. Similar results are reported in chapter 3 of this volume at the top of table 1.

3. The degree of "accommodation" is critical. Short-term forecasters often assume "accommodating" monetary policy and thus unchanged *r* (IMF WEO). With "reasonable" degree of accommodation, we get about 100 basis points rise in G3 *r* per $100 billion rise in government spending, on average over the first three years (less in short run). (See table 2 of my paper.) The third Brookings conference in Korea showed similar results.

4. These effects are large. They reflect low *r* elasticities of IS and LM curves in most estimated models. This has consequences for LDC growth. Bank estimates show that increase in real LIBOR of 100 basis points, sustained over 10 years, reduces LDC growth *rate* by 0.2 per cent per annum. Thus, even if the increase in income in the United States were sustained, income in LDCs would soon be less than baseline, since the *level* of G/y is directly related to the *level* of *r* and *y* in the United States, which is inversely related to the *level* of I/y in LDCs, which is inversely related to the growth rate in LDCs. In addition, leading models predict that, in the medium term, the *level* of *y* in the United States probably *falls*. Moreover, *r* may continue rising for many years, especially if Debt/GNP ratio is permanently raised. This worsens implications for LDCs, via their markets, debt burden, and also terms of trade. My paper sticks to short-run analysis, with no

treatment of growth of capital. But in the medium term, with capital stocks variable, shocks in G and in I are very different. Whereas higher G crowds out I, higher I raises income, lowers the PSBR and the stock of public debt, thus damping any rise in *r*. This will be accentuated if higher I raises technical progress, creates process innovations, and builds human capital. By raising the growth *rate* of productivity, the shock to I may keep *r* from rising significantly. The implications for LDC growth are very different from the rise of US government spending. Interest rates may be higher, but not *much* higher; and export markets are bigger and terms of trade more favourable to primary producers.

Against this, contrast the implications of Taiwan's investment programme and a programme of large-scale lending to the USSR, etc. Taiwan's programme raises TFP growth. Transfers to the USSR *could* be more like an increase in US consumption.

Estimated and operational global models, so far, do not tell us much about these longer-run relations between growth, investment, savings, factor productivity, and public policy for growth. Public or publicly guaranteed spending programmes that *complement* investment and that speed up TFP are difficult to introduce into the neoclassical paradigm. Yet much of the capital spending programme looming ahead, especially in the ENV area, is precisely aimed at generating a self-perpetuating process of growth. The Bank associates these efforts with programmes to achieve low long-run ICORs. This process is more elegantly formulated in the New Growth Theories of Maurice Scott and others.

So, in conclusion, a challenge ahead for global modellers is to integrate the new growth theories with the neoclassical paradigm, in its modern dress of dynamic inter-temporal equilibrium. Until we accomplish this integration, global models will continue to overstate the dangers to LDCs of well-conceived investment programmes in the rest of the world. This integration will be a big hill to climb, and I want to assure Professors Klein, Hickman et al., who started all this, that the profession of global modelling is still young.

Note

1. Dr. de Souza gave the opening remarks at the Conference.

Comments on chapter 3

Warwick J. McKibbin

This paper explores the impact on world interest rates and economic activity of an increase in the global demand for capital. The reason for focusing on this issue is the recent projections of increased capital demands in several regions of the world over the next decade and the concern that this will have significant consequences for world growth and development. Many current models that capture interdependence in the world economy primarily through trade flows are not well suited to this type of analysis and I applaud the attempt to integrate asset flows into a model of trade linkages. The joint determination of saving and investment decisions and the explicit treatment of these links between countries is crucial in today's world of high capital mobility among major economies. I have found in my own work that integrating the flow of assets and goods is crucial to understanding many of the features of the 1980s where monetary shocks have been dominated by real shocks that have altered the savings/investment balance in major countries. I believe that it is also crucial to understanding the next decade where savings/investment shocks are again likely to dominate the world economy.

There seem to be two goals in the paper. The first is to provide a rule of thumb for calculating the change in world interest rates for a change in the demand for capital. The second is to provide a way of introducing capital markets into global models where interdependence is primarily modelled through flows of goods rather than flows of assets such as the initial version of the new World Bank Global Economic model.

The approach taken in this paper is first to specify a simple static IS-LM model. This is then calibrated using simulation results from the McKibbin-Sachs Global model. Finally the author uses some series data from 1962 to 1989 to estimate econometrically the key parameters in the theoretical model. The results are surprisingly consistent across approaches.

My comments will be on the general approach followed in the paper, how it achieves the apparent goals of the author, as well as on particular questions raised by the study. To anticipate my conclusion, I found the approach reasonable for finding a rule of thumb for analysing certain types of shock. In fact the approach gave better results than I had anticipated. But there are some crucial caveats required on using the results of such an approach as the basis for a global simulation model.

Theoretical model

The theoretical model is clearly presented although it would be useful to distinguish between real and nominal short and long rates. For the purpose of the study, if expected inflation is unaffected and the shocks are permanent, the lack of distinction is less of a problem. Care should be exercised, however, when taking the results from the MSG model in calibrating the theoretical model, since these distinctions do matter in the MSG model especially for the first two or three years of the shocks and especially for shocks that are not permanent.

In addition, the reader should be careful to note that all variables are in levels rather than logs and therefore coefficients are not elasticities, which is different to the empirical implementation. In the calibration exercise, I would have found it easier to interpret the parameter values if elasticities had been used.

Calibration exercise

The MSG model is shocked by changing real government spending in the United States by $100 billion for 10 years. Despite the comment made in the paper, one can in fact have a permanent fiscal expansion in the MSG model which leads to a permanently higher fiscal deficit. The fiscal closure which prevents this from being unstable is that taxes are raised to service the permanently higher debt. The debt to GDP ratio stabilizes but at a higher level. This stock effect is important for the outcome for long-term real interest rates. The results will be quite different if the level of debt to GDP is returned to baseline. I assume that Armington does indeed let the debt to GDP rise and then stabilize at a new higher level.

The exercise itself raises the question: Can one calibrate a static model with results from a dynamic model with rational expectations? In general, I would have said no to this. It is only going to be reasonable for shocks that are permanent and unanticipated and there would need to be some way to net out the dynamic adjustment path. Given this, I was surprised at the results in the paper. To smooth out the dynamics, Armington has taken an average result for the first few years. There is still a good deal of adjustment in later years, but for the question of what happens to interest rates over the first few years the approach seems to work. Again, if the shock was temporary or changed over time, the technique would have given a misleading interpretation of the coefficients relevant for the theoretical model.

In addition, there is the problem with carrying out the calibration exercise. For example, the money-demand equation is almost identical to that in the MSG model. Why not take the same parameter values that are in the model and then calibrate the others residually from the simulation results?

The second question is whether the effects of a US fiscal expansion will have the same impact on world interest rates as an increase in funds flowing into the developing regions that Armington is concerned about. Developing countries, Eastern Europe and the Commonwealth of Independent States (formerly USSR) and Eastern Germany are in the MSG model and I was curious why Armington did not actually run the simulation directly of increased demand for funds by these regions. I have done a similar set of simulations in a recent Brookings Discussion Paper.[1] The following graphs (see figure 1) give an indication of the results for output, employment, short and long interest rates and exchange rates for a number of economies/regions.

The shock is not exactly the same as Armington's. In these graphs it is a rise in funds flowing into Eastern Europe and the USSR of $60 billion per year for five years, commencing in 1991. These funds can be thought of as loans or increased private flows because they do

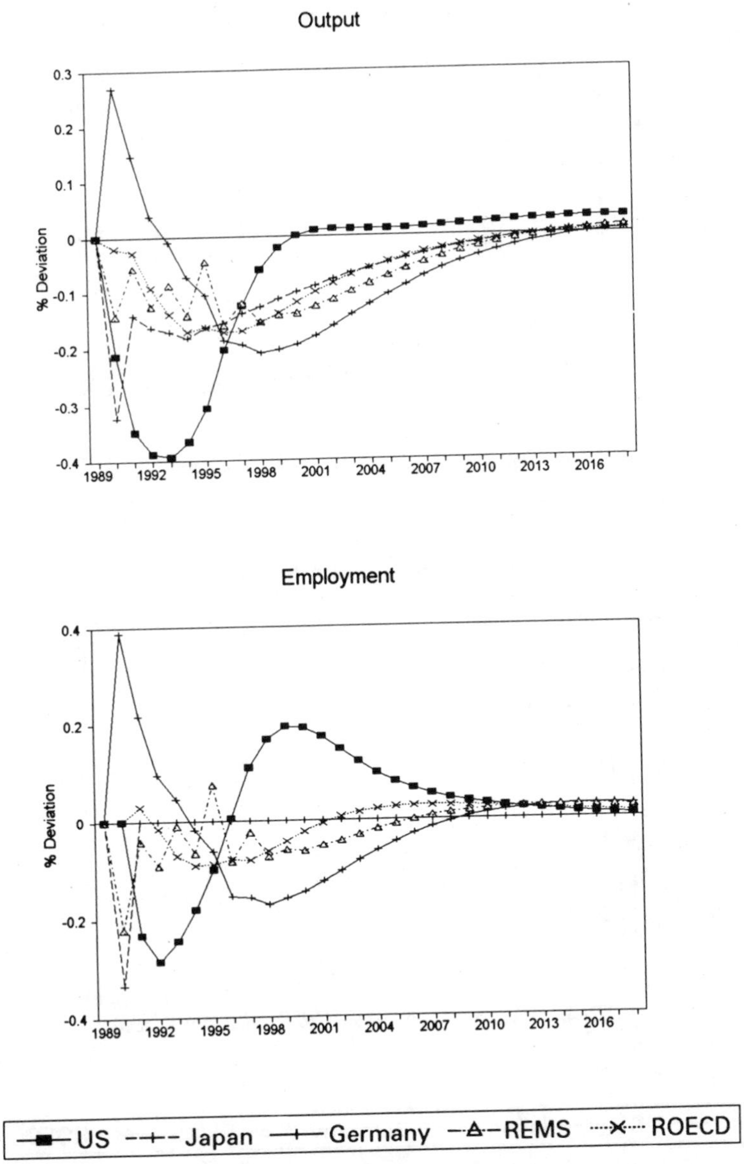

Fig. 1 **Increasing financial flows to Eastern Europe and the USSR**

have servicing requirements. This increase in funds lasts until 1995 and then subsequently declines by $20 billion per year until its return to the baseline by 1998. All variables in these figures are expressed as deviations from a baseline projected from 1089 to 2050.

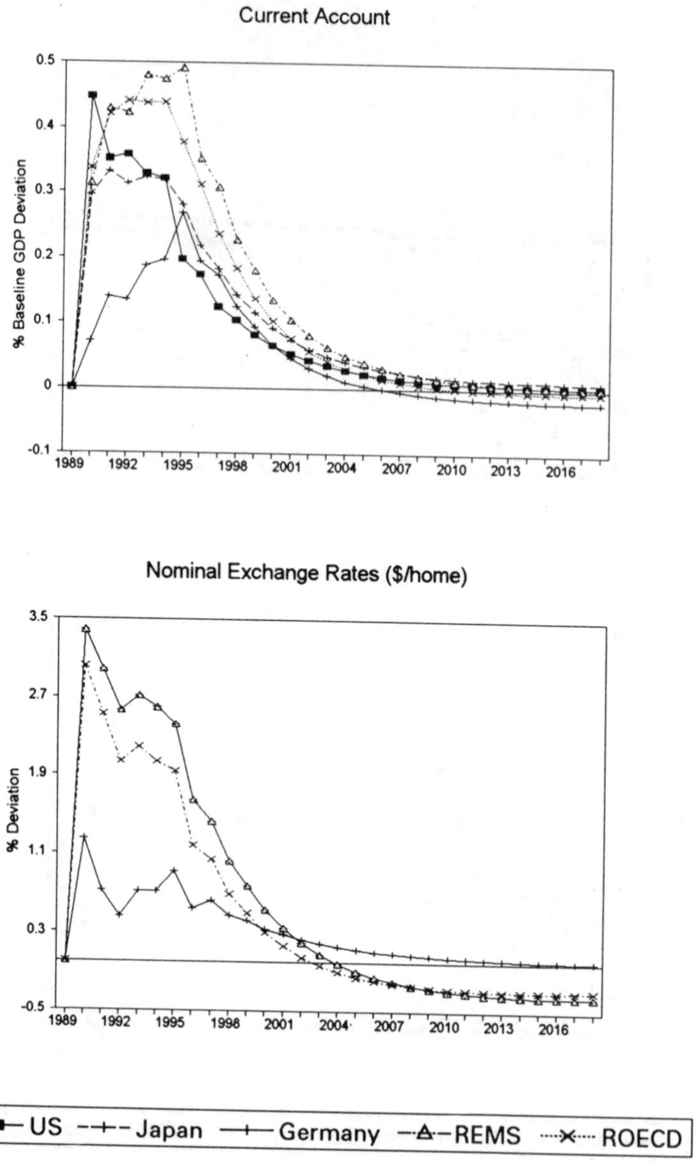

Fig. 1 **(cont.)**

Several points can be made about these results. First the effect on average long-term interest rates is initially around 110 basis points falling gradually over the first five years. This is proportionately larger than Armington's results because with a US fiscal shock, there

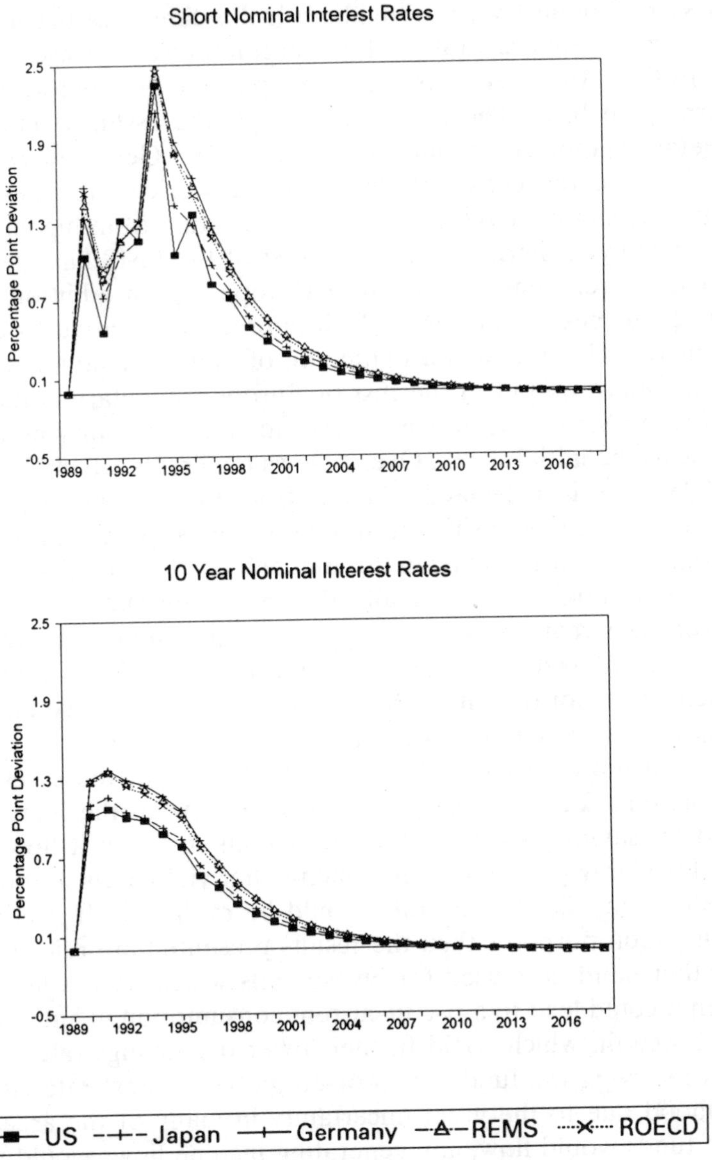

Fig. 1 **(cont.)**

is a partial rise in US private saving in anticipation of future taxes required to service the permanently higher government debt. In the scenario I have done, there is no adjustment of private saving in the regions receiving the funding to cover future servicing costs.

A second point I wish to highlight is the difference between short- and long-term interest rates. Short-term interest rates are more volatile. Initially they rise then fall then spike in 1995 before gradually returning to base. The reason for this is the assumed reactions of monetary authorities. In most countries except Germany, real output falls because the consequence of higher world long interest rates dominates any increase in trade flows resulting from higher demand for goods by Eastern Europe. The rest of the EMS have less significant trade relations with Eastern Europe, but in addition they are assumed to peg to the DM, which appreciates relative to all major currencies. This requires a tightening of monetary policy which further dampens output in the rest of Europe. Monetary authorities in the United States and Japan attempt to relax monetary policy in response to the initial shock. Over time as long rates fall, and especially in 1995 there is a demand stimulus from the expected fall in rates. This leads to a rise in short-term interest rates. Although private behaviour is forward-looking in this model it can be seen that the extent of forward-lookingness is really dependent on the relatively short horizon of a year or two. Finally, note that although the results for long-term interest rates tend to confirm Armington's analysis, the consequences for output exchange rates and current account changes are quite different across countries.

Several more caveats should be stressed about these results and Armington's for US fiscal policy. It matters what the increased demand for savings is used for in the regions in which it flows. If it is used for highly productive investments that yield a quick return then the effect on real interest rates could be mitigated. If it is used for consumption purposes then the results presented are relevant. If, on the other hand, it is used for investments which have a large future return it could lead to a rise in current consumption in anticipation of future wealth, which could further lower the savings rate of the regions receiving the funds and worsen global interest rate rise. In all likelihood due to the great uncertainty in many of the areas where these funds would flow, any generating income flows would result in higher saving rates.

Growth implications

Armington correctly makes the points that there is a trade-off for developing countries between higher growth due to the short-run demand stimulus of a reduction in global savings, and the growth-retarding consequences of higher world interest rates. In stressing this though, it is worth pointing out that there are three factors that matter and these can be different depending on whether the shock is a US fiscal expansion or a rise in lending to Eastern Europe and the Middle East. The three important factors are: the location of the demand for developing country exports, the consequences for world interest rates, and the effect on the exchange rate in which the debt is denominated. The trade patterns are obviously important. Developing countries, especially in Latin America, are more stimulated by a US expansion than by greater spending in Eastern Europe. The interest rate effects have already been covered. The final effect on a change in the exchange rate is less important now than it was in 1982 through 1985 because less debt is now denominated in US dollars. But it is worth pointing out that in the case of a US fiscal shock the US dollar appreciates significantly, which is bad for countries whose debt is denominated in US dollars because more of their own resources are required to service the debt. For the scenario of lending to Eastern Europe the US dollar depreciates, which helps these countries relative to the case of a US fiscal expansion.

Estimation of the global interest rate equation

I only have a few brief comments on this section. First, why estimate the interest rate equation with the level of money balances rather than the change, since as is correctly pointed out in the paper, the equation is really an equation for the change in interest rates? I was intrigued by the result for oil in the interest rate equation. In the MSG model a permanent rise in oil prices of 100 per cent raises world interest rates by about 300 basis points in the long term and short rates by about 200 basis points on average over the first three years. This is very close to the estimated effect in the equation. This result in the MSG model is due partly to the fall in public-sector saving as a result of the revenue loss from lower output and the assumed fiscal reaction. It is also crucially dependent on whether the shock is perceived to be permanent or temporary. Extending the sample by one year to cover the oil spike due to the Iraqi war could have quite an effect on this coefficient. In the estimation technique the difference between permanent and temporary and anticipated and unanticipated is not allowed for. This could bias the estimates over a historical period if indeed the MSG model is correct and some shocks were believed to be temporary. It would be worth attempting to allow for this. An intriguing aspect of the estimation results is that the parameters imply multipliers that are so close to the MSG multiplies for permanent shocks that perhaps this indicates that indeed most shocks were perceived to be permanent during the sample period.

Conclusion

Finally, despite the surprisingly consistent results in the paper, I am still not convinced that a rule-of-thumb approach can be useful for a global model. As I have argued above, it will at best be relevant only for permanent shocks. As the paper points out, the *Z* matrix linking the interest rate and growth will be changing over time. Why not allow a structural approach in the MSG model to capture it? It seems to give the same results as the estimate rule of thumb but allows more flexibility in handling temporary and anticipated shocks.

Note

1. See W. McKibbin, "The New Europe and Its Economic Implications for the World Economy," (Brookings Discussion Paper in International Economics No. 89, Tokyo Club Papers, 1991).

4

On the impact of a cut in the US budget deficit on the world economy: A simulation with the EPA world model

Yasuhiro Asami, Jun Nakano, Toshie Iwase, Akira Katayama, Atsuo Nakagawa, Tsuyoshi Okawa, and Norio Terashima

I. Introduction[1]

1. From the viewpoint of demand-side economics, US budget deficits in the middle of the eighties contributed to an increase in US imports and subsequently to economic growth in the countries that pursued an export-oriented policy.

2. In recent years, the size of US budget deficits has begun to increase again (see table 9). The US current account, however, has shown an improvement (see table 11), mainly due to increases in exports.

3. Prospects for the world economy in the 1990s indicate new potential factors which may increase the demand for world saving, such as the demand of countries in Central and Eastern Europe, in the transition from planned to market economies.

It is uncertain that the United States can continue to increase net exports.

4. The reduction of US budget deficits has been important and will continue to be so.

According to the Economic Declaration of the London Economic Summit 1991, continued progress in reducing budget deficits is essential.

5. However, it may also be possible that in the short term, the US cut in budget deficits would decrease US imports and consequently transmit deflationary effects on countries that are strongly oriented to the US market. Those countries would face decreases in their export volumes and/or the deterioration of trade balances, if the United States were to cut budget deficits.

6. Thus, the main purpose of this paper is to consider, by model simulation techniques

i. what impacts US reductions in budget deficits would have on the supply-demand situation of global saving[2] and also on the economies of the developing countries.

ii. what kind of policy coordination among the industrialized countries would be appropriate to mitigate the deflationary effect of US policy on developing countries.

7. Before explaining the simulation results, it may be useful to show briefly the structure and properties of our model for their better understanding. The readers can then be aware of the advantages and limitations of the model for the above analytical purpose. We will then explain the simulation results, focusing on the impact on developing countries. They are most likely to be influenced by the deflationary effect of the US budget reductions.

II. An outline of the EPA world economic model

Structure

1. The EPA world economic model has (i) macroeconomic models of nine individual countries, i.e. the G7 countries, Australia, and Korea, (ii) six regional models,[3] and (iii) a trade-linkage model (see table 1).

2. In the EPA world economic model the consistency between world aggregate import and export volume is kept. The currency exchange rates of the G7 countries and Australia to the US dollar are endogenously determined.[4]

It should be possible to estimate the effect of the US budget deficit reduction on the export volume of each area in the world in a systematic way.

3. The individual country models of the EPA world economic model are basically the demand-determined, Keynesian type, with the estimation period from the first quarter of 1979 to the fourth quarter of 1988.

Table 1 **The structure of the EPA world economic model**

	US	Japan	Germany (West)	France	UK	Italy	Canada	Australia	Korea	Trade-linkage	Total
The number of structural equations	70	65	51	17	19	19	18	17	11	24	311
1. Final expenditure	7	8	6	3	3	3	3	4	3	0	40
2. Employment	6	5	5	1	1	1	1	2	1	0	23
3. Wage and price	15	13	11	6	6	7	5	5	5	0	73
4. Income distribution	9	10	3	0	0	0	0	0	0	0	22
5. Public finance	6	7	6	1	1	1	2	2	0	0	26
6. Finance	14	7	10	2	2	1	2	2	1	0	41
7. Balance of payments	13	15	10	4	6	6	5	2	1	24	86
Identity	122	144	86	37	38	40	36	33	38	325	899
Endogenous variables	192	209	137	54	57	59	54	50	49	349	1210
Exogenous variables	92	49	23	17	16	20	18	21	23	1	280

Note: In this table, six regional models are included in trade-linkage for convenience.

It is difficult to estimate the effect of US policy on the supply-side of the US economy. There is a possibility of parameter shifts, if the United States should cut the budget deficits drastically.

4. As for the export volume equations *for the six regions*, the export volume is explained by world demand for the region's product[5] and a relative price term.

The import volume of the six regions is explained by the lagged dependent variable, a relative price, and an income constraint, approximated by the export of the region. Thus, the repercussions of the impacts of the decrease in US imports on developing regions could be analysed.

As for the modelling of the six regions in our model, however, the only endogenous variables are those related to the trade balance.

5. The US short-term interest rate is originally estimated on the basis of the money-market approach. That is, the short-term interest rate is determined by the balance of free reserves. M2 (money demand) is basically explained by the nominal GNP and the short-term

Table 2a **Export volume equations of the six regions**

	Income	Price	Accumulated current deficit
Asia (excl. Korea and Japan)	1.83	0.72	–
Latin America	1.48	0.20	0.84
Middle East	0.47	0.20	–
Soviet Union and Eastern Europe	0.52	0.58	–
Western Europe (excl. 4 major countries)	0.98	1.62	–
Other areas	0.88	1.09	–

Table 2b **Import volume equations of the six regions**

	Income	Price	Lagged dependent variable
Asia (excl. Korea and Japan)	0.32	0.29	0.61
Latin America	0.65	0.43	–
Middle East	0.09	0.12	0.87
Soviet Union and Eastern Europe	0.13	0.12	0.85
Western Europe (excl. 4 major countries)	0.34	0.74	0.56
Other areas	0.19	0.74	0.61

interest rate. The long-term interest rate is explained by the term-structure relationship.

In the following simulations, however, because M2 is held constant under the assumption of an unaccommodating monetary policy, the short-term interest rate is determined basically by nominal GNP.

6. Finally our model is not a rational expectation type, because it was originally developed for short-term forecasting.

Properties

The following are pointed out as characteristics of the properties of our model, which seem to be important for understanding the simulation results in the following section.

i. The first characteristic is that the effect of a US fiscal policy change on world imports and the real GNP of other countries is more significant than that of the other countries (see table 3). This is mainly because the share of the US GNP to the world aggregate GNP is the highest, and also because the US import elasticity with respect to income is relatively higher (see table 5 and Akihiro 1988).

   With regard to the effect of US monetary policy on other countries (see table 4), the increase in money supply in the United States causes a decline in US interest rates and subsequently causes the US dollar's depreciation. Therefore the United States increases its export volume, while the German export volume shows a decrease. However, Japan increases its export volume at the initial stage, probably due to the increase in US domestic demand.

ii. The second characteristic is that when there is a fiscal expansion with a non-accommodating monetary policy,[6] the individual country's model shows a crowding-out effect (see table 6).

iii. The third characteristic is that although our model is originally developed for short-term forecasting, long-run neutrality is prevalent as much as possible. For example, when money supply is increased by 2 per cent from the baseline (see table 7):

   a. the real GNP shows an increase at first, but returns to the baseline level by the sixth year;
   b. the long-term interest rate shows a decrease at first, but returns to the baseline level by the sixth year;
   c. the exchange rate of the US dollar depreciates at first, but returns to the baseline level in the sixth year.

Table 3 **The effect of fiscal policy (an increase in government expenditure by 1% of real GNP) (see note 1)**

		Country initiating the policy					
		Real GNP			Exchange rate		
Country affected	y	US	Japan	Germany (West)	US	Japan	Germany (West)
USA	1	1.39	0.05	0.02	–0.34	0.24	0.03
	2	1.38	0.15	0.08	–1.50	1.05	0.26
	3	1.28	0.23	0.14	–2.17	1.38	0.43
	4	1.03	0.26	0.16	–3.32	1.44	0.37
	5	0.91	0.26	0.12	–3.42	1.22	0.06
	6	0.95	0.21	0.04	–2.85	0.80	–0.20
Japan	1	0.27	1.26	0.04	0.25	–0.83	–0.04
	2	0.44	1.27	0.09	1.69	–3.48	–0.28
	3	0.68	1.11	0.10	3.08	–4.58	–0.48
	4	0.80	0.95	0.10	4.51	–4.53	–0.45
	5	0.85	0.77	0.07	5.16	–4.33	–0.23
	6	0.80	0.70	0.05	3.62	–3.39	0.01
Germany (West)	1	0.19	0.02	0.99	1.33	–0.01	–0.06
	2	0.96	0.07	1.18	5.00	0.02	–1.24
	3	1.05	0.14	1.08	5.82	0.20	–1.71
	4	1.30	0.20	1.03	8.27	0.50	–1.90
	5	1.39	0.25	1.07	7.91	0.76	0.47
	6	1.38	0.31	1.17	7.52	1.09	1.69
World import	1	0.63	0.15	0.26			
	2	0.93	0.23	0.39			
	3	1.28	0.23	0.30			
	4	1.41	0.25	0.22			
	5	1.52	0.29	0.17			
	6	1.51	0.32	0.18			

1. The figures in this table are the percent deviation from the baseline of real GNP in the USA, Germany (West), Japan, or the percent deviation of world import, when each of three countries increases real government expenditure by 1% of real GNP of the baseline respectively.
2. This table assumes each country increases real government expenditure by 1% of the baseline real GNP.
3. These multipliers are calculated from the full-link simulation.
4. The exchange-rate of each currency (yen, D-Mark, French franc, pound, Italian lira, Canadian dollar, and Australian dollar) to the US dollar is endogenous.
5. M3 in Germany and France, M2 in the USA, Italy, and Japan, and M1 in the UK are kept at baseline values.

Table 4 **The effect of monetary policy (an increase in money supply by 2% from the baseline)**

		Country initiating the policy					
		Real GNP			Exchange rate		
Country affected	y	US	Japan	Germany (West)	US	Japan	Germany (West)
USA	1	0.60	−0.04	−0.06	0.97	−0.37	−0.48
	2	1.29	−0.10	−0.11	2.84	−1.09	−0.32
	3	1.34	−0.10	−0.05	2.84	−0.67	0.04
	4	1.15	−0.04	0.03	2.84	−0.38	−0.01
	5	0.65	0.03	0.07	1.71	−0.30	0.03
	6	0.16	0.08	0.06	0.75	−0.15	−0.02
Japan	1	0.13	0.17	−0.06	−1.06	1.33	0.07
	2	0.15	0.29	−0.06	−4.64	3.81	0.14
	3	−0.13	0.61	−0.03	−5.26	2.53	−0.18
	4	−0.31	0.44	−0.02	−5.37	1.31	−0.14
	5	−0.48	0.20	0.02	−4.57	1.14	−0.09
	6	−0.27	−0.06	−0.01	−1.97	0.76	−0.33
Germany (West)	1	−0.06	−0.01	0.55	−2.70	−0.01	4.86
	2	−0.32	−0.03	0.86	−5.38	−0.07	2.57
	3	−1.35	−0.06	0.59	−3.54	−0.24	0.15
	4	−1.19	−0.06	0.57	−2.82	−0.19	1.32
	5	0.00	−0.04	0.53	−0.52	−0.11	1.25
	6	0.19	−0.02	0.49	−0.02	−0.28	1.97
World import	1	0.29	−0.01	0.07			
	2	0.47	0.01	0.27			
	3	0.20	0.06	0.20			
	4	0.15	0.03	0.14			
	5	0.08	0.00	0.11			
	6	0.11	−0.01	0.07			

1. The figures in this table are the percent deviation from the baseline of real GNP in USA, Japan and Germany (West), or the percent deviation of the world import, when each of three countries increases money supply by 2% from the baseline respectively.
2. This table assumes each country increases money supply by 2% from the baseline real GNP.
3. In Germany and France, M3 is constant, in the USA, Italy, and Japan M2 is constant, and in the UK M1 is constant.
4. These multipliers are calculated from the full-link simulation.
5. The exchange-rate of each currency to the US dollar is endogenous.

Table 5 **Exports and imports function of the nine countries in the EPA world model**

(1) Income and price elasticities of the nine countries' *exports*

Country	Income	Price
USA	1.09	0.67
Japan	1.47	1.09
Germany	1.15	0.82
France	1.41	0.49
UK	1.19	1.06
Italy	1.75	0.56
Canada	0.88	0.18
Australia	0.43	–
Korea	0.97	1.25

(2) Income and price elasticities of the nine countries' *imports*

Country	Income	Price
USA	1.75	1.06
Japan	1.14	0.40
Germany	1.52	0.30
France	1.36	0.69
UK	1.41	0.48
Italy	1.23	0.49
Canada	1.40	0.85
Australia	0.69	0.53
Korea	0.76	0.37

Table 6 **The size of crowding-out effect of the four countries**

Year	USA	Japan	Germany (West)	Korea
1	0.10	0.02	0.09	0.01
3	0.33	0.14	0.53	0.20
6	0.75	0.47	0.58	0.24

1. The above figures in this table are calculated as follows:
   [GNP(A) – GNP(B)]/[GNP(A) – GNP]
   GNP: actual real GNP
   GNP(A): real GNP estimated under the two assumptions (1) government expenditure is increased by 1% of real GNP of the baseline; (2) nominal short-term interest rate is held constant.
   GNP(B): real GNP estimated under the increase in government expenditure by 1% of real GNP of the baseline.
2. This simulation is carried out under the single country mode with the starting year of 1983.
3. The exchange rate of yen and D-Mark to the US dollar is endogenous. The effective exchange rate of the US dollar and the exchange rate of Korean won to the US dollar is exogenous.

III. The trade structure between the United States and the developing countries

1. Before the explanation of the simulation results, it may be also useful to review the trade structure between the United States and other countries or areas, based upon EPA trade-linkage data.

2. Because the magnitude of the effect of a US policy change on a region is partly explained by the degree of dependence of the region

Table 7 **The effect of the increase of money supply in the USA on its economy**

Year	Real US GNP	Nominal US GNP	US GNP deflator	US nominal long-term interest rate	Effective exchange rate of the US dollar
1	0.60	0.58	−0.02	−0.54	0.97
2	1.29	1.38	0.09	−0.63	2.84
3	1.34	1.87	0.52	−0.56	2.84
6	0.16	2.25	2.09	0.15	0.75

1. The figures in this table excluding nominal long-term interest rate are the percent deviation from the baseline, when the US money supply (M2) is increased by 2 per cent from the baseline.
2. The figures of nominal long-term interest rate are the absolute deviation from the baseline.
3. This multiplier's test is carried out under the full-link mode.
4. The exchange rate of each other currency to the US dollar is endogenous.

on the US economy through the region's exports, the following items deserve to be mentioned:

i. The economies of the Asian countries, the Latin American countries, and the group of other countries depend highly upon the US economy through their exports (see table 8). In CY 1988, 44 per cent of Latin American countries' total export volume, and 22 per cent of the Asian countries' total export volume (excluding Korea and Japan) were shipped to the United States.

   The dependence of the Soviet Union and Eastern Europe on the US economy is relatively lower. In CY 1988 only 5.5 per cent of the Soviet Union's and Eastern European countries' export volume was shipped to the United States.

ii. The G7 countries have accounted for more than 50 per cent of the total export volume of most areas. This indicates the large influence of policy coordination among the G7 countries.

IV. The simulation results

1. The US budget programme and the possible upward pressure on US interest rates from abroad

1.1 *The actual movement of the US budget deficits and US current account deficits*

i. In fiscal year 1990, the US federal budget deficit amounted to $220.4 billion, and their ratio to the nominal GNP reached 4.1 per cent (see table 9).

Table 8 **The share of each area's export by countries in CY 1988**

	Asia (excl. Japan and Korea) %	Latin America %	Middle East %	Soviet Union and Eastern Europe %	Western Europe (excl. four major countries) %	Other areas %
USA	22.1	43.8	15.1	5.5	6.3	17.3
Japan	20.0	6.0	20.3	12.9	1.8	9.8
Germany (West)	4.0	5.3	5.3	10.2	19.3	9.2
France	1.8	2.6	5.6	4.9	11.1	11.2
UK	4.1	2.7	4.1	3.6	11.3	6.9
Italy	1.6	2.8	9.6	5.8	6.8	7.7
Canada	1.3	2.7	0.4	0.9	0.9	1.5
Others	45.1	34.1	39.6	56.2	42.5	36.4
Total	100.0	100.0	100.0	100.0	100.0	100.0

1. The above countries and regions are based on the classifications in our model.
2. Western Europe does not include Germany (West), UK, France, and Italy.
3. The shares in the above table are calculated on the figures of real export (1985 price).
4. The figures of real export are calculated in such a way that the nominal export from "Direction of Trade Statistics" (IMF) is deflated by export price from "International Financial Statistics" (IMF).

Table 9 **The movement of US budget deficits (in billions of dollars)**

Fiscal year	1985	1986	1987	1988	1989	1990
Receipts	734.1	769.1	854.1	909.0	990.7	1,031.5
Outlays	946.3	990.3	1,003.8	1,064.0	1,144.0	1,251.9
Balance	–212.3	–221.2	–149.7	–155.1	–153.4	–220.4
The ratio of the balance to nominal GNP (%)	–5.4	–5.3	–3.4	–3.2	–3.0	–4.1

Source: *Federal Reserve Bulletin.*

ii. Despite this, the ratio of the US current account deficits to the nominal GNP has shown a steady decline to 1.7 per cent in CY 1990 (see table 11), mainly owing to the increase in exports.

1.2 *The US budget programme and our simulation*

i. To curb the large budget deficits, the Budget Enforcement Act was enacted in 1990, and the budget programme and projections have

Table 10 **Maximum deficit amounts of US Federal Government 1992–1996 by OMB (in billions of dollars)**

1992	1993	1994	1995	1996
–348.3	–245.7	–132.1	–73.6	–55.5

Source: OMB, "Mid-Session Review of The Budget" (15 July 1991).

Table 11 **US current and trade deficits**

	1986	1987	1988	1989	1990
	$ bn				
Current account	–145.4	–160.0	–126.2	–106.3	–92.1
The ratio of current account deficit to nominal GNP	3.4%	3.5	2.6	2.0	1.7
	$ bn				
Trade account	–145.1	–159.0	–127.0	–115.9	–108.1

Source: Survey of Current Business.

been published by OMB (table 10) and CBO. According to the above programme, the United States is expected to cut budget deficits for several consecutive fiscal years.

ii. It is, however, difficult to translate these figures of outlays and receipts on the federal budget basis into figures on the GNP statistics basis. Therefore, in the following, only multipliers of US cuts in government expenditures will be shown.[7]

iii. Nevertheless, the multipliers should be helpful for considering the total effect of the cut in US government expenditures.

1.3 *The possible upward pressure on US interest rates from abroad*

i. In this paper, we take the US nominal long-term interest rate as an indicator of the supply-demand situation of money in the world. There are several actual or potential factors which may cause an upward pressure on US long-term interest rates. For example, it has been pointed out that increases in the demand for funds in Germany, the Soviet Union, and Eastern Europe in the transition from a planned to a market economy, will raise interest rates.

In order to evaluate, but very roughly, the effect of a cut in US government expenditures on US long-term interest rates, we tried to

Table 12 **The effect of increases in German government investment on nominal long-term interest rates in the USA, Japan, and Germany (West)**

Year	USA	Japan	Germany
1	0.00	0.02	0.17
2	0.03	0.06	0.46
3	0.08	0.09	0.66

1. The figures in this table are absolute deviations of nominal long-term interest rate from the baseline, when Germany (West) increases government expenditure by 1% of her GNP.
2. The above figures are calculated in the full-link simulation where the exchange rate of each currency to the US dollar is endogenous.
3. In the USA and Japan M2 is held constant, and in Germany M3 is held constant.

compare the magnitude of two opposite effects on the interest rate of the US budget cut and an increase in government investment in Germany.[8]

ii. It is very difficult for us to estimate the total amount of government investment for East Germany. The multipliers of the increase in government investment by 1 per cent of the real GNP in West Germany are shown in table 12.

iii. As regards the effect of the increase in the government investment in Germany on the US nominal long-term interest rate, the multipliers indicate that its magnitude is very small. This may be partly attributed to the fact that impacts are transmitted only through the exchange rate and trade in our model. The transmission mechanism in the model is as follows. The increase in the government investment in Germany raises the German long-term interest rate, and subsequently causes the depreciation of the US dollar against the DM, although the US current balance shows a little improvement (see table 13).

The US could then increase export volume and consequently the GNP. As a result of the increase in US nominal GNP, money demand increases, and finally the US long-term interest rate rises.

2. The size of the effect of the cut in US government expenditure (Case A)

2.1 *The objective*

The objective of the first simulation is to estimate how the US government expenditure cut affects the US interest rate, and also the

Table 13 **The effect of increases in German government investment on the current balance in the USA, Japan, and Germany (West)**

Year	USA	Japan	Germany
1	0.01	0.02	−0.42
2	0.01	0.05	−0.58
3	0.02	0.05	−0.69

1. The figures in this table are absolute deviations of the ratio of current account to the nominal GNP respectively, when Germany (West) increases the government expenditure by 1% of her real GNP.
2. The above figures are calculated in the full-link simulation where the exchange rate of each currency to the US dollar is endogenous.
3. In the USA and Japan M2 is held constant, and in Germany M3 is held constant.

export volumes and trade balances of six regions, without any countervailing policy by the countries affected.

2.2 *The main assumptions*

For the above objective, we assume that the US cuts general government expenditure by 1 per cent of real GNP, together with the unaccommodating monetary policy. We also assume that real general government expenditure and money supply in the other industrialized countries do not change from the baseline.

2.3 *The main results*

i. The US government expenditure cut by 1 per cent of real GNP produces a negative deviation of the long-term interest rate from the baseline (see table 14). This may show that the US cut could ease the tight balance of global saving.

Due to the decline in the US long-term interest rate, although the US current balance is improved, the US dollar depreciates and subsequently the US export volume shows a positive deviation from the baseline. In addition, the US import volume shows a negative deviation from the baseline, owing to the decrease in the US domestic demand and also to the depreciation of the US dollar, which makes imports more costly for the United States. This policy generates positive deviation of the US trade balance, and corresponding negative deviations for the other industrialized countries' trade balances (see table 15).

In comparison with the size of the multiplier of the increase in

Table 14 **The effect of the cut in US government expenditures on nominal long-term interest rates in the USA, Japan, and Germany (West)**

Year	USA	Japan	Germany
1	−0.34	−0.15	−0.07
2	−0.88	−0.43	−0.29
3	−1.27	−0.72	−0.57
4	−1.86	−0.99	−0.86
5	−1.91	−1.32	−1.06
6	−2.25	−1.49	−1.20

1. The figures in this table are the absolute deviations of nominal long-term interest rates from the baseline, when the USA cuts government expenditure by 1% of the US real GNP.
2. The above figures are calculated in the full-link simulation where the exchange rate of each currency to the US dollar is endogenous.

Table 15 **The effect of the US cut in the government expenditure on trade accounts in the USA, Japan, and Germany (West)**

Year	USA	Japan	Germany
1	0.14	−0.14	−0.00
2	0.11	−0.18	0.01
3	0.14	−0.23	−0.18
4	0.11	−0.26	−0.27
5	0.18	−0.28	−0.36
6	0.23	−0.22	−0.35

1. The figures in this table are absolute deviations of the ratio of trade account to the nominal GNP, when the USA cuts government expenditures by 1% of the US real GNP.
2. The above figures are calculated in the full-link simulation where the exchange rate of each currency to the US dollar is endogenous.

West German government investment, which is briefly shown in the previous section, the magnitude of the effect of the US cut in government expenditures by 1 per cent of its real GNP is likely to be sufficient to offset the upward pressure on the US interest rate.

ii. It may, however, be questioned whether the decline in the US interest rate is sufficient for developing countries to offset the deflationary effect of the above US policy on their economy. That is, the US cut in government expenditure causes relatively large negative deviations of export volume for some of the six regions, namely, the Latin American countries, the Asian countries (excluding Korea and Japan), and the other area. This is due mainly to the high US import elasticity with regard to income and the high dependence of these regions on the US economy (see tables 5 and 8). This may cause a deceleration of economic growth rate in those regions. The price of primary products shows a negative deviation from the baseline associated with the decrease in US imports. In addition, due to the depreciation of the US dollar, the import price of the developing countries shows a positive deviation from the baseline. The trade balance of these regions shows a deterioration (see table 16), although they benefit from the decline in interest rates.

iii. The multipliers indicate that for the United States to bring about significant declines in real long-term interest rates immediately, it would have to make relatively bigger government expenditure cuts for the short term. This would produce severe deflationary effects on countries in developing regions.

3. The effect of countervailing policy by the countries affected (Case B)

3.1 *The objective*

The objective of the second simulation is to see to what extent the developing countries that are highly dependent on the United States can mitigate the deflationary effects of US cuts in government expenditures through their own efforts.

3.2 *The main assumptions*

i. In the EPA model only the Korean model is designed as a single country macroeconomic model among non-industrial advanced countries.

ii. Although Korea should perhaps now be classified as a developed country, the Korean economy is treated as *one type*[9] of the developing countries, which in this simulation is highly dependent on the US economy.

iii. In addition to the assumptions in the first simulation, we assume an increase in the Korean general government expenditure by 1 per cent of real GNP with an unaccommodating monetary policy.

3.3 *The main results*

i. If Korea increases government expenditure by 1 per cent of her real GNP when the United States cuts government expenditure by 1

Table 16 **The effect of the US cut in government expenditure by 1% of real GNP (Case A)**

		1	2	3	4	5	6
USA	SG/GNPV*	0.44	0.46	0.59	0.81	0.95	1.05
	Long-term interest rate*	−0.34	−0.88	−1.27	−1.86	−1.95	−2.25
		−0.30	−0.73	−0.90	−1.40	−1.58	−1.87
	Real long-term interest rate*	−1.40	−1.39	−1.31	−1.10	−0.99	−1.03
	Real GNP	−2.98	−3.32	−4.10	−4.40	−4.97	−4.94
	Import volume	0.14	0.11	0.14	0.11	0.18	0.23
	The ratio of trade account to nominal GNP (effective exchange rate of US dollar)*	0.35	1.56	2.23	3.46	3.58	2.98
Japan	Real GNP	−0.27	−0.43	−0.67	−0.78	−0.92	−0.79
	The ratio of trade account to nominal GNP*	−0.14	−0.18	−0.23	−0.26	−0.28	−0.22
Asia	Export volume	−0.58	−0.93	−1.01	−1.26	−1.68	−1.83
	Import price	0.06	0.74	0.98	1.57	1.27	0.56
Latin America	Export volume	−1.51	−1.52	−1.63	−1.62	−1.83	−1.45
	Import price	0.06	0.60	0.68	1.08	0.70	0.04
Soviet Union and Eastern Europe	Export volume	−0.11	−0.13	−0.18	−0.25	−0.33	−0.38
	Import price	0.21	1.19	1.50	2.34	1.99	1.24
6 areas	The ratio of trade account to nominal export*	−0.35	−0.38	−0.43	−0.43	−0.53	−0.57
The price of primary products		−0.91	−0.46	−0.78	−0.02	−0.51	−1.10

1. The above figures are the percent deviation or the absolute deviation from the baseline, when the USA cuts government expenditure by 1% of the US real GNP with US non-accommodating monetary policy.
2. * signifies the absolute deviation from the baseline.
3. SG is the saving-investment gap of US general government; GNPV is nominal GNP.
4. In calculating real long-term interest rate, we deducted the rate of increase in the GNP deflator from the nominal long-term interest rate.
5. The above figures are calculated in the full-link simulation where the exchange rate of each currency to the US dollar is endogenous.

Table 17 **The effect of the countervailing policy by Korea (the increase of government expenditure by 1% of Korean real GNP) (Case B)**

Year	1	2	3	4	5	6
Real GNP						
Case A	−0.34	−0.22	−0.20	−0.04	−0.18	−0.44
Case B	1.03	1.41	1.30	1.25	0.95	0.63
Real government expenditure						
Case A	0	0	0	0	0	0
Case B	6.14	5.97	6.12	6.32	6.64	6.69
GNP deflator						
Case A	−0.02	0.13	0.35	0.59	0.75	0.50
Case B	0.05	0.27	0.76	1.20	1.49	1.30
Short-term interest rate						
Case A	−0.13	−0.05	0.08	0.21	0.27	0.03
Case B	0.41	0.68	0.94	1.04	1.10	0.74
The ratio of trade balance to nominal GNP*						
Case A	−0.21	−0.15	−0.20	−0.14	−0.20	−0.22
Case B	−0.41	−0.43	−0.49	−0.52	−0.62	−0.62
The ratio of fiscal balance to nominal GNP*						
Case A	−0.07	−0.07	−0.08	−0.07	−0.07	−0.07
Case B	−0.79	−0.76	−0.81	−0.83	−0.87	−0.88
Export volume						
Case A	−0.96	−0.69	−0.93	−0.59	−0.83	−1.24
Case B	−0.99	−0.75	−1.13	−0.98	−1.31	−1.76
Import volume						
Case A	−0.41	−0.55	−0.62	−0.57	−0.42	−0.40
Case B	0.13	0.16	0.16	0.17	0.26	0.26

1. The figures of Case B in the above table are the percent deviation or absolute deviation from the baseline, when the USA cuts government expenditures by 1% of the US real GNP and simultaneously Korea increases government expenditure by 1% of the Korean real GNP.
2. * shows the absolute deviation from the baseline.
3. The above figures are calculated in the full-link simulation where the exchange rate of each currency to the US dollar is endogenous.

per cent of US real GNP, the Korean real GNP shows a positive deviation from the baseline in the short term (see table 17).

ii. However, the size of the increment of her real GNP, which is produced by increasing government expenditure, is the biggest in the second year. From the third year, its size becomes smaller, partly due to a crowding-out effect.

iii. The ratio of the trade balance to nominal GNP for Korea shows a deterioration mainly due to an increase in import volume.

iv. The ratio of the budget deficits to nominal GNP also shows a negative deviation from the baseline (see table 17).[10]

v. The GNP deflator shows a positive deviation from the baseline.

vi. Therefore, it may be difficult for the Korean government to continue expansionary fiscal policy for several consecutive years.

4. The effect of the policy coordination of the industrialized countries (Case C)

4.1 *The objective*

The objective of the third simulation is to consider to what extent the industrialized countries, except the United States, could mitigate the deflationary effect of the US cut in government expenditures without causing big fluctuations in their exchange rates to the US dollar, and without any other serious disequilibria in their economies.

4.2 *The main assumptions*

Based on the above idea, we assume that the G7 countries and Australia simultaneously increase their money supply by 1 per cent from the baseline in this simulation in addition to the US cut of government expenditure by 1 per cent of the real GNP. The reason we assume the United States increases the money supply is to prevent bigger interest rate differentials between itself and the other industrialized countries, which would induce the appreciation of the US dollar.

We do not assume expansionary fiscal policies of the other industrialized countries because the increase in government expenditures would be against the Economic Declaration of the London Economic Summit calling for reduced government claims on saving.

4.3 *The main results*

Comparing the third simulation results (Case C) with those of the first simulation results (Case A) in order to analyse the effect of policy coordination among the industrialized countries, we find the following items to be worth mentioning (tables 18, 19, 20).

i. The US long-term interest rate shows a bigger decline in Case C than in Case A. This leads to more improvement in the US fiscal balance in Case C than in Case A.

ii. The US real GNP and real import volume show smaller negative deviations from the baseline in Case C than in Case A.

Table 18 **The effect of policy coordination on the US economy**

Year	1	2	3	4	5	6
SG/GNPV*						
Case A	0.44	0.46	0.59	0.81	0.95	1.05
Case C	0.57	0.81	1.04	1.29	1.32	1.29
Nominal long-term interest rate*						
Case A	−0.34	−0.88	−1.27	−1.86	−1.95	−2.25
Case C	−0.62	−1.28	−1.68	−2.16	−2.07	−2.26
Real GNP						
Case A	−1.40	−1.39	−1.31	−1.10	−0.99	−1.03
Case C	−1.18	−0.90	−0.70	−0.46	−0.54	−0.81
Export volume						
Case A	−0.28	−0.15	0.18	0.73	1.02	1.06
Case C	−0.21	0.26	0.86	1.53	1.60	1.21
Import volume						
Case A	−2.98	−3.32	−4.10	−4.40	−4.97	−4.94
Case C	−2.42	−2.44	−3.59	−4.24	−5.02	−4.88
The ratio of trade balance to nominal GNP*						
Case A	0.14	0.11	0.14	0.11	0.18	0.23
Case C	0.12	0.05	0.10	0.11	0.22	0.27
Effective exchange rate of US dollar						
Case A	0.35	1.56	2.23	3.46	3.58	2.98
Case C	0.25	2.05	3.32	4.78	4.30	3.02
GNP deflator						
Case A	−0.04	−0.19	−0.56	−1.00	−1.35	−1.72
Case C	−0.05	−0.18	−0.42	−0.64	−0.73	−0.85

1. The figures of Case C in the above table are the percent deviation or absolute deviation from the baseline, when the following assumptions are satisfied: (1) The USA cuts government expenditures by 1% of US real GNP and increases money supply by 1% from the baseline; (2) The other 7 industrialized countries (Japan, Germany, France, Italy, UK, Canada, and Australia) increase money supply by 1% from the baseline, together with unchanged real government expenditure from the baseline respectively.
2. * shows the absolute deviation from the baseline.
3. SG: fiscal balance;
   GNPV: nominal GNP.
4. The above figures are calculated in the full-link simulation where the exchange rate of each currency to the US dollar is endogenous.

iii. The ratio of the US trade balance to her nominal GNP shows smaller positive deviations in Case C than in Case A.

iv. Real GNP in the other industrialized countries shows a smaller negative deviation from the baseline respectively in Case C than in Case A (see Table 19). This is because the real long-term interest

Table 19 **The effect of policy coordination on the other industrialized countries**

Year	1	2	3	4	5	6
1. GNP						
Japan						
Case A	−0.27	−0.43	−0.67	−0.78	−0.92	−0.79
Case C	−0.17	−0.19	−0.47	−0.71	−0.97	−0.84
Germany (West)						
Case A	−0.18	−0.62	−1.00	−1.23	−1.32	−1.31
Case C	0.11	−0.40	−0.91	−1.06	−1.08	−0.99
2. Private consumption deflator						
Japan						
Case A	−0.03	−0.16	−0.43	−0.83	−1.35	−1.97
Case C	−0.02	−0.11	−0.34	−0.71	−1.18	−1.70
Germany (West)						
Case A	−0.09	−0.39	−0.65	−1.06	−1.48	−1.99
Case C	0.03	−0.42	−0.67	−0.99	−1.29	−1.68
3. SG/GNPV*						
Japan						
Case A	−0.10	−0.17	−0.17	−0.16	−0.10	−0.03
Case C	−0.03	−0.00	0.00	0.00	0.01	0.06
Germany (West)						
Case A	−0.02	−0.08	−0.14	−0.22	−0.30	−0.36
Case C	0.04	−0.04	−0.09	−0.16	−0.24	−0.28

1. The figures of Case C in the above table are the percent deviation or absolute deviation from the baseline, when the following assumptions are satisfied: (1) The USA cuts government expenditures by 1% of US real GNP and increases money supply by 1% from the baseline; (2) The other 7 industrialized countries (Japan, Germany, France, Italy, UK, Canada, and Australia) increase money supply by 1% from the baseline, together with unchanged real government expenditure from the baseline respectively.
2. * shows the absolute deviation from the baseline.
3. SG: fiscal balance;
   GNPV: nominal GNP.
4. The above figures are calculated in the full-link simulation where the exchange rate of each currency to the US dollar is endogenous.

rate shows a bigger decline in the above countries, and also because the export volume of those countries shows a smaller negative deviation from the baseline in Case C than in Case A.

v. The fiscal balance in the other industrialized countries shows more improvement due to the decline in interest rates.

vi. The export volumes of the developing countries gradually show smaller negative deviations from the baseline in Case C than in Case A (see table 20).

vii. The effective exchange rate of the US dollar shows a smaller

Table 20 **The effect of policy coordination on the export volumes of the developing countries**

Year	1	2	3	4	5	6
Asia (excl. Korea and Japan)						
Case A	−0.58	−0.93	−1.01	−1.26	−1.68	−1.83
Case C	−0.47	−0.58	−0.44	−0.77	−1.39	−1.73
Latin America						
Case A	−1.51	−1.52	−1.63	−1.62	−1.83	−1.45
Case C	−1.18	−1.02	−0.53	−1.86	−2.23	−1.75
Soviet Union and Eastern Europe						
Case A	−0.11	−0.13	−0.18	−0.25	−0.33	−0.38
Case C	−0.06	0.00	0.01	−0.06	−0.23	−0.30

1. The figures of Case C in the above table are the percent deviation or absolute deviation from the baseline, when the following assumptions are satisfied: (1) The USA cuts government expenditures by 1% of US real GNP and increases money supply by 1% from the baseline; (2) The other 7 industrialized countries (Japan, Germany, France, Italy, UK, Canada, and Australia) increase money supply by 1% from the baseline, together with unchanged real government expenditure from the baseline respectively.
2. * shows the absolute deviation from the baseline.
3. SG: fiscal balance;
   GNPV: nominal GNP.
4. The above figures are calculated in the full-link simulation where the exchange rate of each currency to the US dollar is endogenous.

Table 21 **The effect of policy coordination on the trade balances of the six regions as a whole**

Year	1	2	3	4	5	6
Case A	−0.35	−0.38	−0.43	−0.43	−0.53	−0.57
Case C	−0.24	−0.33	−0.43	−0.45	−0.57	−0.54

1. The figures of Case C in the above table are the percent deviation or absolute deviation from the baseline, when the following assumptions are satisfied: (1) The USA cuts government expenditures by 1% of US real GNP and increases money supply by 1% from the baseline; (2) The other 7 industrialized countries (Japan, Germany, France, Italy, UK, Canada, and Australia) increase money supply by 1% from the baseline, together with unchanged real government expenditure from the baseline respectively.
2. The figures in this table are absolute deviations of the ratio of the trade account to the nominal export of the six regions as a whole.

depreciation in the first year in Case C than in Case A. This is due to the smaller long-term interest rate differentials between the United States and the other industrialized countries.[11]

In the above senses policy coordination would effectively lower the

US long-term interest rate and mitigate the deflationary effect of the US policy on the economies of the developing countries, without serious disequilibria in the other industrialized countries.

viii. However there may still be some problems with this policy coordination. One example is that the export volume of the Latin American countries still shows relatively bigger negative deviations from the baseline in comparison with other areas. Their dependence on the US economy is so high that they could not benefit much from the increase in the demand of the other industrialized countries.

V. Concluding remarks

Simulation results are sensitive to the structure of our model as well as to the assumptions. However, it seems to us that the simulation results indicate the following points as policy implications.

1. The first point is that in the medium term a US cut in the budget deficits would be an appropriate policy to improve the demand-supply balance of the global saving.

According to our simulation results, the US cut in government expenditures would reduce the twin deficits and lower long-term interest rates. In addition, this US policy would enable other industrialized countries to lower their interest rates.

2. The second point is that in the short term, the US cut in budget deficits would have a deflationary effect, especially on the developing countries, and it might be difficult for them to sustain economic growth by themselves because of the decrease in US imports.

According to our simulations, the US cut in government expenditure immediately decreases the export volume of the developing countries and gradually lowers real long-term interest rates. This may therefore bring about the deceleration of economic growth and deterioration of trade balance of developing countries, although they could benefit from the decline in interest rates in the later stage.

Also according to our simulation results, Korea has a capability of offsetting deflationary impacts from the US budget cut by increasing government expenditure to sustain economic growth. However, it may not be possible for the country to continue an expansionary fiscal policy for the medium term due to the crowding-out effect and also to the deterioration of the trade and fiscal balances.

In the case of the primary producing countries, they would possibly face a decrease in demand for their products. In this situation it would be difficult for them to raise export prices to cope with the deterioration of the trade balance.

3. Therefore, the third point is that the policy of the industrialized countries should be coordinated with due regard to maintaining economic growth of the developing countries, if the United States cuts budget deficits.

According to our simulation results, policy coordination among the industrialized countries would effectively lower interest rates and mitigate the deflationary effect of the US cut in the government expenditure. If all the industrialized countries in our model increase money supply, together with the US cut in government expenditure, the demand for products of the developing countries in our model would show a smaller decrease. The budget balance in the industrialized countries would show a greater improvement, due to the decline in interest rates.

However, the developing countries that strongly depend on the US economy would still be much influenced by the decrease in US imports. It may be necessary for them to lower the degree of dependence on the US economy, if the United States were to cut government expenditures for several consecutive years (table 10).

Notes

1. The authors are grateful to Mr. Akira Sadahiro and Mr. Yoichi Nakamura for their helpful comments, and to Ms. Yuko Shimokawa for her secretarial skills. The views and quantitative findings should not be interpreted as those of the organization to which the authors belong.
2. In this paper we assume the US nominal long-term interest rate as the indicator of the supply-demand situation of the global saving.
3. The six regions are:
   (i) Asia excluding Korea and Japan
   (ii) Latin America
   (iii) The Middle East
   (iv) The former Soviet Union and Eastern Europe
   (v) Western Europe excluding Germany (West), France, the United Kingdom, and Italy
   (vi) Other countries.
4. (1) The exchange rate of the currencies (Yen, Deutsche Mark, French franc, the pound sterling, Italian lira, Canadian dollar, and Australian dollar) to the US dollar is basically determined by the following three factors:
   (i) the ratio of unit labour cost to that of the United States, as a proxy for the purchasing power parity
   (ii) the differentials between the long-term interest rate of each country and that of the United States
   (iii) accumulated surplus of the current account as a proxy for a risk-premium.

(2) The US dollar is implicitly determined as the effective exchange rate of six currencies (excluding the Australian dollar).

(3) The Korean won is assumed to be linked with the US dollar.

5. The world demand for one country's or region's products is estimated in the following way (see note 2).

   Using the import volume determined by each country model, the world demand volume for each country's export is defined by the following formula:

$$YV+i=\sum_j AO(i,j)\cdot M+j.$$

   $YV+i$ is the world demand volume for ith country's export; $M+j$ is the import volume of jth country; and $AO(i,j)$ is the trade share-matrix in the base year (the ratio of export volume of ith country to total import volume of jth country).

6. In Germany and France, M3 is constant, in the United States, Italy, and Japan M2 is constant, and in the United Kingdom M1 is constant.

7. Needless to say, tax increases are an alternative way to reduce budget deficits. We conducted the simulations only for expenditure cuts because the tax alternative does not substantially affect the results.

   The starting year for the multipliers' test is CY 1983, although economic conditions in CY 1983 are different from those at present, including the US net foreign asset position. The reason why we adopted CY 1983 as the starting year for the multiplier test is that the estimation period of our model is from 1979 to 1988.

   The multipliers in this paper have been derived from sustained change simulations.

8. In the "initial" stage of German unification, its effect is supposed to be shown mainly on the demand side of the economy. Moreover, the effect of the government investment is supposed to be one major part of the "initial" effect of German unification, because the government investment has registered a big increase for infrastructure (see Masson and Wignall 1984; Masson and Meredith 1990).

9. There are two types of developing countries, those that are primary producing countries and those that have a high degree of industrial development – largely in manufacturing and construction lines.

10. In 1988, 0.88 per cent of the nominal GNP was approximately equal to 1,000 billion won. According to the International Financial Statistics, in 1988, the Korean budget surplus was 2,009 billion won. However in 1990, the Korean budget deficit amounted to 1,090 won on a provisional basis.

11. The effective exchange rate of the US dollar shows more depreciation in Case C than in Case A from the second year. This is mainly because the US current balance shows less improvement in Case C than in Case A. This would indicate that to stabilize the exchange rate, it may be necessary to take policy coordination more seriously.

References

Akihiro, Amano. 1988. Comment on Simulation Properties of Three Internationally-Linked Models. Papers and Proceedings of the Fourth EPA International Symposium.

Bodkin, Ronald G., Lawrence R. Klein, and Kanta Marwah. 1991. *A History of Macroeconometric Model-Building*. Aldershot, UK: Edward Elgar.

EPA. 1990. Macroeconomic Linkages and International Adjustment. Paper presented at OECD Informal Workshop C: Tokyo, April.

—— 1991. EPA World Econometric Model Discussion Paper No. 19.

Kato, H. 1991. The Economic Linkage between OECD and DAEs. Mimeo.

Kuczynski, Pedro Pablo. 1990. *Latin American Debt*. The Simul Press.

McKibbin, Warwick J. 1992. "The New Europe and its Economic Implications for the World Economy." *Economic and Financial Computing*, Autumn.

Masson, Paul R., and Adrian Blundell Wignall. 1984. Fiscal Policy and the Exchange Rate in the Big Seven (Transmission of U.S. Government Spendings Shocks). International Seminar on Macroeconomics.

Masson, Paul R., and Guy Meredith. 1990. Economic Implications of German Unification for the Federal Republic and the Rest of the World. IMF working paper, September.

Comments on chapter 4

1. Akinori Marumo

I would like to express my appreciation for the efforts of the EPA team who tried to analyse the possible impacts of the reduction of the US budget deficits on the global economy under the circumstances we are going to face in the near future: possible acute shortage of worldwide savings due to the emerging demand for funds by the developments in Eastern European countries including the former East Germany and the Soviet Union.

It is of the utmost importance that we analyse in an objective, scientific way the possible impacts of the effort to reduce the US deficit, which has been a major concern in recent years for the healthy development of the world economy.

I also appreciate the EPA team's endeavors to uncover the efforts made by major countries in limiting the deflationary impacts of the US budget deficit reduction. However, I have certain doubts and reservations concerning the way the simulations are made and their results.

First, the simulations are made on highly hypothetical assumptions, such as an increase of government expenditures equivalent to 1 per cent of US and German GNP. I believe that the simulations would have been more meaningful if the team tried to adopt more realistic magnitudes in view of the current and prospective situation. Of course, one can argue that, given the multipliers, any reader can estimate possible magnitudes of impacts of any amount of measures to be taken. But I think it would have been much more useful if the simulations were made on the assumption of more realistic magnitudes of policy variables.

Secondly, concerning the simulation Case C, I think it would have been much more realistic if they assumed that the German government spending would increase by an appropriate amount, rather than keeping it constant, because it is already certain that German government expenditures have been increasing significantly.

One of the biggest weaknesses of the simulations, I think, is the asymmetry between the impacts on the "worldwide shortage" of the increases of demand for funds emanating from the United States on one hand and from Germany on the other. According to table 14, a cut in US government outlays equivalent to 1 per cent of her GNP reduces US nominal long-term interest rates by 1.27 percentage points (third year), whereas according to table 12, a cut of government outlays by the German government equivalent to 1 per cent of GNP is estimated to reduce US long-term interest rates by only 0.8 percentage points (third year).

If we take into consideration the differences in size of the two countries ($5.2 trillion for the United States and $1.2 trillion for West Germany, for 1989), it means that the same $52 billion increase in government expenditures in Germany would raise US long-term interest rates by only 0.35 percentage points compared to 1.27 percentage points in the case of the United States. I think the assumption, therefore, that in this model US nominal interest rate represents the "supply-demand situation of global saving" is not appropriate.

2. Warwick J. McKibbin

The authors have chosen an important topic to focus on and I agree with many of the points made in the paper. In particular, I agree with the argument that countries should use monetary policy rather than expansionary fiscal policy to offset any possible negative consequences of a future US fiscal consolidation. There are some advocates of a Japanese fiscal expansion, such as a recent *Economist* editorial, aimed at further reducing the Japanese current account surplus and providing a stimulus to growth in the world economy. In the current environment, with potential increases in the demand for world saving, this policy would be misguided. Some countries need to run a current account surplus to provide the necessary savings for financing the Eastern European and Soviet economies. In this context the EPA paper presents needed empirical results crucial to understanding the policy implications of alternative policy responses to an inevitable adjustment in US fiscal policy.

Despite my general endorsement of the approach taken in the paper and the conclusions reached, I would like to draw attention to some of the simulation results to suggest that some of the quantitative answers in the paper may need to be reconsidered.

First, I would like to focus on table 3. The multiplier effect on US output of an increase in US government spending is large relative to other models. It is also larger than in table 16. I assume that this is because table 3 includes some monetary policy adjustment. The second point from table 3 is that the spillover from the United States to Japan and Germany seems large and ever increasing. In the MSG model and some other multi-country models the spillover becomes negative by five years. This is possibly because the exchange rate of the dollar continually appreciates after the fiscal expansion in the EPA model. The scale of changes in the exchange rate is similar to other models but the trajectory is different. This may be worth looking into and may explain the output results after six years.

Now I would like to turn to table 7 where the results of a US monetary expansion are presented. It is stated in the text referring to this table that the model exhibits monetary neutrality. But this table suggests otherwise. I assume that the effective exchange rate is nominal. In the case of a US monetary expansion of 2 per cent, the US dollar should depreciate by 2 per cent and not return to base as apparently occurs. I am not going to argue that the model should necessarily impose monetary neutrality but it should be clear that it does not currently appear to exhibit it.

I would next like to draw a link between the paper by Paul Armington at this conference and the current paper by using the results of this paper to explore the impact on world interest rates of a change in the demand for savings resulting from changes in fiscal policy in the industrial economies. Table 12 in the paper gives the results for the change in world interest rates for a change in German fiscal policy. The first aspect of this table that is striking and contrasts with the results from Armington's paper is the small effect of the rise in German interest rates on the interest rates of other countries. Rescaling the results in this paper to a rise in the demand for savings of around US$100 billion, it can be calculated that the simple average of world interest rates rises by 120 basis points. This is below the Armington result of close to 200. In contrast, if we use the results for a US fiscal expansion given in table 14, adjusting for the scale of the shock we see that a $100 billion US fiscal expansion raises world interest rates by closer to 170 basis points by the third year. This is much closer to the Armington result and adds further weight to the argument that an increase in the demand for funds can have significant effects on world interest rates. A question still remains as to why the spillover into world interest rates of a German fiscal expansion is much smaller than the US spillover in a world of high capital mobility.

While on the topic of interest rates and exchange rates and how to model exchange rates I would like to address a point raised by Professor Hickman in the session on Paul Armington's paper. Professor Hickman argued that models using the uncovered interest rate parity assumption imply that only interest rates influence exchange rates and that therefore there is no role for other factors such as trade balances. This is not true if the model is specified allowing for the imposition of intertemporal budget constraints. For example, writing the assumption of uncovered interest rate parity as in the MSG model we find:

$$r_t = r_t^* + {}_te_{t+1} - e_t,$$

where r is the domestic nominal interest rate, r^* is the foreign nominal interest rate, ${}_te_{t+1}$ is the exchange rate (in logs) between the two currencies in period $t+1$ expected given information in period t, and e_t is the log of the actual exchange rate in period t. Solving this equation under rational expectations gives that the current exchange rate is equal to the expected interest differentials from period t until some period T plus the expected exchange rate in period T.

$$e_t = e_T + \sum_{s=0}^{T}({}_tr_{t+s} - {}_tr^*_{t+s}).$$

In the MSG model, the equilibrium exchange rate e_T is determined by long-run stock equilibrium and therefore is a function of the flow of trade balances between period t and T. Note that this equilibrium exchange rate is not discounted and therefore changes in trade balances, which affect this equilibrium rate, can have important effects on the current exchange rate. In addition, changes in equilibrium inflation rates also impact on both the nominal interest differentials and the equilibrium nominal exchange rate. This illustrates that as long as intertemporal budget constraints and the treatment of stocks and flows over time are introduced in a consistent manner, as they are in the MSG model, a rich specification of the exchange rate is possible in a way that back-looking models have difficulty in achieving.

This also suggests a possible problem with how the exchange rate adjusts in the EPA model. Many of the short-run responses in the model look reasonable to me. The one area that I have highlighted where foreign GDP appears to keep rising for a fiscal increase is perhaps due to the fact that the exchange rate of the home country appreciates and then continues to appreciate. With a dynamic response of exchange rate appreciation followed by depreciation, the output of foreign economies would rise and then fall. Assuming uncovered interest parity and national expectations is only one way of achieving this type of plausible adjustment. There are other ways which do not rely on national expectations but are partial adjustment models, which perhaps the authors should consider incorporating into the model.

The second part of the paper looks at possible coordinated policy responses to a US fiscal contraction. I agree with many of the qualitative conclusions of this part of the paper but the quantitative conclusions depend on the fiscal and monetary multipliers that I argued above require closer scrutiny.

A good number of improvements have been implemented in the EPA model and I hope my comments will help in the ongoing research effort. The use of a model to explore important and relevant policy scenarios is important both to improve our understanding of these complex issues, as well as learning where possible deficiencies are located in the models we use. In this respect, I found the EPA study both relevant and timely.

3. Guy V.G. Stevens[1]

The paper by the EPA World Economic Model Group presents a set of simulations that are timely and stimulating. The paper challenges us to devise and evaluate programmes that both eliminate the US budget deficit and minimize adverse effects on the world's poorer countries. In examining any simulations, one is necessarily led to an examination of the credibility of the underlying model; I conclude below that the EPA model, for at least the short to medium run, has eminently reasonable properties that lend credence to the reported simulations. I also register concern, however, that recent exercises in multi-country model comparison are straying too far from tests of out-of-sample prediction.

I. The key results of the EPA simulations

The fiscal contractions as simulated in the EPA system succeeds in reducing the US budget deficit and, moreover, significantly reduces the US trade deficit. This latter effect is aided importantly by the depreciation of the weighted average dollar, which reaches 2.2 per cent after three years.

As I will discuss in somewhat more detail below, all of these effects are quite consistent, at least for the first three years, with the views of modellers at the Federal Reserve Board and the average results for multi-country models published in Bryant et al. (1989).

A major potential problem with any programme to cut the US budget deficit and one emphasized in the EPA paper, is the possible negative effect on the developing countries – those least able to afford them. As shown clearly in table 16 of the paper, the volume of US imports decreases for five straight years after the deficit cut, falling 5 per cent below the baseline (4.1 per cent after three years).

Imports from LDCs are hurt less than this average, but the effect is still significant: a 1.6 per cent reduction of Latin American exports

Table 1 **Effects of US fiscal contraction**

Year	1	2	3	4	5	6
			US GNP[a]			
EPA model	−1.40	−1.39	−1.31	−1.10	−0.99	−1.03
Bryant et al. partial average	−1.40	−1.28	−1.03	−0.83	−0.64	−0.46
			Exchange value of dollar			
EPA model	−0.35	−1.56	−2.23	−3.46	−3.58	−2.98
Bryant et al. partial average	−1.86	−2.10	−2.04	−1.95	−1.94	−1.91

Source: Table 16 of EPA paper and Bryant et al. (1989), pp. 106–107.
a. All effects measured as percent deviations from the baseline.

after three years, and a 1 per cent drop in Asian exports. The EPA model does not have the equations to translate the drop in LDC exports into reductions of GNP, but I will assume that the effects would be substantial. I might add that we at the Federal Reserve consider the magnitude of these effects to be eminently realistic; we often use as a rule of thumb that an uncompensated 1 per cent drop in US GNP leads to an average 2 per cent drop in developing country exports; other observers have used ratios as high as 1 to 3.

This potentially disastrous scenario has prompted the EPA modellers to craft two other simulations that attempt to investigate the impact of various unilateral and cooperative policies in reducing the negative effects on developing countries. The composite simulation that adds a 1 per cent increase on Korean government expenditures on to the basic US fiscal contraction shows the strength and weaknesses of unilateral action. As shown in table 17, the Korean action does indeed protect Korean GNP (even increasing it in this case), but at the cost of a significant deterioration of the Korean trade balance. After three years, export volume is down more than in the original simulation (–1.13 per cent versus –0.93 per cent), and imports are increased significantly. Thus, a unilateral response to the US fiscal contraction can work only for a country that has no worries about its trade balance.

The final EPA simulation addresses the trade-balance effect by investigating a coordinate policy that links the US fiscal contraction with a monetary stimulus of 1 per cent for each of the developed countries in the model (the G7 plus Australia). This is one method of trying to shift the burdens of the US fiscal contraction from developing to developed countries. Although the effects are in the direction desired, my interpretation of this simulation is that it illustrates *how difficult* it is to insulate developing countries from the adverse effects of a US contraction. However, I should hasten to add that the adding of other factors, now absent from the EPA and most other models, might change the picture.

As shown in tables 18 and 19, the coordinated action mitigates the fall in GNP in developed countries. Although the adverse trade effects on developing countries are also mitigated, in some cases they are, in my view, still substantial. For Asian developing countries the adverse effect on exports is halved; under policy coordination, exports fall 0.44 per cent after three years, instead of the previous 1.01 per cent. But for Latin America, the improvement after three years is small, an export reduction under policy coordination of 1.53 per cent versus the original 1.63 per cent reduction. If we consider the results after six years, the mitigating effects on all developing-country exports virtually disappear – but, as discussed in the next section, there may be good reasons to ignore this aspect of the simulation.

To me this illustrates the difficulty of designing simulations – and, *a fortiori*, coordinated policies – that eliminate deleterious and unwanted effects on developing countries. This is a problem that goes beyond any particular model and we should be grateful to the EPA team for pointing it out so clearly. I might add that there have been some interesting policy recommendations for solving the US fiscal and trade deficits, while at the same time minimizing the negative effects on developing countries. For example, William Cline (1989) recommends a carefully calculated package of worldwide fiscal actions and exchange rate changes; however, for lack of world model on the order of the EPA model, Cline cannot specify the basic policy changes that can achieve his desired solution. The fully integrated approach allowed by models such as the EPA model suggests that programmes such as Cline's may be more easily said than done.

One channel that the EPA model does not at present possess may lead to a more favourable outlook for coordinated policies in this area. A probably important effect of a US fiscal contraction would be the impact of the attendant US interest rate reduction on interest payments by developing countries.[2] Table 18 indicates that the coordinated policy would reduce the nominal long-term US interest rate by 1.68 percentage points after three years. This could cause a major reduction in developing-country interest payments and a significant improvement in their current-account balance. Once this channel is incorporated into models such as the EPA model, the outcome of a coordinated US fiscal contraction could be much less severe on many developing countries.

II. Evaluating multi-country models

I would like now to turn to a question that has been alluded to above, but not faced directly – the question of model evaluation. How do we know, or how can we find out whether the answers a model is giving are worthy of our attention? This is a question of special interest at this conference where interesting simulations have been presented by some dozen model groups. I would also like to suggest that the area of model evaluation might be a subject of research interest for the future at the UN University.

One of the few ways to evaluate a multi-country model at the present time is to compare its simulation properties to other multi-country models. A few years ago, we had very little in the way of comparative simulation results, but now we do – because of the work led by Ralph Bryant and the cooperation of a large number of modelling groups around the world.[3] Table 1 compares the results of the standard 1 per cent US fiscal shock carried out above for the EPA model with the average of the results of the models studied in Bryant et al. (1989): panels are presented for the effects of the shock on US GNP and the weighted-average dollar exchange rate. It is clear that the EPA model for the first three years has properties that are close to the average for the multi-country model population as a whole. After three years, there does seem to be some tendency for the EPA simulations to show multipliers that are quite a bit larger than the average. The model does seem to be converging, however, although at a quite slow and somewhat worrying rate. For that reason, in the discussion above, I emphasized the results for the first three years of a given simulation. Except for this possible caveat, I conclude that the simulations on which the EPA paper is based are believable, coming from a model that in all major ways is consistent with average results in the field.

But I would like to see more. I want to reiterate that I support the kind of cross-country model comparisons of multi-country models pioneered in Bryant et al. (1988, 1989). But let us not mistake this type of exercise for what it is not; in particular, it is unrelated to crucial time-honoured procedures of scientific verification, procedures that involve confronting a model with data independent of that used in its construction. Rather, these comparisons are the confrontation of a model with the properties of other models – none of which need necessarily be stable or predictively accurate.

Personally, I become uneasy when, in evaluating a model – or a single empirically estimated equation – we neglect prediction. Of course, there are other important characteristics of a good model: for example, consistency with accepted theory and the reasonableness of the estimated coefficients. But to me the touchstone of a scientific approach is the confrontation of a discipline's constructs with independent data.

Thus, I believe that more forecasting should be done as a key part of multi-country model evaluation (both *ex ante* and *ex post* forecasting). I fear that the multi-country model building community may be straying from this goal – although it is well recognized by domestic modellers.[4] In some cases, modellers have even got to the point where the only reported exercise in verification is a comparison of a model's simulations with the averages reported in Bryant et al. (1988, 1989): consider, for example, the otherwise laudatory study by Malley and Foster (1991).

Notes

1. This paper represents the views of the author and should not be interpreted as reflecting the views of the Board of Governors of the Federal Reserve System or other members of its staff.
2. I am indebted to my colleague Jaime Marquez for this point; some of his present work is directed toward incorporating this effect into the Federal Reserve multi-country model.
3. See R.C. Bryant et al. (1988) and R. C. Bryant et al. (1989).
4. See, e.g., Fair (1979) and Chong and Hendry (1986).

References

Bryant, Ralph C., Dale W. Henderson, Gerald Holtham, Peter Hooper, and Steven Symansky, eds. 1988. *Empirical Macroeconomics for Interdependent Economies.* Washington, D.C.: Brookings Institution.

Bryant, Ralph C., David A. Currie, Jacob A. Frenkel, Paul R. Masson, and Richard Portes, eds. 1989. *Macroecoomic Policies in an Interdependent World.* Washington, D.C.: International Monetary Fund.

Chong, Yock Y., and David F. Hendry. 1986. "Econometric Evaluation of Linear Macro-Economic Models." *Review of Economic Studies* 33, November, pp. 671–690.

Cline, William R. 1989. *United States External Adjustment and the World Economy.* Washington, D.C.: Institute for International Economics.

Fair, Ray C. 1979. "An Analysis of the Accuracy of Four Macroeconometric Models." *Journal of Political Economy* 87, August, pp. 701–718.

Malley, James R., David Bell, and John Foster. 1991. The Specification Estimation and Simulation of a Small Global Macroeconomic Model." *Economic Modeling* 8, October, pp. 546–559.

4. Toshihisa Toyoda

Substantial US deficits and their implications for interest rates and aggregate demand, both at home and abroad, certainly remain major issues of the day. The paper by the EPA World Economic Model Group offers a clear and useful simulation analysis of the reduction of the US budget deficits. The recent budget agreement in the United States, if implemented in full, is a significant step toward coping with the federal fiscal problem in that country. The feasibility of cutting the budget deficits has been increased by the recent mutual proposals for the reduction of armaments between the United States and the Soviet Union (the present CIS). Therefore, it is very timely for us to understand possible scenarios for cutting US budget deficits and their potential effects both on the United States and world economies.

The main message of this paper will be that, although a US cut in the budget deficits is an appropriate policy for improving the demand-supply balance of global saving, policy coordination among the industrialized countries (in the form of increases in the money supply) is necessary to lower interest rates effectively and mitigate the deflationary impacts on the world economy (particularly on developing countries).

My first comment concerns the contents of the proposed policy coordination. The authors assume that G7 countries and Australia simultaneously increase their money supply by 1 per cent from the baseline values along with a US cut in government expenditure by 1 per cent of the real GNP. This policy mixture actually improves export volumes in developing countries but the effect on the trade balances of the six regions as a whole is totally unclear (see table 21). As far as the developed countries are concerned, only the effects on Japan and Germany are reported in the paper, but the impact on their GNP is not very clear. It seems that Japan and the other developed countries should initiate more growth and stability. Japan is still deflationary and so is Germany after the second year, as seen in table 19. I would like to propose an increase in the money supply by 2 per cent rather than 1 per cent in each industrialized country which would give more appreciable offsetting effects against the US contractionary policy; interest differentials between the United States and the other industrialized countries, e.g., Japan, will become greater because of the different magnitudes of the slopes of their LM curves. The steeper the slope of the LM curve, the greater will be the increase in the interest rate for a 1 per cent shift in the IS curve, mitigating the over-devaluation of the dollar exhibited in table 8.

As my second comment, I would like to point out that, comparing the present fourth version with the former third one, a big "structural change" has been embodied in the Japanese model, which naturally plays an important role in this world model. After a rather detailed study of the simulation properties of the present fourth version of the EPA model, including some multipliers not reported in this paper, I find that fiscal expansion carried out by the Japanese government causes an appreciation of the yen/dollar exchange rate which has not been observed in the previous three versions. To my understanding, actual "structural change" in the Japanese financial sector has caused this new simulation result. Over the recent sample period, 1979Q1–1988Q4, many attractive time deposits have been created in Japan, making the interest elasticity of money demand substantially lower. The resultant LM function is steeper, so that a fiscal expansion raises the interest rate more than before to bring about an appreciation of the exchange rate. The result also supports the Japanese coordination policy choice of monetary rather than fiscal expansion to alleviate possible pressures for worldwide interest hikes.

Finally, I would like to note the issue of the supply-demand relation of global saving. The authors simply assume that the US long-term interest rate works as the indicator of the supply-demand situation of global saving. However, this assumption may be legitimated only under the situation of constant demand for world saving, including the demand by Eastern European countries. More work will be called for in the future if the authors want serious studies on the supply-demand situation of global saving as they claim in the introduction to the paper, although I do realize the limited availability of the necessary data.

5

Development and the environment: Extending the Global Input-Output modelling system

Faye Duchin and Anatoly Smyshlyaev

I. Introduction[1]

As part of the world community's efforts to determine policies for economic development that will also be ecologically sustainable, the United Nations Department of International Economic and Social Affairs (DIESA) and the Institute for Economic Analysis (IEA) of New York University are carrying out a three-year study to upgrade and extend the Global Input-Output modelling system originally developed for the United Nations by Professor Wassily Leontief and his associates in the 1970s. The GIOM system is currently being used by the IEA team to evaluate strategies for environmentally sound economic development in the world economy over the next several decades based on a macroeconomic outlook provided by DIESA.

Some environmental problems – notably those associated with the effect of greenhouse gases on the climate – are global in both origin and impact. While the rich countries now have the greatest emissions of greenhouse gases, the developing countries may catch up quickly. International agreements will probably be needed to motivate governments to take the politically difficult steps to alter their economic production techniques and consumption patterns enough to reduce or at least limit these emissions. Other problems are more localized, such as water pollution in regional seas or international river valleys, and some are essentially national or sub-national, such as disposal of solid waste (though even this can be an international issue, as with the export of hazardous waste). The present UN/New York University study is focused mainly on energy use and the related global problem of CO_2 emissions and the more local or regional problems of SO_x and NO_x emissions.

This paper describes some of the major methodological issues involved in developing the necessary database and specifying appropriate global macroeconomic scenarios, both of which are vital for obtaining projections from the GIO model that can be relevant for policy formulation. The detailed scenarios, which are the basis for model calculations, are not discussed in this paper.

The first generation models of the world economy and the associated databases were built in the 1970s and, by and large, underwent little additional development in the 1980s. Current concerns about the global environment, however, provide the opportunity for incorporating substantial improvements in their conceptual design and in sharpening the division of labour, geographically and by area of expertise, in the construction of a world database that can be widely shared.

Questions of sustainable development involve a joint concern with natural resource scarcity and prices, on the one hand, and pollution "externalities" on the other. Accustomed ways of dealing with these topics are being rapidly extended, both by those who would modify the usual approaches to determining optimal rates of depletion and optimal pollution controls (e.g., Barbier 1989) and those who advocate different approaches based, for example, on the close collaboration of economists with ecologists and the rethinking of each discipline's notions of equilibrium and optimality that this would involve (Costanza 1991a,b). There are, however, strong common elements in all of this work. Some of the most important, especially for the purposes of this paper, are the need to integrate resource use and pollution through their connection to material transformation, notably in production; the need to replace the unlimited substitution possibilities represented in many models by concrete instances of substitution; and the conceptual accommodation within the analytic framework of variables that are not necessarily traded in markets, such as water. The GIOM system is able to satisfy many of these requirements in both conceptual and practical ways.

II. History of the Global Input-Output modelling system

The UN Global Input-Output modelling system was built and first used in the mid-1970s by Wassily Leontief et al. (1977) and their colleagues according to a general design that had been sketched by Professor Leontief in his Nobel lecture (1973). The original system distinguished 15 geographic regions and almost 50 goods and services and covered the period from 1970 to 2000. The model and database were used in a number of subsequent, more specialized investigations (such as Leontief and Duchin's work on military activities (1983) or Leontief et al. on non-fuel minerals (1982) and were extended and updated in each instance. None the less, the basic design remained unchanged throughout this period.

The fundamental building block of the GIO model is the familiar open, static input-output model. This building block is also used in most other world models, and it is for this reason that they will be able to share a world input-output database. The input-output sub-model provides a means of disaggregating to the sectoral level the results obtained with an econometrically estimated macroeconomic model. Input-output detail has also been absorbed into aggregated production functions in general equilibrium models. The level of sectoral detail in both these kinds of models is generally much lower than that of, for example, the GIO model, but it is likely to increase as more researchers address problems about sustainable development.

For the GIO model, Leontief used this building block in another way and achieved, in a preliminary fashion, a multi-sectoral linkage over time (a dynamic input-output model) and among regions (international trade and capital flows). He also insisted on the technological significance of input structures. This concern with technological content had found expression in the earlier interest in process analysis and materials balances. Construction of input-output matrices from engineering information has not received a lot of attention over the past few decades. However, the usefulness of input-output data and models for analysing relationships between the economy and the physical world based on technical information is now being rediscovered and is likely to revive this line of work.

Input-output tables are published on a periodic basis by statistical offices in over 100 countries and should, in principle, form the building blocks for a world input-output database describing the past. These tables contain only current account information and would need to be supplemented in various ways – for a dynamic model, for example, by data describing capital stock requirements per unit increase in output, not to mention the need for information about the sectoral generation of pollutants. Even for deriving exclusively economic, current account coefficients, however, the original GIOM database for 1970 did not rely directly on these tables for several reasons. Tables for different countries (and even the same country in different years) still use different accounting conventions, definitions, and classifications, making it impractical to combine national tables into regional tables.

A more fundamental problem is posed by the fact that each country's table is valued in the currency of that country. While the mechanics of conversion to a single currency are easily achieved if the conversion factors are given, defining and measuring these conversion factors in a way that does not distort the relative prices of individual countries proves to be a difficult exercise. For these reasons, a few representative tables, supplemented by a great deal of additional information, were used as the basis for estimating "synthetic" input-output parameters for the base year in the original GIOM database. Quantities were measured in physical units (like tons) or in constant US 1970 prices (using various conversion factors). Projections for 1980, 1990, and 2000 were based on technical assumptions that are documented in some detail by Carter et al. (1977).

III. Simplifying, and simultaneously extending, the structure of the Global Input-Output model

The description of the World Model in Leontief et al.'s *Future of the World Economy* (1977) consisted of 175 equations. The original model has recently been rewritten in a handful of matrix equations that clearly emphasize the nature of its simplified dynamics and interregional linkages and that generalize all the other relationships. Besides simplicity, this representation has the added advantage of using the same notation as other input-output literature, both theoretical and applied.

Over the past decade, progress has been made in the formulation and implementation of the dynamic input-output model (in the one-country context) and of the integrated physical/price/income model, both static and dynamic (see Duchin and Szyld 1985) and Duchin 1988; for applications see Leontief and Duchin 1986 and Duchin and Lange 1992). The mathematical model of the current implementation of the GIO Model is easily generalized to accommodate these advances; this design, and the subset of it that is currently in use, are shown in the Annex. Separate but integrated dynamic physical/price/income models will be implemented for the GIOM at the next opportunity.

The work of Leontief (1956) and that of Jones (1961) provides many of the elements for the determination of patterns of international trade based on a direct comparison of cost structures in the many-country, many-commodity case. However, this work (and other, earlier contributions along similar lines) has not been developed to the point where it can be directly incorporated in an operational model. This development has perhaps been postponed by the widespread use in models of the world economy of practical devices such as treating otherwise similar products as different products according to their place of production (Armington 1969) or the use of exogenous export-market shares and import-to-use parameters that bypass the direct comparison of cost structures: the latter approach is used in the GIO model. With the current revival of interest in world models, the earlier line of theoretical work is again being taken up. Further development of the GIO database – the proposed world database – could provide the empirical content required for calculations within such a framework.

IV. Global economic outlook

A multi-regional, multi-sectoral model that is to be used for a several-decade period extending into the future, like the GIO model, requires a database containing parameters governing sector-level production, consumption, and trade. The database also needs to be able to accommodate different sets of parameters corresponding to alternative assumptions about the future. Each set of parameters and exogenous variables constitutes a scenario.

The construction of a scenario also requires projected values for exogenous variables and important related assumptions about policy and behavioural changes and technology transfer that are not generally made explicit: we will call these projections and assumptions, collectively, the global economic outlook. The global economic outlook provides the general economic outlook for the next 30–40 years as well as broad technological assumptions about how the macro-level outlook might be achieved. The global economic outlook should be consistent and its assumptions need to be incorporated, directly and indirectly, into the database. It is difficult, however, for obvious reasons, to ensure its consistency. In fact, one function of computations made with the GIOM system is to provide feedback for adjusting the global economic outlook.

1. Future trends in economic growth and interactions with the environment

The macroeconomic outlook needs to reflect the high probability that future development patterns in all regions will diverge from historical trends. Environmental problems and concerns are likely to accelerate some of the changes in the world economy and trade that began in the 1970s and 1980s. Continuation of current wasteful patterns of world development is not inevitable.

Current patterns of economic development, if they continue unmodified, may cause long-term harm to living conditions, via negative effects on and feedback from the environment. There is evidence that the earth's climate is getting warmer as a result of increasing atmospheric concentrations of CO_2 and other "greenhouse" gases. Warming could be accompanied by significant shifts in regional patterns of rainfall and drought, with mixed effects on agriculture and the biosphere. The increases in greenhouse gases appear to correspond primarily to the burning of fossil fuels and a wide variety of other industrial and agricultural processes, including large-scale clearing of tropical forests. These activities, in turn, respond to the combined forces of growth of population and income and changes in technology and institutional arrangements.

These potential environmental effects are controversial, partly because of uncertainty about the magnitudes and mechanisms of change and partly because of disagreements over the desirability of different possible scenarios for development and the environment. In the case of population growth, more people tend to consume more natural resources – and to deplete the stocks of non-renewable resources and threaten the sustained output of many that could be renewable – given the available store of technologies, the institutional systems for production and distribution, and culturally determined tastes for consumption of various goods and services. In recent decades technology, institutions, and even tastes have changed mainly in ways that increase per capita output of greenhouse gases and other impacts on the environment. But it is possible that the more recent trend toward environmental awareness on the part of governments and individuals could decelerate and even reduce these impacts.

Population growth generates economic activity and income, and consequent environmental impacts, through its effects on consumer demand and on the supply of labour. Conversely, sustained growth of per capita income tends to reduce the so-called "natural" increase in population (births minus deaths) though there may be a lag of several decades, and even a temporary increase in the rate, when a country first emerges from extreme poverty. Continued population growth in the developing countries, together with their understandable desire for a higher standard of living – especially for the billion or more people still living in absolute poverty – almost certainly will increase resource extraction and environmental pressures in many of these countries. More rapid transfer of environmentally sound technologies to these countries and an active role for emerging environmentally sensitive institutions and related public information campaigns could enable these countries to safeguard and even improve the environment. In the developed countries, government policies and individual consumer decisions could reverse the past increases in environmental damage and perhaps lead to significant improvements, as has begun to happen with respect to air and water quality in some areas.

The policy significance of environmental and economic problems depends, or should depend, on how easily they can be modified in the longer term. There is a tendency to exaggerate the significance of relatively sudden changes in long-term trends, e.g., to anticipate a rapid shift from fossil-based to nuclear power following the oil price increases of the 1970s while underestimating the relative availability and safety of natural gas as a substitute. Similarly, many discussions of deforestation assume that recent rates of deforestation will continue unchecked, ignoring the feedback from economic experience, i.e., that cleared tropical forest land has low productivity for many crops. Of course, in many cases, like the latter, it is important to learn the lessons quickly.

2. Key determinants of the global economic outlook

The macroeconomic outlook now being elaborated for the GIOM is intended to serve as a feasible framework within which to consider the impact that different national and international policies and technological developments may have on the future evolution of the world economy. It is assumed that key determinants of future economic growth will not change dramatically in the 1990s from magnitudes observed in recent years.[2] However, initiatives by some governments to reduce emissions of SO_2 and even CO_2 in the beginning of the next century could, depending upon how they are implemented, lead to higher capital requirements and somewhat lower rates of growth.

More significant changes in relationships between macroeconomic variables are expected after the year 2000. Our major assumption is a tendency for the trends in economic growth in different countries to converge, at least among the industrialized countries. A major reason for the convergence is the competition between these countries in global markets, which is leading to greater similarities in production and consumption patterns. This convergence is already evident in the historical trends of a number of parameters. In many countries, public concern for the environment has stimulated a commitment to produce and consume in "cleaner" and more efficient ways. Cleaner production need not be extremely costly, but we do assume that capital per unit of output in these countries will continue to increase while growth in productivity slows down. More detailed assumptions are specified in the individual technical scenarios.

There will be significant differences in rates of economic growth among the developing regions with some changes from recent trends: the rapid growth achieved in some regions in the 1970s and 1980s will be exhausted while other regions will improve. Capital intensity will remain lower than in industrialized countries, but it will steadily increase. We expect that the newly industrializing Asian economies (NIAs) in 30 years will probably be as developed as Japan is today, with comparable capital intensity and labour productivity. Because of the labour surplus in other South and East Asian developing countries, which is expected to persist, it is unlikely that capital-intensive technologies will be introduced on a large scale by the year 2020. Therefore these countries may have reduced rates of growth in the next decades. For most of Latin America, we assume that the external financing crises which characterized the 1980s will not be repeated, and that significant changes in policy will accelerate production in the second half of the 1990s and in the following two decades. While their observed capital intensity is already high, this is probably inflated by the inclusion of capacity idled because of financial constraints during the debt crisis. Therefore, we assume an upturn in the investment share of national income in this region after 2000.

3. Trade patterns

A logic consistent with the above outlook for world economic growth needs to be applied to projecting international trade patterns. Of the 16 GIOM regions, High-Income Western Europe is the largest international market, with 40 per cent of total world trade, although most of that is intraregional trade. Even in this large and growing market, however, shares of imports from developing countries have either stagnated or declined in the last two decades except for the share from the NIAs, which has increased in almost all regional markets. Future exports and imports by region also depend upon assumptions about future terms of trade. It is possible that the declining terms of trade that most developing countries experienced in the 1980s, in relation to the developed countries, fostered the observed increase in trade among developing countries. Exporters mainly of primary commodities were the most affected by the decline. For example, in Sub-Saharan Africa, the share of food and crude materials in exports is more than half, and the export price deflator dropped by over 20 per cent in this region between 1980 and 1987 while the deflator for imports increased by 6 per cent. It seems likely that future world demand for primary commodities will not grow faster than that for processed goods and equipment. Thus, more processed goods in the exports of these countries will be needed to compensate for the losses in their terms of trade. Relatively high rates of productivity growth, especially through more capital-intensive production, are prerequisites for adequate export growth. Overall, there will be a tendency to expand manufacturing in developing countries and to accelerate trade among these countries.

4. Energy use

Any macroeconomic outlook with relevance for environmental problems must include assumptions about energy use both in production and by households. Oil use relative to GDP in developed countries is probably an unreliable guide to the future value of this indicator in the developing countries, despite its frequent use for this purpose. There are large intercountry differences in oil intensity, as measured by the oil/GDP ratio, but in most cases a high proportion of oil products is consumed by passenger cars. While inputs of gasoline are included both in the numerator and the denominator, the value of most of the services of these cars is not counted in GDP.

The problems posed by oil use for transportation are important as it accounts for 30 per cent of total final energy consumption and more than half of total oil use in OECD member countries. Between 1973 and 1988 oil consumption in the transportation sector in these countries increased by almost 2 per cent per year while oil consumption by the industrial, residential, and commercial sectors decreased by over 2 per cent per year. There are many determinants of gasoline consumption that have varying importance even in countries of similar wealth; for example average annual gasoline consumption per car is about 3 tons for North America, 1.2 tons for Europe, and 1.4 tons for the Pacific region, and total gasoline consumption went up about 35 per cent from 1973 to 1988 in Europe and 43 per cent in the Pacific region but only 10 per cent in North America (OECD 1991). Fuel efficiency gains too have been uneven among regions, and the average miles driven per car also varies considerably. These observations suggest that a more elaborated representation of energy use is needed – and one is in fact incorporated in the GIOM database.

Within the framework of an input-output system, reductions or increases in the use of energy can be traced to changes in final deliveries (including investment) of specific goods and services, changes in technologies, or some combination of the two. The ability to compute both direct and indirect requirements makes it possible to quantify the critical links between development and emissions. Even if a sector has low direct energy inputs, it may none the less require a large amount of energy via energy-intensive intermediate inputs.

The relative total energy intensities of the different sectors, including the energy used for intermediate inputs, is an important guide to energy-saving strategies for an economy as a whole and for particular industries. Variations in total energy intensity are evident from an analysis of historical input-output tables carried out by DIESA for 26 selected developed and developing countries, despite some incomparability of those tables. Electricity generation, transport, and oil-refining rank highest in many countries. The next tier often includes the cement industry, iron and steel, nonferrous metals, fertilizers, pulp and paper, and synthetic rubber. There are some other industries, which might be overlooked based only on their direct energy consumption, but which have high total energy requirements that are captured in an input-output computation. For example, in Japan in 1980 direct energy requirements for selected textile goods were 5 to 7 times less (per yen of output) than for basic chemicals, iron and steel, and nonferrous metals; but their total requirements per unit of final product were only 2 to 3 times less. Similarly, selected fibre and textile industries in India in 1979 had direct energy requirements 4 to 7 times less than cement production, but their total energy requirements per rupee of output were only 1.5 to 2 times less energy-intensive. In the USSR automobile production was 9 times less energy-intensive than cement in 1966, but its total energy requirements were only 3 times less because of the high inputs of metals in automobile production.

The GIOM framework captures not only the direct exports of energy but also indirect exports, through export of energy-intensive products. The case of Australia illustrates the importance of this distinction. Australian coal is not only a direct export, it is also used for production and export of extremely energy-intensive commodities such as aluminium.

Another aspect of energy efficiency involves the number of steps in the processing and use of energy products. Because of the energy losses associated with each stage of energy conversion, overall energy efficiency declines when the number of transformations from primary to useful energy increases. This phenomenon is well known. New technologies that are often introduced to reduce the number of transformations of energy and materials have been quite successful (Ayres 1989). One major example is the use of continuous casting in steel production, which reduces energy use per ton of steel by 10 to 15 per cent compared with older processes. Recycling and the use of secondary metals can reduce energy requirements dramatically.

Future patterns of production and energy use will undoubtedly be affected by growing public concerns about the environment. In the developed countries it is reasonable to assume that government policies, and decisions by businesses and local communities, will curtail emissions of air pollutants. The reductions achieved so far in SO_x emissions and in fuel consumption and emissions by passenger cars (per mile of travel) may well be extended to other areas of environmental damage. Significant conservation of energy use in industry is possible at a fairly low capital cost in almost every sector of the economy without retarding economic development, as shown by Japan. Other countries have announced their intentions to reduce emissions of greenhouse gases including carbon dioxide. Some countries already have a carbon tax, and others are considering one.

A challenge in using the GIOM system is to incorporate energy targets and foreseeable technological and policy changes with a feasible macroeconomic outlook. A continuation of energy conservation, capital for energy substitution, and technical change that saves both capital and energy may take place in the most energy-intensive sectors, like metals and chemicals. Given the extreme unevenness in existing technologies across countries and the existing mixture of old and new technologies in a particular country, we may expect different rates of energy saving at the sectoral level across regions.

These considerations raise the issue of how to pay the capital costs for increasing energy efficiency in poor countries. There are already proposals and debates on international trade in emission permits and on modernization of existing establishments in some countries by using technology and capital provided by the countries that suffer from the pollution. Thus the so-called polluter-pays principle might be complemented, at the international level, by the willingness of neighbouring countries to pay for pollution abatement measures. For example, there is a project to modernize nickel smelters in the USSR with technology provided by Finland, Norway, and Sweden in order to reduce SO_2 emissions by a factor of 8, and at a much lower cost than would be required for similar reductions in the donor countries.

The GIOM by itself cannot evaluate whether proposed schemes for a carbon tax of, say, \$100 to \$250 per ton of carbon will be sufficient to encourage energy-saving techniques and substitution of low-carbon fuels or alternative energy sources in the next 30 to 40 years. However, technical information and best-practice examples incorporated in the database, together with an analysis of historical trends, can provide a more accurate evaluation of the range of options available for each sector to contribute to CO_2 reduction than can be undertaken with more aggregated models alone.

Uneven starting conditions – in terms of levels of economic and technological development and, therefore, different potential paths for future development in relation to the environment – will require a wide range of strategies for different regions and countries. For example, protection or sustainable use of tropical rain forests might be the priority area for a number of developing countries in response to the global warming problem. By improving logging practices, upgrading their wood industry, and increasing productivity in agriculture, these countries may also accelerate the industrialization process and expand their export base. These developments are consistent with the macroeconomic outlook developed for the GIOM.

Regarding the assumptions about sectoral energy use, the present

GIOM framework does not distinguish demands for electricity from different types of power plants (coal, oil, natural gas, or nuclear power). This means that changes in the input fuel mix for an economy as a whole, as well as for a particular sector, must be based on information provided by other forecasting techniques. In the general economic outlook, assumptions about energy production cannot simply be extrapolated from recent trends. For example, the future role of nuclear energy is highly uncertain. At the end of 1990 there were 83 nuclear plants under construction, with a total capacity of about 20 per cent of already installed capacity. But the IAEA is considering the possibility that electricity generation by nuclear power plants will be increased by 80 per cent by the year 2005 (IAEA), and ESCAP contemplates a possible 6.5 times increase by the year 2010 in Asian developing countries (ESCAP). In the industrialized countries (except Japan), however, no large-scale growth in new plants for electricity generation is foreseen, including nuclear power plants.

Consistent with historical trends, demand for electricity in developing countries will continue to increase. Consideration of supply-side options in electricity generation needs to be extended beyond the distinction between fossil fuels and other sources (hydro, nuclear, biomass, solar) to include different mixes of fuels and differences in fuel quality and the types of equipment and technologies that can be used in the next 30 to 40 years. In so far as carbon dioxide emissions cannot be reduced dramatically with technologies available for thermal power plants, the importance of even marginal reductions of emissions at the global level through higher conversion rates and fuel switching are very important for many countries, especially those with available natural gas reserves. This option would lead to an increase in international trade in natural gas. Historical trends do not give clear guidance about the feasibility of such an outcome. In the case of electricity there will surely be increases in efficiency of conversion and end-use. Relative increase in energy prices and other policy interventions could accelerate this process.

Detailed case studies have been carried out at the Institute for Economic Analysis about construction, metal processing, electric power, industrial energy conservation, household energy use, transportation, and paper and chemicals to provide parameter projections under a baseline scenario through 2020. In their general orientation, the case studies are consistent with DIESA's global outlook which has been described in this section.

V. Standards for constructing a world database

The need for standards and conventions in constructing a database is widely recognized, and all modelling of the world economy is based on the International Standard Industrial Classification and the Standard International Trade Classification. Some other international classification schemes are also used by economists, although not nearly as extensively, like the Standard Occupational Classification.

There is a need for a Standard Regional Classification System that can be aggregated to different levels as there are unfortunately overlaps in the regional classifications presently used in different world models and databases. The classification system has to include alternative classification schemes to accommodate aggregation principles appropriate for different purposes. These needs will grow stronger rather than weaker as the area of world modelling develops. Descriptive economic databases are often organized on a country basis because countries are the reporting unit; however, world models will remain region-based for a long time to come. The general purpose models will need to maintain enough information and flexibility to shift classification schemes from time to time.

The need for classification schemes and accounting definitions and conventions is evident, but there are other standard requirements that have been almost completely overlooked. Perhaps the most important is the establishment of a set of standard units, one for each variable in the database, and the conversion factors for transforming alternative units to the standards. Units for parameters follow directly from those in which the variables are measured.

Economists generally value variables in what appears to be one unit only, money prices. The estimation and use of deflators, conversion factors relating unit prices in one time period to those in another, is widespread, although they are not systematically assembled on a worldwide basis. The use of a set of "purchasing power parities," or, more generally, conversion factors relating unit prices in one economy's currency to those in another's during the same time interval, is less widespread and much less systematic; a single exchange rate is often used in their place. The root of the difficulty in estimating both types of price conversion factors, is that *there is no vector of unit prices, even for a single base region in a base year, to serve as a starting point.* Consequently, considerable ingenuity is required to compile world data in a single value unit.

For specified regional and sectoral classification schemes, it will be a significant accomplishment to assemble a common, complete, and systematic set of base-year, sector-level unit prices and conversion factors relating unit prices at the sectoral level across regions and over time – say, for 1970, 1980, and 1990 – to the standard prices. While these prices and conversion factors do not now exist as a uniform database, any world model that spans this period has them built explicitly or implicitly into its variables and parameters. In evaluating data coming from different sources (see below), it is much easier and more reliable to reconcile quantities measured in physical units, like tons, than in values, like constant 1987 US prices, because the price conversion factors that are employed by different analysts are rarely explicit, and rarely the same.

Other units need to be defined in addition to price units – units for measuring quantities of such things as raw materials and pollutants, goods, and services. As one moves through the standard classification scheme, a standard unit needs to be associated with the output of each sector. Some will be more difficult than others, and the task can be carried out by stages starting with the easiest. In the GIOM database, for example, processed metals are measured in tons of metal content, fertilizers in tons, and fuels in tons of coal equivalent.

It has proven difficult to define a standard unit for some economic activities. Perhaps the most elusive cases have been the service sectors. There have been promising approaches to defining the typical transaction for a given service sector, but few sustained efforts of measurement have been made along these lines. For this reason the service sector deflators, based on a variety of assumptions, are the most suspect among deflators.

The problems faced in the most difficult instances, however, should not obscure the fact that units are easily defined, and in fact in common use by economists and especially by other analysts, for many sectors. As the value of a standard physical unit for economic analysis becomes clear, progress will also be made in the more problematic instances. The key to this progress will be disaggregation. While it may not be useful to measure output of chemicals in tons, this is the unit of choice for important components like fertilizers or plastics.

Defining the units, and quantifying stocks and flows in terms of them, may appear to be burdensome for statistical offices. However, many accounts are already kept in physical units; for example, worldwide data on items as different as cement (in tons) and automobiles (in number of autos). Keeping separate track of physical quantities and unit prices can be expected to improve the quality of data and will greatly facilitate the task of assembling the unit prices and price conversion factors.

VI. Sources of information and case-studies

The National Accounts, which are collected periodically in most countries following guidelines set out by the United Nations, constitute a descriptive economic database of the world economy. Considerable work would be required to convert it to an analytic database with a uniform classification scheme, compatible levels of aggregation and with variables and parameters quantified (with no "missing data") as required for computations with a specific model. All world models share the National Accounts, but at the present time each model has its own analytic database. The ambition of the further development of the GIOM database is to be part of the analytic database for many world models. A common database will improve the quality and the credibility of the empirical work done with all the models as well as their comparability.

Given the magnitude and the nature of the task, the construction of the new world database needs to be a cumulative effort where one starts from a complete but rough version, which can already be used for analysis, and improves it progressively generally by adding or replacing entire rows or columns, perhaps for several regions at a time. Documentation clearly needs to be developed in parallel. The existing GIOM database can serve as the starting point. It has been significantly expanded and improved through a number of case studies in the course of the present project. We still regard it as a preliminary version, but one that demonstrates the feasibility of the undertaking; the most recent results using this database are reported in Duchin et al. (1992). It will be possible to ask increasingly refined questions, and have more confidence in the results, as the quality of the database is further improved.

Primary data in the physical sciences are obtained using highly specialized instruments under specified, controlled conditions. The closest thing to primary economic data is probably the National Accounts, which are subject to the discipline of double-entry bookkeeping and where the correspondence to the censuses or surveys on which they are based is vouched for by the statistical offices that publish them. These need to be supplemented by other country-reported data, data collected by industry associations or international organizations, and information about input structures provided by technical experts such as engineers, which constitute the principal raw materials for constructing a world database. The challenge is coordinating and integrating this material, some of which is by definition available for past years only. Projections about the future are even harder to come by; they are necessarily fragmentary and based on a multitude of assumptions. Yet parameters and exogenous variables must be quantified for the future if the model which uses the database is to be able to make projections for future years, and this is the ambition of all of the world models. Building the new database will require extensive collaboration.

One advantage of starting from an existing database in building a new one is that one incorporates feedback from the use of the database, with one or more models, in order to improve it. An important form of feedback is comparing computed values for endogenous variables to "control totals." If the discrepancy between computed and control value is too large, some part of the database (or model, but this is not our concern here) may need to be adjusted.

The first step is to evaluate the quality of control totals, for they are not necessarily of higher quality than computed values even if the former are "official." In fact, the perception of discrepancies and oddities resulting from empirical analysis is important for obtaining the kinds of understanding that contribute to the improvement not only of the database but also of the model and sometimes the underlying theory.

However, if the computed figure is deemed to be in need of correction, the reasons for the discrepancy must be determined in order to identify the parameters that have to be changed. This step occupies a good deal of the time of researchers working with multi-sectoral, multi-regional models, and the associated methodological problems merit discussion in the economic literature. Here, the mathematical form of the model is important; the simpler its structure, the easier it is to follow the logic.

Once the problem is identified, there is one basic guideline in changing parameters: not to make any changes that do not improve their quality. This is important in order to maintain the integrity of the database, which gets expressed in a concrete and practical way. Because of the interdependence of the different parts of the economy, if parameters are changed opportunistically, some variables may as a consequence converge toward the controls but others are bound to diverge.

Since the parameters have a technological significance, they can often be estimated directly; for example, tonnage of steel to make 1,000 average automobiles in a particular region in 1990, or the per cent change in this parameter since 1980, assuming that the parameter for 1980 was relatively reliable. In other instances, a parameter for the past can be computed as the ratio of two control totals. Another approach is to compute the ratio of the control total to the *computed* value of the same variable (say, steel production) and multiply the entire steel row by this ratio. The last approach is the weakest but can still improve the database provided there is no reason to believe that the steel coefficients have been systematically over- or underestimated.

Computed values also provide feedback for the global economic outlook (section 4). There may, for example, be inconsistencies between computed investment (based on sector level assumptions and data) and the initial macroeconomic assumption about investment. Alternatively, the initial growth assumptions for different regions may lead to unanticipated accumulation of international debt in certain regions, which is judged to be unrealistic. These inconsistencies are resolved by adjusting either the global economic outlook or the detailed assumptions or both.

A world database capable of providing a structural description for the present and the future needs to be built through case-studies covering all sectors of the world economy. The concept of a case-study is very familiar, and that is a good reason for choosing this name for what turns out to be a rather new enterprise. These case-studies need to be highly structured, requiring the development of a new formalism. Each case-study needs to use the regional and sectoral classification schemes that are agreed upon and the standard units of measure. The ultimate objective is to quantify and document all the relevant variables and parameters directly or to evaluate and improve those already in the database. These variables and parameters, for example, for a case-study of the world steel industry, include regional output, the row and column coefficients, trade shares, and the unit price. Our experience shows that a great deal of the qualitative and descriptive work usually associated with case-studies is in fact required to achieve this goal: technologies in use, levels of recycling, competition with plastics and other materials, and so on. With the added structure provided by the framework that has been described, the case-study is a logical way to parcel up what would otherwise be a daunting task and to ensure that the pieces will fit together when they are individually completed.

Researchers at the Institute for Economic Analysis have carried out case-studies for emissions of three atmospheric pollutants, and for a number of the most energy intensive sectors, at various levels of detail. In the course of this work, the database has, hopefully, been improved. In addition, several conceptual problems have been identified whose resolution requires modification of the model. For example, the use of fuel by motor vehicles depends upon the stock of motor vehicles, not the flow. A large share of motor vehicles in most regions is held by households and government. Yet these are not represented as stock-holding sectors in National Accounts or in the dynamic models with which we are familiar, including our own. The importance of transportation for sustainable development suggests that it may be worth tackling a more realistic representation of the accumulation of capital by households and governments in terms of both modelling and data collection.

VII. On accuracy

Quality control standards for a world database, built with a significant reliance on estimated data not only for the future but even for the past, need to be directly addressed. The standards have to be relevant to this particular undertaking and not borrowed from other sciences where direct measurement is the usual route to quantification.

In their insightful and pertinent book on measurement in science for policy, Silvio Funtowicz and Jerome Ravetz (1990) describe the misleading aura of objective truth of the "magic number" syndrome. They point out that maps, because they are for cultural reasons immune to this syndrome, "... are now generally accepted as being the product of human creation, embodying policies, prejudices, and error" (p. 83). This is true despite the fact that mapping is particularly mature as both an art and a science after several millennia of experience.

The construction of world maps provides an extremely informative comparison for the construction of world models and databases. Maps of the New World and of the polar regions made in the course of the periods of active exploration are of special interest as examples of the successful incorporation of new, increasingly detailed information also needed for a world database. At the earliest appearances of these maps, new features tended to be exaggerated in size and highly stylized in form (for example, the Nile and Amazon rivers). As new information from the ground became available and assimilated by the map-makers, the gross distortions slowly worked themselves out. Even the distorted maps, however, were useful in their time.

Building a world database at, say, a 50-sector level of detail, for a several decade period extending into the future, is perhaps as ambitious as drawing a map of the New World in the early sixteenth century. If, at the present time, our results match control totals only very approximately, "that should be an occasion neither for shame nor for concealment" (as Funtowicz and Ravetz remark in a somewhat different context, 1990, p. 141).

Funtowicz and Ravetz emphasize the role of "rule-of-thumb" estimation in building scientific databases and cite an example from Frederick Mosteller (1977) which is particularly relevant to this paper (because it covers an area where we have indeed had to develop estimates for the GIOM database. The example is about the

> estimation of the number of miles driven annually by American automobiles. This may be done on the basis of various plausible quantitative assumptions: from the total registrations and average use; or from the total fuel consumption and average mileage; or from the total of road space. The first two estimates agree to within 30%, indicating a fairly robust method. (Funtowicz and Ravetz, 1990, p. 104)

Mosteller's judgment (and that of Funtowicz and Ravetz) is that a 30 per cent discrepancy for the type of parameter in question indicates fairly good agreement. Many analysts who do not work with empirically implemented models, perhaps especially experts in narrowly defined areas, still think in terms of "magic numbers" and are intolerant of discrepancies from their preferred standards of even several per cent. However, the large amount of work required to build the world database will be mobilized only if there are realistic expectations about the nature of the task. This requires a community of scholars who support the undertaking and can demonstrate its value through the use they make of the database.

Notes

1. This paper grew out of an IEA project "Strategies for Environmentally Sound Economic Development: An Input-Output Analysis," funded by the Norwegian government and DIESA.
2. This assumption is consistent with that made in the UN report, "Overall Socio-economic Perspective of the World Economy to the Year 2000," 1990.

Annex: A simplified description of the Global Input-Output model

1. Global Input-Output model

The GIO model has been rewritten in the form of four matrix equations, which are given below. This description conveys its salient characteristics and uses familiar notation.

The version given below includes features (like a separate, dynamic price model) that are not yet implemented; otherwise the description would be even more succinct. On the other hand, some important relationships that *are* implemented have been omitted to simplify the exposition, especially those that are not part of a feedback loop (like equations for calculating emissions associated with production), and others are shown in a simplified form (dynamics). The principal departures from the present implementation of the World Model are described below. Some implementation issues are also taken up briefly.

Model

$$(I - A_t - R_t + \hat{M}_t)x_t - B_{t+1}(x_{t+1} - x_t) = c_t + g_t + \hat{E}_t s_t \tag{1}$$

$$(I - A_t - R_t + B_{t+1})' p_t = (I + \hat{\Pi}_{t-1})B_t p_{t-1} + v_t \tag{2}$$

$$\sum_r \hat{M}_t^r x_t^r = \sum_r \hat{E}_t^r s_t \tag{3}$$

$$y = v_t' x_t + \hat{\Pi}_{t-1} p_{t-1}' B_t x_t = p_t'(c_t + g_t + \hat{E}_t s_t - \hat{M}_t x_t) + p_t' B_{t+1} x_{t+1} - p_{t-1}' B_t x_t \tag{4}$$

where all vectors and matrices are indexed by both region (r) (except s which is a global variable) and time period (t). Region superscripts have been omitted from equations (1), (2), and (4) in order to simplify the notation.

$t = 1, ..., T$ and initial values need to be provided for x_1 and p_0

$A = n \times n$ matrix of current-account inputs per unit of output

$R = n \times n$ matrix of replacement of capital per unit of output

$B = n \times n$ matrix of capital stock requirements per unit expansion of capacity

$M = n \times n$ diagonal matrix of import coefficients[1]

$x = n \times 1$ vector of output

$c = n \times 1$ vector of consumption

$g = n \times 1$ vector of government spending

$\hat{E} = n \times n$ diagonal matrix of export shares[2]

$s = n \times 1$ vector of total world exports (or imports)

$\hat{\Pi} = n \times n$ diagonal matrix of rate of return on capital

$p = n \times 1$ vector of prices

y = scalar, gross national product

$v = n \times 1$ vector of other factor payments (labour, indirect business taxes and subsidies) per unit of output

If c^r, g^r, and v^r are exogenous, then x^r, p^r, and s are endogenous.

2. Relations in equations (1)–(4) that are not yet implemented

The fully dynamic input-output physical/price/income model features (included in equations (1), (2), and (4)) have been implemented and used in empirical analyses of the US economy (see references in the text) and are ready to be incorporated in a world input-output model. The income equation has not yet been computed for the GIO model, and a rudimentary form of the price equation (2) was at one time computed but is not part of the model. Very little information that is not already required for equation (1) is needed to implement equations (2) and (4), and the range of questions that could be addressed (for example, about taxes and subsidies or the functional distribution of income) would be considerably expanded.

The representation of expansion investment in equation (1), $B_{t+1}(x_{t+1} - x_t)$, is schematic: it is well known that the model including this expression is unstable and has only a balanced growth solution (see Duchin and Szyld 1985). The expression is used here because it is simple and familiar: this is neither the representation in the GIO model (see below) nor that used in contemporary empirical work which distinguishes capacity from output and multiplies the B matrix by the change in capacity, not the change in output (see Duchin and Szyld 1985). The modern dynamic input-output model accommodates the general case of "uneven" sectoral growth (or decline).

3. Major simplification of equation (1)

The major simplification of the physical model in the current implementation has to do with investment. Instead of the expression from equation (1), $B_{t+1}(x_{t+1} - x_t)$, the GIO model represents the expansion of capacity (or output) in a given region and year by applying an exogenous, sector-specific growth rate to x_t. In addition, the B matrix is decomposed into a vector of sector-specific capital-to-output ratios and a single vector representing the composition of gross investment in that economy.

4. Other important relations in the world model

A number of other equations are included in the GIO model that are important from an empirical point of view but not shown here because of their standard form: these include the labour equations and the pollutant emission equations. Personal consumption of individual goods and services is represented as a function of total consumption and of population (the latter variable is exogenous). The composition of government spending is specified, and the level is represented as a fraction of GDP.

An important equation determines a region's balance of international payments. The debt or credit is accumulated from one decade to the next but does not feed back automatically to the rest of the economy. The equation is of the following form:

$$\text{BOP}_t = p'(\hat{E}_t s_t - M_t x_t) + \alpha F + G,$$

where BOP is short-term credit (or debt), p is the vector of current world prices, F is the stock of foreign capital (which is accumulated in another equation), α is the rate of return on foreign capital, and G is the inflow of long-term capital and of aid (which are determined in other equations). At the present time the world prices are exogenous.

5. Implementing the model

Regional and sectoral classification schemes need to be fixed, and a unit needs to be specified for every variable. The GIOM system uses a mix of physical units (like tons) and constant US prices to measure output variables; it does not now include a price model. With outputs measured in physical units (for example, an average automobile for the motor vehicle sector) and factor payments in current regional prices, the price equation can be used to compute domestic costs of production for given input structures. The physical and price data discussed in the text need to be assembled, however, before this can actually be done.

Notes

1. Import coefficients are defined as import to output ratios while an export share is a region's share of total world exports of that good or service.
2. Ibid.

References

Armington, Paul S. 1969. "A Theory of Demand for Products Distinguished by Place of Production." *International Monetary Fund Staff Papers*, pp. 159–173.

Ayres, Robert. 1989. "Industrial Metabolism." In: J. Ausubel and H. E. Sladovich, eds. *Technology and Environment*, Washington, D.C.: National Academy Press.

Barbier, Edward B. 1989. *Economics, Natural-Resource Scarcity and Development: Conventional and Alternative Views*. London: Earthscan Publications.

Carter, Anne P., Peter Petri et al. 1977. *United Nations World Data Documentation. Vol. 1–11*. Waltham, Mass.: Brandeis Economic Research Center.

Costanza, Robert. 1991a. *Ecological Economics: The Science and Management of Sustainability*. New York: Columbia University Press.

—— 1991b. "Ecological Economics: Creating a New Transdisciplinary Science." *Structural Change and Economic Dynamics* 2(2).

Duchin, Faye. 1988. "Analyzing Structural Change in the Economy," In: Maurizio Ciaschini, ed. *Input-Output Analysis: Current Developments*. London: Chapman and Hall, pp. 113–128.

Duchin, Faye, and Daniel Szyld. 1985. "A Dynamic Input-Output Model with Assured Positive Output." *Metroeconomica* 37, October, 269–282.

Duchin, Faye and Glenn-Marie Lange. 1992. "Technological Choices, Prices and Their Implications for the U.S. Economy, 1963–2000." *Economic Systems Research* 4(1).

Duchin, Faye, Glenn-Marie Lange, Knut Thonstad, and Annemarth Idenburg. 1992. "Strategies for Environmentally Sound Economic Development." Final Report to the United Nations. Contract CPTS/CON/112/91.

ESCAP. 1991. Energy, Technology, and Policy Options in the Asia/Pacific Regions. Paper prepared by the Secretariat of ESCAP for the United Nations meeting in China on Energy and Environment in the Development Process.

Funtowicz, Silvio O., and Jerome R. Ravetz. 1990. *Uncertainty and Quality in Science for Policy*. Dordrecht, the Netherlands: Kluwer Academic Publishers.

International Atomic Energy Association. 1990. *Energy, Electricity Estimates for the Period up to 2005*. Vienna: IAEA.

Jones, Ronald. 1961. "Comparative Advantage and the Theory of Tariffs: A Multi-country, Multi-commodity Model." *Review of Economic Studies*, June, pp. 161–175. Reprinted in: R. W. Jones. *International Trade: Essays in Theory*. 1979. New York: North-Holland.

Leontief, Wassily. 1956. "Factor Proportions and the Structure of American Trade: Further Theoretical and Empirical Analysis." *Review of Economics and Statistics* 38(4): 386–407. Reprinted in: Wassily Leontief. *Input-Output Economics*, 2nd edn (1986) Ch. 6. New York: Oxford University Press.

—— 1973. "Structure of the World Economy: Outline of a Simple Input Output Formulation." *Les Prix Nobel, 1973*. Stockholm: Nobel Foundation.

Leontief, Wassily, A. Carter, and P. Petri. 1977. *The Future of the World Economy*. New York: Oxford University Press.

Leontief, Wassily, J. Koo, S. Nasar, and I. Sohn. 1982. *The Future of Nonfuel Minerals in the U.S. and World Economy: Input-Output Projections, 1980–2030*. Lexington, Mass.: Lexington Books.

Leontief, Wassily, and Faye Duchin. 1983. *Military Spending: Facts and Figures, Worldwide Implications and Future Outlook*. New York: Oxford University Press.

—— 1986. *The Future Impact of Automation on Workers*. New York: Oxford University Press.

Mosteller, Frederick. 1977. "Assessing Unknown Numbers: Order of Magnitude Estimation." In: W.B. Fairley and F. Mosteller, eds. *Statistics and Public Policy*. Addison-Wesley, pp. 163–184.

OECD. 1991. *Fuel Efficiency of Passenger Cars*. Paris: OECD, International Energy Association.

United Nations. 1990. *Overall Socioeconomic Perspective of the World Economy to the Year 2000*, Publication No. E.90.II.C.2. New York: UN.

Comments on chapter 5

1. Iwan Jaya Azis

I believe that an input-output framework, if properly applied, is among the most useful tools by which linking economics and the environment is to be achieved for planning purposes. Therefore, I find this paper important for modellers who have a strong interest in the topic.

Although the model application discussed in the paper is only of an exploratory nature and lacks detailed vigour, I had the opportunity to obtain further explanation about the model from a series of personal discussions with one of the authors during her recent visit to Indonesia. I do not find significant flaws in the modelling itself; the problem seems to lie in the feasibility and operation of constructing an input-output table measured in physical units. As far as I know, no single country's input-output table of that sort has yet been developed.

Along with other colleagues, in Indonesia and abroad, I have been working on the same topic, i.e., linking economics and the environment, although I use a completely different model and approaches. From our experiences it has become very apparent that collecting physical data relevant to the objective of linking economics and the environment is very tedious work. At best such a task could be done only at a particular location and for merely a few selected factors, e.g., water use, energy use, or air pollution. To relate those factors to the corresponding production sector, which is an important step in the input-output analysis, would be another tricky thing to do.

This, however, should not prevent efforts in applying the model for the analysis of linking economics and the environment at the national, and eventually global, level. As long as we can confine ourself at an early stage to only selected environmental factors, I do not see any reason why we cannot make a serious attempt to collect the necessary data. From the positive side, this line of work should effectively open an avenue whereby real collaborative work between economists, engineers, biologists, and other scientists could materialize.

The dynamic input-output model incorporating physical/price/income relations, as represented by equations (1), (2), and (4), requires information on capital stock. It is no secret that these data are practically unavailable in many countries, especially in the developing nations, unless certain models and assumptions are adopted. Furthermore, it still needs some explanation as to what extent the standard assumption necessary for such a dynamic model, i.e., a balanced growth pattern, is verifiable, given the real conditions in many countries. Nevertheless, I remain optimistic and can easily appreciate the significance of applying the approach once the necessary data are collected. The rest of my comments will be more about the implications and assumptions of applying the model for global analysis as the authors have suggested in the paper.

The projection results from the GIOM system appear to depend on the (global) macroeconomic outlook, in which one would capture the association between sectoral levels of production with corresponding energy use and pollution emissions. Interestingly enough, the study assumes a convergent trend in economic growth for different countries, particularly after the year 2000. Among others, the authors attribute this assumption to at least the following two phenomena: first, the increased trend of greater similarities in production and consumption patterns due to competition in global markets; secondly, the presence of a common concern for the environment, which implies an increasing trend of capital-output ratio and slower growth of labour productivity.

I am sure the authors would agree with me that the first phenomenon is not too realistic for many developing countries. In fact, if we refer to the world trend data of the seventies and eighties, one could easily see that within the category of developing nations the trend of GDP growth had varied quite dramatically from one region to another. While the developing South Asia registered a fast-increasing trend of GDP growth in this period, Latin America and the Caribbean experienced decelerating growth in the same decades. A decelerating growth is also observed in Sub-Saharan Africa, while a dramatic acceleration took place in East Asia.

But the authors are quick to point out that the assumed convergence is applied "at least among the industrialized countries" and they are indeed equally quick to state that "there will be significant differences in rates of economic growth among the developing regions." However, from the remarks following this, we seem to be led to accept the assumption that the growth in the NIEs will be higher than that in the South and East Asian countries. As far as the growth rate and not the level of GDP is concerned, I think this point is debatable. In my opinion, it is not at all certain that the growth rate of South and South East Asia in the future will be lower than the rate expected to occur in the NIEs. Many signs have shown that the NIEs are approaching the growth pattern of countries such as Japan and the USA, that is, within the range of a maximum 5 per cent.

It seems that the problem, among others, lies with the assumption adopted by the authors on the use of capital-intensive technologies, i.e., only by the year 2020 would the South and East Asian countries introduce such technologies. I am not so clear what the authors mean by "capital-intensive technologies" here? During the import-substitution period of the seventies many of these countries were already critically viewed as adopting unnecessarily technologies of a capital-intensive nature. Perhaps the statement would be more appropriate if related to the knowledge-intensive or high-tech production process. Given the critical role of the assumption, it would be useful for readers to have a more specific explanation as to the assumed trend of GDP growth being used in the study.

Why is this important? As the paper has indicated, there is a very close link between the macroeconomic outlook and environmental problems. Energy use is perhaps among the most critical factor, reflecting such a link. The strength of an input-output framework in this respect, as we all know, is its ability to capture direct and indirect requirements, suggesting that a sector with low direct energy inputs may be classified as a high energy requiring sector if in fact it uses a large amount of energy-intensive intermediate inputs. Obviously, the sectoral composition and the type of technology adopted will determine the size and the nature of energy use. None the less, the assumption on the macroeconomy will indeed play a critical role in the analysis of energy use.

The authors made another interesting remark in this respect: "Future patterns of production and energy use will undoubtedly be affected by growing public concerns about the environment." I wholly support this assertion. It is in this connection I would like to refer to my recent study on finding the interdependent link between economic, socio-demographic, and ecology-environmental factors.[1] This study was conducted in one region in Indonesia, Riau, with a high potential environmental damage level. We found from the study that there is a two-way link between people's knowledge/awareness towards environmental problems (one of the elements in the socio-demographic block) and so-called environmental welfare. That the former affects the latter almost everyone knows, but not the contrary. It turns out that the knowledge, and hence also the awareness, of the local people towards environmental problems has been greatly enhanced by the seriousness of the environmental damage taking place in the region.

The problem is obviously in the planning implementation. It is not at all easy to have a consensus, for example on the future patterns of production and energy use, especially when information and knowledge about alternative energies are still scanty. The current situation in Indonesia is perhaps worth citing. While many have predicted that oil-based energy will become more limited in the not too far distant future, the government has recently proposed a plan to switch from oil to coal, and to some extent also, nuclear energy. Controversies have naturally emerged. While many countries attempt to reduce the CO_2 emissions, the switch to coal energy in Indonesia is probably considered rather preposterous. But what are the other alternatives for Indonesia given the existing (limited) affordable technology available in the world market?

In this connection it is not yet clear to me what the model assumes about the efficient use of energy in many developing countries. The effects of energy switching and those of more efficient use of energy should not be the same. Some studies have indicated, for example, that the estimated effects on the CO_2 emissions of the two scenarios are clearly not the same.

The next point on which I would like to comment pertains to the authors' assertions on assumed trade patterns, particularly in connection with the future terms of trade. While I fully agree with their suggestion that "more processed goods in the exports of these (primary commodities exporting) countries will be needed to compensate for the losses in their terms of trade," I really question their following remarks "It is possible that the declining terms of trade that most developing countries experienced in the 1980s, in relation to the developed countries, fostered the observed increase in trade among developing countries." I do not think that trade between developing countries has increased faster that trade between developing and developed countries.

In a paper I wrote for another meeting in Japan I showed that while the intraregional trade in Asia-Pacific has increased quite tremendously (by the end of the last decade roughly 70 per cent of the region's total exports are directed to itself), the picture is completely different with respect to trade among the developing members of the region only (in particular when the US and Japan are excluded).[2] A declining intra-Asean trade, despite all kinds of efforts to further increase it, is another cogent example demonstrating the lack of natural complementarity among the developing nations. Thus, it is like a "back to basics," type of international trade theory, where a classical pattern of interregional trade is observed, i.e. between developing and developed countries. It is almost a universal rule that the economies of developing countries often have a tendency to bear low degrees of economic complementarity with each other.

An important consequence of the above points would be the need for a clearer picture regarding the future world trading system. Unfortunately, this is not an easy task given the increasing trend of regional grouping (e.g. Europe 1992 and NAFTA) and the (almost) collapse of the present GATT round.

Another extremely important consequence, especially if the issue is to be related with the environmental problems, is the need to reassess (and hopefully alter) the prevailing import tariff and non-tariff patterns in which the developed nations tend to impose much higher rates for processed goods than for resource-based activities. This has led to further depletion of natural resources in many developing countries (forest and mining depletion is a trenchant example to cite), because no incentives are provided for developing countries to switch from resource-based to resource-saving export activities.

The use of an input-output framework for the GIOM is, again, extremely useful. Basically various new directions as well as variations of analysis can be made. However, we are all aware that when an attempt is made to relate the model to environmental problems, one of the most important early steps would be the conversion of biological materials and wastes to measures of production that will match with the classification in a standard input-output framework. I know that Professor Duchin has done extensive work on this matter and I think it would be useful to many of us if she could elaborate further at least some of the critical points pertaining to this conversion matter. It is with this point that I would like to connect my closing comments on this interesting paper. In the last section of the paper the authors try to remind us that we should be more tolerant of discrepancies in world data to be collected for the GIOM. I believe an even greater tolerance is needed if we wish to construct an IO table in physical units and integrating resource use and pollution through their connection with material transformation.

This point, however, should not be confused with the continued tasks of scholars who have, directly or indirectly, advisory roles to the government for improved policy measures. We are all aware that inaccurate information has the potential for producing incorrect conclusions, unless the conclusion is already predetermined. The resulting policies are too important to be left to rely entirely upon such a conclusion. I believe the authors should not be too worried and place too much stress on the possible discrepancies in the database as long as we can accept that presenting scenarios and analysis is our most important task in applying the GIOM to economic-environment analysis; far more important than the necessary policy recommendations, at least in the early stages of the study.

As to the appeal to widen the efforts of applying the GIOM system for determining policies for economic development that will also be ecologically sustainable, I happily endorse such an appeal. Sharing information and materials is, however, very critical at the early stage if interest among policy makers and scholars throughout the world is to be solicited.

Notes

1. Inter-University Center for Economics (IUC-EC-UI), *The Link Between Economics, Socio-Demgraphic and Environmental Factors in Riau: A Study Based on Local Perceptions* (funded partly by the IDRC, 1991).
2. Iwan J. Azis, *Export Potentials in Asian Market*, ICSEAD conference on "Exports, Foreign Investments and Growth in East and South-East Asia," August 1991.

2. Olav Bjerkholt

The Duchin and Smyshlyaev paper is concerned with the prerequisites for global modelling with reference to, on the one hand, the Global Input-Output model (GIOM) of the Institute for Economic Analysis, and on the other, to applications of this model for the analysis of the global problem of CO_2 emissions and related energy use. The model project aims at reaching decision makers and relates to their problems. The emphasis on prerequisites such as a comprehensive database with an appropriate conceptual structure, conventions with regard to units and accounting principles, etc., is very commendable. An ambition expressed in the paper is to build an analytic database that can be shared by many world models.

The analysis of the global climate change problem is still at an early stage of analysis. A number of different modelling approaches has been attempted. Much of this early modelling and analysis work will serve to improve our understanding of the problem and help focus on the most pertinent questions for further analysis. As more of the uncertainty about the climate consequences of CO_2 is resolved, models addressing the climate issue will influence policy. Different models reflect different approaches to answering the same questions, but models differ also because they focus on different aspects of the same complex issues and hence address different questions. It should be readily accepted that pluralism in modelling approaches is a great advantage. The GIO model underlying the Duchin and Smyshlyaev paper has advantages as well as disadvantages. Among the advantages are the rich descriptive detail of the model with regard to both regions and industries, as well as the focus on technology and material transformation that makes it possible to follow the flow of materials and the direct and indirect pollution from the various economic sectors. Among the disadvantages are the lack of price response in the model and the somewhat crude treatment of international trade. Both are serious disadvantages for the intended application. The paper points, however, to these areas as prime targets for development of the model. The degree of openness in the model implies – as emphasized by the authors – that a considerable effort is necessary to ensure consistency in the formulation of scenarios.

The focus on technology and the amount of detail is open for a wide range of studies and a higher degree of realism at sectoral and regional level than for many other global modelling efforts. Something may be gained by combining models with complementary advantages and disadvantages, not necessarily by formal linking of the models, but, for example, by using results from one model as assumptions in another. It may also be possible to move towards a mutually consistent picture. The GIOM should be open for such linkages.

Modelling the global climate problem

The question of climate change and CO_2 emissions is closely connected to the question of how to reduce the world dependence on fossil fuels. According to current estimates, fossil fuels use amounts of more than three-quarters of the world energy consumption. Almost three-quarters of the carbon dioxide emissions stem from industrialized countries. As fossil fuels are exhaustible resources they would have to be replaced sooner or later even if there were no external effect on the global climate. If the view, held by many scientists of severe degradation of the Earth's ecosystem if fossil fuel burning continues, is correct, the challenge is enormous. In modelling terms, it is primarily a question of studying ways of reducing fossil fuel use by efficiency improvements, shifts between energy sources, and reduced energy dependence.

The total efficiency in energy use in human societies can be measured by energy to GDP ratio. This ratio differs widely between regions. To assess the changes in efficiency that might occur requires an assessment of (1) the autonomous changes in efficiency, (2) the price-induced efficiency improvement, and (3) the diffusion of new and more energy efficient technology throughout the world. The potential for reducing fossil fuel use in industrialized countries over a period of a few decades is probably very great, but so is the need for increased energy use in developing countries. The model has a framework well suited to the integration of the various elements in the global energy and environment picture. I am a little surprised that the authors go no further in indicating and outlining what kind of scenarios they want to generate by means of the model. It is high time these scenarios were developed for studying what this model can contribute to the prime audience in the large gathering of policy makers attending the UNCED conference in Brazil in 1992.

Developing a world database

The ambition to develop a world analytic database that can be used by many world models is an endeavour in which it would be easy to overstretch resources. Models differ and it is hard to design a modelling database that will be sufficient and satisfactory for other models beside the one for which the data were originally prepared.

The paper points out with full justification the importance for analytic economics of the United Nations' leading role in establishing guidelines in the form of statistical conventions. The national accounting standard is, of course, of supreme importance in this context. The double standard of SNA and MPS may soon be a thing of the past as the users of MPS are quickly vanishing. China pursues, in principle, a Chinese way of national accounting, but has for some years emphasized full reconciliation with the SNA system. The authors point to difficulties in reconciling input-output tables from different countries due to different accounting conventions. I think this was more prominent in the past, and such differences are about to disappear as more and more countries compile their input-output tables within the framework and as recommended by the UN Standard of National Accounting.

There is clearly a need for more unified conventions with regard to analytic descriptions in areas that have not been sufficiently codified, such as energy production and use where there is considerable variation in standards and practice and in the description of technologies. As this is a matter of concern for many analytic institutions, not only global modellers, the common interest among such institutions for arriving at practical guidelines should be investigated, and maximum use should be made of already existing and accessible databases.

Scenarios and uncertainty

There is little discussion in the paper about uncertainty, as such, and how it should be dealt with when making projections into the future. The uncertainty of the assumptions that have to be made is considerable for projections in the area considered here: energy use, environmental impact, climate change, and induced technological progress. There is both a substantive issue about how to assess uncertainty, and a question of presentation about how to convey the uncertainty and the choices that have to be made as the resolution of the issues proceeds.

There is probably no need to remind readers that most long-term projections of a global nature have turned out to be failures. The reason for most failures is not the occurrence of unique, unforeseeable events. The failure is often inability to perceive the development of the underlying long-term determinants and distinguish them from the more visible short-term movements of the initial situation. The much-used expression "prolonging current trends" often means extrapolation beyond reason. My own favourite example is the oil-price predictions of 1980/81. DRI International – a very distinguished forecasting company – predicted, for example, in 1981 that the oil price of 1995 would be 168 dollars per barrel. The forecast was clearly unduly influenced by short-term changes in the oil market. Why should the long-term balance in the supply and demand of oil be influenced by events that took place in the Middle East in 1979/80? It should not, but this is the kind of mistake that is made again and again in the history of modelling. This perhaps merely reflects that global long-term modelling is still at an embryonic stage. It is probably fair to say also that there is in long-term modelling a general tendency to underestimate uncertainty.

The main tool for dealing with presentation of uncertainty in modelling is *scenario analysis*, i.e., the selection of a small number of possible paths of development, contingent upon assumptions concerning a number of uncertain variables. Well-formulated scenarios, which require high consistency in the assumptions, may serve to indicate possibilities for the future, thus generating interest in the problems they are intended to illuminate.

In order to form a basis for making decisions, scenario analysis has serious shortcomings. There is not time to pursue the point here, but the main reason is that a typical scenario analysis lets the selected cases fan out in different directions at time $t = 1$, as if all uncertainty of the future were concentrated at that point. I leave the issue here, by just pointing out the importance of facing uncertainty in policy-oriented global modelling.

Transparency and prior beliefs

In the theory of economic policy and the use of models it is usually assumed that the role of the decision maker is to evaluate different outcomes from an empirical model constructed and estimated by economists and econometricians. A striking observation is that politicians and other decision makers often go far beyond the evaluation of outcomes; they engage uninhibitedly in arguing about the effects of different policy proposals.

The reason for this is that politicians have *prior beliefs*. Environmental issues are good examples of problems where prior beliefs are important. The information incorporated in such beliefs may not be amenable to formal analysis, but that is not a sufficient reason for not taking such beliefs seriously if we want models to influence policy.

Debates about the working of the economy based on prior beliefs are not caused, as one might be led to assume, by the fact that the predictions from economic models have often turned out to be unreliable. There are other areas with unreliable predictions where prior beliefs play no role. Consider weather forecasts. Nobody would take seriously a Californian politician who ran his campaign for relaxing water restrictions on the grounds of a firm belief in heavy rain during the coming winter. The reason why he would not be taken seriously is not that we have access to reliable expert forecasts contradicting the claim, but because nobody believes there can be private information of this nature. All prior information is based on statistics that are already included in the available weather forecasting models.

On the other hand consider tax policy. This is an area where politicians feel very free to form their own opinions about the effects of tax changes, whether corroborated by empirical evidence or not. The Laffer argument about the relationship between tax rates and tax revenue is a crude example, but not more crude than when it was taken seriously, at least for a while, by politicians as well as the voting public. Climate change and climate policy might easily be another area where prior beliefs will have great influence when it comes to deciding on policy measures.

The point I want to make is that for a model builder to be *credible*, i.e., to produce something that will be taken seriously by decision makers, it is necessary to pay attention to the fact that there are prior beliefs. One consequence of this is that *simplicity in model structure* is essential. A decision maker cannot relate his prior beliefs either to a complex model structure he or she cannot comprehend or to a "black box model."

Consider the choice in the analysis of a given problem between a large, intricate, and opaque model, on the one hand, and a small, simple, and transparent one on the other. Assume for simplicity that the "large" model gives a perfect description of the workings of the economy, but with unknown parameters. For parameters for which available data are scanty, there may be prior information in the form of Bayesian-type prior distributions.

One disadvantage of the "large" model is the loss of prior information as standard estimation methods will ignore such information.

As the model by assumption is complicated, the decision maker will not be able to relate the results of the model to his prior beliefs. Thus to rely on this model, the decision maker will have to disregard his prior beliefs. There is in practice no way to incorporate them into the analysis.

Another disadvantage of the "large" model is the difficulty of optimizing. A model estimated by econometric methods will include stochastic error terms, hence we have a stochastic optimization problem. Even deterministic optimization of large-scale models is computationally demanding. Furthermore, optimization requires knowledge of the decision maker's preferences, which are usually unavailable. Thus the problem is often solved by presenting a small menu of possible paths of development for different policies, a procedure which is not likely to lead to optimal decisions.

These disadvantages will be less serious for a "small" model. If the model is small, simple, and transparent, the decision maker may get a reasonably good understanding of the model and will be able to incorporate some prior information. This requires that the empirical evidence can be presented in an easily understandable form. Furthermore, it will be easier to get a feeling for the optimal choice in a small model than in the large model.

The disadvantage of the small-model approach will be mainly due to approximation errors. Since the "large" model is assumed to yield a perfect description of the economy, the "small" model must necessarily deviate. Optimal decisions deduced from an erroneous model will necessarily be different from truly optimal decisions.

This somewhat simplistic argument leads to the conclusion that a "small" model is the better choice if the approximation error is small and either the prior information substantial or the optimization procedure is important. That is not exactly where I wanted to finish. Let me just continue by stating that there are other relevant reasons for the choice between a "small" and a "large" model than those included in this line of reasoning.

But suppose we have a "large" model and we are unable to construct a good small-model approximation of it? If that is the case, the decision maker is not likely to understand the assumptions of the large scale model. In practice he may have the choice of relying on the "large" model or turning to somebody he trusts and with whom he shares prior beliefs for informal but perhaps more convincing advice. He may realize that this advice is incomplete and unlikely to lead to optimal results.

The challenge for the builder of a large model is that if he wants the model to provide a basis for policy decisions, he should make an effort to cope with these demands by giving a transparent interpretation of the model, e.g. by making a small "model of the model" (a reduced version). The model underlying the Duchin and Smyshlyaev paper is large and may seem complex, but basically it is a simple model which can be presented in a way that is more transparent for decision makers. I want to draw the authors' attention to the need for doing that.

The authors compare, at the end of the paper, the ambition of building a world database at a 50-sector level for projections stretching several decades into the next century with that of drawing maps of the the American continent in the early sixteenth century. The comparison is fanciful, but well chosen. Map-drawing at that time was imaginative reasoning on the basis of quite scanty and unreliable data. The balance between imagination and facts is certainly different with regard to the database, but the idea of the end product as something to navigate by, until a better picture is drawn, is very attractive.

References

Bjerkholt, O., and K.A. Brekke. 1991. *Practical Aspects of Policy Analysis under Uncertainty*. In: Proceedings from Global Climate Change: Global and Regional Responses. Peder Sather Symposium, Berkeley, California, 16–18 October.

Energy Journal. 1991. Special Issue on Global Warming, 12(1).

WCED. 1987. *Our Common Future*. World Commission on the Environment and Development. Oxford: Oxford University Press.

3. Maurizio Grassini

With all the unbelievable and honestly unpredicted changes which have taken place during the recent past, one must admire the courage of those who are prepared to forecast the world economy in the first quarter of the next century. I should be frightened by the task of commenting on this sort of forecast; however, the paper by Duchin and Smyshlyaev is mainly concerned with a research project (or a methodological issue, as specified by Faye Duchin in her presentation) on a three-year study for upgrading and extending the Global Input-Output Modelling system. The paper makes it clear that the study will afford the development of a database and the specification and the use of appropriate macroeconomic scenarios; at the end, an outline of the Global Input-Output model is given. Jointly with the results of the present study the GIOM is the tool that will be used to explore the near future. Hence, a few comments on the proposed database, the macroeconomic scenarios, and the suitability of the model are in order.

Within the three-year time span, I think that a great impulse can be given to the construction of the database sketched in the paper; since it is claimed that this database is going to be widely shared, the goal to sharpen the division of labour on a geographical base must be clearly pursued from the start; I mean that, from now on, the project should be always accompanied by a chorus of a good, not only a geographical, variety of partners. I do not see any other way to communicate the fact that such a database is going to be built and at the same time to stimulate interest in collaborating with the collection of information, which is inevitably country specific. Beside the team that builds up the database, I suggest planning a special task force with the aim of collecting all the present laws concerning environmental matters and then decoding them in economic terns. I think that this task force will inevitably provide interesting suggestions for shaping the database by revealing the set of instruments that will be actively used all around the world. This investigation, of course, is important for defining the information to be inserted into the database; but I would like to stress that it is even more important to think about the suitability of the present design of the model; in fact, one can figure out the necessary changes to be introduced in order to incorporate the instruments, which will be intensively used in the future.

While I have nothing to say about the suitability of the outlined macroeconomic scenarios, I would like to stress a point which arises from their proposed use. It is said in the paper that the "input-output submodel provides a means of disaggregating to the sectoral level the results obtained with an econometrically estimated macroeconomic model." This is a top-down (from an aggregate to a disaggregate model) approach that in the framework of input-output models is realized as follows: (a) the macroeconomic econometric model is used to predict macrovariables (for instance, private consumption expenditure, total exports, etc.); (b) one or more predicted macrovariables are spread along the input-output sectors according to given (IO table) shares; (c) the input-output model is then solved for some of the (residual) endogenous variables (at least for the total sectoral outputs). If the macroeconomic model supplies all the final demand components, the input-output model gives total production and intermediate consumptions, which, together with the final demand variables, consistently define the balance between total resources and their uses.

In the paper it is said that "the global economic outlook should be consistent and its assumptions need to be incorporated, directly and indirectly, into the database. It is difficult, however, for obvious reasons, to assure its consistency." I think that the "obvious reasons" here deserve a close investigation. The top-down approach (even with a slightly different path with respect to the one described above) necessarily introduces inconsistencies. These are due to any departures from the static input-output model created by Leontief. But it is well known that the static input-output model inserted into a macroeconomic model according to the above mentioned top-down approach does not produce sectorally interesting results; likewise, it is well known that any departure from the static input-output model (for instance, endogenizing one or more final demand components) produces inconsistencies with any given macroeconomic forecasts. Once we deal with a multi-sectoral model with a joint interest in macroeconomic aggregates as well, only a bottom-up approach is able to give meaningful results. In fact, the model is constrained to behave like the real economy, which generates the macroeconomic variables by summing up sectoral values, and not vice versa. Then, if we follow the bottom-up approach we get rid of the (logical and numerical) inconsistencies implied by the top-down one. But there are, of course, other sources of inconsistencies. Some of them can be related to the generation of the global economic outlook; others to the structure of the model. It seems to me that not enough elements are provided to discuss the first source of inconsistencies; I will therefore confine my discussion to the model.

The model consists of four groups of equations. The first group, named the dynamic input-output physical model, has three sets of endogenous variables: (i) sectoral total productions; (ii) sectoral fixed investments; and (iii) sectoral imports. Set (i) is the endogenous variable that in the input-output model is given by default; (ii) is the set of sectoral investments endogenized in the dynamic input-output model; (iii) is the set of sectoral imports endogenized using a particular specification of import equations. Then, equation (1) can be rewritten as follows:

$$x = Ax + c + g + i - m + ex$$

$$i = B(x(+1) - x)$$

$$m = Mx,$$

where all vectors should be indexed by time period ($x(+1)$ is the total sectoral productions vector at the time $t+1$; the matrix replacement R is here ignored without any loss in generality); ex is the vector ES in equation (1). From this representation of the dynamic input-output physical model we clearly see the set of variables involved; but the relationship between this set of sectoral variables and the (I suppose) subset of the corresponding macrovariables supplied by the global economic outlook is not clear (anyway, c and g clearly belong to the global economic outlook). In other words, it is not clear which set of variables will drive the projections and how the "computations made with the GIOM system" are used "to provide feedback for adjusting the global economic outlook." One can only think that, out of a variety of feasible procedures (since all matrices are provided by a time period subscript), a trial-and-error approach could be the way used to assure the balancing of equation (1) time by time; the final result of this work will, then, be poured into the database. At this point, rather than discussing the model, I wish to raise some questions and to make some comments on it.

The sectoral import equation has the following analytical structure

$$m_{it} = M^{*}_{it} x_{it},$$

where M^{*}_{it}s are "import coefficients … defined as import to output ratios"; if we delete subscript t to M, we can say that the import equation implies an elasticity of imports with respect to total output equal to one. It is hard to make such an assumption to represent import equations in GIOM in general; this assumption may perhaps model the asymptotic convergence towards a structural parameter representing the degree of openness "at least among industrialized countries"; at the same time it would preclude any prospect of economic integration for a new industrializing country actively entering international trade. However, parameter M has the subscript t which could hide a subtle import equation model designed to match all the elementary requirements for modelling imports into the framework and the time horizon of GIOM.

Investments are endogenized by means of the matrix of capital stocks requirements per unity expansion of capacity, assuming that investments planned at time t will fulfil the requirements of the expected and realized future level of total output at time $t+1$. This hypothesis is represented by the equation of "expansion investment in equation (1)". But "it is well known that the model including this expression is unstable and has only a balanced growth solution." This problem is the cause for introducing a "major simplification of equation (1)", which seems to be something more than a simplification; first the "expansion of capacity (or output)" is represented by "an exogenous, sector specific growth rate to x_t"; secondly, "the matrix B" is collapsed into "a vector of capital-to-output ratios" and thirdly "a single vector representing the composition of gross investment in [the] economy" is introduced. This means that the above-mentioned investment equation is no longer included into the model and in fact it is used here [only] because it is simple and familiar." Hence, equation (1) should be rewritten in order to include the analytical representation of the sketched "major simplification." I have not afforded this exercise because it is not clear how to couple "an exogenous sector specific growth rate of x_t" with a sectoral total output that turns out to be an endogenous variable.

The use of a vector representing the composition of gross investment in the economy drops a hint about the computation of the investment vector in equation (1); this composition is naturally related to the investment vector in the final demand of the input-output model; namely, investments by sector of origin. Then, it seems that this vector could be used to spread total gross investment computed into a framework similar to the one of equation (1) or supplied by the global economic outlook. This vector reminds that in accounting data, at best, gross investment is disaggregated by sector of origin and destination into a capital flow table; this table provides the composition of gross investment by sector, which is a good statistical base to convert gross investment by sector of destination into gross investment by sector of origin (the input-output investment sectoral disaggregation). Besides this table, time series of investment by sector of destination allows the specification of equations as supported by suitable investment theories; the capital flow table and a system of investment equations could provide a good implementation of the GIOM.

Equation (3) which defines the interregional link model can be rewritten as follows

$$\sum_r M_{tr} x_t = s_t$$

$$\sum_r E_{tr} = I,$$

where index r stands for regions; the splitting of equation (3) into two sets of equations gives evidence of the sequential functioning of the interregional link. The total of world sectoral imports is given by the sum of regional sectoral imports; since the total world imports are equal to total world exports, s is then fragmented among regions using sectoral shares (located along the main diagonal of the matrices Es). All matrices have a time period subscript, but balancing procedures are not made clear; undoubtedly, the fifth equation – the region's balance of international payments – should play an important role in defining regional (sectoral) propensities to import and regional world market (sectoral) export shares. However, the regional balance of payments involves the price vector which leads to equation (2). I am aware that it is declared that the GIOM "does not include a price model" and that "at the present time the world prices are exogenous"; however, this does not justify the undefined relationship between the price vector in equation (2) and the world price vector.

Of course, if equation (2) is not yet included in the model, equation (4) does not belong to the present version of GIOM as well. But, since it is true that "very little information that is not already required for (1) is needed to implement (2) and (4)," and it is planned to deal with questions like taxes, subsidies, and functional distribution of income, I can only suggest adding it to the GIOM equation (2) and, of course, equation (4) as quickly as possible. This is the best way to become aware of how much a redefinition of equation (2) is needed, how large is the amount of information required to model the price equation and how far from the standard equation one must go to deal with questions like taxes (not to say import prices, exchange rates, terms of trade, and the domestic price vector itself).

4. Shuntaro Shishido

The model (GIOM) is a typical multi-country version of a dynamic input-output model that aims at evaluating strategies for environmentally sound economic development in the world economy over the next several decades. Essentially, it is designed to analyse physical relationships of various productive activities and consumption in the global context. This distinctive feature of the model enables the analysis of pollution, especially CO_2 and other important pollutants in different regions of the globe. As stressed in this paper, the statistical information from IO tables, especially in terms of physical units for selective industries by region becomes essential and I would like to commend highly the others' endeavours at modelling as well as the database for these strategic industries. The database needs to be strengthened in certain industries through various engineering inputs, especially for those LDC regions where statistical information is still underdeveloped.

Since the model, being more physical-volume-oriented, does not seem to be price-sensitive, unlike the ordinary multi-sectoral econometric models, it seems to me that there is some room for improvement in order to take into account the changes in relative prices such as those caused by carbon tax, exchange rate adjustment, etc. In my opinion, these additional needs can be met by introducing adequate submodels that have explicitly prince-sensitive behavioural equations on household consumption, exports and imports, and fuel consumption of selective industries.

In forecasting the model over the next several decades, a forecast of technical progress becomes of vital importance. In view of the broad range of difference between optimism and pessimism on technical progress, alternative assumptions need to be used in the form of sensitivity analysis so as to make flexible the global scenarios produced by the model. The appearance of an electric car and its widespread use might make CO_2 forecasting more optimistic in industrial countries, while the difficulty of environmental technology transfer to the LDC might delay the achievement of CO_2 reduction.

Two additional comments on the database: first, the PPP approach by the UN has achieved great success in measuring the expenditure side of GNP on an internationally comparable basis. Very little effort, however, has been made concerning PPP on the supply side. This approach is of vital importance in preparing an international IO table and its modelling. I strongly hope that the GIOM project stimulates the UN's project on International Price Comparison (IPC) toward the supply-side approach. Otherwise, the IO model based on the official exchange rate would be significantly biased in terms of the physical unit (see my paper of the UN expert group on IPC, 1991).

United Nations University Press
53-70, Jingumae 5-chome
Shibuya-ku, Tokyo 150
Japan

Reader's Reply Card

Modelling Global Change
Edited by Lawrence R. Klein and Fu-chen Lo
UNUP-880 ISBN 92-808-0880-X

Name

Address

Country

How did you come to know about this book?

- ☐ UNU Press Publications Catalogue
- ☐ Advertisement in ....
- ☐ Distributor ....
- ☐ Bookstore ....
- ☐ Other ....

The information on this card will help us to improve our publishing programme. Please complete the card and return it to the United Nations University Press.

What are your areas of interest?

- Development .... ☐
- Social Sciences .... ☐
- Natural Resources .... ☐
- Economics .... ☐
- Food and Nutrition .... ☐
- Energy .... ☐
- International Law .... ☐
- Politics .... ☐
- Culture .... ☐
- Science and Technology .... ☐
- Other .... ☐

I am interested in information about the UNU .... ☐

Please add my name to the catalogue mailing list .... ☐

Secondly, the economic data on pollution abatement cost per unit of CO_2 needs to be strengthened. The cost varies according to different countries and different sectors. So far, very few data are available on an internationally comparable basis. It would be much appreciated by global researchers if such data could be made available in the course of GIO modelling by the DIESA/IEA team.

6

Economic interdependence in the Asia-Pacific region: A study with application of bilateral international input-output tables

Takao Sano, Chiharu Tamamura, Koji Nishikimi, Ikuo Kuroiwa, and Masahiro Mimura

I. Introduction

The Asia-Pacific region is experiencing a historical drama as it moves towards the twenty-first century. The rise of Asian Newly Industrializing Countries (ANICs) and the growth of the Association of Southeast Asian Nation (ASEAN) countries, which are rapidly catching up with ANICs, have been making the regional economy more and more powerful and dynamic.[1]

This paper attempts to analyse the patterns of interdependence behind the dynamism of the Asia-Pacific economy and their transition in the recent years. It depicts the relationship of production among different countries in the region with reference to the "intra-regional" division of labour, which is considered to be formed through the acceleration of both production and international trade. The following discussion highlights the structure of international sectoral linkage of production between Japan and each of those three countries, namely South Korea, Thailand, and Indonesia, which are selected for analytical purposes of applying bilateral international input-output tables covering the three pairs of countries[2] for both 1975 and 1985.

It is very important, and necessary in a sense, to analyse the dynamism of the Asia-Pacific economy from every aspect of economics. In fact, many academicians, in particular those in the field of macro-economics and international trade, have so far investigated it from various points of view. We would like to contribute to these continuous efforts by presenting this paper, maintaining that the indirect effect of intermediate goods, as well as the direct effect of final goods, on sectoral production plays a key role in the determination of "intra-regional" division of labour and that analysing international input-output relationships is indispensable for grasping the reality of the Asia-Pacific economy. Understanding the reality, we believe, should be the first step in analysing its dynamism.

II. An overview of the economic growth experience of Asia-Pacific countries

The Asia-Pacific region consists of countries at different stages of economic development. Table 1 shows gross national product (GNP) per capita for major developing Asia-Pacific countries,[3] Japan, the United States, and the EC for the period of 1968–1989. It is useful as an indicator for roughly classifying the stages of economic development among them. According to the latest figures for 1989, Hong Kong and Singapore reached the stage of $10,000 (dollars are US dollars) while South Korea, another ANIC, just exceeded the stage of $4,000, which is less than half the level of the leading ANICs. Following are Malaysia at the stage of $2,160, almost half the level of South Korea, and Thailand at the stage of $1,220, which is slightly more than half the level of Malaysia. Indonesia and the Philippines are catching up with the other ASEAN countries, but at a slower pace, at the stages of $500 and $710, respectively.

As for our three selected countries during the 1970s and 1980s, South Korea was at the stage of $270 in 1970. In the 1970–1980 period, its GNP per capita increased to $1,630, which was six times as high as the 1970 level. In the 1980–1989 period, it continued to grow further to $4,400. Thailand started from the stage of $210 in 1970, which was 78 per cent of Korea's 1970 level. It reached the stage of $670 in 1980, which was only 41 per cent of South Korea's 1980 level. Although it developed to the stage of $1,220 in 1989, against South Korea's level its percentage dropped further to 28 per cent. The divergence has been becoming greater during the two decades. Indonesia's GNP per capita was $80 in 1970. It increased nearly sixfold

Table 1 **GNP per capita (in US dollars)**

	Republic of Korea	Thailand	Indonesia	Japan	United States	EC	People's Republic of China	Hong Kong	Malaysia	Philippines	Singapore
1968	180	190	60	1,440	4,440	2,020	90	690	370	230	740
1969	220	200	70	1,680	4,760	2,190	110	790	380	250	840
1970	270	210	80	1,940	4,950	2,360	120	900	390	230	950
1971	310	210	90	2,140	5,310	2,590	130	1,020	410	220	1,080
1972	330	220	90	2,540	5,780	2,940	130	1,220	450	220	1,270
1973	390	250	110	3,230	6,410	3,570	150	1,570	550	250	1,580
1974	480	300	150	3,820	6,890	4,250	160	1,900	700	300	2,020
1975	580	360	210	4,490	7,400	4,900	180	2,180	820	360	2,540
1976	750	410	270	4,970	8,180	5,440	170	2,700	920	420	2,760
1977	910	460	320	5,690	9,040	6,000	190	3,200	1,000	450	2,940
1978	1,190	530	370	7,020	10,100	6,790	220	3,750	1,140	500	3,310
1979	1,510	590	400	8,620	11,150	8,220	260	4,260	1,400	590	3,880
1980	1,630	670	470	9,870	12,000	9,760	300	5,210	1,680	680	4,550
1981	1,830	750	560	10,390	13,270	10,230	320	6,080	1,890	770	5,450
1982	1,930	780	610	10,280	13,620	9,850	320	6,330	1,910	800	6,160
1983	2,100	810	580	10,320	14,510	9,090	320	6,140	1,900	740	6,930
1984	2,230	840	550	10,580	15,910	8,730	330	6,330	2,040	630	7,730
1985	2,310	800	520	11,250	16,770	8,590	330	6,080	1,970	570	7,610
1986	2,550	800	490	12,840	17,530	9,400	310	6,910	1,850	560	7,450
1987	2,920	850	440	15,840	18,590	11,270	310	8,180	1,830	590	8,010
1988	3,550	1,000	440	21,050	19,870	14,200	340	9,230	1,940	630	9,100
1989	4,400	1,220	500	23,810	20,910	15,980	350	10,320	2,160	710	10,450

Source: World Bank. *World Tables* (1989–1990 and 1991 edns).

to $470 in 1980. In the period 1980–1988, its per capita GNP continued to go up to its highest level of $610 in 1982, but after that it began to decline to $440 in 1988.

Table 2 displays annual growth rate of real gross domestic product (GDP) at 1980 constant prices for the period 1978–1988 for the same countries as table 1. Apart from the GDP level, total production of goods and services in the major developing Asia-Pacific countries grew higher than that of the mature industrialized economies during the 1970s and 1980s. In the 1970s, South Korea, Hong Kong, and Singapore enjoyed a long expansion at the rate of more than 9 per cent per year on average while the economies of Thailand, Indonesia, Malaysia, and the Philippines grew by 6 to nearly 8 per cent per year on average. The Japanese economy expanded at the annual average rate of 5.3 per cent whereas the United States and EC economies grew by 2.7 per cent and 3.3 per cent per year on average during the same period. These relatively lower growth rates for the industrialized countries reflects negative GDP growth recorded in the deep recession of 1974 and 1975. The favourable growth of the developing Asia-Pacific economies was accordingly interrupted by the recession, but they recovered their original growth path very shortly.

The period of the 1980s is the decade of global adjustment and structural change. The economic slowdown of the industrialized countries in the early 1980s is symbolized by a curious state of high unemployment accompanied by high inflation, "stagflation," particularly for the United States and the EC countries. The GDP growth rate for the EC was 0.1–1.2 per cent per year in the first three years of the 1980s while the United States experienced negative GDP growth twice during the same period. The growth path of the developing Asia-Pacific countries was again pushed downwards, but the power for a quick recovery was not damaged. However, the sharp decline in world commodity prices in the mid-1980s certainly did a lot of damage to the developing Asia-Pacific countries, which still owed much of their earnings to the export of primary commodities. Actually in 1985 and 1986, most of the countries recorded very low, or even negative, GDP growth rates. After the Plaza Accord in September 1985, in which the exchange rate realignment of devaluing the US dollar against other major currencies was agreed upon, Japanese foreign direct investment surged into the developing Asia-Pacific countries, taking advantage of the high yen, which made their factor prices appear cheap. Both the devaluation of the US dollar and foreign direct investment in the region are important factors of the re-

Table 2 **Annual growth rate of real GDP (at 1980 constant prices; %)**

	Republic of Korea	Thailand	Indonesia	Japan	United States	EC	People's Republic of China	Hong Kong	Malaysia	Philippines	Singapore
1968	10.6	8.5	13.9	12.9	4.1	5.2	–6.5	NA	8.0	5.5	NA
1969	13.5	8.0	8.8	12.5	2.5	6.0	19.2	11.8	4.9	4.9	12.9
1970	8.2	9.2	9.1	10.7	–0.3	4.4	23.4	9.4	6.0	4.7	12.5
1971	9.6	5.0	6.5	4.3	2.7	3.2	7.0	7.3	5.9	4.9	11.2
1972	5.6	3.9	9.5	8.4	4.9	4.1	2.9	11.0	9.4	5.6	13.2
1973	14.6	9.8	11.3	7.9	4.9	5.9	8.4	12.7	11.7	8.5	9.0
1974	8.9	4.3	7.7	–1.2	–0.7	2.0	1.1	2.3	8.2	5.0	6.1
1975	7.7	4.8	5.0	2.6	–1.0	–1.1	8.3	0.2	0.8	6.6	8.0
1976	13.5	9.4	6.9	4.8	4.8	4.7	–5.4	17.1	11.7	7.8	5.5
1977	11.0	9.7	9.0	5.3	4.6	2.8	7.9	12.5	7.8	6.3	7.1
1978	10.9	10.6	7.7	5.1	5.2	3.1	12.5	9.5	6.8	5.5	9.6
1979	7.5	5.0	6.2	5.2	2.1	3.4	7.0	11.7	9.5	6.3	9.1
1980	–3.3	4.7	7.9	4.5	–0.1	1.2	6.4	10.9	7.5	5.3	6.1
1981	6.9	6.3	7.4	3.9	2.0	0.1	4.9	9.4	6.9	3.8	9.2
1982	7.4	4.0	–0.4	2.8	–2.5	0.9	8.3	3.0	6.0	2.9	8.1
1983	12.1	7.2	3.3	3.2	3.7	1.6	9.8	6.5	6.4	1.1	10.8
1984	9.6	7.1	6.1	5.0	7.0	2.4	13.5	9.5	7.9	–6.3	11.0
1985	6.9	3.6	2.5	4.7	3.6	2.4	13.1	–0.1	–1.1	–4.5	0.1
1986	12.6	4.4	4.0	2.5	3.0	2.6	8.0	11.9	1.3	1.4	1.9
1987	11.9	8.1	3.4	4.2	3.8	2.7	10.5	13.8	5.3	4.9	9.0
1988	11.3	10.9	5.5	5.7	4.4	3.8	11.2	7.4	8.9	6.5	10.8

Source: World Bank. *World Tables* (1989–1990 edn).

cent five years' economic expansion of the developing Asia-Pacific countries.

III. Production and external trade

1. Historical overview

The economic growth of the developing Asia-Pacific countries is closely associated with external trade. Traditionally, as mentioned earlier, most of the countries have depended on primary commodities to gain revenues from the export of foodstuffs and raw or lightly processed materials, taking full advantage of abundant endowments of natural resources. Although exporting such commodities as tin, rice, rubber, coconut, sawlog, and crude petroleum is a short cut for leading to high value added, it is not favourable for a developing economy to depend too much on them because the degree of uncertainty is also high in the world market.

In the 1950s to 1960s, most of the Asia-Pacific developing countries implemented economic policies embodying import substitution industrialization programmes to set up the manufacturing sector as a more powerful engine generating higher value added in the domestic economy. Industrialization was required for these countries to provide employment opportunities, in the first place. On the other hand, the policies aimed at switching the allocation of the very foreign exchange reserves earned by the export of primary commodities from the import of consumer goods to that of those intermediate and capital goods, which were necessary as inputs for production but could not be produced in domestic industries due mainly to the lack of technology.

The import substitution industrialization strategy was almost successful, particularly in the sense of establishing domestic manufacturing industries. Although it was often criticized for causing unfavourable conditions of inefficiency and the distortion of price and resource allocation for the domestic economy due to heavy industrial protection posed by the government, most of the manufacturing industries that had been established in the import substitution phase managed to survive and some of them started exporting their products to the world market. The first import substitution phase has shifted to the export promotion phase in the 1970s and 1980s, in which new development programmes were carried out to draw a potential for higher growth and further development in the future from the export of manufactures.

2. A macroeconomic perspective

Figure 1 depicts the share of exports and imports of goods and services in GDP for major developing Asia-Pacific countries,[4] Japan, and the United States. In 1970, the share of exports in GDP was in the range of 13 to 19.1 per cent for South Korea, Thailand, Indonesia, and the Philippines, with the exception of Malaysia at 42 per cent, whereas Japan and the United States earned 11.3 per cent and 6.8 per cent of their GNP, respectively, from the export of goods and services. On the other hand, the share of imports in GDP was from 15 to 23.8 per cent for the above four countries and 37.8 per cent for Malaysia, while only 10.2 per cent and 5.9 per cent of GNP was reduced by imports for Japan and the United States. According to the latest data for 1989, the export share in GDP went up gradually to the levels of 25.2 to 36.3 per cent for the four countries and tremendously to the level of 73.8 per cent for Malaysia. For Japan and the United States, the export share in GNP rose relatively slightly to 14.2 per cent and 12.1 per cent, respectively. The import share in GDP too rose to the levels of 23.1 per cent to 38.6 per cent for the four countries and to the level of 70 per cent for Malaysia. Japan's import share in GNP increased slightly to 12.3 per cent while that of the Unites States jumped to the level of 13.1 per cent, compared with the 1970 level.[5]

It is concluded that an upward trend of the export and import shares in GDP (GNP) is observed, though it sometimes fluctuates, for all the above seven countries during the 1970s and 1980s. This means that the growth of exports and imports is faster than that of GDP. In particular, South Korea, Thailand, Indonesia, and Malaysia are remarkable for their steeper upward trends. This fact indicates that more and more goods and services come into and out of the world market and flow into and out of the production processes of each country. In addition, exports and imports are two sides of a story. Behind the export promotion, there should be "import promotion" for producing exportable goods. On the other hand, the higher the export earnings, the larger become the foreign exchange reserves to be used for importing intermediate and capital goods for production. This "virtuous" circle of export, import, and production has

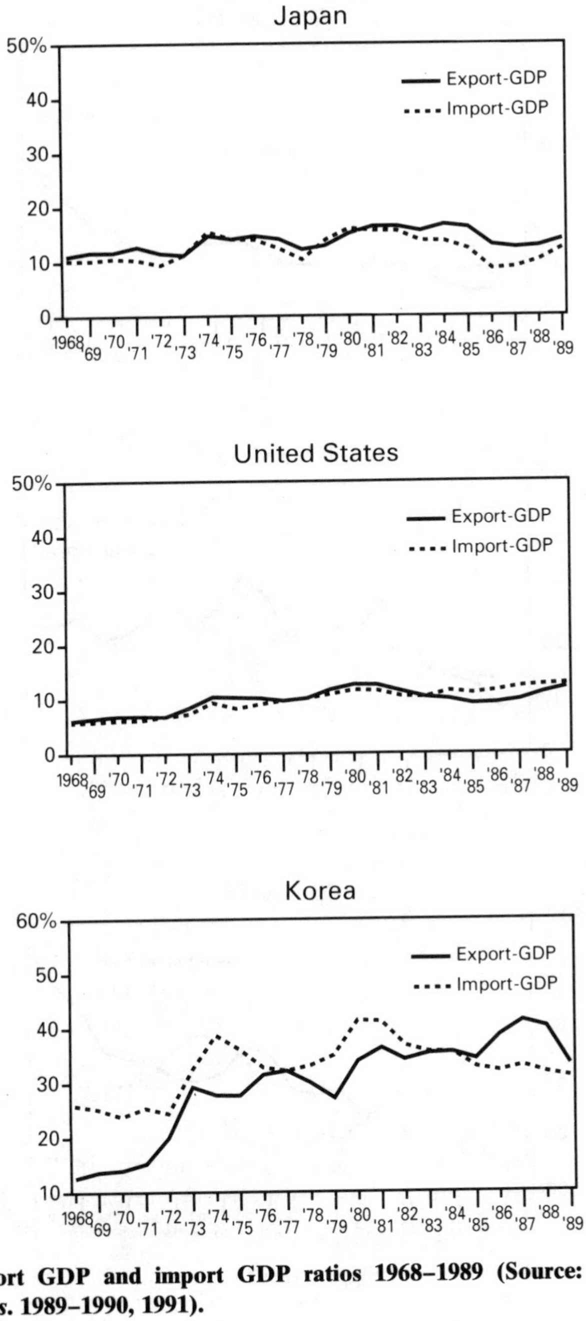

Fig. 1 **Export GDP and import GDP ratios 1968–1989 (Source: World Bank, *World Tables*. 1989–1990, 1991).**

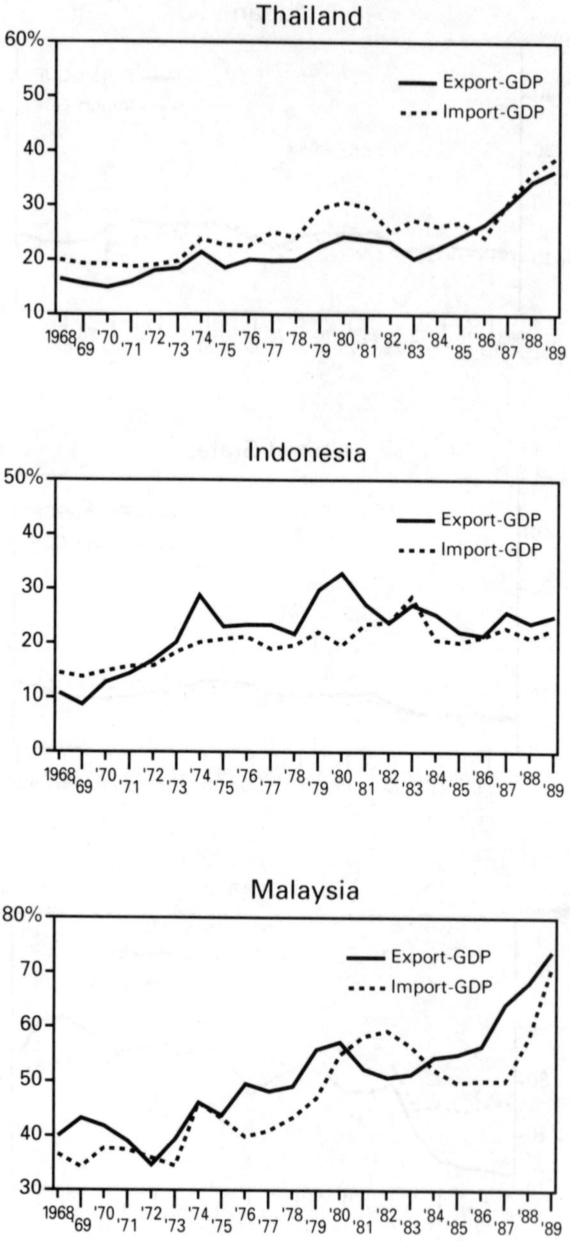
Thailand
60%
50
40
30
20
10
Export-GDP
Import-GDP
1968 69 '70 '71 '72 '73 '74 '75 '76 '77 '78 '79 '80 '81 '82 '83 '84 '85 '86 '87 '88 '89
Indonesia
50%
40
30
20
10
0
Export-GDP
Import-GDP
1968 69 '70 '71 '72 '73 '74 '75 '76 '77 '78 '79 '80 '81 '82 '83 '84 '85 '86 '87 '88 '89
Malaysia
80%
70
60
50
40
30
Export-GDP
Import-GDP
1968 69 '70 '71 '72 '73 '74 '75 '76 '77 '78 '79 '80 '81 '82 '83 '84 '85 '86 '87 '88 '89

Fig. 1 **(cont.)**

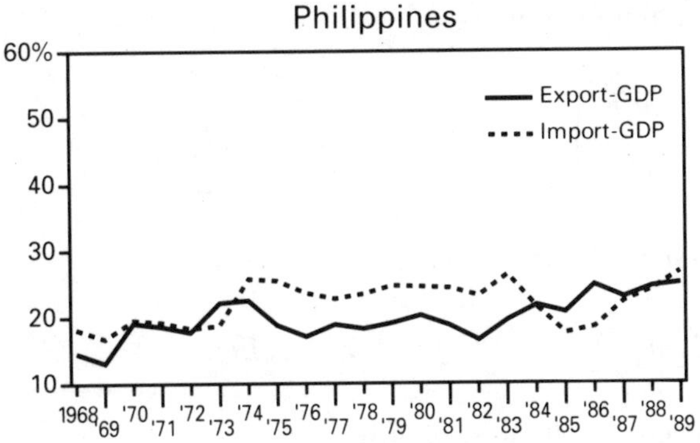

Fig. 1 **(cont.)**

sustained the dynamism of high growth performance in the Asia-Pacific region.[6]

IV. Economic interdependence among Asian countries

The rapid economic growth in the Asia-Pacific countries has appeared with a simultaneous increase in export and import. This indicates that production in these countries was interrelated through the trade between them. The economic interdependence across countries can be analysed with international input-output tables, which depict the flows of commodities for the trades within and between countries. In this section, the aspects of the interactions of production and external trade in the selected Asian countries are investigated in detail by using the three bilateral input-output tables already available, i.e., the Indonesia-Japan, Korea-Japan, and Thailand-Japan tables.[7] First, we will look over the features of comparative advantage for the above four countries and explore how much per cent of their production was induced by export to the world market. In the section on "production and import" below, we will investigate how these countries depended on each other through the importing of intermediate and final goods.

Throughout this section, we use the following notation for the input coefficient matrix, the import from the rest of the world (ROW) matrix, the value added coefficient vector and the inverse matrix, where the superscripts and subscripts represent countries and sectors respectively.[8] For instance, a_{ij}^{JP} shows the input of Japanese ith product to jth sector in P country.[9]

(1) input coefficient matrix

$$A = \begin{pmatrix} a_{ij}^{JJ} & a_{ij}^{JP} \\ a_{ij}^{PJ} & a_{ij}^{PP} \end{pmatrix}, \qquad (i,j = 1,2,\ldots,17),$$

(2) import (from ROW) matrix

$$A^W = (a_{ij}^{WJ}\ a_{ij}^{WP}), \qquad (i,j = 1,2,\ldots,17),$$

(3) value added coefficient vector

$$r^J = (r_1^J, r_2^J, \ldots, r_{17}^J)$$
$$r^P = (r_1^P, r_2^P, \ldots, r_{17}^P),$$

(4) inverse matrix

$$B = (I - A)^{-1} = \begin{pmatrix} b_{ij}^{JJ} & b_{ij}^{JP} \\ b_{ij}^{PJ} & b_{ij}^{PP} \end{pmatrix}, \qquad (i,j = 1,2,\ldots,17).$$

1. Export and production

The production in each country is determined by reflecting the pattern of international division of labour formed by the world market. This pattern can be depicted, to some extent, by the composition of exports and imports. But actually, the existence of intermediate goods makes matters somewhat complicated. For example, the competitiveness of the automobile may come from production processes not only in the automobile industry but also in other industries such as steel, plastic, rubber, and so forth. Therefore, we must make it clear what production activity holds comparative advantage by examining each industry's value added contained in the tradable goods. Equation (1) shows the amount of ith industry's value added included in the f_j unit of the jth commodity.

$$v_{ij} = r_i b_{ij} f_j, \qquad (i,j = 1,2,\ldots,17). \tag{1}$$

When a country engages in the world market, production will be specialized in the activities with comparative advantage. Therefore, we can observe what production activity the world market assigns to the country, by comparing the value added composition of export with that of total final demand. Figure 2 shows, country by country, the specialization ratios in production for each industry in 1975 and 1985 (sr_i), which are calculated in equation (2).

$$sr_i = \log \frac{r_i \sum_j^{17} b_{ij} f_j^e \Big/ \sum_k^{17} r_k \sum_j^{17} b_{kj} f_j^e}{r_j \sum_j^{17} b_{ij} f_j \Big/ \sum_k^{17} r_k \sum_j^{17} b_{kj} f_j}, \qquad (i = 1, 2, \ldots, 17), \qquad (2)$$

where f_j^e is the jth product exported to ROW and f_j is the total final demand for the jth product.

In 1975, Indonesia specialized production in the industries related to petroleum such as crude petroleum, natural gas, and chemical industries, but it obtained competitiveness in textile and other light industries in the next 10 years. This fact indicates that the Indonesian economy stepped into the stage of industrialization, shifting from a simple industrial structure depending on primary commodities. The specialization patterns in Korea and Japan were fairly stable in this period. In both years, Korea had advantages in textile and other light industries, and also in heavy industries such as chemical, metal, machinery, and transport equipment, while Japan specialized its production mainly on heavy industries. In Thailand the specialization ratios are fairly evenly distributed among industries and, accordingly, show that production in Thailand was more diversified than in any other country. But it also had advantages in agriculture, fishery, and forestry, and the food industry, in contrast with the other three countries. As a whole, it can be said that the above four countries had comparative advantages in the different production activities and, accordingly, that they probably complemented each other rather than conflicted as competitors in the world market. This provided the basis for the economic interdependency among these countries.

Appropriating their comparative advantage observed above, the Asian countries rapidly increased production in recent decades. Table 3 shows the contribution ratios of export to ROW which represent what percentage of value added was induced by export to ROW in 1975 and 1985. In the tables for Indonesia, Korea, and Thailand, the first two columns present the effects of export from own country, while the third and fourth columns show the effects of Japan's exports.

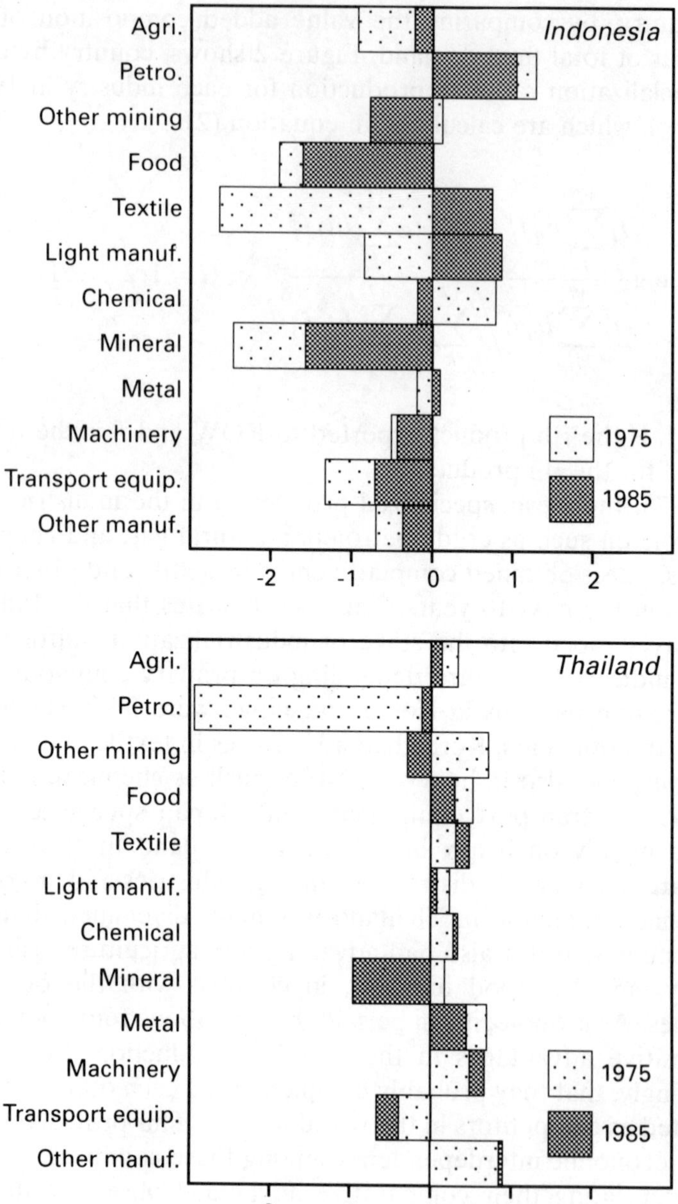

Fig. 2 **Specialization ratio**

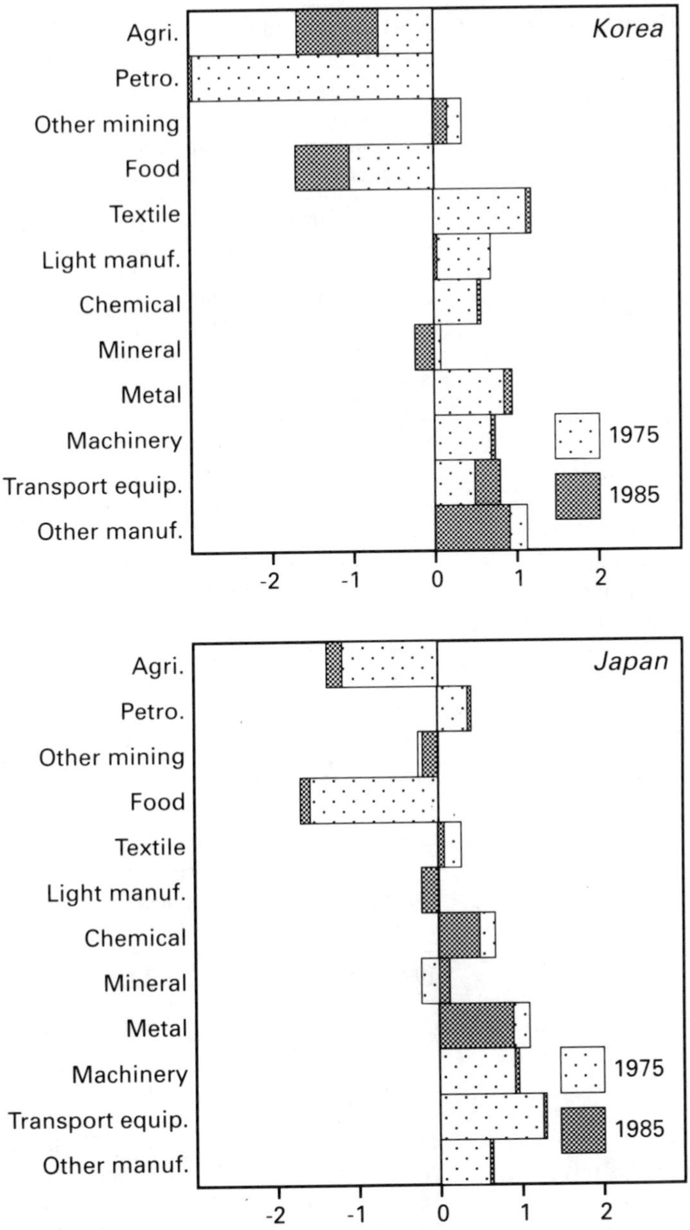

Korea
Agri.
Petro.
Other mining
Food
Textile
Light manuf.
Chemical
Mineral
Metal
Machinery
Transport equip.
Other manuf.
1975
1985
-2
-1
0
1
2
Japan
Agri.
Petro.
Other mining
Food
Textile
Light manuf.
Chemical
Mineral
Metal
Machinery
Transport equip.
Other manuf.
1975
1985
-2
-1
0
1
2

Fig. 2 **(cont.)**

Table 3 **Contribution ratio of export to value added (%)**

(1) Indonesia

Sector	Export of Indonesian products 1975	Export of Indonesian products 1985	Export of Japanese products 1975	Export of Japanese products 1985	Total 1975	Total 1985
Agriculture, fish, and forestry	5.70	9.67	0.21	0.13	5.91	9.80
Crude petroleum	49.26	34.11	8.33	8.43	57.60	42.54
Other mining	15.52	5.68	6.97	5.69	22.49	11.37
Food	2.13	2.48	0.03	0.04	2.19	2.52
Textile	0.98	25.28	0.06	0.23	1.04	25.52
Other light industries	6.08	28.59	0.22	0.26	6.30	28.85
Chemical	30.41	10.21	2.16	1.70	32.57	11.91
Non-metallic mineral	1.18	2.55	0.09	0.11	1.27	2.66
Metal	11.57	13.58	1.53	4.99	13.10	18.57
Machinery	8.83	7.86	0.96	0.52	9.79	8.38
Transport equipment	3.72	5.94	0.21	0.55	3.94	6.49
Other manufacturing	7.06	8.44	0.21	0.33	7.27	8.76
Electricity, gas, and water	7.80	4.93	1.06	0.49	8.80	5.42
Construction	0.56	0.68	0.05	0.08	0.60	0.76
Trade and transport	9.82	10.20	0.47	0.48	10.29	10.68
Services	3.99	6.42	0.20	0.37	4.19	6.79
Public administration	0.00	0.00	0.00	0.00	0.00	0.00
All industries	13.68	12.04	1.78	1.75	15.47	13.79

(2) Korea

Sector	Export of Korean products 1975	Export of Korean products 1985	Export of Japanese products 1975	Export of Japanese products 1985	Total 1975	Total 1985
Agriculture, fish, and forestry	7.29	3.60	0.19	0.21	7.48	3.81
Crude petroleum	0.00	0.00	0.00	0.00	0.00	0.00
Other mining	20.02	23.11	1.83	0.94	21.85	24.05
Food	5.00	3.55	0.05	0.08	5.06	3.63
Textile	43.42	62.36	0.83	0.48	44.26	62.84
Other light industries	28.91	19.80	0.39	0.29	29.29	20.09
Chemical	24.00	32.90	0.57	0.81	24.58	33.71
Non-metallic mineral	15.70	14.90	0.33	0.61	16.03	15.52
Metal	31.93	50.32	0.77	1.71	32.70	52.02
Machinery	28.49	40.65	1.09	0.87	20.58	41.52
Transport equipment	22.83	43.77	0.08	0.08	22.91	43.85
Other manufacturing	45.06	49.06	0.41	0.29	45.47	49.35
Electricity, gas, and water	12.09	23.86	0.29	0.47	12.38	24.33
Construction	1.18	2.49	0.02	0.02	1.20	2.51

Table 3 **(cont.)**

(2) Korea

Sector	Export of Korean products		Export of Japanese products		Total	
	1975	1985	1975	1985	1975	1985
Trade and transport	17.04	25.45	0.38	0.27	17.42	25.73
Services	8.75	10.90	0.36	0.20	9.11	11.09
Public administration	0.00	0.21	0.00	0.00	0.00	0.21
All industries	14.38	19.12	0.36	0.34	14.74	19.46

(3) Thailand

Sector	Export of Thai products		Export of Japanese products		Total	
	1975	1985	1975	1985	1975	1985
Agriculture, fish, and forestry	12.95	24.50	0.18	0.22	13.13	24.72
Crude petroleum	0.00	18.80	0.00	0.56	0.00	19.36
Other mining	19.14	16.06	1.35	1.05	20.49	17.12
Food	15.72	28.59	0.12	0.12	15.84	28.71
Textile	11.70	34.10	0.18	0.10	11.88	34.20
Other light industries	11.47	22.86	0.10	0.17	11.58	23.03
Chemical	11.93	29.32	0.79	1.38	12.72	30.70
Non-metallic mineral	11.11	8.12	0.04	0.05	11.16	8.17
Metal	18.75	32.93	1.61	3.28	20.36	36.22
Machinery	13.57	41.62	0.13	0.20	13.71	41.81
Transport equipment	6.20	11.01	0.08	0.07	6.27	11.09
Other manufacturing	20.27	51.29	0.10	0.64	20.38	51.94
Electricity, gas, and water	8.64	14.72	0.22	0.24	8.86	14.96
Construction	0.84	0.97	0.02	0.01	0.86	0.98
Trade and transport	6.43	27.65	0.26	0.14	6.69	27.79
Services	7.09	9.43	0.05	0.06	7.14	9.49
Public administration	0.00	0.00	0.00	0.00	0.00	0.00
All industries	9.45	21.18	0.21	0.23	9.65	21.40

Table 3 **(cont.)**
(4) Japan

Sector	Export of Indonesian products 1975	Export of Indonesian products 1985	Export of Korean products 1975	Export of Korean products 1985	Export of Thai products 1975	Export of Thai products 1985
Agriculture, fish, and forestry	0.00	0.00	0.03	0.04	0.00	0.01
Crude petroleum	0.08	0.02	0.15	0.29	0.02	0.03
Other mining	0.01	0.01	0.10	0.28	0.01	0.02
Food	0.00	0.00	0.01	0.02	0.00	0.00
Textile	0.01	0.02	0.34	0.60	0.02	0.04
Other light industries	0.01	0.01	0.07	0.11	0.01	0.01
Chemical	0.05	0.04	0.30	0.41	0.04	0.05
Non-metallic mineral	0.01	0.01	0.11	0.23	0.01	0.01
Metal	0.03	0.03	0.22	0.55	0.04	0.08
Machinery	0.01	0.01	0.10	0.28	0.01	0.01
Transport equipment	0.03	0.02	0.03	0.09	0.01	0.01
Other manufacturing	0.01	0.01	0.10	0.26	0.01	0.02
Electricity, gas, and water	0.01	0.01	0.08	0.16	0.01	0.02
Construction	0.00	0.00	0.00	0.01	0.00	0.00
Trade and transport	0.01	0.01	0.06	0.11	0.01	0.01
Services	0.00	0.00	0.04	0.07	0.01	0.01
Public administration	0.00	0.00	0.00	0.00	0.00	0.00
All industries	0.01	0.01	0.07	0.13	0.01	0.01

Sector	Export of Japanese products[a] 1975	Export of Japanese products[a] 1985	Total 1975	Total 1985
Agriculture, fish, and forestry	3.33	3.33	3.36	3.38
Crude petroleum	15.43	18.73	15.68	19.07
Other mining	8.93	10.87	9.05	11.18
Food	2.24	2.46	2.25	2.48
Textile	14.53	14.35	14.90	15.01
Other light industries	9.14	10.86	9.23	10.99
Chemical	22.36	21.37	22.75	21.87
Non-metallic mineral	9.13	15.09	9.26	15.34
Metal	33.18	33.04	33.47	33.70
Machinery	25.78	35.04	25.90	35.34
Transport equipment	38.79	49.02	38.86	49.14
Other manufacturing	20.42	25.53	20.54	25.82
Electricity, gas, and water	12.08	12.92	12.18	13.11
Construction	0.58	1.01	0.58	1.02
Trade and transport	11.97	14.51	12.05	14.64
Services	6.74	6.92	6.79	7.00
Public administration	0.00	0.20	0.00	0.20
All industries	11.12	13.04	11.21	13.19

a. The figures for the effect of Japan's export are obtained from the Indonesia-Japanese tables.

In Indonesia, the export of their own products mainly contributed to crude petroleum and natural gas (49.3 per cent), chemical (30.4 per cent), other mining (15.5 per cent), and metal (11.6 per cent) in 1975. In total, 13.7 per cent of GDP in 1975 was induced by exports. Although the contribution to GDP declined to 12 per cent in 1985, the effects on textile and other light industries jumped to 25.3 per cent and 28.6 per cent respectively, reflecting the changes in the comparative advantage. This forms a striking contrast to the decrease in the contributions of crude petroleum and natural gas, other mining, and chemical.

In addition to the contributions of their own exports, 1.8 per cent of the Indonesian GDP was achieved through Japanese exports in both years. This provides evidence that some part of the competitiveness of Japanese products was formed by production in Indonesia. The reason why the effect of Japanese exports did not shift to textile and other light industries in spite of the changes in comparative advantage in Indonesia is that, in this period, Japanese exports always specialized in heavy industries, which generate little intermediate demand for such products. It is notable, however, that the effect of Japanese exports on the other mining sector was slightly larger than that of Indonesian exports in 1985. It can be said that production in Indonesia and Japan helped each other to supply more competitive goods to the world market.

Korean economy depends more on export as a source of demand. In 1975, most of the manufacturing sectors attained more than 20 per cent of their value added from export to ROW and, in total, 14.4 per cent of GDP was gained through exports. These contribution ratios rose further in 1985, especially, in textile (62.4 per cent), metal (50.3 per cent), machinery (40.7 per cent), transport equipment (43.8 per cent), and other manufacturing sectors (49.1 per cent). As a result, 19.1 per cent of GDP in 1985 came from exports. The export of Japanese products did not bring much production to Korean industries, unlike the Indonesian case. But these exports were gradually expanding their influence on the production in the chemical, non-metallic mineral, and metal industries.

Thailand is a country that experienced the most drastic change in export intensity. In 1975, the contribution of export of GDP in Thailand was the smallest (9.5 per cent) among the four countries obtainable from the bilateral tables. In the next 10 years, however, the contribution ratios in almost all the industries increased to twice the size of those in 1975. Consequently, the effect on GDP shot up to

21.2 per cent in 1985, which was the greatest among the four countries. The influence of Japanese exports on production in most of the Thai industries was generally insignificant. But the influence was not negligible for some specific industries, namely, other mining, chemical, and metal industries to which Japanese export contributed 1.05, 1.38 and 3.28 per cent, respectively, in 1985.

The last part of table 3 shows the contribution of each country's export to Japanese production. The contribution ratio of own export for each industry was quite stable in the period 1975–1985, compared with the other three countries. In this period, those sectors which earned more than 20 per cent of value added from own exports remained unchanged, i.e., chemical, metal, machinery, transport equipment, and other manufacturing sectors. The contribution to GDP increased a little from 11.1 per cent in 1975 to 13.0 per cent in 1985. The influence of the other three countries' exports was generally slight. This is chiefly because their export level was low relative to Japanese production. However, textile and transport equipment industries in Japan were more affected by Korean exports than those in Korea by Japanese exports.[10] This cannot be explained by the relative size of the economies. The influence on Japanese transport equipment is attributable to its competitiveness in the world market. But the textile industry in Japan had little advantage both in 1975 and 1985. This problem should be examined further in detail.[11]

2. Production and import

In this section, we investigate how the production in one country depends on production in other countries. Most industries use imported intermediate goods, and such demand induces the value added abroad. Equation (3) shows the total amount of Japanese value added required for producing a unit of *j*th commodity in *P* Country.

$$v_j^{JP} = \sum_i^{17} r_i^J b_{ij}^{JP}, \qquad (j = 1, 2, \ldots, 17). \tag{3}$$

It also requires product of ROW in the amount of v_j^{WP} presented in equation (4).

$$v_j^{WP} = \sum_i^{17} \sum_k^{17} a_{ik}^{WP} b_{kj}^{PP}, \qquad (j = 1, 2, \ldots, 17). \tag{4}$$

The sum of v_j^{JP}, v_j^{WP} and the value added in P Country induced by a unit of jth product (v_j^{PP}) must be equal to unity. In other words, jth product in P Country comprises ($v_j^{JP} \times 100$) per cent of Japanese value added, ($v_j^{PP} \times 100$) per cent of P Country's value added, and ($v_j^{WP} \times 100$) per cent of ROW products. They represent the dependency ratios of jth industry on the production in Japan, P Country, and ROW, respectively.

Table 4 shows the dependency ratios for each industry in Indonesia, Korea, and Thailand. The last three rows in each table provide the averages of the dependency ratios for all industries. The first one presents the simple average, while the second and the third show the averages weighted by each industry's share in the domestic final demand and in export to ROW, respectively. Therefore, the latter two show the degree of dependence for the two kinds of final demand as a whole. It can be said that they provide the actual pictures of economic interdependence, whereas the figures in the upper rows in the table indicate the underlying structure of the industrial linkage for each industry.

In Indonesia, the dependency ratios on Japan were relatively high in such industries as metal (15.01 per cent), machinery (14.73 per cent), transport equipment (19.74 per cent), and other manufacturing (11.76 per cent) in 1975. These industries generally required products of heavy industries where Japan held a comparative advantage. In 1985, however, intermediate goods for the metal industry were substituted by domestic goods and those for other manufacturing by the products in ROW. On average, the dependency ratio on Japan decreased from 5.37 per cent in 1975 to 2.76 per cent in 1985. On the other hand, the dependency ratios on ROW are generally high in the textile through construction industries. In this period, the average dependency ratio on ROW remained almost unchanged (14.97–14.94 per cent), but industries such as machinery and other manufacturing exceeded 40 per cent in 1985.

For the final domestic demand, the dependency ratios on Japan declined from 3.00 per cent to 1.73 per cent, and it signifies that the Indonesian economy in 1985 actually induced less value added in Japan than in 1975. The dependency ratio on ROW also decreased from 9.16 per cent to 8.60 per cent.

As for the dependency ratios of the exports to ROW, that for Japan decreased (0.98–0.85 per cent), while that for ROW increased (3.79–6.50 per cent). In this connection, what is noticeable about the structure of the Indonesian economy is that, in both years, Indo-

Table 4 **Dependency ratio (%)**

(1) Indonesia

	Indonesia		Japan		ROW	
Sector	1975	1985	1975	1985	1975	1985
Agriculture, fish, and forestry	98.09	97.07	0.37	0.28	1.54	2.65
Crude petroleum	99.01	97.74	0.16	0.31	0.83	1.95
Other mining	94.53	95.41	1.10	0.73	4.37	3.86
Food	94.44	93.82	0.57	0.39	4.99	5.79
Textile	64.51	71.62	6.69	2.42	28.80	25.96
Other light industries	82.47	88.23	4.17	1.09	13.36	10.68
Chemical	85.11	77.07	2.78	1.71	12.11	21.22
Non-metallic mineral	87.39	85.83	2.25	1.69	10.36	12.48
Metal	59.45	71.71	15.01	4.53	25.54	23.76
Machinery	46.25	47.50	14.73	11.02	39.02	41.48
Transport equipment	52.16	71.20	19.74	10.24	28.10	18.56
Other manufacturing	54.35	50.27	12.03	5.59	33.62	44.14
Electricity, gas, and water	77.26	81.99	2.04	1.63	20.70	16.38
Construction	74.89	82.93	7.15	3.90	17.96	13.17
Trade and transport	92.22	93.00	1.47	0.82	6.31	6.18
Services	91.97	93.68	1.10	0.56	6.93	5.76
Public administration	100.00	100.00	0.00	0.00	0.00	0.00
Average	76.65	82.30	5.37	2.76	14.98	14.94
Domestic market	87.84	89.67	3.00	1.73	9.16	8.60
Export to ROW	95.23	92.65	0.98	0.85	3.79	6.50

(2) Korea

	Korea		Japan		ROW	
Sector	1975	1985	1975	1985	1975	1985
Agriculture, fish, and forestry	82.33	90.36	1.25	0.93	6.42	8.71
Crude petroleum	–	–	–	–	–	–
Other mining	87.92	88.40	2.25	1.59	9.83	10.01
Food	75.88	80.94	1.50	1.09	22.62	17.97
Textile	63.85	60.12	9.26	5.68	26.89	34.20
Other light industries	53.03	61.67	4.07	2.50	42.90	35.83
Chemical	46.31	45.74	7.07	3.70	46.62	50.56
Non-metallic mineral	76.59	74.72	3.92	2.59	19.49	22.69
Metal	48.12	59.80	18.24	8.15	33.64	32.05
Machinery	57.27	60.48	15.29	12.49	27.44	27.03
Transport equipment	58.31	65.01	16.35	10.96	25.34	24.03
Other manufacturing	62.65	68.10	11.76	7.83	25.59	24.07
Electricity, gas, and water	67.51	78.75	8.34	1.36	24.15	19.89
Construction	76.70	80.56	6.27	3.47	17.03	15.97

Table 4 **(cont.)**

(2) Korea

Sector	Korea		Japan		ROW	
	1975	1985	1975	1985	1975	1985
Trade and transport	89.36	84.18	1.98	2.01	8.66	13.81
Services	88.36	90.94	1.98	1.03	9.66	8.03
Public administration	100.00	78.22	0.00	4.47	0.00	17.31
Average	67.31	68.70	6.44	4.11	26.25	27.19
Domestic market	78.67	80.24	3.94	3.04	17.39	16.72
Export to ROW	67.52	65.20	7.83	6.43	24.65	28.37

(3) Thailand

Sector	Thailand		Japan		ROW	
	1975	1985	1975	1985	1975	1985
Agriculture, fish, and forestry	95.53	89.17	0.67	0.83	3.80	10.00
Crude petroleum	–	94.01	–	0.42	–	5.57
Other mining	93.70	86.63	0.97	0.86	5.33	12.51
Food	93.18	88.47	0.79	0.82	6.03	10.71
Textile	73.47	74.93	4.77	2.24	21.76	22.83
Other light industries	82.54	70.52	2.76	1.77	14.70	27.71
Chemical	53.27	53.34	3.00	1.41	43.73	42.25
Non-metallic mineral	81.47	78.91	2.38	1.56	16.15	19.53
Metal	68.96	63.99	11.14	8.21	19.90	27.80
Machinery	61.96	66.67	12.37	6.66	25.67	26.67
Transport equipment	54.77	58.31	16.17	9.84	29.06	31.85
Other manufacturing	82.65	79.27	3.46	2.21	13.89	18.52
Electricity, gas, and water	77.74	86.49	2.24	0.81	20.02	12.70
Construction	80.11	76.52	5.10	3.89	14.79	19.59
Trade and transport	92.92	84.44	1.04	0.92	6.04	14.64
Services	94.20	90.91	0.88	0.64	4.92	8.45
Public administration	100.00	100.00	0.00	0.00	0.00	0.00
Average	75.67	78.97	3.98	2.53	20.35	18.50
Domestic market	88.49	84.28	2.23	1.70	9.28	14.02
Export to ROW	86.98	80.59	2.32	1.76	10.70	17.65

nesia's export to ROW had a tendency to require less production (or induce less value added) abroad than the domestic final demand. This is mainly because a primary exported commodity for Indonesia was crude petroleum, and it required a relatively small amount of intermediate goods from either the own or the other countries.[12] This suggests that Indonesia could earn foreign exchanges rather efficiently, that is, it could expand its export without importing a lot of intermediate goods from abroad.

In Korea, the industries where dependency ratios on Japan were relatively high in both years are, as in Indonesia, metal, machinery, transport equipment, and other manufacturing. However, the figures for most industries in Korea decreased in this period. Nevertheless, Korea's average dependency ratios on Japan as well as on ROW were still higher than those of Thailand and Indonesia in both years. This indicates that Korea has been more dependent on intermediate goods procured from abroad than the other two countries.

As for the dependency ratios on ROW, those industries that use a large amount of primary commodities (e.g. crude petroleum) as well as industrial intermediate products show relatively high figures. They include textile, other light industries, chemical (more than 50 per cent in 1985), and the industries mentioned above on Japan. In contrast to the dependency ratios on Japan, those on ROW, on the average, slightly increased (26.25–27.19 per cent). This signifies that Korea diversified its procurement of intermediate goods and became less dependent on Japan.

We can understand another aspect of the Korean economy by comparing the dependency ratios of the domestic final demand with those of the exports to ROW. That is, in contrast to Indonesia, Korea's exports to ROW had a tendency to induce more value added in Japan and ROW than did the domestic final demand. It is supposed that the competitiveness of Korean products was achieved, to a large extent, by appropriating the advantage of the other countries. In other words, it obtained much benefit from the world market in procuring intermediate goods as well as in selling its products. But it is true, on the other hand, that Korea's economic structure made it rather difficult to enjoy a current account surplus, compared with the case of Indonesia.

In Thailand, such industries as metal, machinery, and transport equipment had relatively high dependency ratios on Japan in both years. However, like the other two countries, those ratios declined in most industries. The average dependency ratio on Japan also decreased from 3.98 per cent to 2.53 per cent.

As for the dependency ratios on ROW, we can find that, as in Korea, those industries that use a large amount of primary commodities as well as industrial intermediate products show relatively high figures. They include textile, other light industries, chemical (more than 45 per cent in 1985), and the industries mentioned above on Japan. The average dependency ratio on ROW decreased from 20.35 per cent to 18.50 per cent.

Comparing dependency ratios of the domestic final demand with those of the exports to ROW, we can observe a relationship similar to that of Korea, that is, Thailand's exports to ROW had a tendency to induce more value added in Japan and ROW than the domestic final demand did. However, the differences between those figures are not as large as in Korea.

It is also noticeable that Thailand lowered its dependency ratios on Japan with regard to both the domestic final demand and the exports to ROW, while the dependency ratio on ROW was, instead, considerably raised.

As is shown in the previous discussion, the procurement of intermediate goods from abroad formed an important facet of economic interdependence for these countries. However, the role of the final goods trade should be considered as well. Therefore, we will discuss below how these countries depended on imports to procure not only intermediate goods but also final goods.

Table 5 shows total import ratios from the world (ROW plus Japan) and from Japan. The total import ratios presented here show how much per cent of final demand consumption (private plus government) and capital formation, respectively for each product, was ultimately fulfilled by import. Generally, import from abroad is induced through two routes, that is, (i) some products are imported to be consumed as final goods, and (ii) others are imported to be used as intermediate goods so that domestic industries can produce final goods. Separating these two routes, total import ratios for final demand are calculated as follows:

(i) Products imported[13] as final goods for jth industry

$$= f_{jC}^{WP} + f_{jC}^{JP}.$$

(ii) Products imported as intermediate goods for jth industry

$$= \sum_{i}^{17} \sum_{k}^{17} (a_{ik}^{WP} + a_{ik}^{JP}) b_{kj}^{PP} f_{jC}^{PP}.$$

(iii) Total import ratio for ith industry

$$= \frac{f_{jC}^{WP} + f_{jC}^{JP} + \sum_{i}^{17} \sum_{k}^{17} (a_{ik}^{WP} + a_{ik}^{JP}) b_{kj}^{PP} f_{jC}^{PP}}{f_{jC}^{WP} + f_{jC}^{JP} + f_{jC}^{PP}} \times 100.$$

Besides the above figures, total import ratios for all the industries are presented at the bottom of the table, and the ratios of import from Japan are given inside the parentheses. The total import ratios for all the industries show how much per cent of each item of final demand, as a whole, was ultimately fulfilled by import.

In table 5, the total import ratios for capital formation concerning all the industries are about two to three times higher than those for consumption in all the countries. This suggests that import generally played more import role for capital formation than for private consumption. Among the industries, metal, machinery, transport equipment, and other manufacturing have extremely high total import ratios for capital formation; note that some of them even exceed 90 per cent. As for the ratios for all the industries, Korea showed the greatest figure (44.78 per cent) in 1975, but Thailand surpassed Korea in 1985 and reached 38.65 per cent.

The total import ratios from Japan for capital formation are also high in the industries mentioned above, namely, metal, machinery, transport equipment, and other manufacturing. While those ratios for import from Japan declined sharply in all the countries, the shares that Japan holds in the total import ratios for capital formation are still high. For instance, in 1975, as much as 45.18 per cent of Korea's total import ratio for capital formation concerning all the industries was held by Japan. Although it declined to 35.38 per cent in 1985, these shares were about twice as great as the shares for consumption (22.41 per cent and 17.20 per cent in 1975 and 1985, respectively). Such a relationship can be also seen in the other two countries. Therefore, we can conclude that Japan has been playing an especially active role in promoting capital formation in these countries, and, although this Japanese role has become smaller, it is thought to be still important.

As for consumption, such industries as chemical, metal, machinery, transport equipment, and other manufacturing present relatively high figures. Those for imports from Japan are also generally high in metal products, machinery, transport equipment, and other manufacturing.

Table 5 **Total import ratio (%)**

	Indonesia				Korea				Thailand			
	Consumption		Capital formation		Consumption		Capital formation		Consumption		Capital formation	
Sector	1975	1985	1975	1985	1975	1985	1975	1985	1975	1985	1975	1985
Agriculture, fish, and forestry	1.78	3.22	1.70	31.99	8.44	10.75	8.80	12.19	4.44	13.92	6.07	36.50
	(0.49)	(0.38)	(0.49)	(0.26)	(1.82)	(1.21)	(1.82)	(1.27)	(0.98)	(1.12)	(0.99)	(1.16)
Crude petroleum	0.00	0.00	0.00	0.00	–	–	–	–	–	0.00	–	0.00
	(0.00)	(0.00)	(0.00)	(0.00)	–	–	–	–	–	(0.00)	–	(0.00)
Other mining	19.74	19.31	0.00	0.00	11.58	10.80	0.00	0.00	6.60	14.30	0.00	0.00
	(2.54)	(2.11)	(0.00)	(0.00)	(2.97)	(1.96)	(0.00)	(0.00)	(1.25)	(1.14)	(0.00)	(0.00)
Food	7.90	7.43	0.00	0.00	24.37	18.41	23.76	17.43	7.29	12.53	0.00	0.00
	(0.83)	(0.56)	(0.00)	(0.00)	(2.17)	(1.45)	(2.10)	(1.40)	(1.14)	(1.25)	(0.00)	(0.00)
Textile	30.88	28.65	73.03	36.04	36.49	36.77	42.63	40.86	24.60	24.19	25.53	21.79
	(9.85)	(3.75)	(24.09)	(4.06)	(14.16)	(8.06)	(21.10)	(7.72)	(7.87)	(3.37)	(7.05)	(2.91)
Other light industries	17.88	14.60	15.51	11.47	47.58	38.61	48.33	35.68	24.12	33.36	16.95	30.39
	(6.84)	(1.97)	(6.23)	(1.53)	(6.84)	(4.56)	(7.86)	(3.27)	(5.02)	(3.08)	(3.71)	(2.56)
Chemical	42.07	33.59	12.29	22.47	52.43	51.77	0.00	0.00	59.05	58.38	64.98	70.25
	(6.25)	(3.81)	(4.44)	(2.60)	(11.43)	(5.89)	(0.00)	(0.00)	(7.32)	(4.45)	(15.78)	(9.70)
Non-metallic mineral	66.29	30.80	28.37	18.30	26.05	33.98	0.00	0.00	37.52	34.73	43.92	63.42
	(14.02)	(6.12)	(7.19)	(3.03)	(8.15)	(8.29)	(0.00)	(0.00)	(12.05)	(8.35)	(17.14)	(24.70)
Metal	43.49	54.77	49.26	62.26	52.53	46.84	64.01	–	51.16	59.52	48.12	65.49
	(21.99)	(10.81)	(23.50)	(13.02)	(25.03)	(13.32)	(30.31)	–	(18.77)	(16.38)	(18.35)	(15.93)
Machinery	51.52	55.82	94.14	81.63	46.07	41.58	82.79	64.71	57.43	59.76	92.20	81.72
	(20.41)	(17.19)	(36.79)	(21.72)	(21.46)	(19.13)	(39.09)	(30.43)	(23.84)	(15.55)	(32.47)	(23.98)
Transport equipment	35.06	34.90	52.27	66.37	41.12	31.69	66.68	41.68	41.67	37.95	71.59	56.64
	(24.04)	(10.61)	(29.13)	(8.02)	(21.61)	(13.01)	(41.70)	(13.79)	(24.14)	(15.79)	(34.02)	(23.98)

Table 5 **(cont.)**

Sector	Indonesia				Korea				Thailand			
	Consumption		Capital formation		Consumption		Capital formation		Consumption		Capital formation	
	1975	1985	1975	1985	1975	1985	1975	1985	1975	1985	1975	1985
Other manufacturing	46.50	49.53	96.93	94.19	40.06	36.86	83.91	75.62	38.03	43.19	88.29	76.47
	(22.41)	(10.61)	(36.45)	(26.73)	(18.94)	(14.60)	(38.66)	(28.67)	(7.56)	(5.76)	(20.76)	(19.10)
Electricity, gas, and water	20.58	17.14	0.00	0.00	32.11	20.17	57.88	51.29	20.56	18.25	0.00	0.00
	(2.79)	(2.12)	(0.00)	(0.00)	(10.93)	(1.82)	(6.78)	(1.11)	(3.09)	(0.97)	(0.00)	(0.00)
Construction	20.18	16.02	20.18	16.02	21.87	17.83	21.85	17.78	16.99	20.45	16.99	20.45
	(8.86)	(4.74)	(8.86)	(4.47)	(8.01)	(4.17)	(8.01)	(4.17)	(6.36)	(4.74)	(6.36)	(4.74)
Trade and transport	9.05	10.17	10.70	10.99	11.18	16.56	28.56	22.60	7.48	16.17	10.22	18.63
	(1.87)	(1.05)	(6.04)	(5.56)	(3.56)	(3.06)	(22.65)	(11.22)	(1.58)	(1.45)	(5.47)	(6.04)
Services	11.47	12.56	0.00	0.00	12.17	9.47	11.18	8.37	8.04	11.57	4.98	8.11
	(1.40)	(0.67)	(0.00)	(0.00)	(2.67)	(1.47)	(2.63)	(1.28)	(1.20)	(0.93)	(1.15)	(0.80)
Public administration	0.00	0.00	0.00	0.00	0.00	20.38	0.00	0.00	0.00	0.00	0.00	0.00
	(0.00)	(0.00)	(0.00)	(0.00)	(0.00)	(5.18)	(0.00)	(0.00)	(0.00)	(0.00)	(0.00)	(0.00)
All industries	10.48	11.07	33.63	28.06	20.26	18.90	44.78	31.94	11.87	16.87	36.23	38.65
	(2.42)	(1.38)	(15.07)	(7.11)	(4.54)	(3.25)	(20.23)	(11.30)	(2.77)	(2.01)	(14.14)	(11.29)

Note: Figures inside parentheses are the ratios for imports from Japan.

Among these three countries, Korea, in both years, had the greatest total import ratio for consumption for all industries (20.26–18.90 per cent). However, that of Thailand increased the most (11.87–16.87 per cent) during this period.

V. Summary

The Asia-Pacific economies have attained remarkable growth with intensive foreign trading over the last two decades. In this process, the world market encouraged production by making a greater demand for their products and by providing them with various intermediate and capital goods.

According to estimates in the bilateral tables, 10–20 per cent of GDP in Indonesia, Korea, Thailand, and Japan was generated by the demand from ROW in 1975 and 1985. Especially, in 1985, more than a half of production in the textile (62.4 per cent) and metal (50.3 per cent) industries in Korea, and other manufacturing (51.3 per cent) in Thailand as created by exports to ROW. On the other hand, the industries in these countries were greatly dependent on industries in ROW for the supply of intermediate goods. The average dependency ratios on ROW for industries in Indonesia, Korea, and Thailand were 15–30 per cent in both 1975 and 1985. Among them all, the ratios for the chemical industry in Korea exceeded 50 per cent in 1985.

The specialization ratios in production show that, in 1975 and 1985, the above four countries had comparative advantages in different production activities. Such a situation is likely to provide a basis for international interdependence through complementary trading among the countries. In fact, as in shown by the dependency ratios on Japan, many of the heavy industries in Indonesia, Korea, and Thailand were dependent on Japan as a supplier of intermediate goods. On the other hand, production in these countries was induced by Japanese export. This indicates that some part of the competitiveness of Japanese products was created by the industries in those countries. In other words, shared production processes made their products more competitive in the world market. A similar case can be found in Korea, where dependency ratios for exports were much greater than those for domestic final demand in both 1975 and 1985.

Besides the procurement of intermediate goods, each industry enjoyed the benefits of "intraregional" division of labour for capital goods as well. In 1975 and 1985, the total import ratios for capital growth were, on average, 30–45 per cent in Indonesia, Korea and,

Thailand. This is 1.5 to 3.5 times as large as those for consumption. Capital growth in these countries relied largely on Japanese industries mainly because of Japan's comparative advantage in heavy industry, although Japan's share gradually declined in this period.

It is often emphasized that exporting is the powerful engine for economic growth. This was apparently true in the case of the Asia-Pacific region. Furthermore, the "intraregional" division of labour made it possible for each country in the region to supply more competitive products to the world market by working not only to its own advantage but also to the advantage of others. The dynamic structure of this region has been constructed on the basis of interdependence among countries.

Notes

1. A number of books and papers on the dynamism of the Asia-Pacific economy have been mushrooming for the past few years. See, for example, Miyohei Shinohara and Fu-chen Lo, eds., *Global Adjustment and the Future of Asian-Pacific Economy*, Asian and Pacific Development Centre and Institute of Developing Economies, 1989.
2. The analysis in this study is not complete and is still preliminary in the sense that it does not cover other major countries in the Asia-Pacific region such as China, Taiwan, Hong Kong, Singapore, Malaysia, the Philippines, etc. However, this arbitrary selection of reference countries, we believe, will not affect the conclusions we are going to draw from the analysis. Complete and more detailed studies will be expected after the international input-output table for 1985 covering such countries is ready for use.
3. These are member countries of the Asian international input-output table for 1985.
4. The real GDP growth rates may be different from the official figures released by each government.
5. In 1970, Singapore's export-GDP and import-GDP ratios were already more than 100 per cent. Hong Kong's ratios exceeded 100 per cent for the first time in 1984. These two countries, specializing greatly in international trade, are omitted in this section.
6. Strictly speaking, the upward trend of the export-GDP and import-GDP ratios over years should be tested statistically. In addition, the role of the exchange rate should be carefully examined in discussing the effect of international trade on the macroeconomy.
7. All the analyses in this section are based on 17-sector classification as follows; (1) agriculture, fishery, and forestry, (2) crude petroleum and national gas, (3) other mining, (4) food, (5) textile, (6) other light industries, (7) chemical products, (8) nonmetallic mineral products, (9) metal products, (10) machinery, (11) transport equipment, (12) other manufacturing products, (13) electricity, gas, and water supply, (14) construction, (15) trade and transport, (16) services, (17) public administration.
8. ROW includes all the countries except Japan and the counterpart country in a bilateral table. Therefore, the members of ROW are different for each table.
9. *P* Country stands for each of Indonesia, Korea, and Thailand.
10. Though the figures for Japanese crude petroleum and natural gas are also greater than those for Korea, it is simply because such an industry did not exist in Korea.
11. Japanese textile industry might produce something essential for Korean export.
12. Total intermediate input coefficients for crude petroleum were 3.16 per cent and 16.57 per cent in 1975 and 1985 respectively.
13. The second subscript *C* represents either *P* Country's consumption or capital formation.

References

Institute of Developing Economies. 1981. *International Input-Output Table, Indonesia-Japan, 1975.* Tokyo: Institute of Developing Economies.

—— 1991. *International Input-Output Table, Indonesia-Japan, 1985.* Tokyo: Institute of Developing Economies.

—— 1981. *International Input-Output Table, Korea-Japan, 1975.* Tokyo: Institute of Developing Economies.

—— 1991. *International Input-Output Table, Korea-Japan, 1985.* Tokyo, Institute of Developing Economies.

—— 1981. *International Input-Output Table, Thailand-Japan, 1975.* Tokyo: Institute of Developing Economies.

—— 1991. *International Input-Output Table, Thailand-Japan, 1985.* Tokyo: Institute of Developing Economies.

Miyohei Shinohara and Fu-chen Lo, eds. 1989. *Global Adjustment and the Future of Asian-Pacific Economy.* Tokyo: Asian and Pacific Development Centre and Institute of Developing Economies.

World Bank. 1990, 1991. *World Tables, 1989–1990 and 1991.* Washington, D.C.: World Bank.

Appendix A

Format of *P* Country-Japan bilateral input-output table

The 1985 *P* Country-Japan international input-output table (*P* Country stands for Korea, Thailand, or Indonesia) is a commodity table in which all of the economic transactions undertaken, in 1985, in and between the territories of *P* Country and Japan are expressed in a manner similar to a national input-output table. Table A1 illustrates the format of the 1985 table.

In Table A1, the first column shows the input structure of industries in Japan. A^{JJ} ($n \times n$ matrix) depicts the flow of goods and services produced and used by the Japanese industries (at producers' value). A^{PJ} ($n \times n$) gives the flow of goods produced by *P* Country's industries but used by the Japanese industries, i.e., the import matrix from *P* Country (also at producers' value). The row below, B^J ($l \times n$), is for the freight and insurance on imported goods from *P* Country. A^{WJ} ($n \times n$) is the import matrix from the rest of the world (ROW). Therefore, A^{WJ} is, in appearance, similar to A^{PJ}, but it is valued at c.i.f. and the imports of services from *P* Country are also contained in A^{WJ}. In A^{PJ}, only the domestic trade margin and transportation costs on the imported goods from *P* Country are presented, expressed as imports of services from *P* Country. D^J ($l \times n$) represents the customs duties and commodity taxes on the total imports in Japan. And V^J ($k \times n$) and X^J ($l \times n$) are, respectively, value added and total inputs.

The second column shows the input structures of industries in *P* Country. A^{JP} ($n \times n$) is the import matrix from Japan. A^{PP} ($n \times n$) is the intermediate transaction matrix of *P* Country's domestic goods and services. The explanations for the first column also apply to the other parts of the second column (B^P, A^{WP}, D^P, V^P, and X^P). The third and fourth columns show the flow of goods and services produced for final demand in Japan and *P* Country. F^{JJ} ($n \times m$) is the final demand for Japanese

Table A1 **Format of *P* Country-Japan bilateral IO table**

		Interim demand			Final demand					Export to ROW		
		Japan	P Country		Japan	P Country						
Intermediate inputs		A AA J JJ 0 9 0 … n0 1 0	A AA P PP 0 9 0 … n0 1 0	E T 9 0 0	F FF J JJ 0 9 0 … m0 1 0	F FF P PP 0 9 0 … m0 1 0	F X 9 0 0	G J 9 0 0	G P 9 0 0	L LL C WX 0 09 0 … 00 1 10	Q X 0 0 1	X X 6 0 0
Japanese products	AJ001 : AJ n AJ900	A^{JJ}	A^{JP}		F^{JJ}	F^{JP}				L^{J}	Q^{J}	X^{J}
P Country's products	AP001 : AP n AP900	A^{PJ}	A^{PP}		F^{PJ}	F^{PP}				L^{P}	Q^{P}	X^{P}
Freight and insurance	BF001	B^{J}	B^{P}		BF^{J}	BF^{P}						
ROW products	CW001 : CW n CW900	A^{WJ}	A^{WP}		F^{WJ}	F^{WP}						
Tariff	DT001	D^{J}	D^{P}		DF^{J}	DF^{P}						
Total	ET900											

Value added	VV001 : VV k VV900	V^J	V^P
Total input	XX600	X^J	X^P

Row	Column	Description
AJ001	AJ001	Intermediate sectors, Japan
:	:	
AJ n	AJ n	
AJ900	AJ900	Sub-total (AJ001-AJ n)
AP001	AP001	Intermediate sectors, P Country
:	:	
AP n	AP n	
AP900	AP900	Sub-total (AP001-AP n)
BF001		International freight and insurance premiums
CW001		Imports from the ROW of the world
:		
CW n		
CW900		Sub-total (CW001-CW n)
DT001		Custom duties and import commodity taxes
ET900	ET900	Total intermediate input or output
VV001		Value added items
:		
VV k		
VV900		Total value added
	FJ001	Final demand items, Japan
	:	
	FJ m	

Row	Column	Description
	FJ900	Total final demand, Japan
	FP001	Final demand items, P Country
	:	
	FP m	
	FP900	Total final demand, P Country
	FX900	Total final demand (FJ900 + FP990)
	GJ900	Total demand, Japan (AJ900[COL.] + FJ900)
	GP900	Total demand, P. Country (AP900[COL.] + FP900)
	LC001	Export to China
	LH001	Export to Hong Kong
	LI001	Export to Indonesia
	LK001	Export to Korea
	LM001	Export to Malaysia
	LN001	Export to Taiwan
	LP001	Export to Philippines
	LS001	Export to Singapore
	LT001	Export to Thailand
	LU001	Export to USA
	LW001	Export to other countries
	LX900	Export to ROW (Total of LC001-LW001)
	QX001	Statistical discrepancy
XX600	XX600	Total input or output

domestic goods and services and F^{PJ} ($n \times m$) that for imported goods from P Country. In contrast, F^{JP} ($n \times m$) is the final demand for imported goods from Japan and F^{PP} that for P Country's domestic goods and services. The same explanation for the first and the second columns can be applied to the other parts of the third and the fourth columns (BF^J, F^{WJ}, DF^J, BF^P, F^{WP}, and DF^P).

L^J ($n \times 10$) and L^P ($n \times 10$) are the export matrices for Japan and P Country to 10 countries or regions – China, Hong Kong, Indonesia, Korea, Malaysia, Taiwan, the Philippines, Singapore, Thailand, the United States (excluding P Country), and ROW. Q^J ($n \times l$) and Q^P ($n \times l$) are the statistical discrepancies. Finally, X^J ($n \times l$) and X^P ($n \times l$) are the total output figures for Japan and P Country.

Appendix B

Procedure of compilation of *P* Country-Japan bilateral IO table

Based on P Country's and Japanese national IO tables for 1985 compiled by P. Country's institute and the Japanese government, respectively, the 1985 *P* Country-Japan bilateral IO table was compiled and it included the following procedure:

1. *Construction of the uniform input-output sector classification*
   The uniform input-output sector classification (UIO) was prepared for converting the national input-output tables into one bilateral input-output table. Also, several converters which link the input-output tables and the foreign trade statistics were prepared here.
2. *Conducting the special survey*
   A special survey was conducted by the counterpart institute in *P* Country to investigate the shares of imported goods, by country of origin, which were used in producing goods in *P* Country. On the other hand, the Ministry of International Trade and Industry (MITI), Japan, conducted a survey to investigate the distribution ratios, by input sector, of imported goods in Japan.
3. *Compilation of the import matrices*
   The import matrices by country of origin were compiled to link the national input-output tables. In this step, the results of the special survey mentioned above were used.
4. *Consistency check of the converter system*
   The foreign trade statistics between the two countries, Japanese exports with *P* Country's imports and *P* Country's exports with Japanese imports, were compared, in US dollars, at the UIO level to check the consistency of the UIO "National IO" CCCN converters.
5. *Conversion of valuation of import transaction tables*
   (from c.i.f. values to producers' (values)
   The import transaction tables obtained at step 3 were all valuated at c.i.f. and in order to convert to producers' prices, the following two substeps done:
   (1) Subtraction of international freight and insurance premiums (conversion from c.i.f. to f.o.b. values)
   (2) Subtraction of domestic freight and trade margins in counterpart country (conversion from f.o.b. to producers' values).
6. *Conceptual adjustments of national input-output table*

Since the *P* Country's and the Japanese input-output tables do not necessarily match each other in regard to format and concept, it is necessary to make adjustments to either one. For this purpose, both the concept and format of the Japanese table were adjusted.

(1) Business consumption
Business consumption has its own sector in the Japanese input-output table, whereas it is not separated from the others in the Thai and Indonesian tables. Therefore, the column and row for business consumption in the Japanese table were removed by distributing them proportionately (based on the compositions of the row and the column) to each element of the matrix in constructing Thailand-Japan and Indonesia-Japan bilateral input-output tables.

(2) Repair of general machinery and electric machinery
In the Japanese table, repairs are separated from production in the sectors grouped as general machinery and electric machinery and have their own sectors, repair of general machinery and repair of electric machinery, whereas they are not separated from the sectors mentioned above in the Thai and Korean tables. Therefore, in the Japanese table, these two sectors were removed by distributing them to those elements that are considered to be closely related to the use of the respective machinery in constructing the Thailand-Japan and Korea-Japan bilateral input-output tables.

(3) Dummy sectors
In the Japanese table, services produced for own use, such as self-education, are separated from their main activities and have their own dummy sectors. Therefore, these dummy sectors were removed by distributing them proportionally (based on the compositions of the row and the column) to each element of the matrix. Another sector provided with a dummy sector in the Japanese table is office supplies, and it was removed in the same way.

(4) Public administration
In the Japanese table, portions of government expenditures are expressed as the intermediate input of the public administration sectors, whereas, in the Thai and Indonesian tables they are expressed as the input of government consumption expenditures (final demand). Therefore, in the Japanese table, the columns (except for value added) for the public administration sectors were removed by merging them into the government consumption expenditures in constructing the Thailand-Japan and Indonesia-Japan bilateral input-output tables.

(5) Others
- Bank service charges (for the Thailand-Japan table)
- Imports of banking, postal, and telecommunication services (for the Korea-Japan table)

7. *Compilation of export matrices*
The bilateral table shows, in matrix form, the *P* Country's and Japanese exports of commodities by country (China, Hong Kong, Korea, Indonesia, Malaysia, Philippines, Singapore, Taiwan, Thailand, USA, and the ROW). This matrix was constructed by decomposing the export column of the national input-output table using foreign trade statistics. All the exports to countries other than Japan and *P* Country were included in the columns of exports to the ROW (LC001, LH001, LI001, LK001, LM001, LN001, LP001, LS001, LT001, LU001, and LW001).

8. *Linkage of the two national IO tables*
   The final compilation step was to link all the data compiled through steps 1–7 – transaction matrices of domestic goods, import matrices, etc. – into one bilateral input-output table. At the same time, the valuation of the national input-output tables (=local currencies) were converted into US dollars. After the linkage, some adjustments were made to balance the bilateral table.

7

Towards an international input-output model: Fact-findings on trade patterns and production technologies

Iwao Ozaki, Masahiro Kuroda, and Masahiko Shimizu

I. Introduction

The pattern of international trade among various types of countries including industrialized countries (ICs), newly-industrializing countries (NICs) and developing countries (DCs) has, through the 1970s and 1980s, greatly changed.[1] These changes have affected economic performance and may help account for the slowing growth, price inflation, and rising unemployment observed in Asian countries as well as NICs in recent years, especially since 1985 (the year of the Plaza Agreement). The deteriorating performance of these countries stands in marked contrast to their earlier growth, and is related to the burgeoning interdependency amongst various countries, particularly the expansion of free trade between ICs. Consequently, it is vital to investigate both analytically and empirically recent patterns of international trade. We attempt, in this study, to observe patterns and features in the international division of labour between these countries and to move in a theoretical direction towards international input-output modelling in order to describe the differences in economic activity among various countries at different stages of economic development. We begin with examining empirically the relationship between the technological features of commodities as determined statistically and the various patterns of international trade among different countries as revealed by the international input-output tables compiled by Ministry of International Trade and Industry (MITI) and Institute of Developing Economy (IDE) in Japan.

The study follows two propositions, one of which is methodological and the other is more substantive. The former, the methodological proposition, is divided into two parts. The first concerns the methodology used to investigate directly the different patterns of international trade among various countries, which was accomplished by analysing nine bilateral international input-output tables (IIOTs 1985). These nine bilateral tables consist of data for Japan–United States, Japan–South Korea, Japan–Thailand, Japan–Indonesia, Japan–China, Japan–Philippine, Japan–Malaysia, Japan–Singapore, Japan–Taiwan for the year 1985, where each national input-output table is bilaterally combined with the Japanese table through international trade matrices of intermediate commodities. Since each bilateral table attempts to describe international transactions as concerns intermediate and final demands in a form of the non-competitive type input-output table, it reveals patterns of international trade and its differences both by countries and by commodities as shown in section 2.1.

The second methodological proposition is the determination of the type of production technology for each commodity. We can directly investigate patterns of production technology by commodity concerning the intermediate input structures by using the IIOTs. The IIOTs provide empirically international comparisons among countries regarding intermediate input structures by commodity and interdependency among commodities in each country. As we mention in section 2.2, we can clearly observe the similarity of technologies concerning the intermediate inputs not only from the viewpoint of the input structure in each commodity, but also from the viewpoint of the inter-industry dependency among commodities. We also try to investigate structures of factor inputs such as labour and capital in order to specify the type of technology by commodity. These types of technology must be determined statistically at the most disaggregated level of commodity-classification. Although this will be discussed in detail in section 3, broadly speaking the results support the hypothesis that a factor-limitational type production function exists in the highly industrialized sectors of an economic system, while in many other traditional sectors, a factor-substitutable production function prevails. These highly industrialized sectors are characterized by the technology which is referred to as K-type technology, indicating its large plant-scale, capital intensive nature. Traditional sectors utilize L-type technology, or small plant-scale, labour intensive technology.

Moreover, it is shown in section 4 that characteristics in the trade patterns of each country are closely related to the features of the technology adopted by the country. Finally, in section 5, we try to connect these fact findings on the technological structure of the production with the factor price differentials in order to explain the differences in trade patterns by countries. We have to introduce the somewhat controversial substantive propostion, in which highly industrialized sectors dominated by the large plant-scale, capital intensive production techniques assume to minimize their unit cost for production in the determination of the optimum plant size, instead of the standard assumption regarding the rational behaviour of the profit maximization in both domestic and international markets. Of course, in the case of L-type technology, the standard assumption of profit maximizing behaviour is appropriate since the determination of optimal plant size is not an issue. For industries with K-type technology, the unit-cost minimization behaviour of firms determines the optimum level of unit cost for each commodity in each country corresponding to different factor prices. The levels of unit costs so determined are comparable across countries and represent an index of the competitive power of each commodity supplied in international markets. The introduction of K-type technology implies not only a scale effect that appears in these sectors of an economy as it industrializes, but also implies the difficulties that less developed countries have in producing products which embody such K-type technology. That is, less developed countries can lose whatever competitiveness they might have had in commodities characterized by K-type technology because of rising wage costs with relatively higher unit capital cost. This framework tentatively gives us a prototype model in order to provide an interpretation for various patterns of interdependency, which were observed in the IIOTs framework as international trade patterns between ICs and DCs.

II. Differences in trade patterns and similarity in the structure of technologies

1. Differences in trade patterns by country

The international input-output table provides us with international trade matrices of intermediate input transactions and final demand between Japan–United States, Japan–South Korea, Japan–Thailand, and Japan–Indonesia bilaterally. As we mentioned in the papers which are presented by our collaborators, MITI and IDE, four bilateral international input-output tables (1985) are re-compiled to be mutually compatible and readjusted among various countries. At first, we begin with confirming trade patterns as concerns intermediate input transactions between two countries based on observations obtained from IIOTs. Figures 1a through 1d give us summaries of the differences of trade patterns in bilateral trade between Japan–United States, Japan–South Korea, Japan–Indonesia, and Japan–Thailand. Each figure represents main commodities in the bilateral trade and their share of exports and imports respectively. According to these summaries, the Japanese trade reveals the enormous advantage in trade of commodities such as transportation equipment, machinery, and metal products. The Japanese export share of transportation equipment amounts to 9.0 per cent of the total export to the United States, 9.8 per cent to South Korea, 10.1 per cent to Indonesia respectively. In addition, that of machinery amounts to 16.4 per cent to South Korea, 15.3 per cent to Indonesia, and 11.9 per cent to Thailand, while that of metal products reaches 17.0 per cent to Indonesia and 17.4 per cent to Thailand respectively. On the other hand, the figures show that each bilateral trade country such as the United States, South Korea, Indonesia, and Thailand has different advantages in trading with Japan. The US export to Japan includes other machines, which share 12.6 per cent of the total amount and forestry products, which share 9.8 per cent. The South Korean export of textile products to Japan shares 1.1 per cent of the total. Crude petroleum and natural gas accounts for 17.5 per cent of the total export of Indonesia to Japan. Additionally, shares of food product exports from Thailand to Japan amount 0.4 per cent of the total. It should be noted that the bilateral trade patterns designate differences of the comparative advantages in each country, where Japan–US trade as equally developed countries is bilaterally shared by the technology intensive commodities like machinery, while Japan–South Korea, Japan–Indonesia and Japan–Thailand trades, which include countries in different stages of development, are clearly characterized by the different type of labour division internationally. In the latter cases, Japan exports the more technology intensive commodities such as machinery and metal products to the less developed countries, while the less developed countries export light manufacturing products such as textiles and food products and raw materials such as crude petroleum and natural gas. When it comes to imports from the rest of the world, the Japanese import is strongly characterized by raw materials and energy resources. These features are also observed in the trade patterns in South Korea and Thailand. It should be noted that the trade patterns in each country are dominated by the factor endowment of natural resources such as energy and mining.

These fact findings in the differences of trade patterns by country give us the starting point of our analysis. How can we explain the differences of these trade patterns from the viewpoints of the technology of production by commodities and the differences of the factor endowment including primary factors and natural resources?

2. Similarity in the structure of technology

Based on the observations mentioned above, in this section, we attempt to confirm the two aspects of technology systems and trade patterns among the various countries based on international input-output tables. The first aspect concerns the similarity in the structure of technologies. The technology system [A] is described by the matrix of input-output technology coefficients $[a_{ij}]$, where the dominant input coefficients of more than 0.01 are plotted in the intermediate transaction matrix. In each table commodities are rearranged in triangular order from the end-use products to the primary-use products. This triangularity designates the hierarchical structure of the intermediate inputs among commodities, where the hierarchical structure is characterized by the inter-block hierarchy among and within certain commodity groups. From the viewpoint of this technological hierarchical structure, a comparison of these matrices shows a strong similarity in the structure of technologies among these national economies. This is one support to the hypothesis that different countries have a similar system of technologies with regard to interdependency between commodities in the national economy.

Next, we can compare the volume of the input coefficients in each commodity in order to check the similarity of input structure by commodity. Although it is fairly difficult to compare exactly because of the differences of the commodity classification in each table, broadly speaking we can confirm the similarity of the volume of the input coefficients in the same commodity among countries. It implies that the assumption of fixed coefficients in intermediate input by each commodity's technology is empirically adoptable and constant returns to scale technology are assumed to be dominant in the inter-

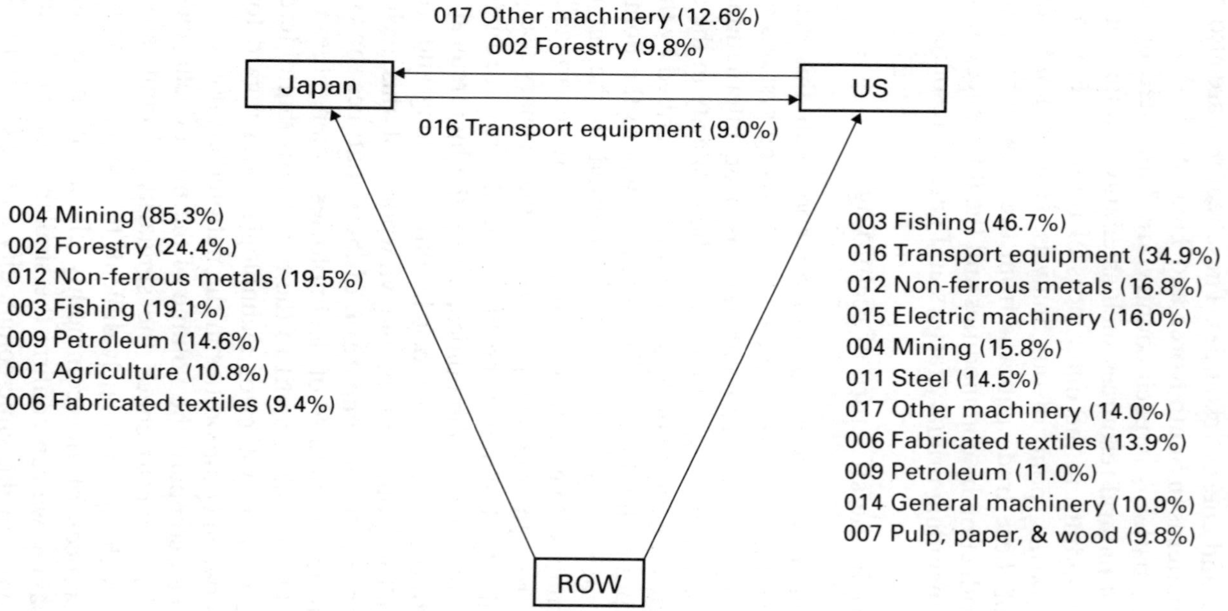

Fig. 1a **Transactions of intermediate goods between Japan, United States, and ROW**

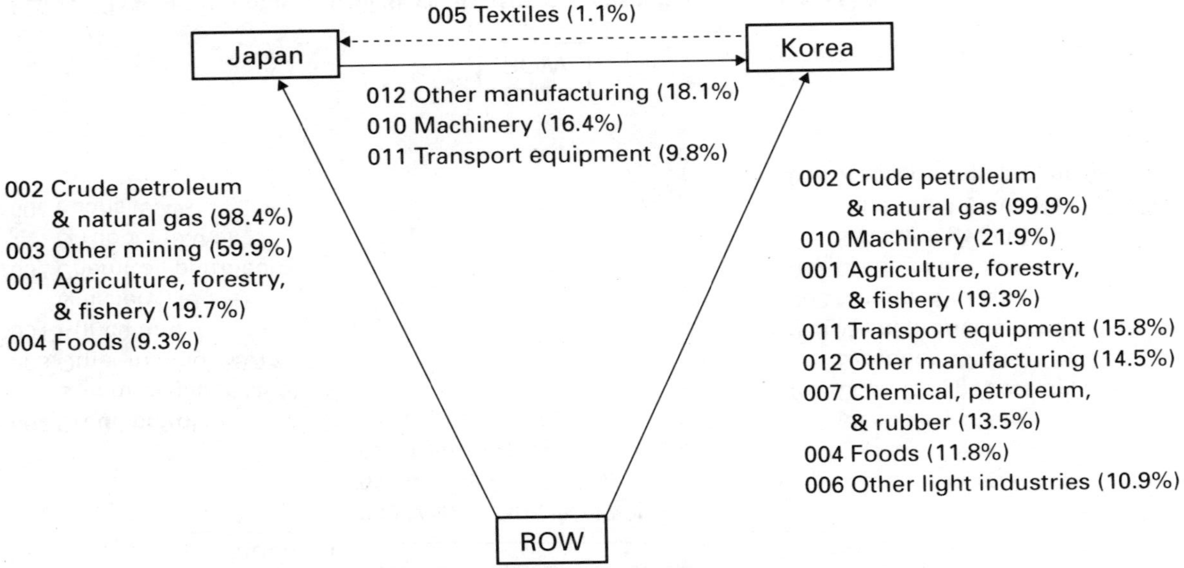

Fig. 1b **Transactions of intermediate goods between Japan, Korea, and ROW**

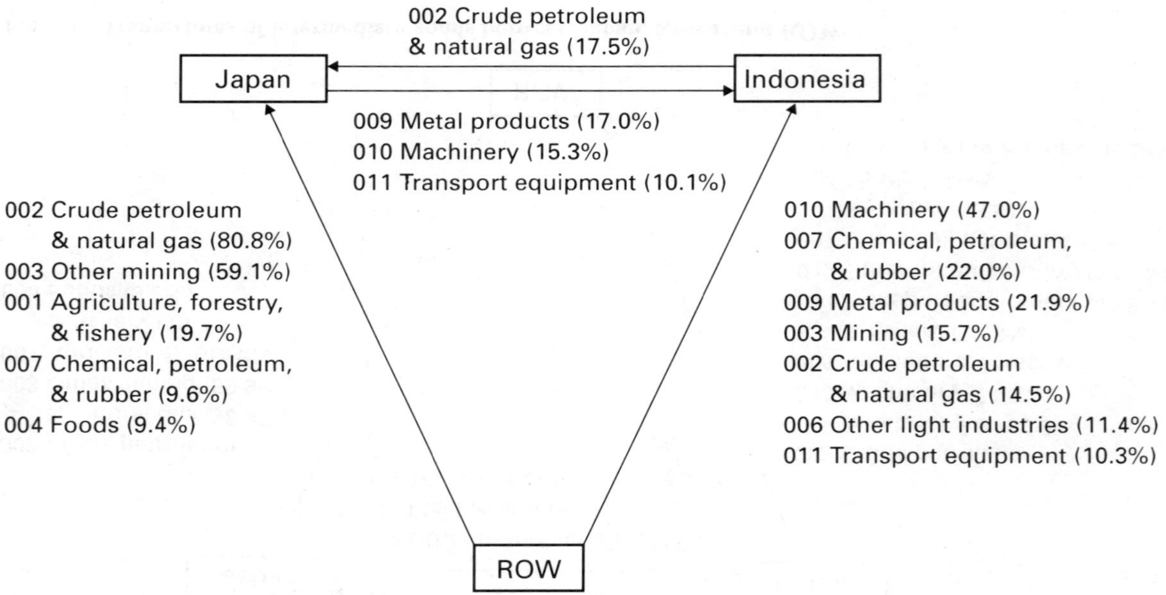

Fig. 1c **Transactions of intermediate goods between Japan, Indonesia, and ROW**

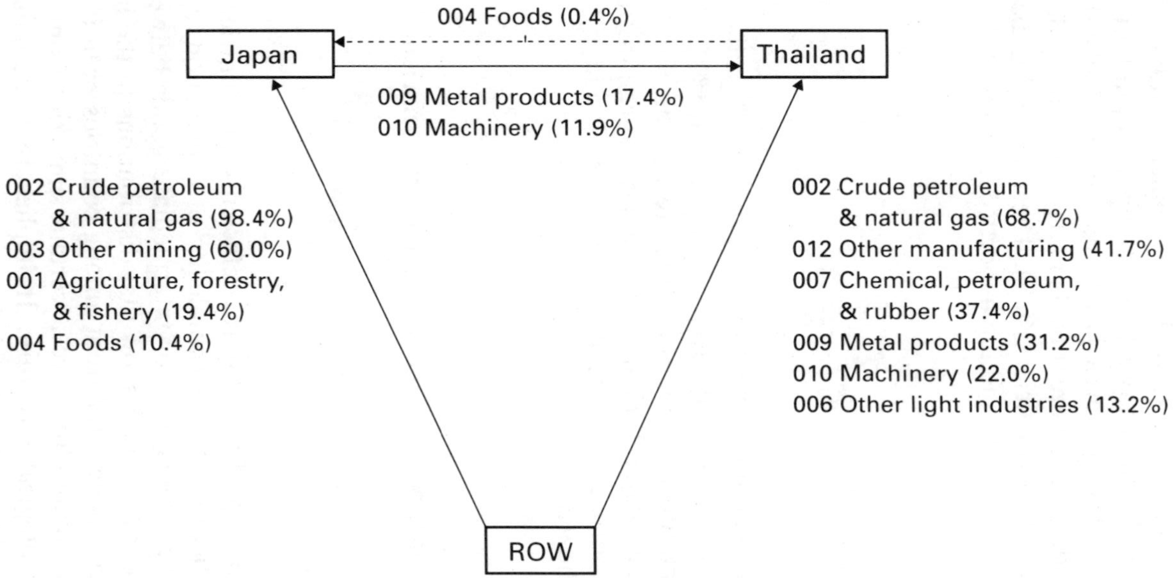

Fig. 1d **Transactions of intermediate goods between Japan, Thailand, and ROW**

mediate transaction. This is another support to our hypothesis that different countries have a similar technology with regard to the input structure of the intermediate transactions by commodities.

On the other hand, the second aspect concerns trade patterns between countries. Using the two bilateral input-output tables (BIOTs) including Japan–South Korea [J-K] and Japan–Thailand [J-T], we can clearly distinguish different trade patterns which are described by the matrix of import coefficients $[a_{ij}^m]$. The relationship between the technology coefficients a_{ij} and the import coefficients a_{ij}^m is as follows.

$$a_{ij} = a_{ij}^d + a_{ij}^m. \tag{1}$$

$$a_{ij}^d = \frac{x_{ij}^d}{X_j}, \quad a_{ij}^{mk} = \frac{x_{ij}^{mk}}{X_j}, \quad a_{ij}^{mr} = \frac{x_{ij}^{mr}}{X_j}, \tag{2}$$

where x_{ij}^d is the amount of the domestic product; x_{ij}^{mk} is the amount of imported intermediate goods from country k; and x_{ij}^{mr} is the amount of imported intermediate goods from the rest of the world.

Based on the bilateral input-output tables, we can distinguish between x_{ij}^{mk} imported from the partner country k and x_{ij}^{mr} imported from rest of the world.

$$x_{ij}^m = x_{ij}^{mk} + x_{ij}^{mr}. \tag{3}$$

At the same time, we can obtain two import coefficients, $[a_{ij}^{mk}]$ and $[a_{ij}^{mr}]$.

$$a_{ij}^m = a_{ij}^{mk} + a_{ij}^{mr}. \tag{4}$$

The detailed map of the import coefficients by countries has been omitted here because of the complexity of explanation, each country's import coefficients, $[a_{ij}^m]$ or intermediate goods between Japan and each partner country k show that distributions of the import coefficients are completely different among countries even if the input coefficients by commodity have a certain similarity from the viewpoint of technological structure. It implies that the international transaction is influenced by the difference in technological advantage and the factor endowment, even in the intermediate transaction.

We are unable to reproduce here in sufficient detail the maps of the technology coefficient matrices $[a_{ij}]$ and the import coefficient matrices $[a_{ij}^m]$ because of limitations in printing techniques. Our findings from these tables are summarized in the following four points.

(a) A comparison of the technology systems [A]s for each country shows that there is a strong similarity among various countries from the viewpoints of the interdependency of the technology among commodities.
(b) Intermediate input coefficients by commodity have a similarity among countries from the viewpoint of technological structure by commodity. It implies that the assumption of the fixed coefficients in the intermediate inputs by commodity is adoptable in each commodity.
(c) On the other hand, the configurations of domestic input coefficients $[a_{ij}^d]$ and import coefficients $[a_{ij}^m]$ differ greatly by country.
(d) Highly industrialized countries export heavy industry products (machinery, iron and steel, chemical products, etc.) to developing countries (DCs) and import light industry products (textiles, foods, and primary products, etc.) from DCs, while DCs export light industry products and import heavy industry products, particularly capital goods (machinery).

III. Determination of type of technology

As we mentioned in the previous section, the international trade in each country is characterized by different patterns, where it seems to reflect the differences of the technology by commodities and the factor endowment by countries. As concerns the intermediate input structure by commodity, we can confirm the similarity among countries, as we showed above.

In this section, we try to categorize commodities on the basis of their technology features which are determined statistically from the viewpoint of factor input structure such as labour and capital for each single commodity. The types of technology were empirically determined for each sector by estimating production functions. Using these results, all commodities were grouped into the following six technology types:

(A) Type K(I-B) technology; (large-quantity processing technology)
(B) Type K(I-M) technology; (large-scale assembly technology)
(C) Type K(II) technology; (capital intensive technology)
(D) Type (L-K) technology; (Cobb-Douglas-type technology)

(E) Type L(I) technology; (labour-intensive technology)
(F) Type L(II) technology; (labor-intensive technology)

Briefly, we refer to types (A)–(C) as K-type technology and types (D)–(F) as L-type technology.

Production functions were estimated using time series data of the Japan Data Development Center, which covers 500 commodities. Observations covered production X, labour L, and the capital stock K.

We estimated the parameters of the production functions for all sectors corresponding to the Japanese 54 × 54 input-output table by using time series production data for the period 1951 to 1968. Experimental equations are as follows:

Factor-limitational type

$$L = \alpha_L X^{\beta_L}, \quad K = \alpha_K X^{\beta_K}, \tag{5}$$

Linear homogeneous Cobb-Douglas type

$$X = \alpha_0 L^{1-\beta_0} K^{\beta_0}, \tag{6}$$

Generalized Cobb-Douglas type

$$X = \alpha L^{\gamma_L} K^{\gamma_K}, \tag{7}$$

where X is the gross output, L is the labour, K is the capital stock, and α, β, γ are parameters.

On the basis of the results from this estimation, the above six types of technology were identified: K(I-B), K(I-M), K(II) (L-K), L(I) and L(II). Table 1 shows a summary of these results. Each technology type has the following features:

(A) Type K(I-B) technology

This is the case where $\beta_L < 1$ and $\beta_k < 1$, but particularly the value of β_L is much less than unity in equation (5). Hence, economies of scale prevail in both labour and capital inputs, but are especially strong for labour inputs, regardless of any changes in the factor-price ratio. Accordingly, for sectors with K(I-B) type technology, there would always exist incentives to expand the production scale for the purpose of reducing unit cost. Only the saturation of demand would halt the expansion of production scale.

In (A) of table 1, we observe that K(I-B) type technology sectors include (1) electric power supply; (2) gas and water supply; (3)

petroleum refining products; (4) basic organic chemicals; (5) artificial fibre materials; (6) iron and steel; and (7) non-ferrous primary products. Therefore, the basic intermediate goods sectors are represented by K(I-B) type technology. K(I-B) type technology is also referred to as large-quantity processing technology because the required massive investment in these areas allows drastic labour saving.

(B) Type K(I-M) technology

This is also the case where $\beta_L < 1$ and $\beta_K < 1$ in equation (5), but the value of β_L for this technology type is slightly larger than that for the previous type K(I-B). Type K(I-M) technology sectors include the following: (1) ships and ship repair; (2) motor vehicles; (3) machinery; (4) electrical machinery; (5) precision instruments; (6) fibre spinning; and (7) beverages and alcoholic drinks. Most of these sectors are machinery sectors except fibre spinning and beverage and alcoholic drinks. This K(I-M) type technology can be called large-scale assembly production technology.

(C) Type K(II) technology

Type K(II) technology is characterized by $\beta_L < 1$ and $\beta_K > 1$ in equation (5). In this case, diseconomies of scale occur in the use of capital inputs, while economies of scale prevail for labour inputs. Consequently, in these sectors, the tendency toward substitution of capital for labour through the expansion of scale production prevails as the factor-price ratio (w/r) increases and as demand expands. The substitution occurs because of the incentive for introducing labour-saving techniques in order to lower the unit cost of these products at a time when wage rates are rapidly increasing. We call this type of technology capital intensive technology.

(D) Type (L-K) technology

Type (L-K) technology is characterized by $\beta_0 < 1$ in equation (6), $X/L = \alpha_0(K/L)^{\beta_0}$. This is the classic linearly homogeneous Cobb-Douglas production function, which is often observed in pre-modern sectors, where the term "pre-modern sectors" is defined here as those small-scale industries that have divisible technology and a low capital-labour ratio, as shown in columns (1) and (2) of table 1. The group includes the agriculture sector, the mining sector, and the other traditional sectors.

(E) Type L(I) technology

Type L(I) technology is the case where $0 < \gamma_L < 1, 0 < \gamma_K < 1$, and $\gamma_L + \gamma_K > 1$, in equation (7), $X = \alpha L^{\gamma_L} K^{\gamma_K}$. This is the ordinary type of the generalized Cobb-Douglas production function with increasing returns to scale and factor substitutability. The sectors included in this type of technology are shown in table 1.

(F) Type L(II) technology

Type L(II) technology is the case where $\gamma_L > 1$ in type L(I) technology. In this case, an increase in the marginal productivity of labour seems to take place. We call L(I) and L(II) types "labour-intensive technology."

Time-series data consists of the aggregate amount of labour, capital, and gross output in each of various industries yet at the same time it contains impacts of technical change. From these we may derive another variant of the production function. Although the estimated values of β_L and β_K obtained from time series analysis were substantially less than those obtained from cross-section analysis, nevertheless we can confirm obtaining similar results from the cross-section analysis in another of our experiments.

IV. Trade patterns of intermediate goods by type of technology

Summaries of our observations of the international transactions of intermediate inputs in the bilateral input-output tables are provided in tables 2a–d. Each table represents the transactions of intermediate goods which are classified by the technological properties of the production functions. Intermediate goods are thus divided into five types; K(I-M), L, K(I-B), agriculture (Cobb-Douglas type), and energy. Table 2a represents the bilateral intermediate transactions between Japan and the United States, which are aggregated into the above five types of commodities. The first column shows the transactions of intermediate goods in Japanese industries, where the intermediate input amounts to \$1,209.8 billion (in US dollars) in 1985. Of this, \$1,083.9 billion is supplied domestically, \$17.1 billion is supplied by the United States and the rest of the world provides the remaining \$108.7 billion. In percentage terms, this is equivalent to 89.6, 1.4, and 9.0 per cent respectively (second column). On the

Table 1 **Production technology types**

(A) Large-quantity processing technology: K(I-B) type

Technology type k(I)	Sector	(1) Production function parameters β_L $L = \alpha_L \times \beta_L$	(1) Production function parameters β_K $L = \alpha_K \times \beta_K$	(2) $\left(\frac{\overline{K}}{\overline{L}}\right)j$ 1951–68 Average	Technological characteristics
K(I-B)	1 Electric power supply	0.12	0.80	17.43	(i) Measuring formula:
K(I-B)	2 Gas & water supply	0.68	0.73	2.59	$L = \alpha_L \times \beta_L$, $K = \alpha_K \times \beta_K$
K(I-B)	3 Petroleum refining products	0.27	0.65	14.76	(ii) Parameter characteristics:
K(I-B)	4 Basic organic chemicals	0.33	0.72	5.70	$\beta_L < 1$, $\beta_K < 1$
K(I-B)	5 Artificial fibre materials	0.10	0.84	3.89	(iii) Parameter value: $\beta_L = 0.2–0.3$
K(I-B)	6 Iron and steel	0.30	0.80	3.86	(iv) Capital intensity: $(\overline{K}/\overline{L})$ value is
K(I-B)	7 Nonferrous primary products	0.38	0.73	3.84	large (> 3)

(B) Large scale assembly production technology: K(I-M) type

Technology type k(I)	Sector	(1) Production function parameters β_L $L = \alpha_L \times \beta_L$	(1) Production function parameters β_K $L = \alpha_K \times \beta_K$	(2) $\left(\frac{\overline{K}}{\overline{L}}\right)j$ 1951–68 Average	Technological characteristics
K(I-M)	8 Ships & ship repairing	0.07	0.80	1.19	(i) Measuring formula:
K(I-M)	9 Motor vehicles	0.46	0.70	2.12	$L = \alpha_L \times \beta_L$, $K = \alpha_K \times \beta_K$
K(I-M)	10 Machinery	0.52	0.88	0.62	(ii) Parameter characteristics:
K(I-M)	11 Electrical machinery	0.55	0.91	1.00	$\beta_L < 1$, $\beta_K < 1$
K(I-M)	12 Precision instruments	0.53	0.97	0.59	(iii) Parameter value: $\beta_L = 0.3–0.5$
K(I-M)	13 Fibre spinning	0.26	0.59	2.07	(iv) Capital intensity: $(\overline{K}/\overline{L})$ value is
K(I-M)	14 Beverages and alcoholic drinks	0.33	0.79	2.26	median (< 3)

Table 1 **(cont.)**

(C) Capital-intensive technology: K(II) type

Technology type	Sector	(1) Production function parameters β_L $L = \alpha_L \times \beta_L$	β_K $L = \alpha_K \times \beta_K$	(2) $\left(\frac{\overline{K}}{\overline{L}}\right)j$ 1951–68 Average	Technological characteristics
K(II)	15 Paper	0.13	1.03	3.07	(i) Measuring formula: $L = \alpha_L \times \beta_L,\ K = \alpha_K \times \beta_K$
K(II)	16 Pulp	–0.29	1.23	3.94	(ii) Parameter characteristics: $\beta_L < 1,\ \beta_K > 1$
K(II)	17 Cement	0.08	1.03	9.07	(iii) Parameter value: $\beta_L < 1$
K(II)	18 Basic inorganic chemicals	0.04	1.01	2.71	(iv) Capital intensity: $(\overline{K}/\overline{L})$ value is large
K(II)	19 Chemical manure	–0.71	1.71	4.97	
K(II)	20 Miscellaneous coal products	–0.09	1.67	1.50	
K(II)	21 Tobacco	0.18	2.30	1.83	

(D) Cobb-Douglas constant (returns to scale type)

Technology type	Sector	(1) β_0 $\frac{X}{L} = \alpha_0\left(\frac{K}{L}\right)^{\beta_0}$	(2) $\left(\frac{\overline{K}}{\overline{L}}\right)j$ 1951–68 Average	Technological characteristics
(L-K)	22 Agriculture, forestry, & fisheries	0.67	0.46	(i) Measuring formula: $\frac{X}{L} = \alpha_0\left(\frac{K}{L}\right)^{\beta_0}$
(L-K)	23 Coal & lignite	0.56	0.90	(ii) Parameter characteristics: simple and symmetrical
(L-K)	24 Mining	0.64	0.56	(iii) Parameter value: $\beta_0 > 0.5$
(L-K)	25 Silk reeling & spinning	0.70	0.59	(iv) Capital intensity: $(\overline{K}/\overline{L})$ value is small (< 1)
(L-K)	26 Vegetable & animal oil & fat	0.69	1.91	
(L-K)	27 Wood milling	0.78	0.68	

Table 1 **(cont.)**

(E) Labour-intensive technology (increasing returns to scale): types L(I) and L(II)

Technology type	Sector	(1) $X=\alpha L^{\gamma_L} K^{\gamma_K}$ γ_L	γ_K	(2) $\left(\frac{\overline{K}}{\overline{L}}\right)_j$ 1951–68 Average	Technological characteristics
L(I)	28 Building & construction	0.75	0.45	0.25	(i) Measuring formula: $X = \alpha L^{\gamma_L} K^{\gamma_K}$
L(I)	29 Meat	0.44	0.61	1.52	(ii) Parameter characteristics: $\gamma_L + \gamma_K > 1$
L(I)	30 Seafood, preserved	0.90	0.48	0.59	(iii) Parameter value: $\gamma_L < 1,\ \gamma_K < 1$
L(I)	31 Transport services	0.70	0.67	1.04	(iv) Capital intensity: $(\overline{K}/\overline{L})$ value is about 1
L(I)	32 Paints	0.58	0.73	1.51	
L(I)	33 Rubber products	0.99	0.63	0.99	
L(I)	34 Glass products	0.44	0.88	1.46	
L(I)	35 Miscellaneous industrial products	0.83	0.93	0.78	
L(II)	36 Other transport equipment	1.31	0.54	1.01	(i) Measuring formula: $X = \alpha L^{\gamma_L} K^{\gamma_K}$
L(II)	37 Metal products	1.35	0.30	0.49	(ii) Parameter characteristics: $\gamma_L + \gamma_K > 1$
L(II)	38 Leather products	2.21	−0.07	0.40	(iii) Parameter value: $\gamma_L > 1,\ \gamma_K < 1$
L(II)	39 Furniture & fixtures	1.82	0.44	0.40	(iv) Capital intensity: $(\overline{K}/\overline{L})$ value is small (< 1)
L(II)	40 Other wood products	2.33	0.68	0.26	
L(II)	41 Paper articles	1.29	0.56	0.72	
L(II)	42 Pottery, china, & earthenware	1.39	0.55	0.51	
L(II)	43 Structural clay products	1.59	0.96	0.57	
L(II)	44 Other non-metallic mineral products	1.87	0.19	1.15	

Table 1 **(cont.)**

(E) Labour-intensive technology (increasing returns to scale): types L(I) and L(II)

Technology type	Sector	(1) $X = \alpha L^{\gamma_L} K^{\gamma_K}$ γ_L	γ_K	(2) $\left(\frac{\overline{K}}{L}\right)_j$ 1951–68 Average	Technological characteristics
L(II)	45 Medicine	1.20	0.80	1.25	
L(II)	46 Weaving & other fibre products	1.75	0.63	0.79	
L(II)	47 Footwear & wearing apparel	1.93	0.28	0.31	
L(II)	48 Printing and publishing	1.43	0.27	0.57	
L(II)	49 Other food, prepared	1.26	0.35	0.65	
L(II)	50 Trading	1.95	0.84	0.65	
L(II)	51 Finance & insurance	1.60	0.22	0.70	
L(II)	52 Communication services	3.38	0.08	0.17	

Source: Summaries of the results presented at the Sixth International Input-Output Techniques Conference (Ozaki, 1976).

other hand, the corresponding transaction in the United States totals \$2,882.3 billion, of which 93.1 per cent is domestic, 0.7 per cent comes from Japan and 6.2 per cent is provided by the rest of the world (fourth column). These figures show that the share (89.6 per cent) of the domestic supply in intermediate transactions in the Japanese economy is slightly smaller than that (93.1 per cent) in the US economy. This result obtains from Japan's high level of dependency (85.3 per cent) on foreign supplies of energy. Thus, excluding energy, the amount domestically supplied for intermediate goods production is 91.1 per cent, while that in the United States is 87.1 per cent. More than 90 per cent of intermediate inputs of K(I-M), L, and K(I-B) type commodities in Japan are supplied domestically while only 76.8 per cent of the K(I-M) type commodities in the United States are supplied domestically and less than 90 per cent of the K(I-B) and L types' commodities are supplied domestically. In other words, as regards K(I-M), L, and K(I-B) types' commodities, the US economy is more dependent on the rest of the world than is Japan. As concerns agricultural goods and energy, however, the Japanese economy is more dependent on foreign supply than is the United States.

As we can see from tables 2a–d, less developed economies such as South Korea, Indonesia, and Thailand largely depend upon foreign countries, especially Japan, for the supply of K(I-M) and K(I-B) type goods. Of the K(I-M) type goods, only 63.3 per cent are domestically supplied in South Korea, 78.5 per cent are domestically supplied in Thailand, and 62.2 per cent are domestically supplied in Indonesia. For K(I-B) type goods, the percentages supplied domestically are 82.6 per cent in South Korea, 61.3 per cent in Thailand, and 72.0 per cent in Indonesia. These countries are particularly dependent on Japan as a supplier of the K(I-M) and K(I-B) type commodities.

According to the transactions divided by the technological properties of commodities, we can summarize our fact-finding in the previous sections as follows:

1. There is a strong similarity of input coefficient patterns for each commodity across all countries, implying the similarity of production technologies as concerns intermediate inputs.
2. Concerning the technical interdependency of the intermediate inputs that are revealed among commodities we can observe similar linkages within industries in each country.
3. As concerns the input functions of labour and capital, each commodity has a stable technology. We can classify these technologies into K(I-M) type, K(I-B) type, and L type: K(I-M) type and K(I-

Table 2a **Transactions of intermediate goods ($100,000)**

		Japan (%)		United States (%)	
Japan	K(I-M)	700,790	(91.9)	105,633	(4.8)
	L	1,811,025	(93.9)	15,137	(0.6)
	K(I-B)	2,454,116	(91.2)	63,133	(1.3)
	Agri.	536,605	(81.4)	2,674	(0.2)
	Subtotal	5,502,536	(91.1)	186,577	(1.6)
	Energy	81,884	(13.6)	33	(0.0)
	Total	10,839,017	(89.6)	201,519	(0.7)
USA	K(I-M)	32,658	(4.3)	1,686,058	(76.8)
	L	23,309	(1.2)	2,334,578	(87.4)
	K(I-B)	40,092	(1.5)	4,457,236	(89.6)
	Agri.	31,820	(4.8)	1,413,328	(93.8)
	Subtotal	127,879	(2.1)	9,891,200	(87.1)
	Energy	6,482	(1.1)	1,683,633	(84.2)
	Total	171,785	(1.4)	26,830,678	(93.1)
ROW	K(I-M)	28,731	(3.8)	404,649	(18.4)
	L	94,111	(4.9)	321,063	(12.0)
	K(I-B)	197,883	(7.4)	455,163	(9.1)
	Agri.	90,665	(13.8)	91,093	(6.0)
	Subtotal	411,390	(6.8)	1,271,968	(11.2)
	Energy	512,845	(85.3)	315,957	(15.8)
	Total	1,087,216	(9.0)	1,790,932	(6.2)
Total	K(I-M)	762,179		2,196,340	
	L	1,928,445		2,670,778	
	K(I-B)	2,692,091		4,975,532	
	Agri.	659,090		1,507,095	
	Subtotal	6,041,805		11,349,745	
	Energy	601,211		1,999,623	
	Total	12,098,018		28,823,129	

B) type technologies are identified by their technological relationships between output scale and individual input scale. Their input functions are specified by the following relationships:

$$L = \alpha_L X^{\beta_L}, \tag{8}$$

$$K = \alpha_K X^{\beta_K}, \tag{9}$$

where β_L and β_K are dominantly estimated as $0 < \beta_L < 1.0$ and $1.0 < \beta_K$.

4. According to our international input-output tables, we can observe

Table 2b **Transactions of intermediate goods ($1,000)**

		Japan (%)		Korea (%)	
Japan	K(I-M)	188,975,795	(97.1)	1,789,289	(15.9)
	L	170,315,324	(93.5)	641,893	(3.2)
	K(I-B)	367,239,560	(93.3)	2,457,902	(6.2)
	Agri.	60,066,242	(79.9)	24,039	(0.2)
	Subtotal	786,596,921	(93.0)	4,913,123	(5.9)
	Energy	8,203,450	(13.4)	32,209	(0.4)
	Total	1,401,356,361	(91.5)	5,616,072	(4.5)
Korea	K(I-M)	308,955	(0.2)	7,134,972	(63.3)
	L	483,566	(0.3)	17,168,255	(86.6)
	K(I-B)	1,224,996	(0.3)	32,763,535	(82.6)
	Agri.	359,865	(0.5)	10,568,149	(80.5)
	Subtotal	2,377,382	(0.3)	67,634,911	(80.6)
	Energy	37,479	(0.1)	1,454,574	(16.2)
	Total	2,886,178	(0.2)	100,253,984	(79.5)
ROW	K(I-M)	5,400,678	(2.8)	2,356,219	(20.9)
	L	11,428,210	(6.3)	2,006,232	(10.1)
	K(I-B)	25,022,911	(6.4)	4,430,719	(11.2)
	Agri.	14,789,367	(19.7)	2,538,802	(19.3)
	Subtotal	56,641,166	(6.7)	11,331,972	(13.5)
	Energy	52,925,191	(86.5)	7,473,351	(83.4)
	Total	127,410,550	(8.3)	20,246,166	(16.1)
Total	K(I-M)	194,685,428		11,280,480	
	L	182,227,100		19,816,380	
	K(I-B)	393,487,467		39,652,156	
	Agri.	75,215,474		13,130,990	
	Subtotal	845,615,469		83,880,006	
	Energy	61,166,120		8,960,134	
	Total	1,531,653,089		126,116,222	

the international interdependency in the intermediate transactions among countries. In spite of the similarity of the technological input coefficients, a_{ij}, each country has a different structure as concerns the shares of imported commodities in intermediate transactions, which are observed by the differences in the scale of the coefficients, a_{ij}^{d} and a_{ij}^{m}. These differences largely depend upon the domestic production structure of the country, which might be attributable to differences in factor endowment and in the scale of demand in the domestic market by countries.

5. Import coefficients, a_{ij}^{m} can be broken down by country of origin. Our bilateral international input-output tables represent the struc-

Table 2c **Transactions of intermediate goods ($1,000)**

		Japan (%)		Indonesia (%)	
Japan	K(I-M)	181,938,550	(97.2)	586,531	(12.3)
	L	199,908,107	(94.2)	99,972	(1.5)
	K(I-B)	337,758,893	(92.9)	996,026	(7.9)
	Agri.	60,053,187	(79.8)	404	(0.0)
	Subtotal	779,658,737	(93.0)	1,682,933	(4.4)
	Energy	8,202,241	(13.5)	2,990	(0.0)
	Total	1,312,933,828	(91.1)	1,810,004	(3.0)
Indonesia	K(I-M)	393	(0.0)	2,975,856	(62.2)
	L	249,689	(0.1)	6,239,356	(92.2)
	K(I-B)	1,078,135	(0.3)	9,050,277	(72.0)
	Agri.	246,505	(0.3)	13,144,143	(95.5)
	Subtotal	1,574,722	(0.2)	31,409,632	(82.9)
	Energy	7,499,274	(12.4)	5,976,026	(85.3)
	Total	9,375,495	(0.7)	52,721,332	(86.0)
ROW	K(I-M)	5,186,131	(2.8)	1,222,481	(25.5)
	L	12,009,284	(5.7)	425,335	(6.3)
	K(I-B)	24,606,635	(6.8)	2,530,192	(20.1)
	Agri.	14,928,937	(19.8)	623,072	(4.5)
	Subtotal	56,730,987	(6.8)	4,801,080	(12.7)
	Energy	44,884,281	(74.1)	1,029,546	(14.7)
	Total	119,042,233	(8.3)	6,804,198	(11.1)
Total	K(I-M)	187,125,074		4,784,868	
	L	212,167,080		6,764,663	
	K(I-B)	363,443,663		12,576,495	
	Agri.	75,228,629		13,767,619	
	Subtotal	837,964,446		37,893,645	
	Energy	60,585,796		7,008,562	
	Total	1,441,351,556		61,335,534	

tures of interdependency among the corresponding countries and the rest of the world.

V. A tentative approach toward the model of technology choice

In section 2, we observed the technological properties of the intermediate input structure of each bilateral input-output table and the characteristics of the bilateral international linkages of the intermediate inputs through the import transactions. In section 3, we outlined the properties of the production functions estimated from Jap-

Table 2d **Transactions of intermediate goods ($1,000)**

		Japan (%)		Thailand (%)	
Japan	K(I-M)	125,915,790	(97.5)	145,295	(9.0)
	L	227,795,458	(93.8)	119,642	(1.5)
	K(I-B)	368,759,616	(93.3)	5,021,141	(6.5)
	Agri.	57,167,149	(80.5)	5,981	(0.1)
	Subtotal	779,638,013	(93.0)	773,059	(3.3)
	Energy	8,202,283	(13.4)	1,796	(0.1)
	Total	1,305,960,260	(91.0)	945,783	(2.6)
	K(I-M)	3,241	(0.0)	1,261,533	(78.5)
Thailand	L	296,089	(0.1)	6,900,698	(88.7)
	K(I-B)	361,372	(0.1)	4,732,964	(61.3)
	Agri.	122,583	(0.2)	5,448,533	(93.5)
	Subtotal	783,285	(0.1)	18,343,728	(79.4)
	Energy	11,788	(0.0)	1,373,769	(48.5)
	Total	834,092	(0.1)	296,124,650	(82.0)
	K(I-M)	3,217,043	(2.5)	200,975	(12.5)
ROW	L	14,709,266	(6.1)	936,712	(11.8)
	K(I-B)	26,210,620	(6.6)	2,480,043	(32.1)
	Agri.	13,688,571	(19.3)	370,197	(6.4)
	Subtotal	57,825,500	(6.9)	3,987,927	(17.3)
	Energy	52,958,192	(86.6)	1,458,514	(51.4)
	Total	128,220,998	(8.9)	5,576,108	(15.4)
	K(I-M)	129,136,074		1,607,803	
Total	L	242,800,813		7,957,052	
	K(I-B)	395,331,608		7,715,148	
	Agri.	70,978,303		5,824,711	
	Subtotal	838,246,798		23,104,714	
	Energy	61,172,263		2,834,079	
	Total	1,435,015,350		36,134,351	

anese time-series data. In the previous section we try to understand our observation of international trade patterns from the viewpoint of the technogical properties estimated in section 3.

Finally, the purpose of this section is to propose a tentative analytical framework under which we can describe the differences in industrial structure among countries consistent with the above facts. The similarity of intermediate input coefficients, a_{ij}, which are confirmed by observation, reinforces our assumption that technological structures as concerns intermediate inputs are the same across countries. On the other hand, labour and capital inputs as concerns primary inputs for commodities classified into K(I-M) and K(I-B) are dependent upon the scale of output, while those for commodities classified into L types are characterized by constant returns to scale. As mentioned in tables 2a through 2d, commodities classified into the K(I-M) and K(I-B) type technologies are mostly supplied by developed countries such as the United States and Japan. Although these commodities are also produced in South Korea and other less developed countries such as Indonesia and Thailand, the scale of production in these latter countries is relatively smaller than that in the developed countries. On the other hand, such commodities produced by L type technology could be produced in any country on any scale, because of the technological properties of constant returns to scale.

When it comes to explaining the determination of the scale in K(I-M) and K(I-B) type technology in each country, we have to introduce another hypothesis concerning the producer's behaviour. Hence, the production scale for K(I-M) and K(I-B) type commodities is determined by minimization of unit cost by producers as follows.

By definition the unit cost of the factor inputs, labour and capital, is given by

$$\frac{C}{X} = \frac{Lw + Kr}{X}, \tag{10}$$

where C and X represent total cost and output scale, L and K, and w and r stand for labour and capital inputs and their prices respectively.

Minimizing the unit cost subject to the input functions (8) and (9), we can deduce the following unit cost minimizing scale of production assuming that w and r are given exogenously:

$$X_0 = \left[\frac{\alpha_L(1-\beta_L)}{\alpha_K(\beta_K-1)}\right]^{1/(\beta_K-\beta_L)} \left[\frac{w}{r}\right]^{1/(\beta_K-\beta_L)}. \tag{11}$$

The unit cost function can be derived as follows:

$$\frac{C}{X} = c = \alpha_L X_0^{\beta_L-1} w + \alpha_K X_0^{\beta_K-1} r,$$

$$= w^{\delta} r^{1-\delta} A, \tag{12}$$

where

$$\delta = \frac{\beta_K - 1}{\beta_K - \beta_L},$$

$$A = \alpha_L a^{\beta_L - 1} + \alpha_K a^{\beta_K - 1},$$

$$a = \left[\frac{\alpha_L(1-\beta_L)}{\alpha_K(\beta_K - 1)}\right]^{1/(\beta_K - \beta_L)}.$$

Given factor prices in each country at a certain period, we can derive the unit cost and the output scale from minimizing the unit cost given in equations (10) and (12). We can also derive the contour of the unit cost function, which is estimated from the parameters of input functions and the given factor prices. Figure 2 represents the model of the contour of the unit cost function, which corresponds to two sets of parameters of input functions. The vertical axis and horizontal axis stand for the factor price of labour (wages), and the factor price of capital (unit capital cost), respectively. Lines A-A and B-B represent two contour sets, which correspond to two different sets of technology parameters. As concerns parameters, both β_L and β_K in line A-A are larger than those in line B-B. Line B-B, the slope of which is relatively steeper than that of line A-A, is expected to correspond to the large scale output technology. We assume that the wage level of country X (the developed country) is observed at the level w_X and that of country Y (the less developed country) is observed at the level w_Y. As concerns the production of commodity B, where the contour of the unit cost in the developed country is depicted by the line B-B, if the unit capital cost of country Y is higher than the level of r_B^*, the unit cost of production in country Y is expected to be higher than that in country X. This implies that the unit capital cost of country Y has to be lower than the level of r_B^*, if country Y wants to produce the commodity B at the competitive level of cost in the market. On the other hand, as concerns commodity A, the level of the unit capital cost at which the production cost of commodity A in the country Y is comparable to that in country X has to be lower than the level of r_B^{**}, which is higher than the level of r_B^*.

Moreover, this analysis implies that the underdeveloped country will probably be competitive in commodity A rather than commodity B, if the conditions of competition are equal in countries X and Y. Production technologies are assumed to be the same across countries. For cases in which the domestic supply of K(I-M) and K(I-B) type commodities are relatively small, the unit capital cost will probably be higher than that in the developed countries. Hence, these countries will not have any competitiveness in markets for K-type products (investment goods). Even if the level of unit labour cost is low

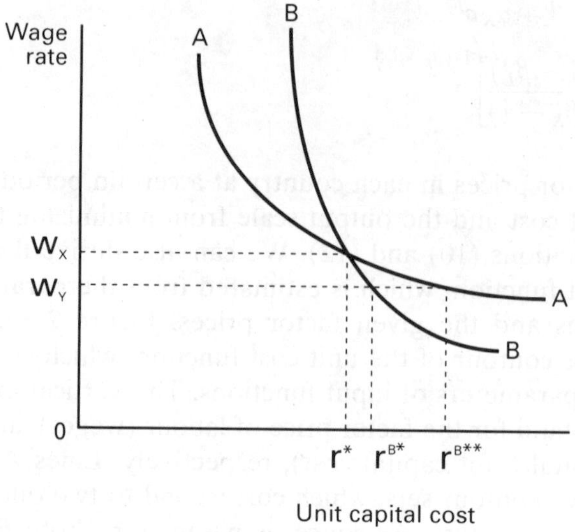

Fig. 2 **Contour of unit cost**

enough to offset the relatively higher level of the unit capital cost, so that the unit cost of production is competitive, the scale of output in the underdeveloped countries will be smaller than that of the developed countries. This theoretical framework thus helps to explain the observations both of relatively smaller production of K(I-M) and K(I-B) type commodities in less developed countries and of their relatively greater production of L-type commodities.

This analytical framework cannot yet be directly tested. To do so would require time-series data about the distribution of factor prices across countries.

V. Conclusion

In this paper we examined and attempted to explain the differences in the industrial structures and the trade patterns of developing and developed countries. Analysis was based on the observation contained in the international input-output tables as well as the estimation of the input functions for production technologies. These production technologies together with the characteristics of factor markets in each country generated the observed differences in the industrial structures and trade patterns. We can summarize our results as follows:

1. According to observations from the international input-output

tables, enormous differences exist in the trade patterns amongst countries, especially in cases of trade between developing countries and trade between developed and developing countries. For intermediate goods, developing countries are characterized by their high import dependency on developed countries, while light manufacturing commodities, which are produced by traditional sectors, are generally provided domestically. On the other hand, trade between developed countries is characterized by bilateral transactions of high technology commodities.

2. Input coefficients patterns for each commodity as shown by the intermediate input structure is similar across countries. In addition, the technological interdependency of intermediate inputs, as revealed by the unit structure of each commodity, shows a similar linkage among industries regardless of country. These facts suggest that production technologies do not vary by country.

3. As concerns input functions of labour and capital, we determined stable input properties for each commodity. Technologies are divided into six types according to the relationships between output scale and input scale. K(I-M) and K(I-B) type technologies characterize capital intensive commodities such as investment goods including machinery and steel. The input functions for these types of commodities are subject to scale effects and can be specified by factor limitational functions. On the other hand, commodities produced with L-type technology are characterized by constant returns to scale and a Cobb-Douglas-type production function.

4. We can explain differences in trade patterns and industrial structures by consolidating these findings about input technologies into a theoretical framework. Production under K-type technology is dominated by relative factor prices. Different levels of factor prices will lead to different levels of output as determined by the minimization of unit cost. Developing countries are less likely to produce commodities involving K-type technology since unit costs in these countries are likely to be higher given their relatively higher capital costs. Even if the lower wages in developing countries are enough to offset this disadvantage, the optimal scale of production of such commodities in developing countries will necessarily be on a relatively small scale.

Although this analysis provides an explanation for the trade patterns revealed by the international input-output tables, sufficient data are not available to test the model outlined here. Consequently, this model remains tentative.

Note

1. KEIO, together with MITI and IDE, has been constructing international input-output tables since 1986. This paper is a joint work with other members of Keio Economic Observatory, Yoshio Akabayashi, Ayu Ikeda and Takeshi Ōtsu. The authors also are highly appreciative of valuable comments from James E. Vestal, Keio University.
   This study was financially supported by the Matsushita International Foundation.

References

Ozaki Iwao. 1976. "The Effects of Technological Changes on the Economic Growth of Japan, 1955–1970." In: Karen R. Polenske and Jiri V. Skolka, eds. *Advances in Input-Output Analysis*. Ballinger Publishing Company.

—— 1983. "Impact of Energy Costs on Industrial Activity." In: *Energy and Structural Change in the Asia-Pacific Region*. Philippine Institute for Development Studies and Asian Development Bank.

Ozaki Iwao, and Shimizu Masahiko. 1984. Technological Change and the Pattern of Economic Development. In Proceedings of the Seventh International Conference on Input-Output Techniques, United Nations.

Dale W. Jorgenson and Kuroda Masahiro. 1992. "Productivity and International Competitiveness in Japan and the United States, 1960–85." In: Bert G. Hickman, ed. *International Productivity and Competitiveness*. Oxford University Press.

Comments on chapters 6 and 7

1. Clopper Almon

The papers presented in this session offer some interesting results and embody an enormous effort in the collection of data. I have neither space nor competence to comment on all of the issues raised but must limit myself to one: the accounting scheme used as the basis for the models. More precisely, I wish to compare this accounting scheme (a) with the one used by the model described at this conference in the Duchin-Smyshlyaev paper and (b) with that aspired to in the Inforum international system. I shall argue that the scheme used in the present papers places an unnecessary burden of "creative statistics" on the authors while that of the Duchin-Smyshlyaev paper does not use some highly relevant and fairly easily available data. The alternative is a "golden mean" treatment which uses all the relevant data but avoids the burden of data manufacture.

The papers of this session use what I shall call "maxi" accounting, because its construction requires the maximum amount of information. Although all of the papers use only two countries, the full implications of this approach are more clearly seen when it is extended to the case of three countries. I shall, therefore, show all three methods for the three-country case. For this case, the maxi system may be summarized in the following social accounting matrix.

$$
\begin{array}{ccc}
\left[\begin{array}{ccc} A_{11} & A_{12} & A_{13} \\ A_{21} & A_{22} & A_{23} \\ A_{31} & A_{32} & A_{33} \end{array}\right] & \left[\begin{array}{ccc} f_1 & & \\ & f_2 & \\ & & f_3 \end{array}\right] \\
\begin{array}{ccc} V_1 & & \\ & V_2 & \\ & & V_3 \end{array} &
\end{array}
$$

Here A_{ij} denotes a flow matrix of products produced in country i and consumed in country j, while f_1 represents the vector of final consumption in country i and v_j represents the (row) vector of value added by each industry in country j. As usual in social accounting matrices, the equations are obtained by requiring that the sum of each column should equal the sum of the corresponding row.

Now the first thing to be noted about this accounting system is that there is no necessity that the sectoring plan of the different countries should be the same or even have the same number of industries. The diagonal matrices in the above social accounting matrix will, of course, be square, but there is, as far as I can see, no reason whatsoever that the off-diagonal matrices should be square. I emphasize this point because the authors of the papers have gone to some pains to make definitionally comparable tables for the pairs of countries involved in their models. One of their computations, however, requires this comparability. Of course, one may want to compare input-output coefficients for other reasons, but it is not necessary to do so for the logical soundness of this approach. This point is also relevant to the authors' stated intention of going beyond two-country studies. So far they have made a number of studies of Japan and one other country. In each case, they appear to have devised a comparable sectoring plan for the two countries in the model. If they proceed to using the approach for a number of countries all in the same social accounting matrix, they should keep firmly in mind that there is no logical necessity for having the same sectoring plan in the different countries.

On the other hand, the data requirements for this approach are heavy, even without comparability. One must ascertain how much each product produced in country 1 is used by each industry in country 2. There are no official statistics collected on these flows. In some cases, special studies have been conducted by MITI to ascertain, say, the US industries to which Japanese steel is sold. In most cases, however, one suspects that it must have been necessary to do a lot of pro-rating in making up the off diagonal A_{ij} matrices. In short, this scheme goes well beyond regularly collected data and must rely on a substantial amount of "creative statistics".

The accounting scheme used in the Duchin-Smyshlyaev paper, by contrast, may be called the "mini" scheme because it requires the minimal amount of information. It would look like the following:

$$
\begin{array}{lllllll}
A_{11} & & & X_1 & f_1 & & \\
 & A_{22} & & X_2 & & f_2 & \\
 & & A_{33} & X_3 & & & f_3 \\
M_1 & M_2 & M_3 & & & & \\
V_1 & & & & & & \\
 & V_2 & & & & & \\
 & & V_3 & & & &
\end{array}
$$

Here the Ms are matrices of imports. Their rows must be in an "international" classification comparable across countries, but the columns need not be the same in different countries, just as the A matrices need not even have the same dimensions for different countries. The X_i matrix shows the exports of country i; its rows are in the classification of country i while its columns are in the same "international" classification used for the rows of the Ms.

Here the data problems will be principally in making up the Ms and Xs. Currently, most countries are collecting export and import information in the "harmonized" system, which would naturally form the basis of the "international" classification mentioned above. The problem, therefore, is in converting data from this "harmonized" system to the domestic classification. But, since the data are actually collected in the harmonized system, that problem must somehow be solved by the makers of the domestic input-output table, who must have, therefore, implicitly made the necessary M and X matrices. In the United States, the making of these matrices through "concordances" is a subject of considerable interest and some debate at the moment. Nevertheless, these matrices can be regarded as fairly well known.

This "mini" scheme, therefore, lives well within knowable data. Indeed, its problem is that it lives too far within those limits. For when the accounting scheme is converted into a model, it will imply that Italy's clothing exports will be affected just as much by an increase in clothing imports by the United States as they would by the same increase in German imports of clothing. Why? Because the accounting scheme has ignored all of the extensive data on bilateral trade. We know that a much larger fraction of German than of US clothing imports comes from Italy, but that fact cannot be reflected in the "mini" scheme.

That problem leads to the "midi" scheme. Its social accounting matrix looks like this:

$$\begin{bmatrix} A_{11} & & \\ & A_{22} & \\ & & A_{33} \end{bmatrix} \begin{bmatrix} 0 & X_{12} & X_{13} \\ X_{21} & 0 & X_{23} \\ X_{31} & X_{32} & 0 \end{bmatrix} \begin{bmatrix} f_1 & & \\ & f_2 & \\ & & f_3 \end{bmatrix}$$

$$\begin{bmatrix} M_1 & & \\ & M_2 & \\ & & M_3 \end{bmatrix}$$

$$\begin{bmatrix} v_1 & & \\ & v_2 & \\ & & v_3 \end{bmatrix}$$

This scheme is almost as well within the limits of collected statistics as is the "mini" scheme. It simply adds the data on the destinations of the exports of each product. (I say "almost as well within" because of the well-known differences between "the imports of *X* by country *A* from country *B*" and "the exports of *X* by country *B* to country *A*.") In this scheme, an increase of clothing imports by Germany will affect the Italian clothing industry more than would the same volume increase by the United States.

Now I must confess a strong preference for modelling using this midi scheme. Why? The mini scheme simply disregards too much relevant data, that is, in principle, available. Namely, it pays no attention to bilateral trade flows. The maxi scheme forces us into the manufacture of data on slim evidence. The midi scheme not only uses all the data we generally have; it also makes evident the major relations to be modelled. These relations are the shares of different suppliers in the imports of a given country (seen by comparing each *M* matrix with the *A* matrix above it. The maxi scheme compounds these two relations into one, thereby making modelling more difficult. Thus, changes in the A_{12} matrix can come about both by changes in the import-to-domestic-purchase ratio in country 2 (on which there is data) and by changes in the share of country 1 in country 2's imports (on which there is also data). These two observable components are visible separately in the midi system but not in the maxi system. Since we are working with available data, we may as well work at a fairly high level of detail in the industry definitions. For Japan, rice is quite clearly a special commodity to say the least, and could easily be given its own sector. If it and a few other similarly special products were so treated, it appears to me that all of these interesting examples could be handled satisfactorily by the "midi" system.

In the Inforum international system, we would have liked to have used the midi system. In fact, however, the cost of data from the United Nations and the OECD has been extremely high. We have, therefore, had to make do with relations which used this full bilateral information for only one year. We hope that new arrangements can be made to make the required data available to researchers at affordable costs. If that is possible, we will move to linking our models with a full system of bilateral trade flows based on the midi accounting scheme.

2. Faye Duchin

These papers are products of the ambitious and important World Input-Output Table project that is being carried out jointly by MITI (Ministry of International Trade and Industry), Keio University, and the Institute for Developing Economies (IDE). The aim of the project is to build and use compatible input-output (IO) tables, starting wherever possible from existing tables. The intention is presumably to cover all or most of the national economies, or at least Japan's trade partners, and study the effects on one economy of economic activities taking place in another. The empirical results reported in these papers about the interdependence of Japan and the US economy, on the one hand, and Japan and the developing economies of the Asia-Pacific region, on the other, will be of great interest quite apart from the methodological issues raised below.

The analysis of interdependence offers considerably more insight into economic relationships than does the more common approach of a comparative study, and the kind of work reported in these papers will take on increasing importance in the analysis of global problems such as environmental pollution. For this reason, I have chosen to pay particular attention to the most important unresolved methodological issues that are raised directly or indirectly in these papers.

Documenting the problem encountered in producing compatible input-output tables

A number of operations were necessary to render detailed tables of different countries compatible; apparently the most time-consuming part of this effort consisted of converting an existing table to the common classification scheme. Since this has by now been done at least a dozen times, the team has acquired considerable experience as to where the greatest discrepancies among existing classification schemes lie, the reasons for them, and how to reconcile them. Some of the most important outcomes of the present exercise should be a set of guidelines for other researchers attempting to reconcile existing tables and a set of guidelines for avoiding at least some of these discrepancies in the first place. Providing these guidelines make sense from a scientific point of view, so others can build upon, rather than replicating, what has already been done, as well as from the practical point of view of improving the standards established by the international statistical community.

Comparative advantage and homogeneous commodities

Many countries decompose the inter-industry portion of their input-output tables into two tables: one shows the domestically-produced inputs and the other, the imported inputs. For those countries that do not (like the United States), the study team has estimated the import table. The rationale for creating two tables is that, even at the finest levels of disaggregation, an imported item appears to have a different distribution among using sectors than does the similar, domestically produced item. Researchers who have compared domestic input tables and import tables for various countries have come to the conclusion that there are decidedly different distributions of imported and domestically produced versions of most items (at a 46-sector level of detail) in the US and Japan.

This body of empirical results is consistent with one of two theoretical explanations: (1) even physically identical items are distinguished by users according to their place of production; (2) no matter how finely one disaggregates a sector, it will produce a mix of products such that domestic producers will specialize in one subset of products while imports will be concentrated in another subset. The conviction that one or both of these propositions are true provides a justification for models of international trade that do not rely on comparative advantage (see, in particular, Armington 1969).

None of the world models in use today incorporates a general theory of international exchange based on comparative advantage. One reason for this is that the theoretical work on comparative advantage has been limited to the case, of limited use in empirical analysis, of two countries and two commodities. (A paper by Milberg [1992] describes why economists generally have the mistaken impression that a multi-country, multi-commodity problem has been resolved by theorists.) However, if either of the propositions listed above is true, there *can* be no general theory of comparative advantage, or at least no empirically operational theory, because it would not be possible to define a sector such that different producers compete on the basis of their respective costs of production of the homogeneous output of this sector. The authors of one paper under review fail to appreciate the implications of the work reported in the other when they make the familiar claim: "When a country enters in the world market, production will be specialized on the activities with comparative advantage" (Sano et al. ch. 6 above). If trade were based essentially on comparative advantage, as this statement implies, there would be no need to distinguish inputs by their place of production – and no need for import tables – provided the classification scheme was sufficiently disaggregated.

I believe that the resolution of this quandary requires more empirical work. Before we draw the conclusion that comparative advantage has only limited explanatory power, here is an important experiment that needs to be carried out. Perhaps the distributions of imported and domestically produced goods appear different because the data are prepared using classification schemes that group together items with similar input structures but impose no constraints about commonality of attributes (like substitutability or complementarity) in use. In Japan, on the other hand, three-fourths of domestically produced electronic equipment is delivered to final users while only 60–65 per cent of its imports are (table 3). Japanese production, whether for domestic use or for export, appears to emphasize consumer electronics relative to US production.

It would be interesting to see the distributions in both countries, of intermediate use and final use of domestically produced and of imported items, if the classification scheme distinguished two sectors, industrial electronics and consumer electronics, instead of just one.

The creators of industrial classification schemes are well aware of the conceptual distinction between a classification based on input structure and one based on use; see, for example, Triplett (1990) or McGuckin (1991). However, I have never yet seen an empirical assessment of the importance of this conceptual distinction. What is needed is a classification scheme that explicitly groups by commonality of both input structure and use, and a comparison of the domestic and the import tables based on input-output tables built using this classification.

Distinguishing quantities and prices

The authors have "linked" the tables for different economies by matching up, for example, Japan's imports of petroleum from Indonesia (reported in the Japanese table) with Indonesia's exports of petroleum to Japan (reported in the Indonesian table), and Indonesia's imports of automobiles from Japan (in the Indonesian table) with Japan's exports of automobiles to Indonesia (in the Japanese table). This linkage was accomplished by valuing all reported flows in a common currency, US dollars, using official exchange rates for the conversions from yen and rupiahs, respectively. International freight and insurance premiums and domestic freight and trade margins were explicitly taken into account to ensure that the flows reported in both directions are measuring the same thing. In cases where the value of the flow as reported in one direction still did not equal the value of the same flow as reported in the other direction "some adjustments were made to balance the bilateral table" (Sano et al. ch. 6 above).

The problem is that, especially in the case of trading partners at different stages of development, relative prices even of traded goods are significantly different because of duties, taxes, and subsidies; petroleum and automobiles in Japan and Indonesia are excellent examples. One needs to account directly for these duties, taxes, and subsidies, but no details are reported in these papers about how the "balancing" was done. This accounting needs to be accomplished by incorporating additional information: either by estimating these charged directly or by utilizing exogenous, sector-specific "purchasing power parities", rather than exchange rates against the dollar, to convert the tables to a common currency. There are, in turn, different ways to estimate purchasing power parities. A new way is proposed by this reviewer: associating a *standard physical unit* with each sector included in the industrial classification scheme (for example, petroleum would be measured in BTUs and automobiles in a number of units). Then each national Statistical Office (or, in this case, the team building the compatible tables) would be expected to report not only the value of sectoral output but also the average unit price (or, alternatively, the physical volume of output). Purchasing power parities would be computed as the ratios of the price vectors in different countries. There are many conceptual and practical problems that need to be resolved if we choose to proceed in this way, but the advantages of systematically distinguishing prices and quantities in economic databases will be enormous; these advantages include basing the "linkage" of trade flows on the physical quantities transferred. There is no national Statistical Office better placed to take the initiative in this regard than that of Japan.

The role of trade in development

The paper by Sano et al. concludes that the developing countries of the Asia-Pacific region have achieved remarkable growth through their trade with Japan. While trade has surely been important, the analysis ignores the roles played by the growth of domestic markets, especially in the larger countries like Indonesia, and the importance of investment and the acquisition of new technologies. It also fails to mention the problems associated with this remarkable growth, like water pollution and the clearing of forests, or the barriers faced by these countries in their attempts to export processed goods instead of raw materials to Japan and other developed economies. All of these issues will have to be addressed by the community involved in modelling the world economy as we refine our models and databases for analysis intended to deepen our understanding of the major global problems of our time. These two papers have demonstrated the feasibility of undertaking the magnitude of data work that will be required and have also exhibited the kind of empirical analysis that will then be possible.

References

Armington, Paul S. 1969. "A Theory of Demand for Products Distinguished by Place of Production." *International Monetary Fund Staff Papers*, 159–173.

McGuckin, Robert H. 1991. "Multiple Classification Systems for Economic Data: Can a Thousand Flowers Bloom? And Should They?". *1991 International Conference on the Classification of Economic Activity.* U.S. Bureau of the Census.

Milberg, Will. 1992. Toward a Generalized Ricardian Trade Model. Working Paper, New School for Social Research, New York, NY.
Triplett, Jack. 1990. The Theory of Industrial and Occupational Classification and Related Phenomena. Presented at the March 1990 Census Annual Research Conference of the U.S. Bureau of the Census.

3. Wassily Leontief

In contrast to the partial equilibrium approach in which the conventional concept of "elasticity of substitution" involves treatment of prices as independent variables, in the general equilibrium formulation of input-output analysis all prices are treated as dependent and only the wage rates and the rate of return on capital are treated as independent variables. Thus, incidentally, this allows taking implicitly into account the interdependence between the technological choices made in the different sectors of the economy.

Input-output methodology provides a convenient conceptual framework for empirical analysis of the important relationship between the rate of interest, i.e., the rate of return on capital, investment, and technological changes.

The state of technology, i.e., the methods of production, used at any given time in a sector (industry i) of a multi-sectoral economy can be concisely described by set of input coefficient $a_{1i}, a_{2i} \ldots a_{ji} \ldots a_{ni}$ where a_{ji} represents the number of units of goods or a service j used, say per year, to produce one unit of good i and by a corresponding set of capital coefficients, $b_{1i} \ldots b_{2i} \ldots b_{ji} \ldots b_{ni}$, where b_{ji} represents the stock of good j (for example, of a particular type of machines or building structures) required for production of one unit of good i per year.

It has to be noted that in this terminology substitution of any specific kind of input by another is called technological change. A typical classical production function describing all different input combinations that can be used to produce one unit of a particular good i would have to be represented by a set of many alternative vectors of flow and capital coefficients.

The input-output terminology is, incidentally, much closer to that actually used by engineers and managers practically engaged in the process of production than that used in economics textbooks.

Let $P_1, P_2 \ldots P_n$ be the vector of prices of all goods, $1_{1i} \ldots 1_{2i} \ldots 1_{ki}$, the vector of labour input-output coefficients for k different type of labour; t_i the dollar amount of taxes paid or subsidies (received or paid per unit of output of industry i), many $W_{1i} \ldots W_{2i} \ldots W_{ki}$ wage rates per unit of labour of different kinds and r, the rate of return on capital invested in various industries.

The following equation describes the relationship between the price P_i of one unit of good i and its total costs of production.

$$P_i = \sum_{j=1}^{n}(a_{ji}p_j) - r\sum_{j=1}^{n}(B_{ji}P_j) - 1_i w_i - t_i. \tag{1}$$

With wage rates and taxes considered as given the following matrix equation can be solved for the unknown prices of all goods

$$l - A' - \hat{r}B')P - V = 0, \tag{2}$$

where each element $(V_i = 1_i w_i + t_i)$ of the column vector V represents the wages and taxes paid out (per unit of its output) by each sector.

For any given rate of return on capital r, and a given set of money wage rates, $\bar{w}$, this system can be used to compute all the prices (p). The prices of consumer goods can then be used to compute a corresponding cost of living index. Dividing the given monetary wage rate by this index, we can compute the corresponding index of the level of real wage rates, say, $\bar{w}$.

Thus, with the state of technology concisely described by the flow and capital matrices, A and B, one can compute a corresponding functional relationship between the rate of return on capital r, and the level of real wages, $\bar{w}$. The higher is the return on capital the real wage rate, of course, must be lower; the higher the wage rate, the lower the corresponding rate of return on capital. A change even in a single a or b coefficient is bound to affect indirectly the prices of all commodities and consequently, the cost of production in all sectors. The choice of technology in one sector is consequently bound to be affected, to some extent, by choices made in other sectors.

On the attached graph, each of the two sloping curves presents all possible combinations of the rate of return on capital r, and the corresponding level of real wages, w attainable with the use of one particular combination of sectoral technologies.

Curve i–i describes, for instance, all the alternative combinations of r and w attainable with given A_1 and B_1. Thus, if the rate of return is 3 per cent the level of real wages is 100. Curve q–q describes on the other hand what combination of r and w would be attainable if all sectors of the economy were employing technologies described by A_q and B_q.

Shifting from point *b* to point *c* would permit a rise in the rate of return on capital from 3 per cent to 4 per cent without any reduction in real wages; a shift from point *b* to point *d* would permit a rise in real wage rate from 120 to 140 without any reduction in the rate of return on capital.

In general a shift from point *b* on curve i–i to any point (technology, A_iB_i) was on point *e* a shift to curve q–q, (i.e., technology A_iB_i) would be clearly not advisable.

Empirical input-output computations of this kind were performed to analyse the choice between "old" and "new" technology in the American economy.

Far from neglecting the possibility of substitution of one method of production for another, the input-output approach provides the sole theoretical basis for empirical analysis of substitution of one combination of inputs for another.

4. Byung-Nak Song

The papers provide very sensible interpretations of economic interdependence and trade patterns among various countries. They are

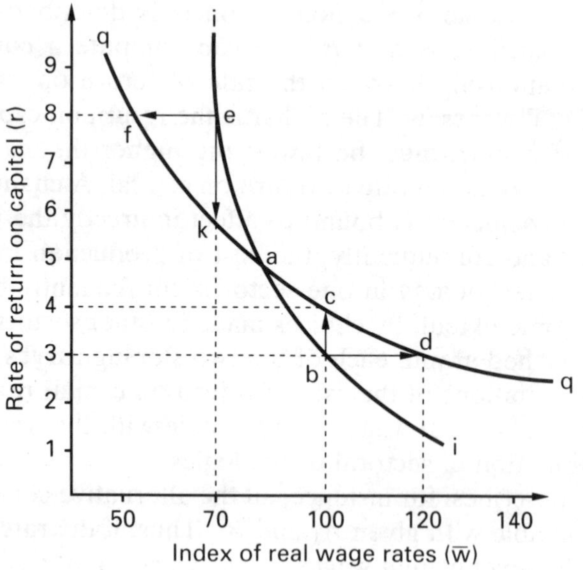

Fig. 1 **All possible combinations of capital return rate and real wages level**

based on an extensive analysis of international inter-industry relations using input-output tables of various countries.

I would like to address my remarks largely to more general issues with regard to the bilateral input-output (IO) relations in the East Asian region, rather than to technical aspects of the papers. The studies that are referred to in this volume were conducted by the research teams of famous institutions in Japan, namely, IDE (Institute of Developing Economies) and Keio University. Both did a remarkable job in analysing extensive amounts of statistical data. I am in agreement with most of their views and findings. However, in the manner of emphasis and of suggesting additional ideas, I would like to touch on some of the findings.

The paper by the Keio team (Iwao Ozaki, Masahiro Kuroda, and Masahiko Shimizu) uses the international IO tables developed by MITI and IDE "to explain the differences in the industrial structures and trade patterns between developing and developed countries." It also examines these structures in relation to production technologies. Their findings sound very sensible. However, there is one point that is not clear to me. The paper indicates that production technologies, as indicated by input-output coefficients, do not vary by country. This is the point that has already been confirmed by Hollis Chenery, myself, and others. But they also state that "the optimal scale of production of such commodities (involving capital-intensive technologies) in developing countries necessarily will be on a relatively small scale." I wonder whether the optimal scale of production of capital intensive commodities also does not vary by country.

As to the IDE paper, I understand that the team also undertook special surveys in Thailand and Indonesia, to supplement the existing data set. In Korea my colleagues and myself attempted some time ago this kind of bilateral IO study for the East Asian region, but because of the time and budget constraints, we were unable to complete it. In this regard, I would like to praise them for their enormous efforts. I think the UN University is in an excellent position to encourage this kind of study. I have personally been looking forward to seeing the results of the bilateral IO study by the IDE team.

I am familiar with the IDE study because I have been involved in this study in the past, and agree with many of their findings. But as my role as a commentator is to criticize, I have three comments to make on the IDE paper. My first comment is concerned with sectoral classification. For this kind of study examining countries at different stages of development, sectoral classification appears to be very important. Takao Sano and other IDE researchers use the 17-sector classification. This classification looks very meaningful in that it starts from developing country sectors such as agriculture, petroleum, and other primary commodities. Then, it moves on to NIC factors such as textiles, chemicals, and other manufacturing industries. Lastly it covers advanced country sectors such as machinery, metals, etc.

But from the point of view of the Korean economy, I think that the advanced country sectors may need reclassification, especially for the Japan-Korea bilateral analysis. We might need sectors such as electronic industries, automobiles, computers, etc., which become increasingly important in the case of Korea. Because of the rapid growth of these industries, Korea's dependence on Japan increases rapidly. Korean industries need to import an increasing amount of capital goods and parts to promote high-tech industries.

We need also to be careful about distinguishing between tradables and non-tradables for the bilateral international input-output study. If we classify the non-tradable sectors in great detail, we may end up with some computational problems.

My second point is related to the major causes for increasing interdependence among EA countries. I believe that the factors that cause increasing interdependence among the EA countries are the following three, namely, trade, tourism, and technology. The paper by Sano and others (ch. 6) has shown that trade alone expanded international interdependence among these countries substantially between 1975 and 1985. But I think tourism and technology also caused increasing interdependence in this region. In the future, it will be more so. In fact their analysis may be interpreted as including the impact of tourism on inter-industry and intercountry interdependence in this region. If we look at the figures in table 3 concerning trade and transport, we can easily discover that in Thailand and Korea, the importance of these sectors expanded rapidly between 1975 and 1985. I believe that these sectors are closely related to tourism and that this trend continued after 1985. In the coming era of increasing interdependence, the service sectors will also play important roles. They may be the sectors that will bind people and activities together in this region. The IDE paper can support this explanation of the impact of tourism and other services on inter-industry relations in the region.

As to the role of technology, I think it is the major factor that closely ties the Korean economy to the Japanese economy. Because of the large technology gap between the two countries, Korean industries rely heavily on Japanese industries for capital goods. As the technology gap between the two countries is expected to expand, so will the dependence on Japanese industries by Korean industries increase. I am afraid to say that the technology gap between Japan and all other countries in the East Asian region will continue to widen in the future.

My last point is concerned with the concept of international inter-industry linkages versus domestic inter-industry linkages. I thought that this might be especially important for the Japan-Korea bilateral study. We would like to know the changing pattern of dependence by Korean industries on various Japanese industries. With this information, Korea will be in a better position to understand interrelations between the two countries at the industry-specific level. Computation of these two types of linkage involves much work and is a somewhat technical matter.

8

Economic impacts of carbon reduction schemes: Some general equilibrium estimates from a simple global model

John Piggott and John Whalley

Abstract

The possibility that over the next decade or two a major global initiative will be adopted to reduce (or, at least, slow the rate of growth of) carbon emissions because of concerns over global warming is now taken sufficiently seriously for economists to study the consequences. The focus of most work thus far has been the global costs of such a measure, while noting the incentives, especially for smaller countries, to free ride. Typically, no explicit treatment of benefits is offered.

This paper presents preliminary results from a computable general equilibrium model with a stylized treatment of preferences towards reduced global carbon use, and compares them with those from a corresponding model with no representation of benefits. Results suggest that the inclusion of the benefit side can substantially affect the assessment of the welfare consequences of alternative global and unilateral carbon reduction initiatives.

I. Introduction

Over the past several years, expert bodies and international forums have issued various calls for dramatic cuts (of up to 50 per cent) in carbon emissions over the next decades to reduce the severity of the greenhouse effect. The policies to be used to implement these cuts, however, have not usually been specified in such calls. And the effects of such cuts on resource allocation and income distribution have not usually been considered or assessed in any detail. These unknowns pose challenges to the economics profession. Policies to implement carbon reduction schemes must be designed, and the economic impacts of alternative policies assessed.

The purpose of this paper is to illustrate how applied general equilibrium (AGE) modelling can be used to explore the economic implications of policies directed towards controlling greenhouse, particularly carbon, emissions. The appeal of the AGE approach in this context lies in its ability to capture far-reaching interactions and feedbacks that the implementation of carbon reduction initiatives of the severity proposed imply. More particularly, however, AGE models can handle simultaneously the effects of trade, tax policies, and quota type instruments; and can incorporate public goods. Policies aimed at curtailing carbon emissions will almost certainly take the form of restrictions on trade, or the imposition of taxes or quotas; the abatement (or reduction in the growth) of carbon emissions is by its nature a global public good. AGE models give economists an appropriate conceptual framework within which to analyse quantitatively the impact of carbon reduction policies.

The AGE approach will be exemplified here by a model originally due to Whalley and Wigle (1991), which has been extended in Piggott, Whalley, and Wigle (PWW) (1992). It should be noted that there are now a number of other AGE models constructed to analyse greenhouse policies (e.g., Jorgenson and Wilcoxen 1990, Nordhaus 1991, Perroni and Rutherford 1991, Burniaux et al. 1991). These and other modelling efforts are surveyed in Dean et al. (1990) and Winters (1991). Two important differences between the PWW model and many of the others are that, first, PWW have no dynamics in their model; and secondly, they give some representation to the benefits of carbon emission reduction. The elimination of dynamics is just a simplification: for our purposes, little is added by an explicit intertemporal specification. The representation of benefits in the model allows a variety of issues to be analysed that cannot be addressed in a model confined to the cost side.

Results reported in the present paper focus on national carbon taxes[1] (that is, taxes where the revenue is returned to the jurisdiction levying the tax). They suggest the following:

1. If national carbon taxes are introduced on a coordinated global basis, then the form of the tax (whether it is levied on consumption or production) plays a crucial role in determining the gainers and losers from such a policy.
2. If single regions undertake cuts in consumption or production, then other regions will face a change in world prices that lead them to increase their own consumption or production. The net global reduction in carbon emissions may be very small, and may even be negative.[2] This raises the question of whether unilateral action such as that undertaken by Sweden has any appreciable effect on global carbon emissions.
3. Terms-of-trade effects can be important in determining the overall outcome when one region cuts its consumption or production.
4. Inclusion of a representation of benefits has a substantial impact on the pattern of gainers and losers, and the extent of gain or loss.

II. A numerical general equilibrium model for analysing carbon reduction initiatives

The model described here is originally due to Whalley and Wigle (1991), and has been extended by Piggott, Whalley, and Wigle (1992).[3] It incorporates trade, production, and consumption of both energy and non-energy products for a number of countries (or groups of countries) over a single 40-year projection period of 1990–2030,[4] which is treated for analytical convenience as a single period; i.e., the model incorporates no explicit dynamics. The model also does not incorporate existing taxes on energy products, although these vary by region, and would affect results. To further keep the model manageable, we do not identify fuel types within the broader category of carbon-based energy products, even though various elements within this category (oil, coal, natural gas) have different carbon content.

In the model, the world is divided into six regions, indicated in table 1. These are the European Community, North America, Japan, other OECD, oil exporters (including all OPEC countries and major non-OPEC energy exporters), and a residual rest of the world, representing most developing countries (those who are not oil exporters) along with the centrally planned economies. Nested CES functions are used to represent production and demand in each region; the nesting structures are set out in table 2. Each region is endowed with four non-traded primary factors: (i) primary factors, exclusive of energy resources; (ii) carbon-based energy resources (deposits of oil, gas and coal); (iii) other energy resources (hydro-electric and nuclear capacity); and (iv) sector-specific skills and equipment in the energy-intensive manufacturing sector. Both energy resources are treated as able to be converted into the relevant energy products through a refining/extraction process that uses other resources (primary factors). There are three internationally traded commodities: carbon-based energy products, energy-intensive manufactures, and other goods (all other GNP). Details of trade patterns are reported in Whalley and Wigle (1991). However, given the aggregation in the present model, direct trade in carbon-based energy products amounts to EC and JPN imports from the oil-exporting region. Energy-intensive manufactures, other goods, and the composite energy product (carbon-based and noncarbon-based energy) enter final demands.

For each of the five produced goods in each region (listed in table 1), production is represented by nested CES functions. Carbon-based and noncarbon-based energy products use the respective energy resources and primary factors. Noncarbon-based energy products are non-traded, since hydro-electric, solar, and nuclear power are not traded in significant quantities between the regions as defined. A domestic energy composite is produced by a third (energy conversion) industry, using the two energy products as inputs. The two final goods

Table 1 **Regions in the global equilibrium model used to evaluate incentives to participate in carbon reduction initiatives**

Regions
1. European Community (of the 12) (EC)[a]
2. North America (US, Canada) (NAM)
3. Japan (JPN)
4. Other OECD (ODV) Austria, Switzerland, Finland, Iceland, Norway, Sweden, Australia, New Zealand
5. Oil exporters (OPEC countries, plus major non-OPEC exporters) (OEXP) Algeria, Libya, Nigeria, Tunisia, Mexico, Venezuela, Indonesia, Iran, Iraq, Kuwait, Saudi Arabia, United Arab Emirates
6. Rest of the world (developing countries and centrally planned economies) (ROW) This is a residual category containing all other countries including USSR, Eastern Europe, China, Brazil, India, and other developing countries not in category 5.

a. Abbreviations in parentheses are those used in the results tables to follow.

(energy-intensive manufactures and other goods) use primary factors and the composite domestic energy product as inputs. Perfect competition is assumed throughout in all regions and for all sectors.

For the two non-traded goods (noncarbon-energy products and composite energy) there is domestic-market clearing separately within each economy. Since prices in this system are treated as completely flexible, they will adjust to the levels required to clear the relevant international and domestic markets.

Counterfactual analyses with the model for any hypothesized policy change involve the computation of a new equilibrium model solution. Policy evaluation with the model is based on a comparison between counterfactual model solutions and the base data to which the model has been calibrated.

The base-case equilibrium solution for the model represents an assumed future evolution of the global economy over a 40-year period between 1990 and 2030. This is based on an assumption of continuing growth in OECD countries at annual rates reflecting the late 1980s, unchanged energy use, and consumption and production of other goods. Hicksian neutral (factor augmenting) growth is assumed to occur in each of the regions in the model at average annual rates reported in the 1989 World Development Report, which are assumed to apply over the entire period under consideration. The oil-exporting region is assumed to grow at 2.5 per cent, the rest of the world (ROW) at 2.7 per cent, and the remaining regions at 2.3 per cent. Each region's endowment of non-produced factors in the model thus reflects the present value of their resources (at constant prices) over the entire 40-year period. We assume that a 5 per cent real discount rate applies for all years in the period considered in the model. The model is then solved to yield a 40-year baseline solution representing an equilibrium in the world economy in the absence of any response to global warming over the period 1990–2030 (in discounted present value terms at 1990 prices, and in $US billion). Policy experiments are then evaluated relative to this baseline, with a comparison of base and counterfactual equilibria.

The structure of the regional economies in the base data used in the model largely corresponds to data available for 1982, projected forward to 1990. Data for regional population and GNP in 1982 are obtained from the 1987 World Tables. Value-added, production, and trade in energy-intensive manufactures (primary metals, glass, ceramics, and other basic manufactured products) are obtained from

Nguyen et al. (1990). These are identified as those industries having the highest energy input requirements. Input ratios from Whalley and Wigle (1991) are used to infer energy input requirements for energy-intensive and other industries.

Production, consumption, and trade in carbon-based energy products and noncarbon-based energy (for 1982) come from UN Energy Statistics. Raw data are in (metric) kilotons of coal equivalent. The carbon content of production and consumption for the regions in the model are determined using the same conversion coefficients as those in Whalley and Wigle (1991). To convert production data into value terms, we use price information from World Resources 1990–1991.

To incorporate the benefit side of slowed global warming, we have modified the preference functions for each of the regions identified in the earlier Whalley-Wigle model so as to include not only goods directly consumed, but also an argument reflecting the level of global carbon emissions. This, in effect, involves an additional nesting level within the utility function U_i, as depicted in table 2. For each region, goods consumed, G_i, are region-specific, but the global CO_2 emission level is common to all regions. G_i is a composite of the goods identified in table 2, i.e. $G_i = G_i(EI_i, \mathrm{OG}_i, E_i)$. Hence, through each region's utility function, U_i externality effects associated with global warming are directly incorporated in the model,

$$U_i = U_i(G_i, \mathrm{CO}_2) \qquad i = 1, \ldots 6. \tag{1}$$

While this change in the model is conceptually straightforward, and parallels the analysis of public goods in the public finance literature (see Atkinson and Stiglitz 1979), there are major problems with numerical specification of these preference functions in a model such as this. As is by now well known, there are no widely agreed estimates as to how large or small the benefits from a slowing global warming are. There are suggestions, such as those by Nordhaus (1991) and Schelling (1991), that the benefits of slowing global warming are likely to be quite small. Nordhaus puts these at no more than 0.75 per cent of GDP for the United States over a 75-year period, whereas Schelling suggests that these are so imperceptibly small and likely to take place over such a long period of time (say, 75 years) that they would be little noticed by most individuals. On the other hand, economists such as Cline (1991) have argued that with a possible sextupling in levels of atmospheric carbon dioxide by the end of the next century, the potential costs are so large that some emission reduction should be undertaken immediately. He emphasizes how most debate on global warming has focused on the consequences of a doubling of atmospheric CO_2 by the middle of the next century, for which temperature rise could be modest, rather than on the larger increases in CO_2 content which would follow out into the next century and for which the consequences are potentially more alarming.

At this point, the sum of marginal benefits from CO_2 reduction is equal to marginal cost. Regional marginal valuations of CO_2 emissions are determined by assuming that the income elasticity of demand for CO_2 abatement is 1.5, and by taking into account regional population levels in 1990.

Our specification of preferences towards global warming would undoubtedly be more convincing if there were a clearer consensus on the size of possible benefits from slowing global warming on the demand side. At the same time, the profile of the policy debate on the issue is such that it still seems worthwhile to make calculations based on various assumptions, even if these are sometimes strong.

Our procedure is to assume that calls for emission reductions voiced at various international conferences are consistent with a global optimal allocation on a full participatory basis if they were implemented. Taking this as our reference point, we evaluate the incentives for regions or countries to participate in various arrangements. The call for emission reductions emerging from the 1988 Toronto conference of a 20 per cent emission reduction by the year 2005, and a 50 per cent emission reduction to follow to stabilize CO_2 content provides the basis for our preference parameterization; namely, that a 50 per cent carbon emission reduction by all regions corresponds to a global full participation global externality correcting intervention. Using this strong assumption we are then able to analyse what the incentives are for various countries to participate in reduction initiatives of different forms.

The parameterization of this extended version of the Whalley-Wigle model is based on standard calibration (see Mansur and Whalley 1984), with the preference parameters towards climate change being correspondingly generated. Counterfactual analysis then allows us to compute new equilibria under carbon emission reductions of various forms, given various assumptions as to what form of region participation is involved.

Table 2 **Production and demand structures in the global general equilibrium model used to evaluate carbon reduction initiatives**

A. *Factors and goods in each region*

Endowments	*Produced goods*
Carbon-based energy resources (CR)	Carbon-based energy products (CP)
Non-carbon-based energy resources (ER)	Non-carbon-based energy products (EP)
Sector-specific factors in energy-intensive manufacturing (SF)	Composite energy (E)
Other primary factors (PF)	Energy-intensive goods (EI)
	Other goods (OG)

B. *Structure of production in each region*
(CES[a] functions used at each stage; figures in parentheses give assumed elasticities of substitution)

Stage 1: production of energy products

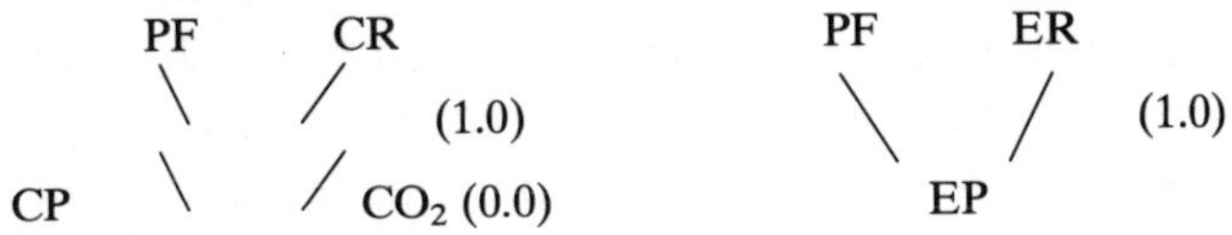

Stage 2: Productions of composite energy

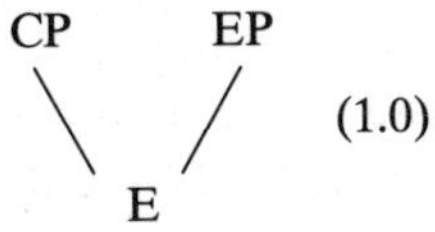

Stage 3: Production of energy-intensive and other goods

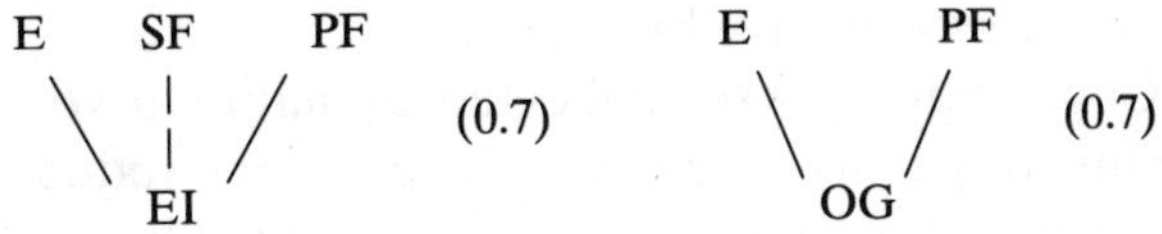

C. *Structure of final demands*
(Nested CES[a] functions used; figures in parenthesis give assumed elasticities of substitution)

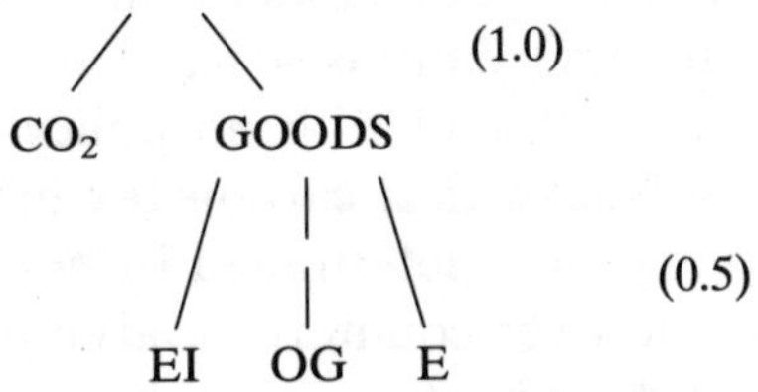

a. CES denotes "constant elasticity of substitution."

III. Results

In this paper, various model results are reported that are intended to illustrate the application of an applied general equilibrium model to the global warming issue.

We have used the model to evaluate possible international incidence, trade, and welfare effects, which would follow the introduction of alternative carbon tax schemes. The results that follow evaluate a target of a 50 per cent cut in carbon emissions relative to the baseline model solution over the period 1990–2030. This target is met either by all countries simultaneously, or by a single country (or region) acting unilaterally. The policy instrument used is in all cases a national carbon tax (or taxes), levied on either consumption or production. A 50 per cent cut in emissions from the baseline is on the high side of the range of targets currently used by other modellers evaluating carbon tax proposals, but corresponds approximately to that called for in the 1988 Toronto Conference statement.

In all our model runs, we endogenously determine the *ad valorem* carbon tax rate, which, in this structure, applies to all fuels at the same rate. However, the rate may vary somewhat across regions.

The carbon tax variants we consider are as follows:

1. Production-based carbon taxes collected by national governments. The emission target assumed is a 50 per cent reduction in each region's production of carbon-based energy. Under this scheme, tax rates will vary by region.
2. Consumption taxes collected by national governments. The emission target assumed is a 50 per cent reduction in each region's consumption of carbon-based energy. Under this scheme, tax rates will vary by region.

These tax schemes are each evaluated using the general equilibrium model in counterfactual mode. The model is first calibrated to reproduce the original (benchmark) data as a baseline equilibrium solution over the period 1990–2030, and with no policy changes in effect. The model is then re-solved with a carbon tax in place. The impacts of any of the tax schemes are determined by comparing the original (benchmark), and the new (or counterfactual) equilibria.

The left panel of table 3 reports our estimates of the gains or losses for the regions identified in the model under each of the tax options, when they are undertaken on a coordinated global basis, that is, with all regions fully participating. The welfare measures capture the combined gains or losses to regions from the production and sale of carbon-based products, as well as the consumption side gains associated with price changes. They also capture the economy-wide effects of energy price changes as they feed through the model. In the model variant in which the benefits from carbon emission reduction are captured, the value of the benefits is included in the results.

The right side of table 3 reports some trade impacts flowing from the implementation of these policies. While the trade patterns of all three traded goods in the model change substantially with the introduction of globally coordinated carbon taxes, the *direction* of trade also alters in a number of cases for energy-intensive goods. These changes in direction are reported, together with the terms-of-trade index.

As can be seen from table 3, the implications of a globally coordinated initiative of this kind are large. Consider first the welfare impacts generated by a model variant in which the benefits of reduced carbon emissions have not been incorporated. World welfare is estimated to have fallen by 3.4 per cent as a result of these taxes.

While the world welfare change is approximately the same under production- and consumption-based taxes, effects by region differ dramatically. North America loses 3.5 per cent of income under a national consumption tax, while the ROW loses 7 per cent of income under such a tax. Oil exporters gain substantially from a national production-based tax, while they lose dramatically from a national consumption-based tax.

These results, therefore, strongly underline the point we emphasize above; namely, that the form any carbon tax takes will have major implications for the international incidence effects of the tax. Under a national production-based tax, energy producers collect tax revenues; hence oil exporters gain. Under a national consumption tax, oil importers collect revenues, and hence Europe gains, North America loses only marginally, while oil exporters lose.

The welfare losses we have been discussing are in model terms the costs of introducing a distortion, or distortions, into an otherwise undistorted competitive market system. The policy proposal itself, however, is motivated by concerns that there is market failure in the form of an externality, in that carbon emissions, while imposing an economic cost, are not priced. It is possible to interpret carbon tax proposals as alternative formulations of a Pigovion tax, designed to correct this market failure. Given the parameterization procedures on the benefit side outlined in section 2, a single-rate tax which reduced carbon emissions by 50 per cent globally, would indeed be a

Table 3 **Welfare and trade effects of a global scheme of national carbon taxes to implement a 50% cut in carbon emissions**

Region		Welfare effects (Base = 100): Model variant with no representation of benefits from carbon reduction	Welfare effects (Base = 100): Model variant with benefits from carbon reduction incorporated	Trade effects: Direction of trade in energy intensive goods	Trade effects: Terms-of-trade index (Laspeyres) (base = 100)
EC	Production tax	96.1	103.0	Export → Import	46
	Consumption tax	99.0	104.0	Export → Import	433
NAM	Production tax	95.7	102.9	Export → Import	45
	Consumption tax	96.5	103.2	Export → Import	428
JPN	Production tax	96.4	103.1	Export → Import	46
	Consumption tax	100.6	104.6	Export → Import	435
ODV	Production tax	97.7	103.6	No change	84
	Consumption tax	98.0	103.7	No change	127
OPEC	Production tax	104.4	105.9	No change	221
	Consumption tax	81.2	96.1	Import → Export	23
ROW	Production tax	92.9	100.2	Import → Export	71
	Consumption tax	93.3	100.4	Import → Export	125
World[a]	Production tax	95.6	102.3		
	Consumption tax	95.6	102.3		

a. Percentage change in sums of money-metric utilities.

perfect example of such a tax in the model variant in which the benefits of carbon emission reductions have been introduced. In this model variant, such a tax, instead of introducing a distortion, would be removing a distortion, and world welfare would rise rather than fall.

The taxes considered in this paper are not exactly of this form, since each *region* is required to meet the 50 per cent reduction target, and the tax rates required to achieve this will vary across regions. But they are fairly close to such a tax. So, it is to be expected that world welfare will rise under such a policy, as reported in table 3.

It is, however, of greater interest to note that, with one exception, *all* regions gain from both these reduction initiatives. The exception is that oil-exporting nations lose from a globally coordinated consumption tax. This results from the dramatic terms-of-trade loss experienced by the oil exporters under such a policy. The significant net benefits accruing globally from such a cut reflect the falling marginal benefit schedule from emission reductions (given the preferences), and the rising marginal cost schedule of reductions (due to emission reduction interventions of increasing severity).

We now turn to trade effects, reported on the right side of table 3. Here we emphasize those cases where the direction of trade changes, and report the terms-of-trade index change. Both Europe and Japan become net importers of energy-intensive products, where previously they were net exporters. A change also occurs for oil exporters from a net import to a net export position.

The dramatic terms-of-trade changes reflect principally changes in the price of carbon fuels. They serve to emphasize the different international incidence impacts of production- and consumption-based taxes. However, it should be remembered that pre-intervention quantity weights are used in the calculation of these indices, and that carbon-energy production and consumption in the new equilibrium is only half its baseline value.

Table 4 reports the welfare and terms-of-trade effects of national production taxes designed to cut production unilaterally in a single region by 50 per cent. The model variant with the benefit side incorporated is used here, and in all subsequent results. Unilateral cuts of 50 per cent involve losses by the regions making such cuts, except for NAM. In North America, the costs of reducing energy production are relatively low because of the high productivity of mobile factors of production elsewhere in the economy, while the high marginal valuation of the benefits of reduced global carbon use results in benefits outweighing costs.[5] Unilateral cuts also benefit all other regions. But the benefits come not only from shared benefits in emission reductions of the country or region making the cuts, but also from terms-of-trade and other effects. Regions cutting production allow other regions to increase production, as well as raising the world price of energy so as to benefit other energy exporters.

The lower part of table 4 reports the terms-of-trade changes for all regions associated with unilateral production cuts. In all cases, the movements are strongest for the oil exporters, whose terms of trade improve in every case. In corresponding simulations involving consumption taxes (not reported here), the converse result occurs.

The results of table 4 suggest that the net impact on global carbon emissions of unilateral cuts might be much less than the reduction in emissions by the region undertaking the cut, because changes in world prices resulting from the unilateral cut induce other regions to increase their production or consumption. This issue is investigated further in table 5. Reductions in global carbon emissions from unilateral 50 per cent production and consumption cuts are reported, and compared with the percentage global reduction which would

Table 4 **Welfare and terms-of-trade effects of *unilateral* production tax policies to cut carbon emissions by 50% (base = 100)**

	50% national cuts by					
	EC	NAM	JPN	ODV	OEXP	ROW
Region	Welfare effects					
EC	99.9	100.7	100.0	100.1	100.6	101.4
NAM	100.2	100.0	100.0	100.1	100.7	101.7
JPN	100.2	100.6	100.0	100.1	100.5	101.3
ODV	100.2	100.8	100.0	99.7	100.7	101.7
OEXP	100.5	101.8	100.0	100.2	98.0	104.3
ROW	100.2	100.6	100.0	100.1	100.5	99.1
World[a]	100.2	100.6	100.0	100.1	100.4	101.0
	Terms-of-trade effects					
EC	97.3	90.5	99.9	99.1	91.9	79.5
NAM	97.3	90.4	99.9	99.1	91.8	79.3
JPN	97.3	90.6	99.9	99.1	92.0	79.6
ODV	99.6	98.4	100.0	99.9	98.7	96.1
OEXP	102.8	110.6	100.1	100.1	108.9	126.2
ROW	99.0	96.4	100.0	99.7	96.9	91.6

a. Percentage change in sum of regional money-metric utilities.

Table 5 **Impacts on global carbon emissions of national tax policies to cut emissions by 50% (base = 100)**

	Unilateral cuts with no restraint by other regions		Unilateral cuts with other regions constrained to baseline levels	
	Production cuts	Consumption cuts	Production cuts	Consumption cuts
EC	97.4	98.0	96.4	92.9
NAM	91.1	96.0	88.1	86.9
JPN	100.0	99.4	99.9	97.8
ODV	99.2	99.7	89.8	98.9
OEXP	92.6	99.6	89.8	97.3
ROW	81.5	91.6	76.8	76.1

have been achieved had other regions not changed their production or consumption levels. The results clearly show substantial production and consumption spillovers take place.[6]

IV. Conclusion

This paper has attempted to illustrate how applied general equilibrium (AGE) models may be used to shed light on the economic impacts of policies designed to curtail global warming. Using a model originally developed by Whalley and Wigle (1990, 1991), and subsequently extended by Piggott, Whalley and Wigle (1992, 1993), the impacts of policies designed to implement a 50 per cent cut in carbon emissions are investigated.

We stress that in considering major policy initiatives of this kind, it is essential to adopt a technique that is able to capture the interactions and feedbacks between industries and regions that would occur were such policies actually implemented. Applied general equilibrium (AGE) models are able to do this, and in addition are able to focus on relevant aspects of trade and taxation policy, and to incorporate public goods, of which slowed global warming is an example.

Results reported in the paper focus on national carbon taxes. They indicate that the base of the tax (production or consumption) is crucial in determining regional welfare changes, but less important in the determination of global welfare change. Where unilateral cuts in production or consumption are undertaken, other regions will tend to respond by increasing their production or consumption, so that the net impact on global carbon emissions may be much smaller than the cut. Terms-of-trade effects can also be important in determining the pattern of welfare gains and losses resulting from such carbon-reduction initiatives.

Notes

1. For an analysis of global taxes, and detailed discussion of international carbon-tax incidence, see Whalley and Wigle (1991).
2. The possibility that carbon-emission reduction in one region may actually increase global emissions arises because the carbon efficiency of production techniques may vary across regions. In the present model, there are no systematic regional variations in carbon efficiency, and the negative result does not occur.
3. See also the presentation in Whalley and Wigle (1990) for earlier calculations made using an even more simplified version of this model.
4. This has been chosen somewhat arbitrarily to capture the initial period and subsequent intermediate term during which a carbon tax would have its largest effects, since with discounting the significance in present value terms of later-year effects recedes. It is relatively easy to run the model for a longer projection period (say, 80 or 100 years), and were this done we believe that the main themes of our results would remain.

   A weakness of this 40-year projection period approach is that in the base-year data used for these projections, most carbon energy trade takes place in oil rather than in other carbon-based fuels. If, as some expect, trade in oil is slowly replaced by trade in coal into the next century, the data used here may be misleading since the countries that are potential future coal exporters (USSR, Australia, China) are quite different from current oil exporters (OPEC countries, Mexico).
5. Although 50 per cent of unilateral cuts are generally losing propositions for the region undertaking the cut, substantial unilateral cuts can lead to welfare gains, especially for the wealthier regions. Piggott et al. (1993) explore this issue in greater detail.
6. This issue is investigated in more detail by Piggott et al. (1992).

References

Atkinson, A.B., and J.E. Stiglitz. 1979. *Lectures on Public Economics.* New York: McGraw Hill.

Bergman, Lars. 1991. Carbon Taxation in a Small Open Economy: Independent vs Co-ordinated Policies. Paper presented to the 5th IIASA Task Force Meeting on Applied General Equilibrium Modelling, Laxenburg, 27–29 August.

Burniaux, J.M., J.P. Martin, G. Nicoletti, and J.O. Martins. 1991. The Costs of Policies to Reduce Global Emissions of CO_2: Initial Simulation Results with GREEN. OECD, Department of Economics and Statistics, Working Paper 103.

Cline, W. 1991. "Scientific Basis for the Greenhouse Effect." *Economic Journal* 101(407): 904–919.

Dean, A. et al. 1990. OECD Survey.

Jorgenson, D., and P. Wilcoxen. 1990. Reducing US Carbon Dioxide Emissions: The Cost of Different Goals. Mimeo.

Mansur, A., and J. Whalley. 1984. "Numerical Specification of Applied General Equilibrium Models: Estimation, Calibration and Data." In: J.B. Shoven and H. Scarf, eds. *Applied General Equilibrium Analysis*, pp. 69–127. Cambridge.

Nguyen, T., C. Perroni, and R.M. Wigle. 1990. A Microconsistent Data Set for the Analysis of World Trade: Sources and Methods. Working Paper, Wilfrid Laurier University, August.

Nordhaus, W. 1991. "To Slow or Not to Slow: The Economics of the Greenhouse Effect." *Economic Journal* 101(407): 920–937.

Perroni, C., and T. Rutherford. 1991. International Trade in Carbon Emission Rights and Basic Materials: General Equilibrium Calculations for 2020. Mimeo, Department of Economics, Wilfrid Laurier University, Waterloo, Canada.

Piggott, J., J. Whalley, and R. Wigle. 1992. "International Linkages and Carbon Reduction Initiatives." In: K. Anderson and R. Blakehurst, eds. *The Greening of World Trade Issues.* Harvester Wheatsheaf and University of Michigan Press.

—— 1993. "How Large are the Incentives for Sub-global Carbon Reduction Initiatives?" *Journal of Policy Modelling* 15(5, 6): 473–490.

Rutherford, T. 1989. General Equilibrium Modelling with MPS/GE. Mimeo, the University of Western Ontario.

Schelling, T. 1991. "International Burden Sharing and Coordination: Prospects for Cooperative Approaches to Global Warming." In: R. Dornbusch and J. Poterba, eds. *Economic Policy Responses to Global Warming.* MIT Press.

Whalley, J., and R. Wigle. 1990. "Cutting CO_2 Emissions: The Effects of Alternative Policy Approaches." *Energy Journal.*

—— 1991. "The International Incidence of Carbon Taxes." In: R. Dornbusch and J. Poterba, eds. *Economic Policy Responses to Global Warming.* MIT Press.

Winters, L.A. 1991. The Trade and Welfare Effects of Greenhouse Gas Abatement: A Survey of Current Estimates. Paper presented to the Workshop on Trade and the Environment, GATT Secretariat, Geneva, 10–11 June.

Comments on chapter 8

1. Jean Waelbroeck

This is a lucidly written paper, based on an elegant "minimum model" that has just the size and degree of detail needed to investigate the issue at hand. I shall mention but not emphasize some of the model's stark simplifications; for example, the assumption that all types of traded energy are characterized by the same ratio of carbon emission to calories, although there are sharp differences in that ratio between, say, natural gas and coal. The search for realism is a slippery path, which takes the modeller on a road that never ends.

The author's basic idea is to assume that the ambitious goals advocated by the Toronto conference are a correct reflection of the preferences of citizens of the various countries of the world. The model's equations, as formulated, imply that men dislike warm climates. Surely this assumption is "counterfactual", to use a favourite term of the jargon of modellers; if people were truly cold-lovers, Spitzberg would be a more popular vacation spot than the Seychelles, and millions of Americans would be migrating to Alaska rather than to the sunbelt;[1] its only virtue is to make it unnecessary to model the relation between temperature and the productivity of agriculture and other industries.

As the authors point out, the data on the impact of greenhouse gases is very unsatisfactory. To bypass that problem, the utility function is calibrated so that a 50 per cent reduction of emissions is roughly optimal for the world, and (reflecting what political pressure reveals about preferences in various regions) that the citizens of rich countries care more about temperature than those of developing countries.

Formally, we have therefore a public goods problem. Solving this problem would require defining a system of energy cut-backs such that each region bears a marginal burden that matches the marginal disutility to that region of lowering the amount of carbon dioxide, methane, and other forms of "gaseous carbon" that are contained in the atmosphere. This burden, the region's contribution to solving the public goods problem, would be the sum of the marginal efficiency loss to the region of reducing its energy consumption, plus by the terms of trade loss (or minus the gain), plus possibly lump-sum transfers to the other regions. This problem is well defined and could be solved using the author's general equilibrium model. This is not what they choose to do.

Instead they focus on an assessment of the popular idea that the various regions of the world should achieve a 50 per cent cut in consumption or production of energy, via energy taxes of the type envisaged by the European Community (and adopted by Sweden in principle). The required taxes need to be differentiated by regions. This approach is less natural for the economist than one that appeals to the theory of public goods, but has the merit that it is close to the approach that dominates the current political debate.

What I conclude from my reading of the paper is that it demonstrates that this dominant approach is nonsense. It disregards two major problems that are bound to come to the fore if countries begin to negotiate seriously on this issue: the taxes' impacts on efficiency and on the terms of trade. As to efficiency, the taxes that achieve the prescribed goals bring about drastic changes in the patterns of trade, with many sign reversals of net trade for energy intensive goods. Clearly, it is more costly to cut energy emissions in some countries than in others. Those countries are forced to enforce high tax rates, which make their energy-intensive goods non-competitive in a way that bears no relation to comparative advantage. Trade in emission rights offers a ready way to reduce such waste: it would have been interesting to study its implications for the model's results. The value of traded emission rights could be large and it would be interesting to calculate these amounts. Trade in those rights should eliminate most of the net trade reversals that are identified by the present simulations, and could modify significantly the level and international distribution of welfare gains and losses.

Not unexpectedly from the point of view of trade theory, the taxes bring about large change, in the terms of trade, with signs that are obvious. The tax on production of energy, giving rise to an income that is retained by oil producers, is equivalent to what took place during the first two oil shocks; of course, it benefits producers. The tax on consumption, levied by oil consumers, corresponds to the energy taxes that were advocated by economists in OECD countries as a way of undermining and possibly destroying the OPEC cartel; of course, it favours consumers. What this means is that the idea of asking all countries in the world to tax production of consumption of energy is a non-starter; thinking should focus on a scheme that would combine a tax on either production or consumption (or on both) with (very large) lump-sum transfers.

In brief, the paper shows that the policy proposals that dominate today's debate on the greenhouse gas problem are not a sound basis for international negotiations. Implicitly, it suggests a correct approach, based on the theory of public goods, but does not implement it. I hope that the next paper by the authors will do that.

Note

1. Consideration of the likely impact of greenhouse gases on agriculture would also not justify the assumption that the Toronto decisions are an attempt to maximize national preferences by world collective action. Canada and Siberia would benefit strongly from a warmer climate, which would have a disastrous impact on the agriculture of many developing countries.

2. Erno Zalai

The economics profession has been challenged by the growing concern over economic development in many ways and times during the past few decades, especially after World War II. The burning issues of development planning in the former colonies and less developed countries, the emergence of more sophisticated planning practices in the (formerly) centrally planned economies, the growing involvement of the state in regulating economic life in the more developed market economies, the preoccupation of international agencies with universal and global economic problems (just to name the most important new issues) all posed challenging policy questions to the economics profession at large and sought immediate answers. The accumulated theoretical and methodological knowledge was far from being adequate to give accurate answers to the burning questions raised. Nevertheless, the constant challenge of practice gave rise to heroic attempts to use scientific methods to analyse policy-relevant macroeconomic questions, to develop appropriate concepts and tools, measurement techniques, and databases. In this process of development a key role has been played by various types of applied macroeconomic models of general economic interdependence.

Applied (multisectoral) nationwide or regional models of the above type have started from two traditions: the input-output (linear activity) analysis and econometric modelling. Following the mostly linear and deterministic models of the 1950s and 1960s the multisectoral models of the input-output or linear programming type have been developed in various directions during the last two decades. The 1970s and 1980s witnessed the emergence and proliferation of models incorporating more and more non-linear relationships into the description of economic phenomena and employing increasingly the accumulating results of sophisticated econometric/statistical estimates of various functional relationships. On the other hand the econometric model-building practice has also widened its scope and incorporated sectoral phenomena into its models. There have been three distinct approaches characterizing the development of the applied multisectoral macroeconomic models.

1. One of them came from the classical econometric macromodelling tradition, which started to introduce sectoral specification into the formerly sectorally aggregated macro economic models (see, for example, the LINK Project).

2. A second approach started from the traditional input-output analysis expanding its deterministic framework by introducing a number of statistically estimated relationships to describe the development of variables such as consumption, investment, exports and imports, prices and the like, and "wrap" them around the core of the input-output model, the "quadrant" of intersectoral flows (see, for example, Stone's "Cambridge" or Almon's "Inforum" project among others).

3. A third distinctive approach was inspired mostly by the economic interpretation of the solutions (especially that of the shadow prices) of the linear (or non-linear) programming models in the spirit of a competitive general equilibrium, which led to the emergence of the computable (applied) general equilibrium (CGE) models.

Each of these models has its own merits and justification, as a matter of fact all of them have managed to attract the attention of excellent scholars. As a result one could now rightly speak of distinguishable schools and traditions in the area of applied multisectoral modelling. This conference brought together once again the representatives of the various traditions, whose approaches may seem sometimes to compete, but as a matter of fact they are quite complementary in nature. It is interesting to note two things here.

1. First, one could observe a remarkable tendency of convergence during the last couple of years. Model builders brought up in the various traditions have learned from ("cross-fertilized") each other, but these approaches remained nevertheless clearly distinguishable.

2. Secondly, the data sets these models are using have been more or less common, based on standard macroeconomic statistics and in the core of intersectoral and interorganizational relationships they relied more and more on SAMs (Social Accounting Matrix), which, in turn, have been gradually taking over the role of input-output tables (incorporating them into a broader concept and framework of macroeconomic accounts).

In these notes I will concentrate on the approach that was mentioned last, the so-called CGE (computable or applied general equilibrium) models and their potential use in addressing economic policy issues of multisectoral dimension at national or global level. I believe that in a situation when it is practically impossible to hope for reliable statistical estimates and forecasts for some crucial economic variables and relationships, the CGE models seem to offer especially useful frameworks and tools to analyse the problem and its sensitivity to alternative assumptions. In these types of model it is customary and in many cases, in fact, inevitable to use "educated" guesses and expert estimates of some parameters that cannot be "normally" observed (see the issue of calibration briefly touched upon in the paper).

The real strength of these models lies in the consistent theoretical framework they employ, the most widely accepted description of the working of interrelated markets, relative price-induced changes in the use and production of economic commodities and resources. The general equilibrium framework, here and there loosened up to a sufficient degree to allow for incorporating imperfections, non-standard formulations, is the best if not the only "play in town" (Taylor 1975) for the time being, at least in situations characterized by severe lack of data and/or major institutional changes.

Since the pioneering work of Johansen in 1960 building up the first computable model in general equilibrium fashion and the early work of Scarf (1973) presenting the first constructive method for computing the fixed point of a continuous mapping, economists in many countries have devoted increasing efforts to the development of practical general equilibrium models for use in a wide variety of applications. Now that so much experience has been gained with computable general equilibrium (CGE) models, the practice of model building itself is becoming increasingly systematized, as reflected for instance, in the increasing use of standard and rather powerful packages, the compilation of data sets, which make it possible for the modeller to concentrate on the policy issue in question. The same development opened up many new areas of application for the CGE models.

In terms of applications, the relatively new fields that are of interest to policy makers include regional models, in which data problems often force model builders to make very special assumptions about the relationships between the particular region and the wider economy. In particular, multi-country models have been developed to explore trading and other links in greater detail than is possible using single country models which typically treat "the rest of the world" as if it were a household with exogenous income and fixed prices. Models that treat energy and environmental problems in more detail than earlier models could do, increasingly rely on CGEs too, sometimes by integrating a detailed sectoral model with a more aggregated general equilibrium model (see, e.g. Capros et al. 1990 in addition to those quoted in the paper). Another newer development in the area is the emergence of CGEs in the formerly centrally planned economies in transition toward mixed market economies (see, for example, Hare et al. 1991 or Zalai and Révész 1991).

Thus, in short, the use and extension of CGE type of models for the evaluation of the possible economic consequences of policies aimed at the reduction of carbon emission should be potentially of significant value. John Piggott's and John Whalley's paper in discussion is one important step in a series of attempts to demonstrate this potential significance of the applied general equilibrium models. Whalley has been among the pioneers of CGE modelling, especially in the field of multi-regional applications. This work is also based on an earlier study involving him (Whalley and Wigle 1990), which became the starting point of and a point of reference for many recent models addressing the same issue from a global or national point of view.

The writer is not a specialist on the issue of global warming. It seems nevertheless to him, that the profession dealing with the greenhouse effect is divided over the importance and immediateness of the environmental and economic dangers posed by the emission of "greenhouse gases", and the choice of policy to reduce the level of emission especially because of the lack of complete and reliable analysis of the economic consequences of alternative abatement strategies. Further modelling efforts are therefore needed to shed light on various aspects of the problem in order to find effective and acceptable global policies. In this process the present paper is one important step, calling attention forcefully to the danger of potentially highly unequal and asymmetric welfare effects of alternative tax policies on various regions or groups of countries.

The model the authors used was admittedly simple, relative to the complexity and the uncertainty of the whole issue. It is a static general equilibrium model intended to capture the medium-run effects of the imposition of production or consumption carbon taxes. This approach implicitly assumes among other things that in the period investigated (1990–2020) the accumulation of greenhouse gases will not reach any significant threshold, thus the dynamics of the problem are not important.

This may be true, however, some dynamic aspects of the economic problem itself are important, which is not reflected by the static model. The analysis of some US policy options by Jorgenson (1990) in the framework of a dynamic, highly detailed model seems to suggest that the size of the carbon tax necessary to induce the required structural changes to reduce the level of emission critically depends on the time of its introduction. If this is the case, it would be interesting to see the effect of different timing by different regions of the introduction of carbon taxes on the global level of greenhouse gases as well as on the welfare level of the various regions. The lack of proper dynamics means also that the estimates of required tax rates can be misleading.

Very few attempts have been made to account properly for the potential welfare effects of global warming, thus including the potential benefits of emission reduction into the formal analysis. This paper is one of the few exceptions. Other notable exceptions include Nordhaus (1989) and Brendemoen and Vennemo (1991), both using detailed calculations to estimate the benefits of such policies. The paper discussed uses a simple measure based on the "magic" target figure accepted at the 1988 Toronto conference, combined with the benchmark calibration technique of the CGEs.

While this is an ingenious and legitimate illustration of the conventional wisdom, it has a potentially misleading impact on the analysis. Most of all, one must ask the question: whose preferences are represented by the above measure of welfare? Also, what weights should be assigned to the various regions of different levels of development to measure the economic costs and benefits of environmental policies? I believe these questions are especially important to ask in relation to a study that attempts to analyse the income distribution effects of internationally agreed policies.

Moreover, it seems that the above solution does not give much more to the analysis based simply on economic cost considerations alone. The rank order of the regions is the same in both cases, whether they calculate "losses" (no benefit taken into account) or "gains" (implicit benefits taken into account). It seems that the only effect is that of "cosmetics": the measures will duly bring about increases in the welfare levels by assumption.

Nevertheless the results of the model in this rather stylized form already illustrate well the potential usefulness of application of applied general equilibrium models to the analysis of the international economic consequences of alternative planned measures to reduce the danger of global warming.

- The analysis convincingly demonstrates that the gains and losses resulting from the imposition of carbon taxes are allocated quite differently among the different regions, depending on whether production or consumption taxes are introduced, whereas the combined gains and losses are not affected by that choice at all.
- In addition, the terms of trade effects seem to be quite dramatic in both cases (but in reverse), especially in the case of consumption taxes.
- Details of the calculations also seem to indicate that the real loser of an undifferentiated universal imposition of such policies in either case are the "energy and technology poor" less developed countries of the third and second world.
- Interestingly, but not surprisingly, the real economic "tug of war" takes place between the carbon-based energy resource exporters and importers.
- The model simulation also suggests that unilateral national tax policies may result in significant terms of trade changes, but have little or no effect on individual or global welfare.

The above results most probably provide convincing arguments for future policy debates. The analysis, however, has remained somewhat sterile and did not go further to exploit the potential of the simple, but differentiated enough model. Thus, for example, it might be interesting to analyse the effects of various asymmetric policies, in which various countries would face different target levels, or the potential use of compensation schemes to induce less developed countries to introduce abatement measures. For it is highly probable that concerted international measures will be hindered by the pressing needs for development and economic restructuring of the less or medium developed countries, who on the other hand are emitting a significant amount of greenhouse gases leading to global consequences.

References

Brendemoen, A., and H. Vennemo. 1991. A Climate Convention and the Norwegian Economy: A CGE Assessment. Paper presented at the Fourth IIASA Task Force meeting on AGEM. Mimeo, Research Department, Central Bureau of Statistics.

Capros, P., P. Karadeloglou, and G. Mentzas. 1990. New Developments for the MIDAS Medium-term Energy Modelling Project of the EEC: The Energy Supply Model and the Supply-Demand Pricing Linkage. IFORS 1990 Conference Paper. Mimeo, Athens.

Hare, P.G., T. Révész, and E. Zalai. 1991. Modelling an Economy in Transition: Trade Adjustment Policies for Hungary. Paper presented at the Fourth IIASA Task Force meeting on AGEM. Mimeo.

Jorgenson, D.W. ed. 1990. *General Equilibrium Modelling and Economic Policy Analysis.* Oxford: Blackwell Publishers.

Nordhaus, W.D. 1989. *The Economics of the Greenhouse Effect.* Cambridge, Mass.: Center for Energy Policy Research, MIT.

Scarf, H.E. 1973. *The Computation of Economic Equilibria, with the Collaboration of Terje Hansen.* Cowles Foundation for Research in Economics at Yale University, Monograph Series, No. 24.

Taylor, L. 1975. "Theoretical Foundations and Technical Implications." In: C. Blitzer et al., eds. *Economy-wide Models and Development Planning.* Oxford: Oxford University Press.

Zalai, E., and T. Révész. 1991. "Trade Redirection and Liberalization: Lessons from A Model Simulation." AULA: *Society and Economy*, 13(2): 69–80.

9

Modelling future greenhouse gas emissions: The second generation model description

J.A. Edmonds, H.M. Pitcher, D. Barns, R. Baron, and M.A. Wise

Introduction

The analysis of greenhouse gas emissions has made enormous progress during the course of the past decade.[1] Analysis has progressed from the use of simple time-trend extrapolations to the analysis of emissions of several greenhouse gases with parallel but independent behavioural and optimization models of energy, manufacturing, agriculture, and land-use systems. But our ability to examine potential future scenarios of greenhouse gas emissions is limited because modelling tools adequate to the task of integrating analyses of technologies and human activities on a global scale with regional detail, including energy production and consumption, agriculture, manufacture, capital formation, and land-use, along with the interdependencies between these categories, do not yet exist.

The first generation of models were specialty models which focused on a particular aspect of the emissions problem without regard to how that activity interacted with other human and natural activities. The Edmonds-Reilly model (ERM) (Edmonds and Reilly 1985), for example, is a global energy model in which the production of commercial biomass has no interaction with the agriculture sector or land-use in general. The Global 2100, Manne and Richels (1990a,b,c,d,

1991) is a computable general equilibrium model, but is limited in its applicability beyond energy-related issues. Other computable general equilibrium models such as Jorgenson and Wilcoxen (1990a,b) focus exclusively on national issues. Other modelling systems such as the Atmospheric Stabilization Framework (ASF) (Lashof and Tirpak 1989), utilize a system of models that provide global coverage of all emissions generating human activities, but do not provide a consistent analysis system in which the interaction between human activities can be analysed. The number of models in use to analyse greenhouse gas emissions reductions is large and growing, including for example: Nordhaus and Yohe (1983); Fossil2, AES (1986, 1991); GREEN, Burniaux et al. (1991), OECD (1991); CETA, Peck and Teisberg (1991); GEMINI, Scheraga et al. (1991); and IMAGE, Rotman et al. (1989).

The current state of understanding of the natural science of the global environmental change issue indicates that a variety of gases are associated with potential changes in the radiative composition of the atmosphere. These gases include: CO_2, CH_4, CO, N_2O, NO_x, SO_2, VOCs, chlorofluorocarbons (CFCs) and CFC substitutes. These gases are released in the process of a wide variety of human activities including: fossil fuel production, transfer and oxidation, land-use change, silvaculture, the application of some fertilizers to crops, the husbandry of ruminant livestock, the cultivation of wetland rice, and specific manufacturing processes such as cement manufacture, nylon manufacture, and chemical manufacture. Moreover, though local air chemistry plays an important role with regard to very short-lived[2] gases, it is the sum of all releases and absorptions of all gases by all human activities that governs the short-term[3] rate of change of the atmospheric composition of radiatively important gases, and the earth's atmospheric radiation profile. In addition, the human activities that govern emissions are interdependent. That is actions that are taken in one segment of the economy affect other segments of the economy. These interactions are likely to become extremely important if policies are undertaken to reduce potential future emissions. For example, carbon taxes raise great quantities of revenue. While the disposition of tax revenue can generally be assumed to be unimportant to the scale of macroeconomic activity, this is certainly not the case with carbon taxes (Bradley et al. 1991; Brinner et al. 1991; and Scheraga et al. 1991). Other potential policy actions such as tree planting to enhance the carbon sink and/or the extensive development of potential biomass resources to replace fossil fuel energy sources, can have substantial impacts on land-use, Marland (1988), Kinsman and Marland (1989), Sedjo and Solomon (1989), Moulton and Richards (1990), Adams et al. (1991), Bradley et al. (1991), and Barfield et al. (1991). Finally, it is essential that the relationship between technology, institutions, economics, and human activity be explicitly represented.

No currently existing model is capable of assessing the global emissions from all human activities and the major direct and indirect consequences of potential policies to reduce emissions. Future analysis requires a more sophisticated suite of models. The new suite of models must include both a global integrating model and compatible regional/national models. These new models must be capable of analysing the emissions of all greenhouse gases from all sources, including both those of natural and human origin, and provide an analysis of the interplay between the variety of human and natural activities responsible for greenhouse gas emissions.

The purpose of this paper is to describe the design of a model, currently under development, which is capable of addressing greenhouse gas emissions and the potential consequences of alternative policy options. We refer to this model as the *second generation model* (SGM).

Paradigms for the SGM

The development of SGMs will benefit greatly from the application of three simple principles: problem orientation, minimum modelling, and parametric modelling. The overriding design principle is that the model should be *problem oriented.* That is, the design of the model should be derived from an analysis of the underlying problem. Model design cannot begin with the set of available models and then try to make the problem fit existing model characteristics. For greenhouse gases, the issues to be addressed are: What are global emissions of greenhouse gases likely to be over the course of the next five to 100 years by region and human activity? What effect will the exercise of policy instruments to control emissions have and what will they cost? What effect will new technologies have on emissions?

Beginning with the problem and working to the design of the model allows the implementation of the second design principle, *minimum modelling.* Minimum modelling means that the model contains all of the information pertinent to answer the research question, but no extraneous information. If chemical manufacture of CFCs is an important activity in determining the rate and timing of climate change it should be included. Moreover, the model should be *parametric.* That is, the model should utilize a database in which all parameters are open to examination and change by the user. In addition, the model should be an *open model.* The purpose of the model is not to provide a one-pass forecast of the future. Where complex human activities subject to public policy action are involved, the future is fundamentally unpredictable. The purpose of a formal model is to provide a consistent, reproducible framework in which to examine possible scenarios. It is important that model results be reproducible and that the model be open to public scrutiny, and criticism, and that all of the parameters be available for inspection and alteration by model users. Finally, given the complexity of the model, it is important to use a *sequential model development* process, beginning with a simple model and adding additional important behaviours in a sequential fashion.

In applying the above cited principles, it is necessary to begin by outlining the pertinent dimensions of the greenhouse gas emissions phenomenon. The critical features associated with the emissions of radiatively important gases are as follows:

1. The issue is *global*, emissions from all sources in all regions of the world determine total atmospheric change;
2. the greenhouse results from the emission of *multiple gases* including: CO_2, CH_4, CO, N_2O, NO_x, SO_2, VOCs, CFCs, and CFC substitutes;
3. emissions result from *multiple human activities* including: agriculture (including forestry), energy production and consumption, transportation, manufacture, services, and land-use;
4. emissions depend upon *multiple resources and technologies* including: managed and unmanaged ecosystems, capital stocks, and labour;
5. emissions depend on *international trade patterns*, and possibly, migration patterns;
6. factors 3, 4, and 5 depend upon *institutional arrangements*;
7. policy analysis requires both mid-term (five-year) and long-term (100-year) *time horizons.*

The second generation model

In light of the above discussion we have undertaken the design of the SGM incorporating the above-listed criteria into the model architecture. The model is global in scope, with five-year time steps and a horizon of 2100. All the major sources of greenhouse gases, as well as SO_2 will be modelled. The economic model is a member of the class referred to as computable general equilibrium models. It contains sectoral detail on households, government, agriculture, energy, and other products activities. Capital stocks are kept by vintage, with economic retirement and retrofit options available. Depletable and renewable resources are tracked in addition to land-use. Economic decision makers include households, government, and producers. The model is regionally disaggregated, with key countries represented individually. Trade between the regions occurs in energy, agriculture, and other products.

Model overview

At base the SGM is a very simple model. Figure 1 depicts the basic structure and flows of goods and services within the SGM version 0.0. At the core of the model are three productive sectors: agriculture, energy, and other products. These, as we will discuss, are disaggregated into 10 sectors in SGM version 0.0. The greatest disaggregation, eight sectors, is found in the energy sector. The central focus on energy reflects the central role energy issues play in determining the future release of radiatively important gases into the atmosphere. Agriculture is similarly handled separately due to the importance of agriculture and land-use issues in determining emissions. All other production is aggregated into a single sector, other products, in SGM version 0.0.

The three productive sectors use three primary factors of production: land, labour, and capital, in combination with produced factors: energy, agriculture, and other products, to produce final output. Note that two aspects of land-use are considered: surface land resources, and sub-surface resources, for example, energy resources.

The household sector is assumed to own land, labour, and private capital. The demographic character of the society is determined within this sector. Household supplies of land and labour are determined on the basis of the price of these factors, which in turn determine, with distributed corporate profits, taxes, and subsidies, the income of the household sector. Household savings are also determined in this sector and vary with the interest rate. This sector also determines the mix of final products to consume.

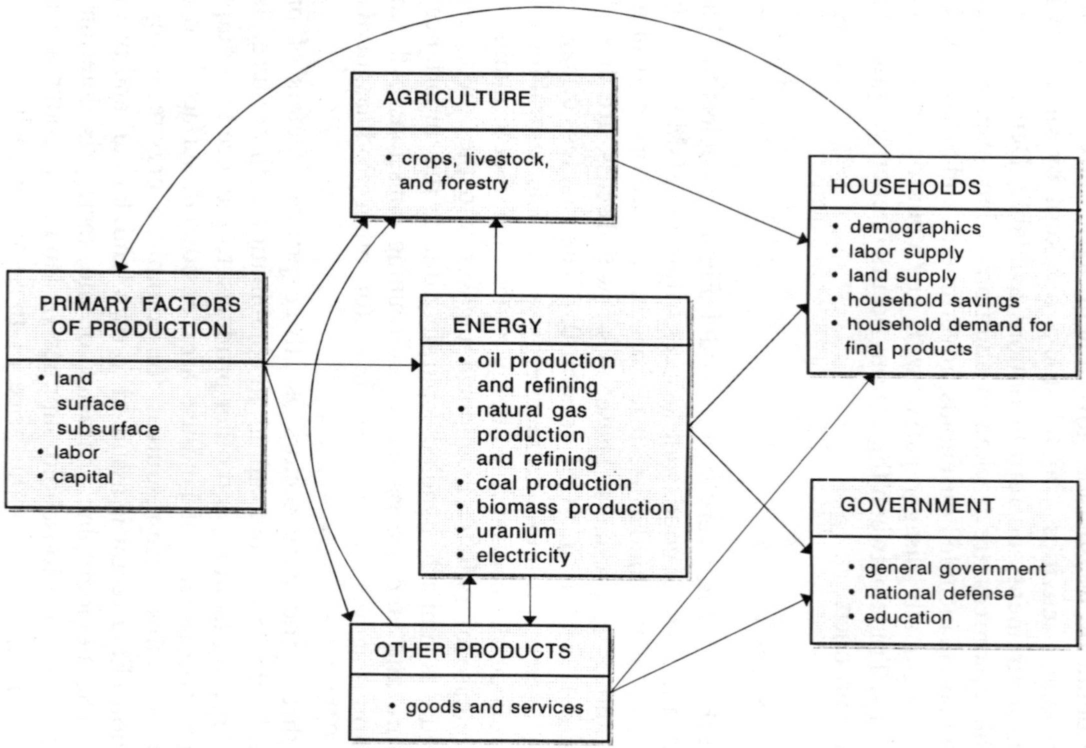

Fig. 1 **The flow of goods and services in SGM version 0.0**

Finally, the government sector obtains tax revenues from other parts of the economy which are either augmented by borrowing (or reduced by government savings). These revenues go to produce three government services: general government, national defence, and education.

The SGM version 0.0 is a self-consistent dynamic model of the relationship between these six general human activities.

Emissions coefficients are applied to each sector's associated subsector and technology activity rates to derive sectoral, regional, and global emissions of radiatively important gases.

Model development strategy

To reflect the current understanding of anthropogenic sources and sinks for radiatively important gases, and to anticipate the potential for new sources, the model has been designed with a generic structure. This structure allows for a flexible number of production activities, consumption activities, and markets. The implementation of this model utilizes the sequential model development principle. That is, the initial model version will be much simpler than the intended final version. Two model versions are currently identified: SGM version 0.0 and SGM version 1.0. SGM version 0.0 is intended to provide a proof in principle for the modelling system. SGM version 1.0 is intended to provide the first full implementation of the SGM system. SGM version 1.0 will be distributed to the public and have a complete documentation set including: theoretical model description, database description, software description, and user's guide.

For both SGM version 0.0 and SGM version 1.0, the energy production, transformation, and consumption activities will utilize databases developed in support of the ERM, Edmonds and Reilly (1985), Edmonds et al. (1986), Edmonds and Barns (1990; 1991). In addition to the energy structure of the ERM, two producing sectors, agriculture and other products have been added for SGM version 0.0. For SGM version 1.0, the number of sectors will be increased to include expanded government, transportation, other products, and agricultural activities. Final demand sectors for investment, government, and households have been developed. Model development is anticipated to proceed beyond SGM version 1.0, but such model designs lie beyond the present planning horizon.

Overview of the SGM structure

Any dynamic model has two problems that it must address. It must describe where the system is at any moment in time and it must describe the process by which it evolves. The SGM is a behavioural model. That is, it attempts to describe how economic systems behave. It is not an optimizing model. The differences between these two approaches are not as great empirically as one might expect.[4] Nevertheless, we have taken the behavioural approach to developing the SGM for two reasons. First, several extremely interesting questions can be addressed in a non-optimizing, imperfect foresight analysis framework. For example, the importance of alternative expectation formation hypotheses can be tested. That is, there is no reason to believe that energy sector decision makers have perfect foresight. In fact, the immediately preceding quarter century of energy history would support the alternative hypothesis, that is that energy decision makers have very imperfect foresight about key future energy parameters such as price. In addition, the behavioural models are computationally simpler in that present behaviour is assumed to be independent of actual future events and decisions. This is of course the domain in which actual decision makers operate. However, the model and its assumed behaviour does depend on anticipated future events and decisions.[5]

Sectors, subsectors, technologies, markets, and accounting

At any moment in time a set of relationships between economic actors can be summarized in a set of accounts that are referred to as an input-output framework. *It is important to emphasize that the SGM is not a traditional static input-output model.* The use of input-output accounting identities to describe economic interrelationships at a point in time does not mean that the SGM simply uses a set of static input-output coefficients that are assumed to remain fixed for an indefinite period in the future to determine production levels and demands. Rather, the simultaneous determination of these input-output coefficients in conjunction with a consistent set of prices is the principal problem facing a computable general equilibrium model like the SGM.

An input-output table shows the relationship between the production, distribution, and use of goods and services in an economy. A row-column entry shows the quantity of a good or service associated with a row by the sector designated by the column. If a good or service is produced in the economy, it will have both a row and column associated with it. Some sectors, for example, households, investment, and government, may be assumed to consume new final goods and services, but to provide no net output for the rest of the economy. Some factors of production, for example, land, labour, and capital, may be utilized for production in a given period, but are not produced using current flows of goods and services.

GNP accounting: The accounting framework for the SGM relies on simple economic relationships. For example, we can define GNP for any region (note we drop the regional subscript to simplify the notation) as the price-weighted sum of net production of all products,

$$\mathrm{GNP} = \sum_{i=1}^{N} P_i\left(X_i - \sum_{j=1}^{N} A_{i,j}\right) = \sum_{i=1}^{N} P_i(C_i + G_i + I_i + \mathrm{EX}_i - \mathrm{IM}_i), \tag{1}$$

where GNP is the Gross National Product; X_i is the gross domestic production of product i; A_{ij} is the domestic use of product i in the production of product j; P_i is the price of product i; N is the number of product; C_i is the domestic consumption by households of product i; G_i is the domestic consumption by government of product i; I_i is the domestic investment uses of product i; EX_i is the gross exports of product i; and IM_i is the gross imports of product i, which in turn is equal to the disposition of net output among final demand sectors. Alternatively, the GNP can be expressed as the sum of payments to the factors of production,

$$\mathrm{GNP} = \sum_{i=1}^{N}\left(P_i X_i - \sum_{j=1}^{N} P_j A_{j,i}\right) = \sum_{i=1}^{N}\left(\mathrm{TXibt}_i + \pi_i + \sum_{j=N+1}^{N+M} P_j A_{j,i}\right), \tag{2}$$

where TXibt_i is the indirect business taxes; π_i is the profits including net interest and capital consumption allowances; and M is the number of primary factors of production (e.g. labour and land).

The fundamental problem that the model must address is finding a set of prices that are consistent with demands by producers and consumers for goods, services, and primary factors of production. The major behavioural components of the model describe the relationship between prices, production, and consumption of goods and services.

Defining sectors, subsectors, technologies, and markets: For the purposes of SGM documentation we have chosen to use several terms in a specific manner.

Sectors
Sectors represent human activities that produce or consume goods and services. There are two types of sectors, producing sectors and final demand sectors;

Producing sectors
Producing sectors combine factors of production, including the products of other producing sectors and primary factors of production, to produce net output. For example, agriculture, energy, and other products are sectors in SGM version 0.0;

Final demand sectors
Final demand sectors provide final demands for final goods and services, and include households, government, investment, and net exports in SGM version 0.0;

Markets/factor inputs
Markets and factor inputs are intimately related in the SGM. A market exists in the SGM whenever production and consumption decisions are determined separately in the model. Each traded good is also potentially a factor of production, although a product may or may not be used in the production process in the implemented model. For example there may be no net demand for agricultural products by any producing sectors. Nevertheless, there will always exist a row entry in the SGM input-output accounting structure even if the element entered there is zero. Markets define the primary level of aggregation in the model. That is, all subsectors and technologies (see descriptions below) in a sector/market produce a single homogeneous commodity. Markets are defined for each producing sector plus for each primary factor of production, for example, agriculture, energy, and other products plus labour and land in SGM version 0.0;

Subsectors
A subsector exists in the SGM whenever two human activities produce the same output. All subsectors within a sector face the same

price for outputs, but would be expected to have different production functions, for example the production of electricity using oil, gas, coal, hydroelectric power, nuclear power, or solar power. Subsectors may be defined for both producing sectors and final-demand sectors;

Technologies

For some human activities an additional level of disaggregation is useful. Whereas, the number of subsectors for an individual sector in a specific region would not be expected to change from analysis to analysis, there will be times in which multiple, non-mutually exclusive, technology options should be considered. These options have the same output price as the subsectors and sector, but would have individual production functions.

SGM sectors, subsectors, technologies, and markets

For SGM version 0.0 sectors, subsectors, and markets have been identified and are listed in table 1. The technology level of the model has not been separately identified here as there is only one technology for each subsector in version 0.0.

Economic sectors

There are eight energy sectors and two non-energy production sectors in SGM version 0.0. Data for the energy sectors is largely drawn from the ERM model, Edmonds and Reilly (1985) and Edmonds et al. (1986) as updated for Edmonds and Barns (1991). The non-energy sector of the economy will be the primary focus of efforts between SGM version 0.0 and SGM version 1.0. Table 2 shows the additional sectors to be added to SGM version 0.0 to create SGM version 1.0. Producing sectors can be roughly categorized as being either agricultural, energy, or other-products related. The level of disaggregation in each area is driven by the need to understand factors affecting potential future emissions of greenhouse gases and the potential consequences of policy actions to reduce potential future greenhouse gas emissions.

Agriculture

The agriculture sector produces food, fibre, and forest products. In version 0.0, there will be only a single aggregate agricultural commodity. In version 1.0 there will be nine outputs, disaggregated primarily on the basis of greenhouse gas emissions. The three sectors

Table 1 **SGM sectors, subsectors, and markets model version 0.0**

Sector No.	Market No.	Sector	Subsector No.	Subsector name
1	1	Agriculture	1	Agriculture
2	2	Crude oil production	1–10	Crude oil production by grade. Each resource grade is modelled as a subsector.
3	3	Oil refining	1	Conventional oil refining
			2	Coal liquefaction
			3	Biomass liquefaction
4	4	Natural gas production	1–10	Natural gas production by grade. Each resource grade is modelled as a subsector.
5	5	Natural gas transformation	1	Conventional gas
			2	Coal gasification
			3	Biomass gasification
6	6	Coal production	1–10	Coal production by grade. Each resource grade is modelled as a subsector.
7	7	Biomass production	1	Traditional biomass
			2	Biomass waste
			3	Biomass farms
8	8	Uranium production and refinement	1–10	Uranium production and processing by grade. Each resource grade is modelled as a subsector.
9	9	Electric power generation	1	Oil
			2	Gas
			3	Coal
			4	Biomass
			5	Nuclear
			6	Solar/fusion
			7	Hydro
10	10	Other production	1	Other production
11	n.a.	Households[a]	1	Consumer demand
			2	Demographics
			3	Land supply
			4	Labour supply
			5	Savings
12	n.a.	Government	1	General government
			2	Education
			3	National defence
n.a.	11	Labour	n.a.	n.a.
n.a.	12	Land	n.a.	n.a.
n.a.	13	Savings/investment	n.a.	n.a.

a. Listed household subsectors represent major decisions made within the household sector rather than subsector as used in the other sectors. See section 'Households' below for further details.

Table 2 **Sectors and subsectors added to SGM version 0.0 to create SGM version 1.0**

Sector SGM version 0.0	Sectors SGM version 1.0	Subsectors
Agriculture		Rice
	Other grains	Other grains
	Ruminant livestock	Ruminant livestock
	Other livestock	Other livestock
	Other food	Other food
	Fibre	Fibre
	Forests	Forests
	Pulp and paper	Pulp and paper
	Wood and wood products	Wood and wood products
	Processed foods	Processed foods
Other production	Manufacturing	Materials intensive
		Other manufacturing
	Passenger transport	Rail
		Air
		Bus
		Other[a]
	Freight transport	Rail
		Air
		Truck
		Other
	Services	Health and other services

a. Passenger automobile in household sector.

closely associated with greenhouse gas emissions are rice (principally CH_4), ruminant livestock (principally CH_4), and forestry (principally CO_2). All sectors are associated with N_2O emissions through the application of fertilizer. Significant quantities of greenhouse gases are also associated with traditional agricultural technology, in particular the practice of slash and burn. The principal inputs in version 0.0 will be land, labour, and energy. In version 1.0 these will be expanded to include fertilizer and materials and land will potentially be disaggregated into multiple categories in accordance with soil types and climate.

Energy

There will be eight energy sectors in the model. Each of these will have subsectors as detailed in table 1 to allow the competing methods for producing the product in question to be accurately modelled.

Two types of energy technologies will be identified, those associated with depletable resources and those associated with renewable resources. All energy technologies will be associated with a resource constraint. A distinction will be made between reserves and resources. Reserves are those resources where two types of energy have been identified and whose location is known and which are known to be producible under present and anticipated economic conditions. Reserves are depleted over time as they are produced. Total reserves are augmented by additions from the resource base. The additions to reserves are determined by grade structure of resources and technologies available to extract them. Renewable resources are handled in a manner similar to depletable resources except that the capacity to produce persists beyond the point of production. Solar energy is an example of a renewable energy resource. A renewable resource may be degraded by production, however. Agriculture, for example, may deplete soils unless investments are made to maintain soil quality.

Other products

In version 0.0, the other products sector will include everything which is neither agriculture nor energy. In version 1.0, the other products sector will be broken down into manufacturing, passenger and freight transportation, and health and other services. There is the possibility of further splitting manufacturing into materials and other manufacturing. Inputs will be capital, labour, and energy in version 0.0 with materials being added in SGM version 1.0. The principal sectors are further disaggregated into subsectors on the basis of their importance to the greenhouse issue, either because they are major energy users, or because they are direct emitters or sinks for a greenhouse gas.

Regions

SGM version 0.0 has 11 regions while SGM version 1.0 will have 20 regions as shown in table 3.

Policy options

Because of the pervasive nature of activities that generate greenhouse gases, a wide variety of policy options needs to be included in the model. Making provision to model these options has had a sig-

Table 3 **Regions in SGM model versions 0.0 and 1.0**

SGM version 0.0	SGM version 1.0
1. USA	1. USA
2. Canada	2. Canada
3. Western Europe	3. European Community
4. Japan	4. Other Western Europe
5. Australia/New Zealand	5. Japan
6. Eastern Europe and Russia	6. Australia/New Zealand
7. China and other planned Asia	7. Eastern Europe
8. Mid East	8. Russia
9. Africa	9. China
10. S. & E. Asia	10. Centrally planned Asia
11. Latin America	11. Mexico
	12. Brazil
	13. Other Latin America
	14. Indonesia
	15. India
	16. Philippines
	17. South Korea
	18. Other S. & E. Asia
	19. Middle East
	20. Africa

nificant impact on the structure of the model. In addition to the usual tax and regulatory options, provisions have been made in the SGM structure to model such strategies as carbon sequestration by reforestation and afforestation, and biomass energy production, and mandated technologies and practices. The SGM is also designed to explore the consequences of changes in real government expenditure patterns/or complementary reductions in non-greenhouse taxes.

Theoretical structure of the model

The SGM employs a generic production-cost structure to facilitate the continued development of the model with a minimum of code changes and a flexible modelling response to the wide variety of potential analyses that may be required. The core of the model is the description of production activities. These activities are described by a generic production-cost relationship. This relationship utilizes the theory of duality to describe production functions alternately in physical or financial terms.

The generic production/cost relationship

The generic production/cost (GPC) relationship uses information about prices, technology, and previous investments to compute levels of production and consumption of commodities as well as demands for investment in new capital stock. Productive activities are described by functional relationships in the SGM which are referred to hereafter as technologies. The term technology is used here to cover a broad array of activities including everything from the production of iron and steel to the production of rice. Technologies, as described earlier, are the fundamental unit of disaggregation in the model. Each sector contains at least one subsector and each subsector contains at least one technology. For SGM version 0.0, there is only one sector, market, subsector, and technology for the production of agricultural output. For the production of electricity, there are seven subsectors each of which can potentially utilize multiple technology options. The SGM keeps all of its information on productive capacity at the technology level of detail.

The SGM uses a vintaged description of technologies. This has a number of important implications. First, it means that history matters. When a technology is installed it remains in existence and can be operated until its retirement. New technologies affect productivity primarily at the margin. They can only affect historical decisions if they are so attractive (unattractive) that they force prices down to the point where existing technologies are retired early (undergo life extension). Another important implication is that once installed, capital stock is not malleable. It cannot be shifted around from one sector of the economy to another. In fact, once installed, capital costs no longer matter. In other words, once the technology is installed the decision to operate or idle a technology depends solely on the ability of the technology to recover its current operating expenses plus taxes and less subsidies.

A technology is described by an array of characteristics including:

1. production function parameters;
2. emissions coefficients;
3. capital investment parameters;
4. installation parameters (e.g. date of first availability, date of removal from the list of options, nominal lifetime, length of installation period); and
5. vintage.

A technology option can be described by the information contained in parameter sets 1, 2, 3, and 4. Once installed, the operating characteristics of a technology can be described by parameter sets 1, 2, and 6.

Within the GPC relationship, the producing sectors all follow the same general structure. There are, of course, some characteristics that are specific to a sector or apply only to a subset of sectors. However, the basic model structure is sufficiently general to accommodate the production/cost and operating characteristics of the various producing sectors in its parameter set.

The sectors represent the highest level of aggregation of production characteristics in the GPC. Within the GPC framework, these production sectors are disaggregated into one or more production/cost subsectors. All sectors, subsectors, and technologies produce a common output and face a common external market price for produced output. The GPC structure allocates investment to technologies based on prior investment history and relative profitability[6] using a logit market-share allocation scheme.

As an example of this sector-subsector hierarchy, consider an electricity production sector with subsectors for coal, oil, natural gas, biomass, nuclear, and hydroelectric power. These subsectors all produce electricity, and they all receive the same price for the electricity they generate. These subsectors do, however, have quite different operating and input requirements for producing electricity, which will in turn affect their relative profitabilities. The allocation of investment among these subsectors in the GPC will reflect these differences in profitability.

Each technology is represented by a vintage-dated, constant elasticity of substitution (CES) production/cost function (one for each vintage of capital stock in operation). For each technology, technological change through time can be captured in the model through the CES production function parameter set. In SGM version 0.0 both an initial set and a terminal set of CES coefficients or parameters is specified for each producing subsector. For any future vintage, the CES coefficients used are a time-dependent interpolation between the initial and terminal values. Different technological change scenarios can thus be modelled in each subsector by varying the terminal coefficient values and the time required to reach these terminal values.

The general execution path for the GPC is to (1) determine desired levels of investment in new capacity, (2) operate the new capacity, (3) retrofit existing capital stocks, and (4) operate or retire existing capital stocks.

The CES production/cost-function

The CES production function can be written,

$$Xs = \alpha_0 \left(\sum_{i=1}^{N} \alpha_i X_i^{\rho} \right)^{1/\rho}, \tag{3}$$

where Xs is the gross output of the process; X_i is the use of input factor i; α_0 is the scale coefficient; α_i is the individual factor coefficients; and ρ is the elasticity of substitution parameter.

Profit maximization implies that,

$$P_i = P_0 \frac{\partial Xs}{\partial X_i}, \qquad i = 1, \ldots N - M, \tag{4}$$

where P_i is the price of ith input; P_0 is the price of output; $N - M$ is the number of variable factors; and M is the number of fixed factors.[7]

Profits can be written as,

$$\pi = P_0 Xs - \sum_{i=1}^{N-M} P_i X_i. \tag{5}$$

By judicious application of algebra, and equation (4), profits can be expressed as a function of price and the quantities of M non-variable factors of production via,

$$\pi = \alpha_0 P_0 \left[1 - (P_0 \alpha_0)^{\mu} \left(\sum_{i=1}^{N-M} \alpha_i^{(\mu/\rho)} P_i^{-\mu} \right) \right]^{-1/\mu} \left(\sum_{i=N-M+1}^{N} \alpha_i X_i^{\rho} \right)^{1/\rho}, \tag{6}$$

where

$$\mu = \frac{\rho}{1 - \rho}. \tag{7}$$

It is well known that the partial derivative of this expression with respect to the price of the ith input is the negative of the total factor demand, that is

$$\frac{\partial \pi}{\partial P_i} = -X_i. \tag{8}$$

The demand for the ith factor input to the production process can therefore be calculated directly as,

$$X_i = \left(\alpha_0 P_0 \frac{\alpha_i}{P_i}\right)^{\mu/\rho} \left(\frac{Y}{Z}\right)^{1-\rho}, \qquad i = 1, \ldots N - M, \tag{9}$$

where

$$Y = \sum_{I=N-M+1}^{N} \alpha_i X_i^{\rho}, \tag{10}$$

and

$$Z = 1 - (\alpha_0 P_0)^{\mu} \left(\sum_{i=1}^{N-M} \alpha_i^{\mu/\rho} P_i^{-\mu} \right). \tag{11}$$

The above equations can be used to model both operational decision making and investment determination.

Expected future profits from the operation of a technology which employs

$$x_k = (X_{N-M+1}, \ldots, X_N)$$

fixed factors over the course of T years of operation is simply,

$$\pi_e(t_0) = \sum_{t=1}^{T} \left(\frac{\pi(x_k, t)}{1 + \text{dis}} \right)^t, \tag{12}$$

where $\pi(x_k, t)$ is the profit rate consistent with expected future prices in future period t and dis is the discount rate.

Investment and operating decisions

Once a technology has been installed, operation is determined by the set of factor prices for variable factors of production, and the quantity of the fixed factor employed. The determination of factor demands is therefore a relatively simple matter. Investment decisions however are not so simple. These are determined both by the present set of factor prices and the set of expected future factor prices extending out over the expected lifetime of the investment. In the SGM, there are two types of investments, investments in new capacity and investments in existing capacity, in the form of retrofit and renovation (life extension) investments. The existence of retrofit and renovation (life extension) investment alternatives means that present operations are never simple, and that the technology chosen for an addition to new capacity may be substantially altered before its ultimate retirement. The analysis of investment alternatives requires a mechanism for the determination of expectations regarding future prices and taxes.

Future price and tax rate expectations

In each sector, investments are allocated among subsectors on the basis of their relative *expected* profitabilities. Therefore, investment decisions for each subsector require expected profit rate calculations, which require expected prices and taxes for all inputs. For an open economy the purchase price of the good produced by the ith sector in region "1" is given by:

$$P_{i,l} = \alpha_{i,l}[P_i(1 + \delta_{i,l}\mathrm{Tr}_i)\mathrm{txa}_{i,l} + \mathrm{txb}_{i,l}], \tag{13}$$

where $\alpha_{i,l}$ is an adjustment factor to reflect markups and intra-regional transport costs; Tr_i is the import transportation costs for the ith good; $\delta_{i,l}$ is a logic driven parameter whose value is 0 if the region is a net exporter, and 1 otherwise, $\mathrm{txa}_{i,l}$ is the proportional tax on the ith product in region 1; and $\mathrm{txb}_{i,l}$ is the additive tax on the ith product in region 1.

Obviously, the price received by the producer of the jth good is simply,

$$P_{i,l} = P_i(1 + \delta_{i,l}\mathrm{Tr}_i). \tag{14}$$

The direct computation of $\pi_e(t_0)$ is cumbersome. An approximation of this value can be obtained by substituting a set of present discounted prices directly into the profit function. This yields an exact solution when $\mu = 1$ (see equation [7]). The present discounted price for product j (either an input or an output), Pe_j, is calculated by,

$$Pe_{j,l}(T) = \sum_{t=1}^{T_{\exp}} P_{j,l}(t_0) \cdot \left(\frac{1 + r_j}{1 + \text{dis}}\right)^t. \tag{15}$$

where $T_{\exp}$ is the nominal life of the investment; r_j is the rate of expected price change; and dis_j is the discount rate for that sub-sector.

As noted above, the nominal life of the investment is a parameter of the technology. This parameter value may be different from the maximum potential life of the technology. The tax rate *tx* is an exogenous variable. Both the rate of expected price change r_j and the discount rate dis are behavioural variables. Expectations of future price and tax rate expectations are assumed to be formed in one of two ways. Either they are given exogenously, and assumed known, or they are formed on the basis of prior experience. This yields four alternative formation assumptions for future prices and taxes of inputs and outputs which can be created by combining assumptions 1, 2, 3, and 4 from the following matrix:

	Formed on the assumption that previous B periods rate of change will continue indefinitely	Given exogenously
Prices	1	3
Taxes	2	4

Note that whenever price of tax expectations are formed on the basis of prior experience, the period of prior experience, *B*, must also be specified. For $B = 0$, present prices or taxes are assumed to remain constant indefinitely. Furthermore, it is possible to run the model in an iterative sequence to develop a perfect foresight set of exogenously specified set of prices. This would be accomplished by specifying prior solution prices as the set of expected future prices and iterating until stability is reached.

We feel that the ability to model behaviour in which price expectations are formed on the basis of imperfect foresight is important. The period of time between 1970 and the present is marked by decision-making on the basis of flawed foresight in energy markets.

Furthermore, the effectiveness of tax and regulatory policies may in fact depend on the expectations formed with regard to long-term commitment.

The relationship between the discount and interest rates

The discount rate and the real interest rate need not be the same. A great deal of behavioural literature suggests that these rates may in fact be significantly different from each other, Lind (1983), Meier and Whittier (1983), Hausman (1979), and Gately (1980). To reflect this phenomenon, the discount rate, dis, will be linked to the interest rate calculated in the model, interest, by a constant factor of addition, fac_r. The sector-specific discount rate for retrofit investments, will therefore be given by,

$$\text{dis}_r = \text{interest} + \text{fac}_r. \tag{16}$$

The add-on factor for retrofit investments need not be the same as the add-on factor for new investments.

The expected future profit rate for a capacity increasing technology

The expected profit rate relative to the capital cost, K, denoted as π_e, is given by,

$$\pi_e = \frac{NR_e}{K} \tag{17}$$

and

$$\frac{NR_e}{K} = \alpha_0 Pe_0 \left[1 - (Pe_0\alpha_0)^{\rho/(1-\rho)} \left(\sum_{i=1}^{N-M} \alpha_i^{1/(1-\rho)} Pe_i^{-(\rho/(1-\rho))} \right) \right]^{(1-\rho)/\rho}$$

$$\times \left(\sum_{i=N-M+1}^{N} \alpha_i x_i^{\rho} \right)^{1/\rho} (1 - tx). \tag{18}$$

where NRe is the expected net revenue, tx is the profits tax rate, there are M fixed factors, and the other $N - M$ factors are variable factors.

In version 0.0, there is only one fixed factor and the fixed factor term reduces to $\alpha_n^{(1/\rho)}$.

When investments in new capacity occur over more than one period

For most investments the decision to invest and the initiation of operation can be assumed to occur within a single five-year time step. This is not always the case. For example, the construction of nuclear electric power plants may require more than five years from start of construction to first production. Forestry similarly requires more than five years between the time of initial investment and the time of harvest. Each of these circumstances requires a somewhat different approach.

Extended construction time

When the construction time for an addition to capacity extends over $T_{\text{construct}}$ periods then there is an evaluation of the investment in each of these periods under the assumption that the fraction of total investment required in each period is equal. That is, if the total investment in the new capacity is taken to be K, and the construction time is $T_{\text{construct}}$, then in each period an investment of

$$K_t = K/T_{\text{construct}}$$

is assumed to be made. If the investment is expected to be profitable in the first period, then construction begins. The present discounted value of the investment requirement is then,

$$K_{e,t} = \left(\frac{K}{T_{\text{construct}}}\right) \sum_{tc=1}^{(T_{\text{construct}}-t)} \left(\frac{1}{1+\text{dis}}\right)^{tc} \qquad t = 1, \ldots T_{\text{construct}}, \qquad (19)$$

where, t is the investment period in which the investment decision is being made, $t = 1, \ldots T_{\text{construct}}$; and tc is an index of periods of investment remaining, $t = 1, \ldots, T_{\text{construct}}$. Note that as each period of construction passes, the expected profit rate will rise, other things being equal, because previous period investments become sunk costs.

Expected net revenues from operation of the investment must also be discounted by a factor,

$$\sum_{tc=1}^{(T_{\text{construct}}-t)} \left(\frac{1}{1+\text{dis}}\right)^{tc} \qquad t = 1, \ldots, T_{\text{construct}}. \tag{20}$$

The growth-harvest decision

The growth-harvest decision problem does not occur in SGM version 0.0, as all agricultural activities are aggregate. In SGM version 1.0, a forestry sector will be disaggregated and this problem will occur. In this case an investment occurs in period t_0, but no revenue is received until T_{harvest}. But T_{harvest} is not predetermined. For growth-harvest production functions the production function given by equation (3) and

$$a_0 = \alpha(C_t, C_{t-1}, \text{Atmos}_t, \text{Atmos}_{t-1}, t - t_0), \tag{21}$$

where α is now a function of a vector of climate and atmospheric state variables, and the amount of time that has elapsed between the initial investment, t_0, and the present period t, C_t is a vector of climate variables such as for example, temperature, precipitation, soil moisture, and evapotranspiration, for $t = t, t-1$; and Atmos_t is a vector of atmospheric state variables such as for example the concentration of atmospheric CO_2, for $t = t, t-1$.

The expected profit rate for an investment in a growth-harvest activity is determined by equations (18) and (21) using the expected price vector for the potential harvest T_{harvest} periods in the future[8] and discounted by the value,

$$\text{discountfactor} = \sum_{t=1}^{T_{\text{harvest}}} \left(\frac{1}{1+\text{dis}}\right)^{t}. \tag{22}$$

The value of π_e can be computed for any two potential harvest periods, T_{harvest_0} and $T_{\text{harvest}_0}+1$, denoted respectively $\pi_e(T_{\text{harvest}})$ and $\pi_e(T_{\text{harvest}}+1)$. The maximum potential value for π_e can be estimated by beginning with $T_{\text{harvest}} = 1$, and increasing the value of T_{harvest} whenever,

$$\pi_e(T_{\text{harvest}}+1) \geq \pi_e(T_{\text{harvest}}).$$

Investments with a maximum value for $\pi_e > 0$ are included in the pool of sector specific competing investments.

Resource constrained technologies

Many economic activities take place against a background of resource constraints. This is of particular interest in the field of energy economics, but is in no way limited to the energy sector. For example, the resource base for conventional oil is ultimately finite, and cumulative production from that resource base may potentially approximate the total resource over the period of analysis. Fossil fuels are an example of a depletable resource. Renewable resources, such as solar, wind, tidal, and ocean thermal energy conversion also exist. For renewable resources the resource is available in each period independent of consumption during the previous period. We will define depletable and renewable resources as follows:

- *Depletable resources*: A depletable resource is one in which the consumption of the resource in one period affects potential consumption in the next period.
- *Renewable resources*: A renewable resource is one in which the consumption of the resource in one period does not affect potential consumption of the resource in the next period.

Describing the relationship between resources and production is important for such activities.

Depletable resources

For depletable resources the total resource available for consumption over all periods is the sum of the resource available in each grade of NG grades,

$$R_i = \sum_{g=1}^{NG} R_{i,g}, \tag{23}$$

where R_i is the total amount of resource of type i which could be potentially recovered under any possible conditions; and $R_{i,g}$ is the total amount resource of type i, found in concentration c_g or higher up to c_{g-1} under any possible conditions. The resource base can be partitioned into discovered and undiscovered resources. Discovered resources are made up of extracted resources, RE, and reserves, RV. Undiscovered resources are denoted as RU. Thus,

$$R_i = RE_i + RU_i + RV_i, \tag{24}$$

$$R_{i,g} = RE_{i,g} + RU_{i,g} + RV_{i,g}. \tag{25}$$

In the model each sector that produces a depletable resource has a different subsector for each grade of the resource. For a given technology, the grade of the resource is reflected in the value of $\alpha_0 = \alpha_{0,g}$ in the production function. Desired extraction from each resource grade is determined by the expected rate of profitability. The production function implicitly includes the cost of converting undiscovered resources into reserves. Production occurs out of reserves as determined by profit maximization subject to the constraint imposed by total investment in each vintage's productive capacity. The production activity occurs only from reserves, and shifts resources from the reserve category to the extracted category.

Because of the multiplicity of resource grades and the existence of substitutes, there is no guarantee that the price of a depletable resource will rise at a rate equal to the rate of interest, the 'hotelling' result.

Competition among capacity increasing investments within a sector

As discussed earlier, the sector is the highest level of aggregation in the model. Subsectors are assumed to produce an essentially homogeneous product within the sector. For example, in SGM version 1.0 it is expected that there will be four different types of freight transport: rail, air, truck, and other. Each will produce a common unit of output, tonne kilometres of freight transport. Obviously, this assumption violates physical reality. Nevertheless, it is intended to capture the essence of the system. For each subsector, there also exists an additional level of disaggregation, which we refer to as the technology level. Technologies compete within the confines of an individual subsector, and in turn determine the overall profitability of the subsector. A logit function is used to determine the share of total sectoral investment each technology obtains. That share is given by:

$$S_{i,\text{tech}} = \frac{(\pi^{\sigma}_{i,\text{tech}}/N_{\text{tech}_i}N_{SS})}{\sum_{j=1}^{NO}(\pi^{\sigma}_{j,\text{tech}}/N_{\text{tech}_j}N_{ss})}, \tag{26}$$

where $\pi_{j,\text{tech}}$ is a metric of the characteristic upon which competition is based for technology, tech, in subsector i, N_{ss} is the number of subsectors, N_{tech_i} is the number of technologies competing in subsector i, σ is a sensitivity parameter, and

$$NO = \sum_{i=1}^{N_{SS}} N_{\text{tech}_i}. \tag{27}$$

The logit function is homogeneous of degree zero. That is, any scaler change in the values of all $\pi_{i,\text{tech}}$ leaves the values of all $s_{i,\text{tech}}$ unchanged. For values of σ equal to zero, $s_i = 1/(N_{ss}N_{\text{tech}_i})$. If greater values of $\pi_{i,\text{tech}}$ enhance market share, then the value of σ is taken to be non-negative. (If greater values of $\pi_{i,\text{tech}}$ diminish market share, then the value of σ is taken to be negative.) As the value of σ approaches ∞, $s_{i,\text{tech}}$ approaches one for the largest value of $\pi_{i,\text{tech}}$.

In this model, we will use the logit function to determine the share of a sector's total investment spending that is allocated to each subsector, that is to say each competing technology option. The independent variables then are the profit rate values of π obtained earlier. In general the value of σ will be set to reflect existing market sensitivity.

Aggregate sector investment in new capacity

Aggregate regional sector investment levels are determined by using an accelerator from the previous periods total investment. Specifically,

$$K_{\text{tot}_{t+1}} = K_{\text{tot}_t} \cdot \text{baserate}_{t+1} \cdot f[\exp(\pi_{t+1})], \tag{28}$$

where K_{tot} is the total new investment in sector i, in period $t+1$; baserate is the base rate of growth of investment; and $f(\exp(\pi))$ is a function of the expected profit rate, $\exp(\pi)$.

We do not prejudice the determination of either baserate or the function $f(\exp(\pi))$. For present model development we use,

$$\text{baserate}_{t+1} = \frac{K_{\text{tot}_t}}{K_{\text{tot}_{t-1}}}. \tag{29}$$

The expected rate of profit is taken to be the average expected profit rate which is given by,

$$\exp(\pi_{t+1}) = \bar{\pi}_{t+1} = \left(\sum_{i=1}^{NO} \pi_{i,t+1}^{\sigma} \right)^{1/\sigma}, \tag{30}$$

where $\pi_{i,t}$ is the profit rate for the ith technology (taken over all subsectors), in period t. This derivation is given in Clarke (1991). For SGM version 0.0 we use,

$$f[\exp(\pi_{t+1})] = \left(\frac{\exp(\pi_{t+1})}{\bar{\pi}_t}\right)^{\alpha}, \tag{31}$$

where α is a sensitivity parameter.

Retrofit and renovation investment decisions and the operation of existing technology vintages

For existing technologies, or technologies with capacity already in place, there are four possible outcomes in any period:
1. *Operate* without change,
2. *Retrofit* and operate,
3. *Idle* the capacity, but do not retire,
4. *Retire* the technology.

The determination of operating mode depends upon the behavioural assumptions. Given the five-year time step in the model, it has been decided to eliminate option 3. In other words, producers will either operate a vintage in the current period or retire that vintage.

For market economies profit maximization is the behavioural paradigm. For investment decisions this means that *NR* is maximized. That is, existing technologies will continue to be operated as long as current operating costs can be covered, unless otherwise prevented from doing so. They will add retrofit technologies either if they are required or if they add to profitability. The behaviour of command economies is similar, except that (1) substantial subsidies, in both the cost of input factors and direct subsidies to total operating costs; and (2) allocation schemes where administered prices do not clear markets are an important determinant of economic behaviour.

Retrofit technologies

Retrofit technologies are the principal complicating factor in the analysis of existing technology operations. The level of operation of the technology is assumed to be identical to the parent technology. The additional capital cost, relative to the original capital cost, is a technology parameter. The presence or lack of presence of retrofit options does not affect the base production or cost functions.

New retrofit options can be incorporated into the operating structure of the technology if they either are required or are determined to be profitable. If retrofit technologies are not required, then it must be determined if the base technology will continue to be operated. If the base technology can cover current costs, it will continue to be operated, even if its present discounted expected future revenues are negative. If it cannot cover present operating costs, then the technology will be retired unless some retrofit package can produce a present discounted expected future profit.

Under some circumstances the present technology may cease to be an option because a retrofit technology must be applied. In such cases the technology will be retired unless some retrofit package can produce a present discounted expected future profit just as if the base technology had been unprofitable in the current period.

To evaluate retrofit technologies we make the following calculations. Consider an existing technology of vintage V, installed in period V, with nominal lifetime T, in existence in period t. To determine the profitability of retrofit options for that technology, we begin by computing,

$$Pe_j = P_j(t) \cdot \sum_{t=1}^{T-t} \left(\frac{1 + r_j}{1 + \text{dis}} \right)^t \cdot [1 + tx(t)], \qquad j = 1, \ldots, N. \tag{32}$$

Note that a set of expected future prices for retrofit technologies may be different from the set of expected future prices for the base technology due to different discount rates for the two activities. That is, some firms may have a higher discount rate for retrofit technologies than for new base load investments.

Because each retrofit technology can affect the original technology is a wide variety of ways, the total technology, that is including both the base technology and a package of retrofit options, is given by a separate CES production function whose net additional capital cost is some fraction of the original capital investment, and whose lifetime is the expected lifetime remaining on the original technology.

The general formulation for profit with a fixed factor CES production function, as given by equation (6), is used to compute a value of π_{retrofit} for each technology with a retrofit option. Note that for retrofit $= 0$, the expected future profit for the base technology is given. If any retrofit technology has a positive present discounted expected profit higher than the base technology, then the retrofit technology package with the highest expected future profit rate is selected. If expected profits are negative no retrofit technology is adopted, and if either the base technology is unable to cover present operating costs, or is no longer available due to mandated retrofit actions, then the technology is retired.

Renovation

Renovation is a special case of the general investment/retrofit problem. At the end of T_{exp} years of service the technology must either be retired or renovated. Renovation takes the form of a one-time capital investment, that occurs in the T_{exp}th year of service. In effect, however, the retrofit option can be thought of as competing with other new investment opportunities with the production function coefficients of the original technology, a capital cost of K_{extend}, and T_{extend} years of expected life. The profit rate is computed using equation (15) and expected future prices based on an expected technology life of T_{extend} years. Of course, more than one life-extension technology option is possible. In the case where multiple options are available, the technology with the highest expected profit rate is chosen.

The present operating profitability, *NR*, is still computed from equation (6). The operation, retirement and retrofit logic diagram is given below:

	$NR > 0$	$NR < 0$
$\pi > 0$	Operate and Retrofit	Retire
$\pi < 0$	Retire	Retire

That is, the technology will be retired unless it both can make money in the immediate period and is expected to add to the wealth of the sector over its expected lifetime.

Greenhouse gas emissions

As discussed earlier, the greenhouse issue is complicated by the fact that a wide array of gases are associated with the effect. We make no attempt to discuss either the nature or the extent of the effect various gases have on the radiative balance of the earth/atmosphere energy balance, but simply note that the following suite of gases will be considered.

- CO_2 emissions from fossile fuel and biomass combustion processes.
- VOC emissions resulting from energy production processes, selected manufacturing processes, some combustion processes (mainly of petroleum based fuel in internal combustion engines), and from selected natural processes.
- CFC emissions from losses from refrigeration and air-conditioning equipment, foam blowing, aerosol propellants, cleaning solvents, and fire extinguishers.
- CH_4 emissions which emanate from the production and distribution of natural gas, mining of coal, from the raising of ruminant animals, the growing of rice, from sanitary landfills, and from combustion processes (principally biomass burning).
- CO emissions, most of which emanate from incomplete combustion of carbon-based fuels, principally in the transportation sector.
- N_2O emissions from combustion processes, fertilizer use, and selected natural sources.
- NO_x emissions from combustion processes – especially from electrical power generation and in internal combustion engines.
- SO_2 emissions and consequent sulphate transformations so that albedo changes can be monitored.

Greenhouse gas emissions coefficients will be included with each technology description. Emissions will be assumed to be proportional to either the scale of input utilization or output of the technology.

Emissions can be calculated simply as,

$$E_{m,1} = \sum_{i=1}^{NS} \sum_{ss=1}^{NSS(i,1)} \sum_{\text{tech}=1}^{N_{\text{tech}}(i,ss,1)} \sum_{v=V_0}^{t} \sum_{j=1}^{NI} \left(e_{m,i,ss,\text{tech},j} X_{i,ss,\text{tech},j,1,v} + f_{m,i,ss,\text{tech},j} Xs_{i,ss}\right), \quad (33)$$

where, $e_{m,i,ss,\text{tech},j}$ is the technology specific emission coefficient for emission m, in sector i, subsector ss, using technology tech, with input j; $X_{i,ss,\text{tech},j,1,v}$ is the input demand for factor j by sector i, subsector ss, using technology tech, of vintage v, in region 1; $f_{m,i,ss,\text{tech},j}$ is the technology specific emission coefficient for emission m, in sector i, subsector ss, using technology tech, producing output j; and

$Xs_{i,ss,\text{tech},j,1,v}$ is the output of good j by sector i, subsector ss, using technology tech, of vintage v, in region 1.

When emissions are released costlessly into the atmosphere they have no effect on either the cost of production or the optimum demand for investment goods. Releases need not be costless. Like other inputs and outputs from the technology, emissions may be priced. Emissions coefficients have been related to individual technologies. This is because the determinants of emissions can be relatively complex. This is even the case for emissions as simple as fossil fuel combustion carbon emissions. In general the release of carbon to the atmosphere is considered to be proportional to the energy content of the specific fuel by a fixed ratio and therefore largely independent of the technology in which the fossil fuel form is combusted. This need not be the case. Emissions capture technologies exist, and the rate of release of carbon to be atmosphere per unit of fossil fuel energy combusted may therefore vary by technology.

On the presumption that emissions can be measured and therefore costs can be associated with them, emissions fees would affect the cost of production. The effect of fees will be reflected in a modification to equations (13) and (14). For consumers of the jth product in the ith sector the cost would become,

$$P_{i,ss,\text{tech},j,1} = \alpha_{i,1}P_i(1+\delta_{i,1}Tr_i)txa_{i,1}+txb_{i,1}+\sum_{m=1}^{EM} e_{m,i,ss,\text{tech},j}\, tx_{m,i,ss,\text{tech}}, \tag{34}$$

where $P_{i,ss,\text{tech},j,1}$ = the price of good j consumed in sector i, subsector ss, using technology tech, in region 1. For producers, the income from the sale of the jth product produced in sector i is,

$$P_{i,ss,\text{tech},j,1} = P_i(1+\delta_{i,1}Tr_i) - \sum_{m=1}^{EM} f_{m,i,ss,\text{tech},j}\, tx_{m,i,ss,\text{tech},j,1}. \tag{35}$$

Final demand sectors

In addition to the sectors that produce goods and services, there are three final demand sectors, households, government, and foreign. As is the case with the directly productive sectors, final demand sectors have demands for goods and services and can produce goods and services. We begin with the government sector, not because the analysis of the behaviour of the government sector is simpler than that of the household, but rather because our modelling approach to this sector is simpler than that of the household sector.

Government

Expenditures by the budget of the government sector must satisfy the following identity:

$$TX_{\text{tot}} - S_{\text{gov}} = TR_{\text{gov}} + \sum_{i=1}^{N} P_i X_{i,\text{gov}}, \tag{36}$$

where TX_{tot} is the total of all net tax revenues, where subsidies are measured S_{gov} is the net government savings, or for negative values equals net government borrowing, and $TR_{\text{gov}} =$ is transfer payments by the government.

In SGM version 0.0, S_{gov} is assumed to be zero. In SGM Version 1.0 this assumption will be relaxed.

In SGM version 0.0 transfer payments are assumed to be a function of demographics,

$$TR_{\text{gov}} = \beta_0 \text{POP}_{\text{tot}}^{\beta_{\text{tot}}} \left(\frac{\text{POP}_{15-} + \text{POP}_{65+}}{\text{POP}_{\text{tot}}} \right)^{\beta_a} \left(\frac{\text{POP}_{25\%y}}{\text{POP}_{\text{tot}}} \right)^{\beta_b} \left(\frac{Y_{\text{personal}}}{\text{POP}_{\text{tot}}} \right)^{\beta_c}, \tag{37}$$

where POP_{tot} is the total population; POP_{15-} is the population under age 15; POP_{65+} is the population over age 65; $\text{POP}_{25\%y}$ is the population whose personal income is 25% or less than the mean; Y_{personal} is the personal income; and β_i is the appropriate empirically determined coefficients.

The government is modelled as producing services. In SGM version 0.0 there are three services produced. In SGM version 1.0 this will be expanded to five. These are given in table 4.

The demand for goods and services by the government sector is modelled as a constrained optimization problem. Government max-

Table 4 **SGM government subsectors version 0.0 and version 1.0**

SGM version 0.0	SGM version 1.0
General, National Defence, Education	General, National Defence, Education, Infrastructure, R&D

imizes a utility function, presumed to be CES in SGM version 0.0, defined over the three subsectors (general government, national defence, and education), and subject to the net income given by equation (36). This can be represented as,

$$G = \left(\sum_{ss=1}^{NGS} \delta_{ss} G_{ss}^{\mu} \right)^{1/\mu}, \tag{38}$$

where G is the government utility, an unobservable variable; G_{ss} is the production of government service ss; δ_{ss} is a scale parameter; μ is an elasticity parameter; and NGS is the number of services produced by the government.

Government services are assumed to be produced with fixed input–output coefficients. Thus the cost of an additional unit of government service, type ss, can be computed as simply,

$$P_{g,ss} = \sum_{i=1}^{N} a_{i,g,ss} P_i, \tag{39}$$

where $P_{g,ss}$ is the cost of the next unit of government service ss, that is P_i is the price of input i in the production process; and $a_{i,g,ss}$ is the amount of input i required to produce government service from government subsector ss.

Because the cost of producing the next unit of government service is constant for any set P_i,[9] the determination of government demands for goods and services is greatly simplified. This problem can be stated as one of maximizing utility subject to a budget constraint, equation (36), maximize $G(G_1, \ldots, G_{NGS})$, subject to

$$TX_{\text{tot}} - S_{\text{gov}} - \sum_{ss=1}^{NGS} P_{g,ss} G_{ss} = 0. \tag{40}$$

This problem has a simple solution,

$$G_{ss} = (TX_{\text{tot}} - S_{\text{gov}} - TR_{\text{gov}})\beta_{ss}P_{g,ss}^{\gamma-1}\left(\sum_{ss=1}^{NGS} \beta_{ss}P_{g,ss}^{\gamma}\right)^{-1}, \tag{41}$$

where $\beta_{ss} = \delta_i^{-1/(\mu-1)}$ and $\gamma = \mu/(\mu - 1)$.[10]

Households

A great number of decisions are carried out in the household sector. These include the following:
1. Demographics
2. Labour supply
3. Land supply
4. Household savings
5. Household demand for final products

In SGM version 0.0 the determination of the demographic characteristics of each region's population, and its supplies of labour, land, and savings are handled sequentially. Only the composition of demand for final goods and services is handled in a holistic utility maximization framework. Because the demographic characteristics of a region's population are an important determinant of other household behaviour we discuss this element of the model first. We then consider labour, land, and savings supplies. These factors determine disposable personal income allocated to consumption. Finally, we describe the determination of final demand for goods and services.

Demographics

The demographic component of the household sector determines population in a region by employing assumptions with regard to three characteristics: survival rates, fertility rates, and migration rates. For any period, *t*, total population is given by,

$$\text{POP}_{\text{tot}_t} = \sum_{\text{age}=1}^{NAGE} \text{POP}_{\text{age, males}} + \text{POP}_{\text{age, females}}, \tag{42}$$

where $\text{POP}_{\text{age, males}}$ is the males in age group age; $\text{POP}_{\text{age, females}}$ is the females in age group age; and *NAGE* is the number of age groups defined.

For the youngest age group, age = 1,

$$POP_{age=1,\,gender,\,t} = \sum_{age=2}^{NAGE} g_{age,\,gender} f_{age,\,t} POP_{age,\,female,\,t}, \qquad \text{gender} = \text{male, female}, \qquad (43)$$

where $POP_{age=1,\,gender,\,t}$ is the population in the youngest age group, age = 1, by gender, in period t; $f_{age,\,t}$ is the fertility rate for females in age group, age, in period t; and $g_{age,\,gender}$ is the fraction of births by gender, with $g_{age,1} + g_{age,2} = 1$, and for other age groups, population is determined by survival via,

$$POP_{age,\,gender,\,t} = SV_{age,\,gender,\,t} POP_{age-1,\,gender,\,t-1} + POPmig_{age,\,gender,\,t}, \qquad c = 2, \ldots, NAGE. \qquad (44)$$

where $sv_{age,\,gender,\,t}$ is the survival rate by gender from age group age to age + 1; $POPmig_{age=1,\,gender,\,t}$ is the net immigration of population into the region in age group, age = 1.

At this point, fertility rates, survival rates, and migration rates are determined exogenously, with the exception that net migration summed over all regions is always zero for each age and gender.

Labour supply

The supply of labour is determined by the working age population, rate of labour force participation, and the wage rate.

$$X_{labour} = \sum_{male}^{female} \sum_{age=1}^{NAGE} \alpha_{age,\,gender} POP_{age,\,gender} [P_{labour}(1 - txa_{labour}) - txb_{labour}]^{\beta_{age,\,gender}}, \qquad (45)$$

where P_{labour} is the wage rate for labour; $\alpha_{age,\,gender}$ is a scale coefficient for the supply of labour, by age and gender; $\beta_{age,\,gender}$ is the price elasticity of supply of labour by age and gender, and txa, txb are proportional and additive tax rates, respectively.

Land supply

In version 0.0, land supply is total land area in the region. All land services are sold on the domestic market. Households supply land on the basis of the rental rate via

$$X_{\text{land}} = \text{LAND}_{tot}\alpha_{\text{land}}[1 - \exp(\beta_{\text{land}}P_{\text{land}})], \tag{46}$$

where LAND_{tot} is the total surface area potentially available for allocation; α_{land} is the maximum potential share of land supplied to the market; β_{land} is a land supply price responsiveness coefficient; and P_{land} is the rental rate on a unit of land.

In SGM version 1.0, the land supply sector will become much richer. One of the potentially most important determinations is the representation of the character of land, and its potential supply and use, and the potential changes to land character as it is affected by human activity. To be most useful, the model of land must be capable of explaining both the present allocation and use of land, how that allocation and use changes with time, and the consequences of land-use for greenhouse gas emissions. Furthermore, the characterization must also be capable of providing a framework for assessing the consequences of potential changes in atmosphere and climate, and of changes in sea level. Several alternative specifications are being considered. A description of land use in SGM version 1.0 will be the subject of future model development reports.

Personal income

Personal income can be computed from the information already developed via the equation,

$$\begin{aligned} Y = {} & X_{\text{labour supply}}[P_{\text{labour}}(1 - txa_{\text{labour}}) - txb_{\text{labour}}] \\ & + X_{\text{land supply}}[P_{\text{land}}(1 - txa_{\text{land}}) - txb_{\text{land}}] \\ & + \pi_{tot}(1 - tx_{\pi} - s_{\pi}) + TR_{\text{gov}} \end{aligned} \tag{47}$$

where Y is the disposable personal income; π_{tot} is the total net profits from the operation of all enterprises; tx_{π} is the profits tax rate; s_{π} is the rate of retained corporate earnings; and txy = income tax rate.

Savings supply

SGM version 0.0 represents savings as a function of present income and the interest rate,

$$S_{\text{hh}} = \alpha_{\text{hhsave}}Y\{1 - \exp[\beta_{\text{hhsave}}(\text{interest} + \text{fac}_{\text{hh}})]\} \tag{48}$$

where S_{hh} is the total supply of savings by households; α_{hhsave} is the maximum potential household savings rate; β_{hhsave} is the price sensitivity of households to the available interest rate; and fac_{hh} is an adjustment factor linking the market interest rate to the interest rate available to households.

While it is usual for a general equilibrium model to maximize a utility function to determine household behaviour, version 0.0 does not do this. The development of a more sophisticated description of aggregate household behaviour is a development task.

Household demand for final products

Own demands for factor inputs labour and land are computed separately from demands for other goods and services.

The own demand for land is a function of the number of households,

$$\mathrm{NHH} = \left(\sum_{\mathrm{age}=1}^{NAGE} \mathrm{POP}_{\mathrm{age}} \right) \Big/ \alpha_{\mathrm{hh}}, \tag{49}$$

where NHH is the number of households; and α_{hh} is the average number of people per household.

Therefore,

$$X_{\mathrm{land,hh}} = \mathrm{NHH}\ \alpha_{\mathrm{land,hh}} P_{\mathrm{land}}^{\beta_{\mathrm{land,hh}}}, \tag{50}$$

where $\alpha_{land,hh}$ is the household land intensity factor; and $\beta_{land,hh}$ is the price elasticity of demand by households for land.

The household demand for labour is a function of the price of labour,

$$X_{\mathrm{labour,hh}} = X_{\mathrm{labour}} \alpha_{\mathrm{labour,hh}} P_{\mathrm{land}}^{\beta_{\mathrm{land,hh}}}, \tag{51}$$

where $\alpha_{labour,hh}$ is the household labour demand intensity factor; and $\beta_{labour,hh}$ is the price elasticity of demand by households for labour.

The total value of consumption can then be calculated by difference

$$Y_c = Y - S_{\mathrm{hh}} - X_{\mathrm{land,hh}} P_{\mathrm{land}} - X_{\mathrm{labour,hh}} P_{\mathrm{labour}}. \tag{52}$$

Consumption of any final product can then be computed using price and income elasticities and an income expenditure normalization via,

$$xd_{i,\mathrm{hh}} = \alpha_{i,\mathrm{hh}} P^{\beta_{i,\mathrm{hh}}} Y_c^{\gamma_{i,\mathrm{hh}}} \left(\frac{1}{\lambda}\right), \tag{53}$$

where $Xd_{i,\mathrm{hh}}$ is the demand for good i by the household sector; $\alpha_{i,\mathrm{hh}}$ is the household demand intensity factor for good i; $\beta_{i,\mathrm{hh}}$ is the price elasticity of demand by households for good i; and $\gamma_{i,\mathrm{hh}}$ is the income elasticity of demand by households for good i, and

$$\lambda = \sum_{i=1}^{NS} \alpha_{i,\mathrm{hh}} P_i^{\beta_{i,\mathrm{hh}}+1} Y_c^{\gamma_{i,\mathrm{hh}}-1}. \tag{54}$$

Each consumption good, which in version 0.0 is identical to a produced commodity in the GPC, is assumed to have an income and a price elasticity of demand.

In version 1.0, the plan is to embed the household decision making process in a cohesive intertemporal decision-making process which includes consumption, savings, and education. Education is important because, at least in the United States, it is the most important determinant of life-cycle labour-force participation. In addition, the subsector structure in the model will be used to expand the number of demographic groups. The number of such groups has not yet been determined but will reflect significant differences with respect to savings and education decisions. In version 1.0 consumption categories will probably be different from production categories, implying the need for a translation matrix from consumption to production commodities. Computationally more versatile forms for the labour and land supplies will also be explored.

General equilibrium

As noted earlier, markets are defined for each of the 10 producing sectors in SGM version 0.0 plus one for each of the three primary factors of production: land, labour, and capital.[11] There are at least 13 markets for the model to clear even when only a single region is being considered. When multiple regions are being considered simultaneously, the number of markets will expand. Land and labour markets are considered to be closed. This increases the number of markets from 13 to $11 + 2NL$, where NL is the number of regions. If capital markets are closed this number increases to $10 + 3NL$.[12] In addition, the model user can open or close any market in any

Table 5 **An example of trading relationship table**

Commodity	Region 1	2	3	4	5	6	7	8	9	10	11
1. Agri.	1	1	1	1	1	1	1	1	1	1	1
2. Crude oil	1	1	1	1	1	1	1	1	1	1	1
3. Oil ref.	1	1	1	1	1	1	1	1	1	1	1
4. Nat. gas	1	1	2	1	2	1	1	1	1	1	1
5. Nat. gas tr	1	1	1	1	1	1	1	1	1	1	1
6. Coal prod.	1	1	1	1	1	1	1	1	1	1	1
7. Biomass	1	1	1	1	1	1	1	1	1	1	1
8. Uranium	1	1	1	1	1	1	1	1	1	1	1
9. Elec.	1	1	2	3	0	2	3	0	0	0	0
10. Other	1	1	1	1	1	1	1	1	1	1	1
11. Labour	0	0	0	0	0	0	0	0	0	0	0
12. Land	0	0	0	0	0	0	0	0	0	0	0
13. Sav/inv	0	0	0	0	0	0	0	0	0	0	0

region relative to the rest of the world, and thus create trading groups. This is indicated through a variable, Mktlink defined over regions and commodities, where if for one of the 13 commodities and 11 regions,

Mktlink $= 0$ indicates that region *L* is permanently closed to trade in commodity *IN*. For example, all regions are closed to trade in land in the above matrix;

Mktlink > 0 indicates that the region trades with all other regions with similar Mktlink values for that commodity.[13]

An example of a trading relationship table is given in table 5.

The number of markets will also vary during the execution of the model. This occurs because transportation costs involved in international trade are non-trivial. It is easily possible to encounter a case in which a region would desire to export a good if the region is treated as an importing region and domestic producers are assumed to be able to obtain the world price of the commodity plus the cost of transportation. On the other hand, if the region is treated as an exporting region, in which domestic producers can obtain only the world price of the commodity, the quantity of the product demanded by the region increases and the quantity supplied decreases to the point where the region would desire to import the good. Under such circumstances, the model will treat that region/commodity combination as if it were temporarily closed.[14]

For each region/commodity combination, an excess demand can be calculated by

$$e_{i,j} = \sum_{s=1}^{Ns} \sum_{ss=1}^{Nss_{i,n}} \sum_{\text{tech}=1}^{N\text{tech}_{i,ss,n}} (xd_{i,s,ss,\text{tech},j} - xs_{i,s,ss,\text{tech},j}), \quad i = 1, \ldots N. \tag{55}$$

where $e_{i,j}$ = excess demand for commodity i in region j.

Consider for a moment the simplest case in which all commodities are traded internationally. For any period, equilibrium exists when a set of prices, $P = (P_1, \ldots P_N)$ can be found for which

$$\sum_{j=1}^{NL} e_{i,j} = 0, \qquad i = 1, \ldots, N. \tag{56}$$

This set of prices is not unique. Walras's law,

$$\sum_{i=1}^{N} \sum_{j=1}^{NL} e_{i,j} P_i = 0, \tag{57}$$

which holds as an identity, and guarantees that if an equilibrium set of prices exists, that any positive scalar multiple of those prices is also an equilibrium set of prices. Any commodity can be chosen as a numeraire and its price determined arbitrarily, set for example to one. The number of independent market prices is always one less than the number of markets.

Similarly, since the unit of measure chosen for commodities is also arbitrary, units can be chosen such that all equilibrium prices are unity in one period.

Solving the SGM

The ERM first generation model, used a Newton search procedure in an elasticity metric. Elasticities were computed numerically by perturbing each market price slightly and re-evaluating the model. This required Nmkt+1 evaluations for each search step. It also created a Nmkt^2 matrix of partial derivatives, which needed to be inverted. With 42 independent markets, this procedure requires a matrix of

1,764 elements to be inverted. The ERM also incorporated a variety of procedures to be invoked in the event that no change in a disequilibrium set of prices could be identified, through the Newton search approach, which reduced the metric of disequilibrium, the sum of squared excess demands.

Increasing the number of markets to 42 in SGM version 0.0 increases the complexity of the problem of finding numerical solutions to the model. The SGM will employ an even more diverse set of solution algorithm alternatives than the ERM. The most important addition to the set of search techniques is the Gauss-Seidel procedure. This solution algorithm begins with an initial price vector, and then updates each element of the price vector individually.[15]

Concluding remarks

This paper describes a new model under development, a second generation model of global energy and other human activities and greenhouse gas emissions. The model addresses the problem of the relationship between human activities in a wide array of domains, and their effect on the emissions of radiatively important gases, and the potential consequences of changes in the atmospheric composition and climate on those human activities. To address the extremely broad scope implied by these objectives, we have begun the development of a global, computable general equilibrium model, which provides insights not possible with linked independent market equilibrium models. It is also designed to address a specific problem. Its level of complexity and disaggregation reflects the character of that problem. Energy is the single most important human activity affecting greenhouse gas emission. It therefore receives the greatest attention in the model. Agriculture and land-use are the next most important issues and receive greater attention than, for example, their value-added contribution to GNP would indicate they warrant. Other sectors of the economy are modelled in relatively aggregate detail.

The model will be exercised for both regional/national economies independently of the world economy, and as a world model. Projects to model the United States, Chinese, and former Soviet Union are underway in partnership with sister institutions in China and Russia. These projects are anticipated to produce results during 1992. This work in turn will help inform the development of the SGM global model. Progress on these endeavours will be the subject of future reports.

Notes

1. The authors would like to express appreciation to the United States Department of Energy, Office of Energy Research and the Office of Policy, Planning, and Analysis, and to the United States Environmental Protection Agency, for support in the conduct of this research. The authors would also like to express appreciation to Yoichi Kaya, Nebojša Nakićenović, Kirit Parikh, Yuangzheng Luo, Bert Hickman, and Ken Ruffing for their thoughtful comments on an earlier draft of this paper.
2. Gases with characteristic *e*-folding or average molecular lifetime values of less than 10 years.
3. Century time scales.
4. For example, control runs using the ERM and GLOBAL 2100 models yield remarkably similar results when standard assumptions are employed in both models. This is despite the fact that the ERM is a behavioural model and GLOBAL 2100 is a dynamic optimizing model.
5. It is always possible to recast a model such as the SGM within the dynamic optimization with perfect foresight paradigm.
6. Compared to competing technologies.
7. Note that the price received by the producers, P_0, is equal to the f.o.b. price. The prices paid by producers are equal to the f.o.b. price plus taxes and markups.
8. Note that in this case the period-specific expected price vector replaces the present discounted price vector given by equation (14).
9. Note that this property is characteristic of any production function which is homogeneous of degree one, such as for example the CES, and not simply the Leontief specification.
10. To see this note that first-order conditions require that

    $$G_{ss} = \lambda^{1/(\mu-1)} G \beta_{ss} P^{\gamma}_{g,ss},$$

    where λ is a Lagrangian multiplier. For convenience define,

    $$Y = TX_{\text{tot}} - S_{\text{gov}} - TR_{\text{gov}},$$

    and note that

    $$Y = \sum_{ss=1}^{NGS} G_{ss} P_{g,ss}.$$

    Substitute (1) into (2) to yield,

    $$\lambda^{1/(\mu-1)} G = Y \left(\sum_{ss=1}^{NGS} \beta_{ss} P^{\gamma}_{g,ss} \right)^{-1}.$$

    Resubstituting (3) into (1) gives the final result.
11. Recall that the capital market is a market for savings and investment. It does not allocate existing capital stocks. Those are quasi fixed as a vintaged capital stock.
12. The relaxation of the assumption that capital markets are closed requires the creation of an investment vehicle. This could be accomplished by the creation of an international bond. This bond would imply a future return flow of resources in exchange for savings. Net interest payments would be added to GNP and household disposable income, assuming households hold the bonds.
13. Note that while model logic will not be affected, there should always be at least two regions involved in a trading group for each commodity. The value of the Mktlink variable gives a reference region whose f.o.b. price of commodity *IN* determines the f.o.b. price for that commodity in all other regions in the trading group. For example, in the matrix above, all

regions, except China, use the f.o.b. price of agricultural products in the United States (region 1) as a common reference f.o.b. price.

The value used in Mktlink should *always* use the lowest region index number of any member of the trading group. For example when regions 3 and 6 form an electricity trading group, both members use the number 3 for their Mktlink values.

We note that a region cannot be open to trade in only one commodity.

14. When a region is temporarily treated as if it were closed to trade in a particular commodity, the value of Mktlink is set to the negative of the reference group number.
15. This procedure has an expected solution rate of between 5Nmkt and 10Nmkt model evaluations. It is thus computationally very efficient. The order in which the Gauss-Seidel algorithm operates may be important. For example, we may wish to solve the world market, then iterate to the regional labour and land markets, and then return to the world market. Some thought needs to be given to getting appropriate output and tracking the solution process with an eye to improving its efficiency.

References

Adams, D., R.M. Adams, J.M. Callaway, C.C. Chang, and B.A. McCarl. 1991. The Economics of Sequestering Carbon on Agricultural Land in the U.S.: A Preliminary Analysis of Social Cost and Impacts on Timber Markets. Mimeo.

Applied Energy Services, Inc. (AES). 1986. *Fossil2 Energy Policy Model Demand Sector Documentation.* 3 vols. Arlington, Va.: AES.

—— 1991. *Fossil2 Energy Policy Model Electricity Sector Documentation.* 3 vols. Arlington, Va.: AES.

Ballard, C.L., D. Fullerton, J.B. Shoven, and J. Walley. 1985. *A General Equilibrium Model for Tax Policy Evaluation.* Chicago, Ill.: University of Chicago Press.

Barfield, B.J., J.F. Clarke, and O.J. Loewer. 1991. *Biomass as Global Energy Source.* In: Technology Responses to Global Environmental Challenges. Proceedings of the IEA International Conference, Kyoto, p. 257.

Bradley, R. A., E.C. Watts, and E.R. Williams, eds. 1991. *Limiting Net Greenhouse Gas Emissions in the United State.* Washington D.C.: U.S. Department of Energy.

Brinner, R.E., M.G. Shelby, J.M. Yanchar, and A. Christofaro. 1991. *Optimizing Tax Strategies to Reduce Greenhouse Gases Without Curtailing Growth.* Boulder, Colo.: Energy Modeling Forum 12.

Burniaux, J.M., J.P. Martin, G. Nicoletti, and J. Oliveire Martins. 1991. *The Costs of Policies to Reduce Global Emissions of CO_2: Alternative Scenarios with GREEN.* Research report to the Policy Studies Branch, Organization for Economic Cooperation and Development, Paris.

Clarke, J.F. 1991. *The Cost and Benefit of Energy Technology in the Global Context – The Case of Fusion Power.* In: Technology Responses to Global Environmental Challenges. Proceedings of the IEA International Conference, Kyoto 1991, p. 364.

Edmonds, J., and D.W. Barns. 1990. *Estimating the Marginal Cost of Reducing Global Fossil Fuel CO_2 Emissions.* Washington, D.C.: PNL-SA-18361, Pacific Northwest Laboratory.

—— 1991. Factors Affecting the Long-term Cost of Global Fossil Fuel CO_2 Emissions Reductions. PNL Global Studies Program Draft Working Paper.

Edmonds, J., and J.M. Reilly. 1985. *Global Energy: Assessing the Future.* New York: Oxford University Press.

Edmonds, J.A., J.M. Reilly, R.H. Gardner, and A. Brenkert. 1986. *Uncertainty in Future Global Energy Use and Fossil Fuel CO_2 Emissions 1975 to 2075*. TR036, D03/NBB-0081 Dist. Category UC-11, National Technical Information Service. U.S. Department of Commerce: Springfield, Va.: 22161.

Edmonds, J.A., and D.B. Reister. 1982. *Characteristics of Nested CES Functions.* ORAU/IEA-82-5 (M) Oak Ridge, TN: Oak Ridge Associated Universities.

Gately, D. 1980. "Individual Discount Rates and the Purchase and Utilization of Energy Using Durables: Comment." *The Bell Journal of Economics* 11: 373–374.

Hausman, J.R. 1979. "Individual Discount Rates and the Purchase and Utilization of Energy-Using Durables." *The Bell Journal of Economics* 10: 33–54.

Henderson, J.M., and R.E. Quandt. 1958. *Microeconomic Theory: A Mathematical Approach.* New York, NY: McGraw-Hill Book Company.

Jorgenson, D.W., and P.J. Wilcoxen. 1990a. The Cost of Controlling U.S. Carbon Dioxide Emission. Presented at a Workshop on Economic Energy Environmental Modeling for Climate Policy Analysis. Washington, D.C., 22–23 October.

—— 1990b. *Global Change, Energy Prices, and U.S. Economic Growth.* Cambridge, Mass.: Department of Economics, Harvard University.

Kinsman, J.D., and G. Marland. 1989. Contribution of Deforestation to Atmospheric CO_2 and Reforestation as an Option to Control CO_2. Presented at the 82nd Annual Meeting and Exhibition of the Air and Waste Management Association, Anaheim, Calif., 25–30 June.

Lashof, Daniel A., and Dennis A. Tirpak. 1989. Policy Options for Stabilizing Global Climate. Draft Report to Congress, U.S. Environmentai Protection Agency, Office of Policy, Planning and Evaluation, Washington, D.C.

Lind, R.C. 1983. *Discounting for Time and Risk in Energy Policy*. Resources for the Future, Washington, D.C.

Manne, A.S., and R.G. Richels. 1990a. "CO_2 Emission Limits: An Economic Cost Analysis for the USA." *The Energy Journal* 11(2): 51–75.

—— 1990b. *Global CO_2 Emissions Reductions – the Impacts of Rising Energy Costs.* Palo Alto, Calif.: Electric Power Research Institute.

—— 1990c. *Buying Greenhouse Insurance.* Palo Alto, Calif.: Electric Power Research Institute.

—— 1990d. *The Costs of Reducing U.S. CO_2 Emissions – Further Sensitivity Analysis.* Palo Alto, Calif.: Electric Power Research Institute.

—— 1991. *Estimating the Energy Conservation Parameters: An Experiment in Backcasting.* Palo Alto, Calif.: Electric Power Research Institute.

Marland, G. 1988. *The Prospect of Solving the CO_2 Problem through Global Reforestation.* DOE/NBB-0082, TR039. Springfield, Va.: National Technical Information Service, U.S. Department of Commerce.

Meier, A.K., and J. Whittier. 1983. "Consumer Discount Rates Implied by Purchases of Energy-Efficient Refrigerators." *Energy, the International Journal* 8(12): 957–962.

Moulton, J.R., and K.R. Richards. 1990. *Costs of Sequestering Carbon Through Tree Planting and Forest Management in the United States.* General Technical Report WO-58. Washington, D.C.: U.S. Department of Agriculture, Forest Service.

Nordhaus, W.D. and G.W. Yohe. 1983. "Future Carbon Dioxide Emissions from Fossil Fuels." In: *Changing Climate.* Washington D.C.: National Academy Press, pp. 87–153.

OECD (Organization for Economic Cooperation and Development) 1991. *The Costs of Policies to Reduce Global Emissions of CO_2: Three Alternative Scenarios with GREEN.* Paris, France: OECD.

Peck, S.C., and T.J. Teisberg. 1991. *CETA: A Model for Carbon Emissions Trajectory Assessment.* Palo Alto, Calif.: Electric Power Research Institute.

Rotman, J., H. de Boois, and R. Swart. 1989. *An Integrated Model for the Assessment of the Greenhouse Effect: The Dutch Approach.* Postbus 1, 3720 BA, Bilthoven, The Netherlands: National Institute of Public Health and Environmental Protection, Rijksinstituut voor Volksgezondheid en Milieuhygiaene.

Samuelson, P.A. 1947. *Foundations of Economic Analysis.* Cambridge, Mass.: Harvard University Press.

Scheraga, J.D., D. Cohan, A. Diener, A. Gjerde, S. Haas, and A. Smith. 1991. "Reassessing the Effectiveness and Cost of Taxes to Reduce CO_2 Emissions." *Gemini Notes.* Washington, D.C.: U.S. Environmental Protection Agency.

Sedjo, R.A., and A.M. Solomon. 1989. "Climate and Forests." In: *Greenhouse Warming: Abatement and Adaptation*, N.J. Rosenberg, W.E. Easterling III, P.R. Crosson, and J. Darmstadter, eds. Washington, D.C.: Resources for the Future.

Shepherd, R.W. 1953. Cost and Production Functions. Princeton, N.J.: Princeton University Press.

Comments on chapter 9

1. Nebojša Nakićenović

The design and implementation of the "second generation" model for analysis of future greenhouse gas emissions is indeed a formidable task. Edmonds et al. (1992) set the goals of such a model well beyond the state of the art by specifying that it should be "capable of analysing the emissions of all greenhouse gases from all sources, including both those of natural and human origin, to provide an analysis of the interplay between the variety of human and natural activities responsible for greenhouse gas emission." Clearly, such models currently do not exist that are capable of "assessing emissions from all human activities and major direct and indirect consequences of potential policies to reduce emission." There are many models that already address some specific parts of the problem, e.g., carbon dioxide emissions associated with energy use or models that cover all anthropogenic sources of emissions and resulting atmospheric concentrations (e.g. EPA's Atmospheric Stabilization Framework, Lashof and Tirpak 1989). They are, of course, still very far from the comprehensive approach suggested by Edmonds et al. Hence, the development of the second generation model of the type proposed by

Edmonds et al. is certainly a most welcome effort, although a very ambitious one.

Undeniably, much could be learned by the modelling community from the exercise proposed by Edmonds et al. In particular, the efforts suggested to endogenize demographic and technological changes merit particular praise and attention. However, within a policy context there is also the issue of how such a model can help reduce the uncertainties inherent in modelling global change.

Alternatively how can the modelling exercise make more transparent and explicit the uncertainties stemming either from our insufficient understanding of natural and social phenomena or their inadequate abstraction (modelling)? Therefore, a word of caution may be in order. The policy dimension of global warming must confront simultaneously the problems of extreme uncertainty, both in the causes and consequences of global warming, and in the future contexts within which policies related to global warming will operate. Thus, there is a need for great flexibility in policy measures since the socio-economic and technological contexts within which any global change policy is situated will clearly vary and alter. We are confronting policy choices related to a global environmental issue whose effects will be measured in decades and centuries. To illustrate the difficulty of this task, imagine confronting similar issues a century before, say in 1892. At that time, electricity did not have a significant role, the motor car had just been invented, the aeroplane was unknown except as a concept, and nuclear weapons were unthinkable due to the lack of basic physics, while major urban problems were particulates from coal and dung from horses. Thus, it should be clear that it is unlikely we will forecast the future evolution of energy systems, technologies, or its social contexts over the next 100 years any more accurately today than if we had performed the same exercise a century ago. Yet, modelling and assessment of strategies for mitigation of climate change require a very long-term view, one which extends far beyond normal planning horizons.

In view of the large and still unresolved scientific uncertainty surrounding greenhouse gas emissions, their sources and sinks, the consequences such as adverse and irreversible climate change and possible response strategies, the development of the second generation model of the parametric type proposed by Edmonds et al. is a very useful effort since it will allow the testing of different hypotheses concerning future energy and greenhouse gas emissions.

In this short commentary we will discuss a few of the salient characteristics of such a model that appear to be required if it is to fulfil the expectations of its authors, but we will not raise the specific technical questions that would need to be resolved before the model can actually be built. The technical questions include, for example, the problem of integrating the global warming potential of emission and concentration of multiple greenhouse gases, or how to account for historical and current N_2O emissions from human activities and natural sources, or how to reconstruct the capital vintage structure for economies in transition and developing countries. These questions are far from being resolved but are the subject of a number of research activities and international efforts from which the proposed modelling exercise could benefit. Let us assume that these uncertainties and unknowns can be resolved by a parametric modelling approach.

We now return to the discussion of important model characteristics which (in order to be brief) we will limit to four issues: (1) population dynamics, (2) endogenization of technology, (3) socio-cultural aspects and (4) provision of energy services. They are important because they are all linked to the requirement of adopting a very long time horizon for model applications, which extends to the end of the next century. The authors are to be complimented for taking the long-term and global view. Models that focus on time-scales of two to three decades can be based on many static assumptions due to the relative stability of demographic trends, social and cultural relations, and the technology base over such periods. Conversely, extension of the time horizon well into the next century means that many of these long-term processes will become fluid and can no longer be treated as constants or "slow variables."

I. Population dynamics

In a century global population could stabilize but during the next few decades it will certainly continue to grow at rates fairly close to the current 1.7 per cent per year. In fact, the momentum behind global population growth is indeed very large. Even if we assume an abrupt change in fertility throughout the world down to or even below the replacement levels of about 2.2 children per woman, as it now prevails in most of the West European countries (and will thus result in a significant population decline), the global population would continue to grow for a few decades as illustrated in figure 1. Thus, the demographic transition is an important issue if a long time horizon is

World: Total Population in Million

	1950	1955	1960	1965	1970	1975	1980	1985	1990	1995	2000	2005	2010	2015	2020	2025
Low Variant	2516	2752	3020	3336	3698	4079	4448	4851	5262	5682	6093	6469	6813	7120	7376	7591
High Variant	2516	2752	3020	3336	3698	4079	4448	4851	5327	5857	6420	6986	7564	8169	8802	9444
Medium Variant	2516	2752	3020	3336	3698	4079	4448	4851	5292	5770	6261	6739	7204	7660	8092	8504

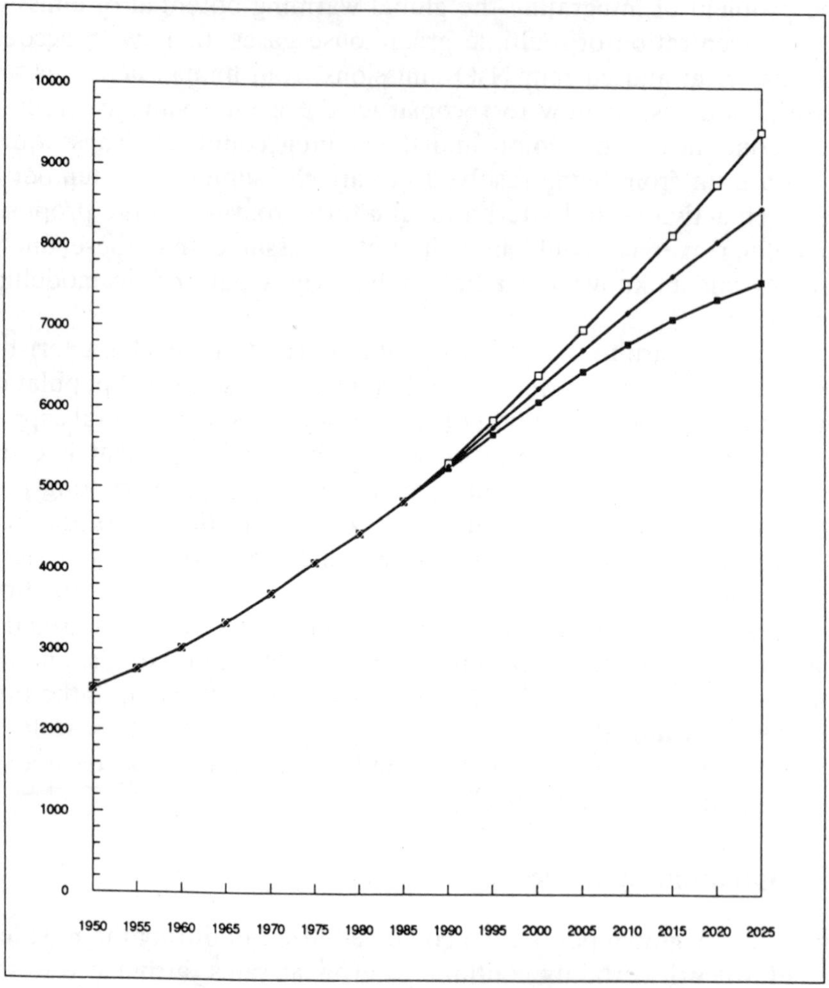

Fig. 1 **World population growth, 1950 to the present and three alternative projections to the year 2025 (*UN World Population Prospects* 1990). In the case of the high variant the population is expected almost to double during the next 35 years. Despite the declining growth rates from now on, the high variant still leads to an increasing absolute population increase. By the year 2020 population increase is still about 40, 80, and 130 million per year in low, medium, and high variant respectively compared to about 100 million increase per year today (Source: Heilig 1992).**

adopted. It is of paramount importance whether the global population will reach 10 billion or grow beyond. What is almost certain is that it can be expected to double during the next 100 years.

The objective to "endogenize" population growth in the next model version is to be welcomed. The actual problem is how to implement the link between development and population: is the demographic transition a prerequisite for rapid development or the other way around? How to account for the diverse experiences among countries and regions with respect to the demographic transition? A critical impasse is how to model these theoretically poorly understood linkages at the global and regional level. For the time being Edmonds et al. plan to include assumptions concerning survival, fertility, and migration rates for individual regions over the time horizon. However, increasing the number of exogenously assumed driving variables does not necessarily lead towards a better understanding of the complex issues between development and demographics. It might, therefore, be simpler and also more transparent to assume different population-growth scenarios exogenously as done by the United Nations population forecasts that are the standard reference in this field (UN 1990). Personally I see little merit in making numerous assumptions in a model without explicitly describing the linkages between the variables. The approach leaves a false impression of certainty and accuracy that does not actually exist. This critically affects particularly the treatment of migration in the proposed model. Clearly, emissions will depend on trade and migration patterns but the problem is that there is no obvious way to model international migration, especially the large movements of people that might be caused by the adverse effects of climate change. Low population growth rates and high levels of affluence in some parts of the world can also be expected to attract additional migration and, this again is a possible linkage between development and population issues.

II. Endogenization of technology

One of the important shortcomings of many energy models is that resource scarcity is one of the central driving forces of future energy development. Once the cheap and clean sources of energy are exhausted, the models "dig deeper" into dirtier and costlier options. This is close to the Malthusian concept of limited resources and has by and large been historically falsified for most factor inputs including energy, minerals, or land. It turns out that in the long run technological change leads to production of more with less rather than of less with more. And yet technological change is still a static concept entirely absent in most models. Fossil energy resources remain static, potentials for technological improvements are ignored, etc. Yet alone since the energy crises of the 1970s the discoveries of additional fossil energy reserves have outpaced their consumption. The resource base continues to increase. Table 1 shows that the known global fossil energy resources are equivalent to about 3,000 gigatons of carbon! The carbon content of the atmosphere is in comparison small with about 760 gigatons of carbon. If the current concerns regarding prospects of global warming are confirmed in the future, it is probable that most of this carbon will remain in the ground. The point here is that technological progress and development are exogenous parameters: as soon as some of these externalities are endogenized, decarbonization strategies will be economically more attractive and less costly than "dirtier" options. In retrospect, we no longer consider technologies that are hazardous to human health as "cheaper" options, but rather as non-options. Therefore, the model needs a "dynamic base" rather than the planned static concept of depletable and degradable resources.

The adoption of a capital vintage approach to endogenizing technological change by Edmonds et al. represents a significant improvement and will undoubtedly produce most valuable insights, as dem-

Table 1 **Fossil energy consumption, reserves and resources (Gt C)**

	Coal	Oil	Gas	Total
1860–1987	114.9	58.2	24.5	197.6
1987	2.5	2.4	1.0	5.9
Reserves	391.6	92.1	58.5	542.2
Resources	2289	622	>115	3026
Additional occurrences	>3500	>1000	>700	>5200

Note: Accounting for historical, present, and potential future carbon emissions from fossil fuel use in gigatons carbon. Historical (1860–1987) and present (1987) carbon emissions from fossil fuel use by source and carbon content in identified, economically recoverable fossil fuel reserves, resources (identified quantities with uncertain prospects of economic recoverability), and additional occurrences (additional quantities inferred from geological information but with speculative technical and economic potential). Compared to historical fossil fuel use, the remaining resources in the ground represent a (perhaps even far too large) "carbon endowment" which is more than a factor 10 as large as the total carbon pool in the atmosphere of around 760 Gt C (corresponding to a present CO_2 concentration rate of about 350 ppm) (Grübler and Nakićenović 1991).

onstrated by similar models for analysing economic structural change. The capital vintage approach can help to model technological change by the introduction of learning and economies-of-scale effects into new additions to the capital stock and the resource base. Nevertheless, the assumption of static resources (even if total potentially recoverable resources are subdivided into reserves and undiscovered resources) over a period of 100 years is indeed a very restrictive constraint that will, no doubt, almost "automatically" lead to high carbon emissions (since cheap and low carbon options are exhausted and renewables and nuclear limited by other "constraints"). For instance, only 10 years ago the existence of methane clathrates was largely unknown. Will they be included as a potential resource base in the model and how is the resource base going to change with the availability of new technologies?

During the next century many new energy systems can also be expected to be introduced that may help avoid the astronomical levels of greenhouse emissions envisaged in many business-as-usual scenarios (e.g., see IPCC 1990). Figure 2 illustrates that even at historical diffusion rates new energy systems can be expected to reach high market shares during the next century. Such systems may include completely new technologies such as carbon removal and deposition (e.g. into the deep ocean) but they will most certainly be also based on improvements and refinements of current technologies such as the electric or hydrogen car (Nakićenović 1992; Nakićenović and John 1991). But even these more evolutionary options will need enabling systems and technologies such as new batteries and fuel cells. The diffusion of whole families of new technologies needs to be modelled both within the energy system and other sectors of the economy. It is not clear how this will be handled in the second generation model, although it is clearly crucial for the understanding of the mitigation and adoption potential offered by new, less carbon-intensive and carbon-free technologies.

III. Socio-cultural aspects

Socio-cultural determinants of future greenhouse gas emissions are also important at all scales but become especially difficult to model when the time horizon is extended to 100 years in the future. Is there cultural convergence over such long periods, especially if the world actually becomes "smaller" through more interaction, global com-

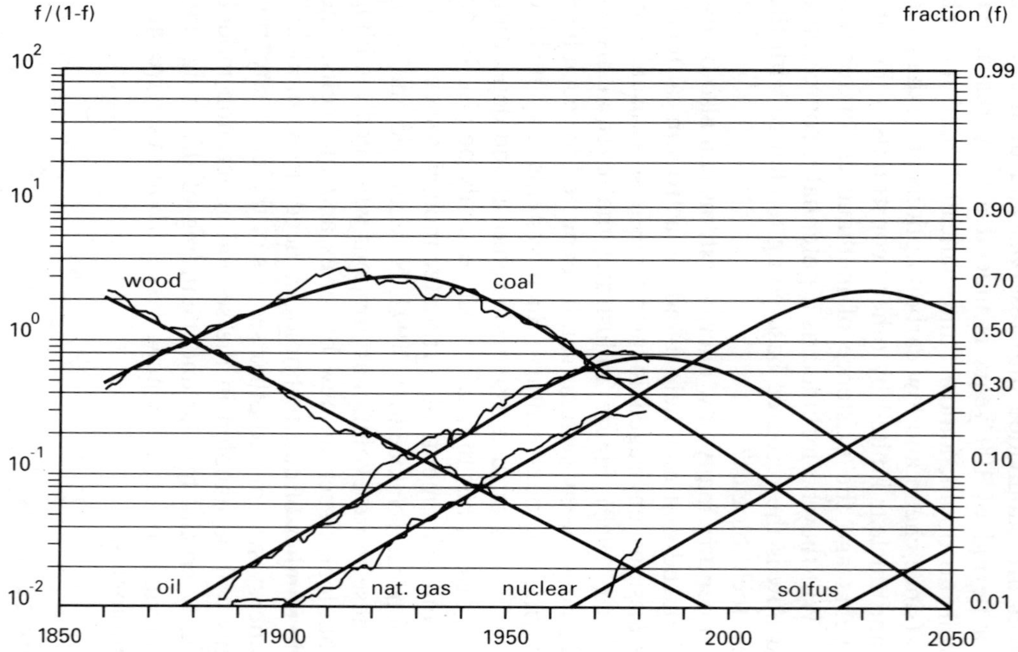

Fig. 2 **World primary energy substitution. Shares of primary energy sources in global consumption. Smooth lines represent model calculations, and jagged lines are historical data. "Nat. gas" is natural gas; "solfus" is a term employed to describe a major new energy technology, for example solar or fusion (Marchetti and Nakićenović, 1979; Nakićenović 1990). It shows that the diffusion of new sources of energy is a very long process lasting many decades. Replacement of other infrastructures such as that of transport systems is also a long process.**

munication, and mobility? At the other extreme, a divergence could be assumed with more heterogeneity and diversity in the world. In fact, this was the historical experience during the last century as illustrated in figure 3 for carbon intensity of value added. In contrast, many of the development strategies and scenario trajectories imply a common global path, e.g., universal adoption of technologies and their transfer despite diverse institutional and regional characteristics, and irrespective of the actual appropriateness of these systems in a given case. The second generation model can be expected to help identify some of the linkages among these issues, but the real problem occurs with the treatment of these social and cultural determinants. For the time being, socio-cultural variables have defined quantifications in most global models and at best have been included as residual values (e.g., derived from general production function approaches). Even if these variables cannot be modelled in the sense of formal abstractions from causality relations, it will be important to make explicit assumptions and scenarios in the model concerning socio-cultural development. This is a potential advantage of a parametric approach.

As another example, is it really reasonable to assume a general equilibrium approach and market-clearing mechanism for analysing the long-term future, when market-clearing mechanism imperfections and regulatory mechanisms are a prevailing characteristic of the world economy rather than an exception? Transfer of "sensitive" technologies is explicitly blocked, diffusion and adoption of technologies can be blocked by local cultures or regulations, and so on. The examples are so plentiful that it is difficult to construct a list of competitive international markets. There are, of course, many methodological reasons for adopting a general equilibrium approach, but the question is whether too much is assumed away by that approach in a model that otherwise includes so much detail. In more aggregate models this might indeed be a very viable and appropriate simplification but in a complex model such as the one proposed it is not clear how to balance detail in some areas against simplistic assumptions in others. In any case, this approach makes the analysis of major and revolutionary changes impossible. Adjustment paths to a low-emissions future is by design at best gradual and excludes socio-cultural diversity. All regions are assumed to have market-based economies and rational, utility maximizing agents (envisaged for version 1.0).

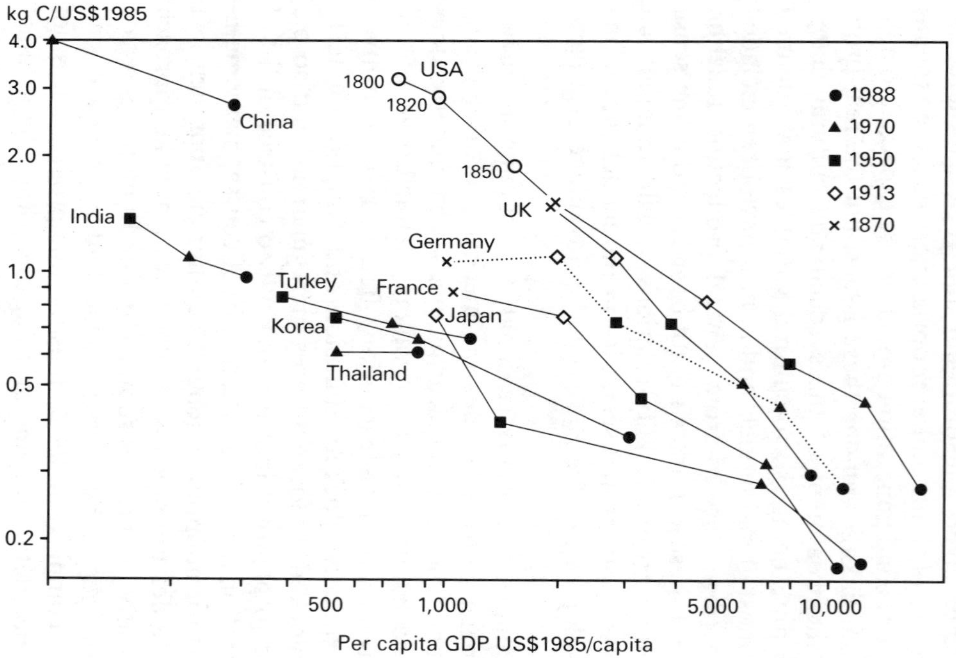

Fig. 3 **Energy CO_2 emissions intensity per constant GDP in kg per constant 1985 US$ versus per capita GDP in constant 1985 US$. Energy data include also non-commercial sources such as fuelwood. In general, carbon intensity of economic activities improves as a function of differences between countries for similar per capita GDP levels. It shows that developed countries had higher specific emissions per unit GDP during early development phases that are comparable to current emission intensities of GDP in developing countries (Source: Grübler and Fujii 1991).**

IV. Provision of energy services

Rationality of agents is in general a very sticky subject when it comes to describing actual energy consumption and end-use behaviours. Conservation and efficiency lag behind what appears to be rational. Often efficiency improvements are offset by increased energy services. For example, new cars are on average more efficient than the old ones in Germany, but they consume more fuel because they are larger, faster, more powerful, comfortable, and safer. Demand for more comfort at home has also increased due to older age structure, smaller family size, and larger dwellings per household, leading again to higher energy services. Figure 4 shows that longer life expectancy and shorter working time have over the last 100 years reversed the share of life spent at work compared to leisure activities from about 80 per cent to about 20 per cent today. This results in more travel, leisure activities, and time spent at home. All of these phenomena are also linked to economic structural changes, productivity increases, and evolving socio-cultural patterns. The problem arises when changes in the end use are observed at the macro-level and explained only by price mechanisms (e.g., elasticities) rather than by changes in human behaviour and social patterns. In those cases fallacies can occur. For example, the price of motor fuel increases but consumers purchase cars that consume more fuel even though they may be more efficient. Perhaps many of these considerations are marginal on a 100-year time-scale. The salient question for personal mobility in the world is rather whether car ownership will diffuse throughout the world to the degree it has in the industrialized countries. Today there are over 400 million cars in the world. Whether this number doubles or increases tenfold during the next decades will have a larger effect than any model variations in the price elasticity of motor fuels. Another example given in figure 5 shows that most of the cars are owned by the male population in Germany, while only a few, mostly young, women own automobiles. Should the ownership rates converge in the future this could almost double the fleet size.

These examples illustrate that the long-time horizon almost inherently demands an interdisciplinary approach in evaluating greenhouse-gas emission mitigation and response strategies. Economic mechanisms alone will not do nor will engineering perspectives. The complex fabric of many dimensions has to be integrated into more holistic approaches for analysing alternative development paths, those that lead to high emissions and those that are responsive to

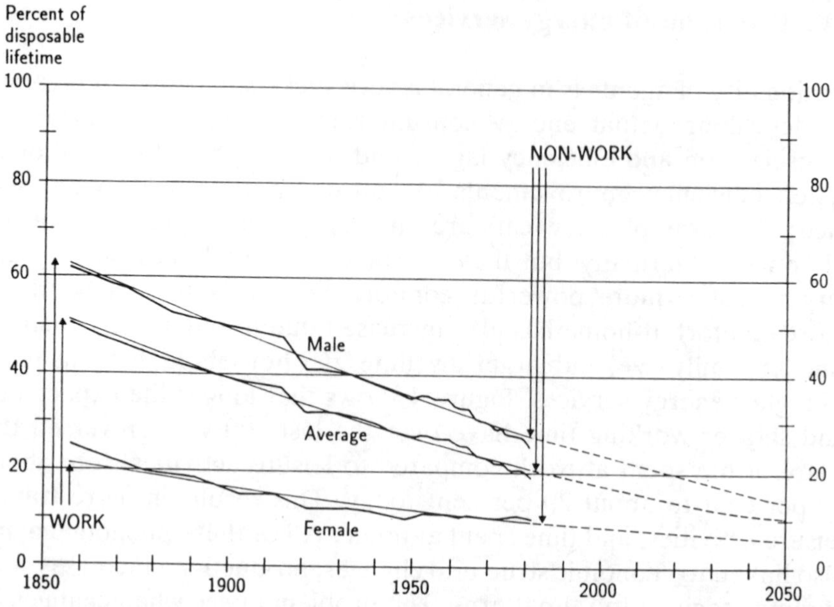

Fig. 4 **Fraction of disposable lifetime spent at work and non-work of female, male, and average working population, UK 1856–1981. Figures are derived by comparing life hours of work to total disposable, active non-work hours for adults. Disposable hours are calculated by subtracting 10 years for childhood and first elementary education and also required "physiological" time, e.g., time required for sleep, eating, and personal hygiene, assumed on average to amount to 10 hours per day. For the average working population in the United Kingdom, working hours decreased from about 124,000 to 69,000 hours between 1856 and 1981, while at the same time disposable lifetime hours increased from 292,000 to 378,000 hours. Thus, non-working hours increased from about 118,000 to 287,000 hours over a lifetime. On average over 60 per cent of the disposable lifetime of male adults was spent working in 1856, this percentage has fallen to less than 20 per cent at present (Source: Ausubel and Grübler 1990).**

climate change. Perhaps creative scenario writing would even further enhance the value of models such as the one proposed by Edmonds et al.

The ultimate question is what is the appropriate model scale (e.g., number of sectors, equations, variables) that is required to capture some of these characteristics? It is clearly undesirable to have a high degree of complexity in treating problems that are poorly understood such as the effect of global warming on international migration patterns. It is better instead to treat with higher accuracy those things that are well known such as the effect of urbanization, mobility, or

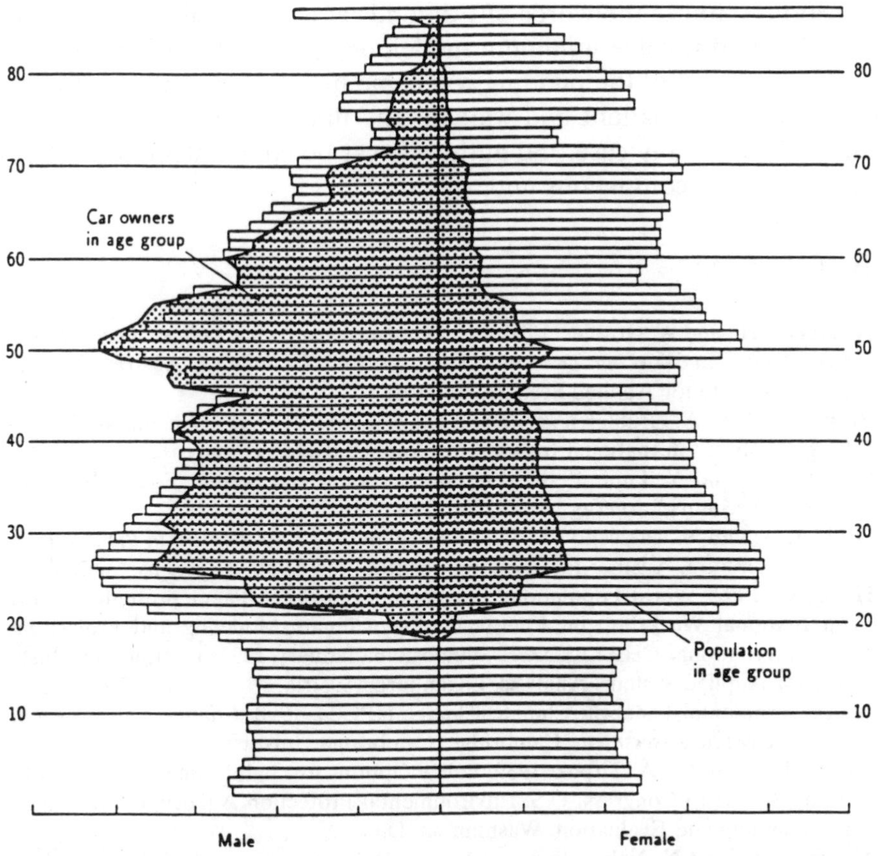

Fig. 5 **Demographics of car ownership in Germany (only former FRG territory) in 1989 revealing significant intergenerational and gender differences in car ownership. Combined with demographic projections scenarios of future car ownership are developed at IIASA based on different scenarios of lifestyle changes of successive cohorts entering driving age. Conversely the ownership (or non-ownership) patterns of older generations are assumed to remain relatively stable, consistent with historical experience (Source: Büttner and Grübler 1991).**

geography and climate on energy end-use patterns. It is a disbenefit to know the magnitude of the global warming potential of multiple gases if carbon dioxide effects and emissions are known with great accuracy while direct and indirect effects of methane and its emissions are very uncertain. In this case, it would be better to know the atmospheric concentrations of these two gases individually. The second generation model can help and improve the analysis of many of these issues provided it is "scaled" appropriately to answer the posed questions – to use the words of Edmonds et al., it should be problem-oriented and involve minimum modelling. I hope that they will succeed. The proof of the pudding will come in eating it – in this case we will have to be patient and wait for the first model implementation and results. In any case, the authors must be complimented on their ambitious and courageous undertaking.

References

Ausubel, J.H., and A. Grübler. 1990. *Working Less and Living Longer. Part I: Long-term Trends in Working Time and Time Budgets.* Laxenburg, Austria: International Institute for Applied Systems Analysis.

Büttner, T., and A. Grübler. 1991. *The Birth of a New "Green" Generation?* Laxenburg, Austria: International Institute for Applied Systems Analysis.

Grübler, A., and Y. Fujii. 1991. "Inter-generational and Spatial Equity Issues of Carbon Accounts." *Energy* 16(11–12): 1397–1416.

Grübler, A. and N. Nakićenović. 1991. *Energy and the Environment in the 21st Century*. Laxenburg, Austria: International Institute for Applied Systems Analysis.

Heilig, G. 1992. World Population: Trends and Prospects. Paper presented at the International Workshop on Energy/Ecology/Climate Modeling and Projections and International CHALLENGE Symposium, January 1992, International Institute for Applied Systems Analysis, Laxenburg, Austria.

Intergovernmental Panel on Climate Change (IPCC). 1990. *Climate Change – The IPCC Scientific Assessment.* Cambridge: Cambridge University Press.

Lashof, D.A., and D.A. Tirpak. 1989. Policy Options for Stabilizing Global Climate. Draft Report to Congress, U.S. Environmental Protection Agency, Office of Policy, Planning and Evaluation, Washington, D.C.

Marchetti, C. and N. Nakićenović. 1979. *The Dynamics of Energy Systems and the Logistic Substitution Model*, RR-79-13. Laxenburg, Austria: International Institute for Applied Systems Analysis.

Nakićenović, N. 1990. "Dynamics of Change and Long Waves." In: T. Vasko, R. Ayres, and L. Fontvielle, eds., *Life Cycles and Long Waves.* Berlin: Springer Verlag.

—— 1992. *Energy Strategies for Mitigating Global Change*, WP-92-1. Laxenburg, Austria: International Institute for Applied Systems Analysis.

Nakićenović, N., and A. John. 1991. "CO_2 Reduction and Removal: Measures for the Next Century." *Energy* 16(11–12): 1347–1377.

United Nations (UN). 1990. *UN World Population Prospects.* New York: United Nations.

2. Kirit S. Parikh

At the outset, let me say that this is an extremely ambitious effort. It is even more ambitious than the one upon which we embarked at the International Institute for Applied Systems Analysis (IIASA) in 1976 in its Food and Agriculture Programme (FAP). We built what we called a Basic Linked System (BLS) of National Food and Agricultural Policy Models.[1] The national models are applied general equilibrium models with a general equilibrium linkage. The system has some 34 models, 20 referring to specific countries or groups of countries having a common agricultural policy and 14 models representing countries of the rest of the world from different regions, grouped according to the similarity of their likely behaviour on the international market. The models distinguish 10 different commodities at the international level (more domestically), of which nine were agricultural commodities and the tenth was a non-agricultural sector to close the system. The parameters of the models were empirically estimated from time-series data. Empirical estimation as opposed to benchmarking was considered essential if the model system were to describe the world with some measure of confidence. It took some 200 person years of effort. The first demonstration version of the model was ready in 1980. A usable one became available in 1984.

However, that was in 1976. Today, it is 1991 and the progress that has been made over these years in computers, algorithms, communication networks, data availability, and the experience obtained with general equilibrium modelling, should make the proposed effort of Edmonds et al. succeed within a reasonable length of time. Without the *Kitty Hawk* of the Wright brothers, 707s would not have come about when they did. With our and similar efforts on building-applied general equilibrium-based linked systems, such an ambitious effort could now be conceived and launched.

My comments on the paper are grouped under different headings. First, I would comment on its approach, then on its scope, limitations, and problem-orientation. These will be followed by some suggestions.

The approach

The approach is a bottom-up approach and the model provides enormous details. With any model that you use, the users always demand more details than what is incorporated into the model. I can confirm that from my personal experience. The model of India that we developed as a part of the IIASA Basic Linked System was one of the more detailed models of the system. I have been using this model for policy analysis and I often find that questions are asked that the model cannot answer without incorporating more details or greater articulation. All the time we keep on updating and modifying the model to address new policy issues as they come up. I am, therefore, sympathetic to the level of detail that is being sought to be incorporated into this model.

There is yet another reason for having a detailed model. A model provides scenarios and these scenarios provide consistent descriptions of a set of variables. These variables can be divided into endogenous and exogenous variables. While a model's solution provides consistency among the endogenous variables, it is not always recognized that consistency among the exogenous variables in specifying a scenario is a difficult and critical task. It does therefore help in specifying for a scenario a set of consistent values for exogenous variables, if their number is minimized. On the other hand this means that the number of parameters to be estimated becomes large. One may also note that when one is exploring long-term strategic alternatives, even empirically estimated parameters cannot be taken to be stable. Even then, the question of descriptiveness of the model cannot be dispensed with: a model scenario is an "if ... then" proposition and the "if" ought to describe the world that we live in if the "then" is to have any relevance.

A simpler CGE model, say of the Manne and Richels, or the Edmonds and Reilly type, provides a starting point for broadly defining some strategic alternatives. However, these models are already available. One should really try to build on them. Moreover, a more detailed model is indeed needed to provide guidance for policy formulations, for international agreements, or to facilitate international negotiations. For these purposes, a model is needed that tells us who gains and who pays under alternative policies and this is where I find some problems with the model.

Problem-orientation, scope, and limitations

I find the model to be what I call a "growth and greenhouse" model and not a "development and environment" model. Its emphasis is largely on loss in economic growth and on the trade-off between economic growth and greenhouse gas emissions. What is required however, is a model that treats both development and environment in a broader perspective. Questions of income distribution, questions of local versus global effects of environmental policy, questions of lifestyles of different groups of people, and questions of consumption patterns and development are very critical and not addressed by the model.

For example, the developing countries do not feel responsible for the current greenhouse problem. Their emissions of CO_2 are less than 30 per cent of the total greenhouse gas emissions in the world, even though they constitute nearly 80 per cent of the world's population. Many of these countries face severe environmental stress in their urban areas due to air pollution, poor sanitation, congestion in slums, use of dirty fuels in poorly ventilated kitchens, and crowded settlements. These environmental issues affect the welfare of their populations in a much more direct way than the consequences of the greenhouse effect. These countries, therefore, rightly feel that they should tackle these local environmental problems before they spend any resources for global environmental problems that in any case they themselves have not created. But, to explore such trade-offs, one needs to incorporate into the model the details of income distribution across different groups in rural and urban areas as mentioned earlier.

To do policy analysis with a model means to compare alternative situations. Some form of comparison of welfare in alternative situations is inescapable. The Edmonds et al. model does not stipulate an integrable demand system without which welfare comparisons would be extremely difficult to make. A consistent integrable demand system is quite essential for such a model. Here, I may also point out that to estimate a consistent demand system that remains meaningful over long periods and large changes in income levels is difficult. Recently, I had occasion to project food demand for the year 2050. When I used elasticities, or a simple linear expenditure system to project these, I got absurd results. The calorie intake implied in these projections was sometimes as high as 10,000 Kcal per day. This is clearly not a feasible intake level. One needs to find an alternative demand system. Here, what we did in the IIASA model is worth noting. We had estimated a separate demand function for each commodity as a function of income and own price. We had also estimated a separate relationship between per capita calorie intake and per capita income. This relationship was asymptotic of what one might consider the physiological limit. For a given target price vector and income level, we estimate an initial vector of demand using each of these individual demand functions. Then we find a vector point that is close to this vector and is such that it satisfies the adding up property as well as meets the aggregate calorie intake constraint. Around the new vector point we then construct a linear expenditure system. Such a procedure was repeated at each time period in IIASA's BLS models. The resulting system can be considered as a local approximation to an underlying utility function and can be shown to be consistent. Such a procedure gave sensible projections for 2050, which were also much more robust to changes in income levels. While the calorie constraint was a logical constraint to impose when dealing with food demand as we were doing in the BLS, it is not adequate for the proposed model, which has many other non-agricultural commodities. It may be necessary to impose some other natural constraint. Perhaps one could impose a constraint on the time required for alternative consumption activities and on the total time available to consume the various commodities. Such a constraint might make the demand system behave sensibly.

It is important that a model does provide insights into trade-offs between alternative development paths, between consumption patterns, between production structures, and across time. Even a long-term model must address some short-term policy issues and the issues of resulting transition costs. If a model does not provide any guidance on what we do now, the model is in some sense useless.

Some points of detail

There are some points of detail which need to be mentioned. First, it is vital to maintain common units for trade of commodities among countries. This is a critical problem and requires much care and data-grubbing work. From the description of the model, I am not sure how these problems are to be handled and how units are going to be kept consistent across different countries.

Secondly, an observation is made in the paper that capital stock data can be "relatively easy to observe." This is not so, as capital stock data are notoriously difficult to obtain. Estimates of total factor productivity growth in Indian industries based on the same data source by two different researchers arrive at two completely contrary results; one saying that factor productivity in India has grown, the other saying that it has not. The difference can be largely ascribed to the way capital stock data are put together from information on the time-series of investment at current prices by assuming certain rates of real depreciation. Unfortunately, the depreciation rates are not observed and a seemingly small change in the rate of depreciation whether it is 3 or 4 per cent per year can make a difference as to whether total factor productivity grew or not.

Thirdly, the model seems to assume that governments do not own land. However, governments can and do own land and substantial amounts of it in many countries. Thus, questions of deforestation and land markets cannot be adequately dealt with without bringing in government behaviour in the land market. Neither do I see fishery mentioned anywhere, and consequences for oceans seem to be left out of the model, hopefully only for the moment.

Some suggestions

I would like to make a couple of suggestions. It seems to me that the agricultural sector model of IIASA's BLS would provide a very good starting point for this modelling work and the authors might explore the possibility of using this model for the agricultural sector. In addition, the algorithm development for IIASA's system has proved over the years to be robust and efficient even when dealing with policy regimes with quotas. They might also explore the possibility of using the algorithm that was developed by Michiel Keyzer[2] using the Kantarovich lemma.

Finally, I would like to emphasize that in using the model, one should keep in mind that no model can address the important question of welfare distribution and responsibilities. We have to keep this earth functioning and we must think in terms of a mechanism, a system that is fair and feasible. I suggest that we think in terms of using market-friendly approaches towards maintaining the global commons at the desired level by giving tradable emission quotas to different countries. Initial allocation of these should be consistent with the carrying capacity of the earth and should be done fairly. I suggest that the allocation based on population would be a fair way. In order not to encourage people to increase their populations, we may keep the allocations to the populations of a past year, say 1990. I hope this model would give us insights into alternative ways of preserving the global commons, of enhancing local environment, and of improving the quality of life for all persons on earth. I congratulate the modellers on their ambitious project and wish them luck.

Notes

1. Fisher, G., K. Frohberg, M.A. Keyzer, and K.S. Parikh. 1988. *Linked National Model: A Tool for International Food Policy Analysis.* Boston, Mass.: Kluwer Academic Publishers and International Institute for Applied Systems Analysis.
2. Keyzer, M.A. 1983. Computation of Fixed Points by Applied Continuation Techniques to the Kantarovich Lemma, Working Paper SOW-83-02. Amsterdam: Centre for World Food Studies.

3. Yuangzheng Luo

Many of the points taken up in the paper are of interest to me and I have yet to digest them. I cannot agree more with the view expressed in that paper that in the process of designing, a new model should be problem-oriented. We should not lapse into the practice of making the problem fit the model. That would be repeating the mistake of the fool in the Chinese fable who chopped off part of his feet so that they could fit the shoes.

In their reconstruction and economic development after World War II, Europe and Japan did not pay due attention to the issue of environmental pollution. Thus it went unheeded until the 1960s when it became an explosive issue. How to control environmental pollution and maintain the ecological balance became a great concern of the United Nations and governments around the world. To this end the United Nations set up the Environmental Council under the Economic and Social Council (ECOSOC). China began to take part in the Council's work in the 1970s. The developed countries have designed a number of models on environmental pollution in addition to formulating relevant policies and legislation. These have proven through practice to be effective in bringing environmental pollution under control step by step. However, from the global perspective, the problem of environmental pollution has not been solved. The global environmental issue has been aggravated as a result of the accelerated transfer by the industrialized countries since the 1980s of highly polluting and energy-guzzling labour-intensive industries to the developing countries and also as a result of the industrial development of the developing countries themselves. Moreover, the emission of greenhouse gases and the depletion of the ozone layer led to global environmental warming. People are becoming increasingly concerned about such global environmental issues. The developing countries have come to see that prevention is better than "cure." But it must be pointed out that the industrialized countries should bear the main responsibility for global environmental pollution and the degradation of the environment. While they seek to protect the environment in their own countries, the industrialized countries must transfer environmentally sound technologies to the developing countries, increase aid to them for environmental protection, and put an end to the transfer to developing countries of industries that pollute the environment.

Great strides have been made in environmental protection since the 1960s when the problem of pollution began to catch the attention of industrialists, policy makers, and the general public. In many countries, effective measures have been taken and laws passed to keep the air and the rivers and lakes clean. Today, more and more attention is focused on the greenhouse effect. I am confident that with a common understanding of the gravity of the problem and through concerted efforts, better technologies will be developed to reduce emissions of greenhouse gases from industrial plants, vehicles, and home appliances and wiser policies adopted to control such emissions.

As a developing country, China is equally concerned about the greenhouse effect and about environmental protection. In its pursuit of a reformist policy and its opening up to the outside world, China has, in the past decade or so, made notable progress in controlling environmental pollution and preserving the ecological balance. China is fully aware of the importance of striking a proper balance between achieving economic and social progress and maintaining a sound ecological system between industrialization and environmental protection. We are ready to learn from other countries whatever is useful to us in preserving our environment. However, due to financial and technological constraints, we cannot apply the same standards of environmental protection that the developed countries use.

You may be interested to learn about China's energy picture. In 1990 China's total energy consumption amounted to 980 million tons of standard coal. The breakdown is as follows: coal, 75.6 per cent; crude oil, 17 per cent; natural gas, 2.1 per cent; and hydropower, 5.3 per cent.

You can see from these figures that coal plays a predominant role in China's energy consumption. There was a time in the 1970s and early 1980s when Chinese factories switched from coal burning to oil burning. But before long, China learnt that it could not afford to do this, since exploration of oil requires far greater capital input than the mining of coal. So we switched back to coal burning. While we continue to rely heavily on coal for energy consumption, we plan to make use of nuclear power and tap China's rich hydroelectric resources on a much larger scale. To this end, a nuclear power station is under construction at Da Ya Wan in Southern China and plans are under way for the building of more hydropower stations. Although economic development remains China's overriding concern, increasing attention is being given to environmental protection. In this regard, there is a great deal for China to learn from the advanced countries. Professor Li and I have briefed our relevant departments on what we discussed here, and are strengthening ties with other countries in the fields of environmental protection and other economic researches. Professor Li Jingwen's Institute, the Institute of Quantitative and Technical Economics, Chinese Academy of Social Sciences, has been engaged in modelling research and application for decades, focusing not only on the Chinese economy but also on global economic issues. The Institute has already learnt a lot from well-known scholars like Professor Klein about international cooperative projects and wishes to extend its international cooperation to a much broader extent.

In June 1991, ministers from 41 developing countries met in Beijing for the Ministerial Conference on Development at the invitation of the government of the People's Republic of China. At its conclusion, the conference issued the "Beijing Declaration." During the conerence the participants discussed important issues such as how developing countries should coordinate their efforts in environmental protection and economic development, how to ensure effective cooperation in this field between the developed and the developing countries. The Beijing Declaration voiced the interests and demands of the developing countries, expressed grave concern over the ever-deteriorating global environment, pointed out that environmental protection and sustained development are the common obligation of all the countries in the world, and urged that the international community take effective action to achieve fruitful global cooperation. It was hoped that the United Nations-sponsored World Summit on Environment and Development held in Brazil in 1992 would address the appeal of the developing countries in earnest.

With the development of science and technology, the world is becoming smaller and smaller, and interdependence is becoming more and more pronounced. It is not only true of economic development, it is also true of the way we live. After all, we have but one planet to share. So let us join hands in a concerted effort to make our planet more habitable for both present and future generations.

10

FUGI global model: Simulations of global CO_2 cut-backs and arms reduction on the world economy

Akira Onishi

Abstract

The purpose of this paper is twofold: to introduce the new generation FUGI global model whose design concepts reflect recent advances in life frontier sciences and AI-oriented expert systems in computer software technology, to make projections of the world economy under alternative policy scenarios for cut-backs of CO_2 emissions to minimize global warming and for arms reduction, in order to assess impacts of global changes in environment and changes in "defence" thinking and military establishments on the development of the world economy.

Global changes and design concepts of the FUGI global model

The trend toward the greater interdependence of the world economy is progressing and is not limited to the exports and imports of goods and capital but has also meant a strengthening of transnational, interdependent relationships through exchanges of information, culture, and individual talents. This in turn has encouraged economics to overcome traditional frameworks which were limited primarily to the economy of one or another single country. In a similar way, the appearance of complex and interrelated problems such as population, environment, food, resources, energy, development, arms competitions, displaced persons, etc. has posed problems whose solution is quite impossible within the old frameworks of an economics dealing for the most part with a single national economy. These facts help explain why, since the early 1970s, research has continued on the design of "FUGI global models."

In my own research on FUGI global models, I have used a "dynamic soft systems approach," progressing from simple conceptual models to more complex theoretical ones, and then to computer models. The "first generation" FUGI global model (1.0) of the early 1970s has developed into an artificial intelligence (AI)-oriented "seventh generation" model (FUGI global model 7.0).

The FUGI global modelling system is supported by the development of both the hardware and the software of high-technology computer systems. Methodologically, the new generation of the FUGI global model represents a new frontier in economics, stimulated by new possibilities in computer science and also by recent discoveries in biotechnology and brain physiology.

Metaphorically speaking, the world's 166-country members of the UN – or more precisely 185 or so countries when we count the non-UN members – can be thought of as "cells," which when separate and isolated can only act in a disconnected way, each in its own fashion. But when given information concerning the global economy, the possibility arises that each country can take in information on what it ought best to do, with the result that through a sort of feedback system the global economy will operate more smoothly. This is one of the hints given by the recent development of life frontier sciences.

The transmission of information is a centrally important aspect of life function, absolutely essential for the existence and continuation of life. Humans furthermore have a capacity through which some information is consciously perceived as signals from the outside, and as a result new and useful information can then be generated from "inside" genetic information, taking on, in other words, a self-organizing capacity. These are vital characteristics of the life phenomenon.

As non-genetic information, our global modelling methodology has also received a large impact from studies of brain physiology. The "right brain" has to do with what we call "pattern recognition," and specializes in the ability to grasp "images" and perceive things as a totality. The "left brain" displays an outstanding capacity to think logically in terms of symbols and words.

The information inputs handled by the left and right brains are linked by a thick belt of neurons known as the inter-brain ridge. Images taken in by the right brain are sent to the left brain, where they are logically analysed and checked out to see if they correspond with reality, and are then "fed back" again into the right brain. In this way, the brain can make judgments about, and therefore "produce," new information. The workings of the human brain, in which the neurons not only form a network but "recognize" each other, has thus provided some very useful hints for the construction of global models.

Global models have the role of offering global information. As each of the countries in the world shares information in the form of a "global communications networking system," information becomes available that can help countries coordinate policies and think about what they ought best to do. If this information undergoes a feedback process reflecting itself in each country's actual policies, the future image of the world economy will have, in effect, changed with the emergence of global information. In the future, mutual understanding can be expected to increase through global information exchanges, and it is only with this base that we can begin to talk about possibilities for global cooperation and policy coordination.

We should at least be aware that the possibilities for global cooperation will be optimized when countries are engaged in dynamic cooperation, recognizing each other's needs and interests, even though we have not yet attained those optimum conditions whereby all countries would optimally adjust their respective interests and adopt an uncompromising posture of coexistence aimed at commonly held objectives for human society.

The UN organization will play "brain-like" roles as one of the world information centres. It would be desirable that the UN and other such brains should, through a process of collection and feedback of various types of information, create an optimally useful information "field" that would indicate how the global economy should be best run for the sake of mankind's survival and smoother coexistence.

The functioning of the individual cells that support human life depends on both genetic information and non-genetic information generated through "creative" endeavours such as learning. It is by using this information that human beings function; but there remains always the question of whether or not the non-genetic information is correct or appropriate. Or put more simply, the question remains whether human beings have lost their freedom of action because of being so bound up in acquired prejudices and stereotypes.

We are by destiny of birth a sort of set system, dependent upon past genetic information. At the same time, each human individual has the capability of self-organization so as to break loose, to some extent, from this destiny, as well as capabilities for controlling and newly organizing his environment. A characteristic of the human individual is, then, that we are not completely determined by fate or destiny, but possess creative abilities, including the ability to effect new transformations.

In the same way, in our information society, trite or trivial information and information with no value for human fulfilment or survival is not really "meaningful information." What the information "field" provided by global models gives us is, par excellence, "real" information, i.e., information that is essential to mankind's coexistence and survival.

It is still in the future for a global model to be developed that will in fact have a capacity for "self-organization" similar to that of living organisms. Perhaps we will first have to develop a global system that will be conducive to the employment of such an avant-garde model. But in this process, it may be nevertheless expected that current global models can give useful policy suggestions.

Today's world is very intricate and hard to grasp, with many phenomena in seeming contradiction. Thus, when one aspect is taken up, certain things can be said, yet if another aspect is taken up, one can often, from this other angle, develop an opposing argument. For progress toward a firm grasp of the reality of things, a certain softness and flexibility is required by which systems of order and correlation can be found within what may appear at first sight to be mutual contradictions.

An important phenomenon discovered through research in bioengineering is the so-called "fluctuation phenomenon." It may be appropriately said that the presence of fluctuations seems to be a basic and necessary element for the evolution of life. And again, this is a very important element in thinking about human societal systems and the global economy. Looking at the present world economy, it is seen that there is a certain sort of "fluctuation" with respect to the future. One or another sort of future is of course inevitable, but humans can at least to some extent "choose" the particular sort of future they will have. There is not a single image of the future but rather plural images, or one might say, images in fluctuation.

What is our present situation? Global models are able to make analyses of this query and to carry out simulations of the future. They are able, first of all, to use knowledge about the present as basic information for making "baseline projections" that assume a continuation of present trends.

Projections based on present baseline scenarios accommodate a large degree of "fluctuation" in light of the current unstable situation. They include, whether we like it or not, the pessimistic possibility, if the present situation should deteriorate, of a world economic and environmental panic accompanied by a collapse of coordination of development and environmental policies at the global level. This possibility cannot at present be discarded.

At the same time, there is of course the possibility of controlling this situation and changing its course through global policy coordination, or, in the terminology of biotechnology, "dynamic cooperation" among countries in the global society. There are indeed many possibilities for keeping sustainable development of the world economy in ways that would make it possible for us to raise the growth rates of the developing economies, greatly reducing risks of seeing enormous numbers of economically displaced persons due to failures in development, and to promote technology transfers from the developed to the developing economies both for improving living standards and for protecting and improving the natural environment.

By demonstrating these possibilities through the dynamic simulations offered by a sophisticated global model, we can produce scientifically elaborated future scenarios for the global economy and can offer meaningful suggestions to those responsible for policy making in the world's various countries.

At the level of mere talk, this will remain nothing but talk. But through the use of a FUGI global model that both utilizes and produces more concrete quantitative information, we can demonstrate various alternative simulations of the future. This information can then be expected to undergo a process of feedback to policy makers and others in the world's various countries and then a further feedback process by which it incorporates itself again into the global model in appropriately revised form. In this way, it will be possible to demonstrate changes in "initial conditions" of global economic systems in a changing global environment.

These initial conditions are in fact constantly changing. Human beings are not wholly determined by fate or destiny of birth, but always have the potential to change their initial conditions through their own initiatives. This situation reflects, we think, the same thing life frontier sciences refer to as the capacity for self-organization possessed by living organisms. And it means very significant challenges for us who are involved with today's global modelling.

A well-constructed global model is not "pie in the sky" – or, as the Japanese might say, a "rice cake in a picture." Rather, it offers the policy-makers of nation states real and utilizable information on the potential for self-organization, which the global economy possesses. In other words, simulations by the FUGI global model can provide global information that is meaningful, value-oriented, and needed for the coexistence and survival of human society.

Though what we call "science" has often been led by traditional patterns, there is probably the need for science, in its newest stage, to incorporate new, alternative ways of thinking. In keeping with these new concepts, it will no doubt advance to new frontiers, while keeping much of its heritage of traditional skills and technology. We ought actively to pursue this vision in a variety of fields, and in this regard we see global modelling as one of the key intellectual challenges.

Outline of the FUGI global model

The FUGI model, whose name is an acronym for "Future of Global Interdependence," was the first global model developed in Japan to make its debut before the global modelling forum at the IIASA in 1977. It was the fruit of joint research done by Professor Yoichi Kaya of the Department of Engineering at the University of Tokyo, Professor Yutaka Suzuki of the Department of Engineering at the University of Osaka, and Akira Onishi of the Department of Economics at Soka University in Hachioji, Tokyo.

Onishi's original FUGI global macroeconomic model (1.0) divided the world into 15 major regions, with the main purpose of drawing attention to future scenarios and policy simulations for alternative paths of the global economy. In particular, a major objective was to shed greater light on alternative "futures of global interdependence," the expression which inspired the name "FUGI." The FUGI global model (1.0) was designed on the basis of Onishi's original multination model, which was applied to the 15 countries of the Asian region in 1965 (Onishi 1976).

The FUGI model project, which was the first such project carried out in Japan to gain attention in international society, continued to develop with successive versions of the FUGI global macroeconomic model using the facilities of, and under the sponsorship of, the Soka University Institute for Applied Economic Research, renamed the Institute for Systems Science at the time of the inauguration of the university's Faculty of Engineering in April 1991. The first-generation FUGI global model (1.0) of 1977 developed into a fourth-generation model (4.0) in 1980–1981, which classified the world into 62 countries and regions and was based on the concept of global interdependence among these various countries and regions. From 1981 it has been used as a long-term policy simulation model by the Projections and Perspective Studies Branch of the Department of International Economic and Social Affairs of the UN Secretariat in New York.

From 1990–1991 a new generation FUGI global model (7.0) was developed at the Soka University Institute for Systems Science (SUISS) in cooperation with IBM Japan, introducing an artificial intelligence (AI)-oriented expert system for global modelling. Though the role of AI-oriented "high technology" is very important for producing these models, expert knowledge is also essential, and in this regard, what must be emphasized is, more than mere mechanical computations, the indispensable role of the economist. In other words, the mechanical computations leave something lacking, and human beings are ultimately the main factors. With respect to the question of how and by what human criteria global information is input into the computers so as to get accurate forecasts, global models are only a very useful tool to assist human judgment.

Especially when global models are used for forecasting, there is the need for special "perceptiveness" in the application of current information to future simulations. To make the most of this perceptiveness, we should think of the future in terms of scenarios, or in other words, various types of policy alternatives that human society could conceivably adopt. We should consider not just a single future but rather various types of future scenarios that might result from human-controlled policy behaviour, and in this connection we should think of global models as a helping tool for thinking about which combinations of these scenarios or types of policy behaviour are most appropriate.

As the FUGI model was originally researched and developed principally around "economic" issues, a task that we have during the past several years put before us is to devise and incorporate subsystems that deal with environmental issues and such areas of concern as "human rights" and "peace and security."

The economic system treated in the newest FUGI model (7.0) is extraordinarily large in scale. Not only is the world subdivided into 180 countries and 80 country groupings, but into each of these 180/80 national regional economic models are incorporated 10 "sub-blocs," as follows: (1) labour and production; (2) expenditures on real GDP; (3) distributions of income: profits and wages; (4) prices; (5) expenditures on nominal GDP; (6) money, interest rates, and financial assets; (7) government finance; (8) international balance of payments; (9) international finance; and (10) foreign exchange rates. The total number of structual equations is more than 150,000 for the M180 model.

The FUGI model (7.0) is designed to respond to the current disequilibrium in the world economy, incorporating varying characteristics of the economic systems in the developed market economies, the developing market economies, and the planned market economies, respectively. With regard, for example, to the developed market economies, for which, relatively speaking, data are most abundant, the fact that the model is constructed so as to be able to utilize an extremely large volume of complex data makes it possible to analyse to an optimal degree the complex systems that characterize these economies, although the model is on the other hand enforced to adopt data situations prevailing in both developing and planned market economies. It is worth noting that the model incorporates dynamic supply-demand integrated systems that allow not only "demand-oriented modelling" but modelling for the supply side as well. If a given country's potential GDP exceeds its real GDP derived from the demand subsystem, the model behaves as if it is a "demand-oriented model" seen in those for the most developed market economies. If a given country's real GDP would exceed its potential GDP derived from a production subsystem, the model works as a "production-oriented model." Both supply–demand features are incorporated into the FUGI global model's system structure, and the model functions for the most part as a "production-oriented model" in the developing market economies as is true also in the case of the planned market economies.

The FUGI global model has country-specific characteristics, although defined in such a way as to allow general applicability. The economic systems of the United States and Japan, for example, are not identical and the system structures of these economies are subject to change over time. Accordingly, by designing a global model that is as far as possible universally applicable, and then choosing from it the most appropriate variables as well as those functions that fit best in making forecasts regarding individual countries or regions in given time periods, modelling can be carried out so that the coherence of the system as a whole may not be lost.

In order to make the computations for such an enormous global model, we require both a very high capacity computer and a specially designed "software package" for use in modelling. This software package, developed according to concepts that we developed in cooperation with IBM at the Soka University Institute for Systems Science, is known as "FUGI/GMS" (FUGI global modelling system).

The FUGI/GMS software system allows highly efficient, large-scale global modelling. It is designed in such a way that the following operations are consistently carried out: (1) serving as a data bank for large-volume data processing; (2) estimating the model's structural parameters; (3) dynamic simulation model testing; and (4) baseline projections and alternative scenario simulations. By applying this software, the necessary manpower needs for global modelling and alternative futures simulations are kept to a minimum, and the work of computation is accomplished quickly and efficiently. Were it not for such progress in software, large-scale econometric modelling for the global economy and reliable forecast simulation would probably be impossible to achieve.

Another characteristic of the FUGI global model is the special attention which it gives to analysing interlinkages of environment, development, peace, and human rights in the relationships between countries.

Simulations of the effects of CO_2 emissions cut-backs on the world economy

In evaluating the impacts of CO_2 emission cut-backs on the world economy in the decade of the 1990s, we have envisaged the following scenarios: (1) the baseline scenario; (2) the introduction of a 100 per cent CO_2 emission tax; and (3) three other alternative scenarios: (A), (B), and (C), each of which supposes that rising global levels of CO_2 emissions during the first part of the decade will be followed by a stabilization at the 1990 level by the year 2000.

Scenarios

Baseline scenario

In order to compare alternative simulation results, we have introduced a "baseline scenario," which is based on the assumption that the policies being followed in the past by each nation will not undergo any drastic change in the future.

100 per cent CO_2 emission tax scenario

In this scenario, we have introduced a "carbon tax" on oil, coal, and natural gas to lessen the consumption of fossils fuels, which produce CO_2 emissions. This is seen as a two-step process, at the end of which a 100 per cent tax is applied to oil, a 120 per cent tax to coal, and an 80 per cent tax to natural gas. The first step, lasting approximately one year, beginning in 1991, involves a 30 per cent increase in the tax on oil, and a proportional increase in the taxes on coal and natural gas. The full taxes are imposed in the course of 1992.

Global cooperation scenarios

Alternative scenario A

It is expected that most of the member countries of the global society would (1) introduce carbon dioxide emission taxes of 10 per cent on oil, 12 per cent on coal, and 8 per cent on natural gas and (2) reduce their economic growth rates though cut-backs of non-housing investment by around 5.0 per cent except the former Soviet Union and Eastern Europe, so as to stabilize their CO_2 emissions at the 1990 level by the year 2000.

Alternative scenario B

In contrast to scenario A, (1) most countries will not introduce carbon dioxide emission taxes. Instead of introducing these taxes, the developed countries will increase by 0.5 per cent of GDP expenditures on R&D, which is aimed at new technologies to reduce CO_2 emissions, and the developed countries will intensify technology transfer to the developing countries by increasing ODA, by amounts equal to 20 per cent over and above total ODA in the baseline scenario, for the specific purpose of reducing CO_2 global emissions to the 1990 level by the year 2000.

Alternative scenario C

It is expected that (1) most countries are likely to cope with global warming effects by reducing CO_2 emissions during the coming decade by introducing carbon taxes of at least 5 per cent on fossil fuels (together with cut-backs of non-housing investment by around 2.5 per cent except the former Soviet Union and Eastern Europe), and that (2) the developed countries will increase R&D aimed at new technologies to reduce CO_2 emissions from the present average of 0.04 per cent of GDP to 0.25 per cent of GDP, and (3) intensify technology transfer to the developing countries by increasing ODA, by amounts equal to 10 per cent over and above total ODA in the baseline scenario, for the specific purpose of reducing CO_2 global emissions to the 1990 level by the year 2000.

Simulation results

Baseline scenario

Since it was projected that the price of oil would increase from 17.9 dollars per barrel in 1990 to 40 dollars per barrel in the year 2000, under such circumstances, the world economy is expected to grow at an average annual rate of 2.9 per cent. The developed market economies will grow at an average rate of 2.6 per cent, while the developing market economies grow at a rate of 4.3 per cent and, the planned market economies at a rate of 2.8 per cent. Within the latter category, the former Soviet Union and Eastern Europe grow at a rate of 1 per cent, while China's growth rate is 4.6 per cent. Among the developed market economies, the average growth rate of the Japanese economy is 3.9 per cent, while that of the US economy is 2.2 per cent. That of the EC is 2.6 per cent. Among the developing market economies, higher-than-average growth performance is expected in the Asia-Pacific region, where the growth rate of the ASEAN countries is 6 per cent. The rate for the Middle East countries is 2.8 per cent, and for Latin America averages 4 per cent.

In the 1990s the world population will grow at a rate of 1.6 per cent per year. The rate of population growth is only an average 0.6 per cent per year in the developed market economies, but is a much higher 2.2 per cent in the developing market economies. Therefore it is hardly to be expected that there will be any further narrowing of the North-South per capita income gap.

Global CO_2 emissions will grow at a rate of 2.3 per cent per year, expanding from 6,118 MT-C (million metric tons in carbon equivalent) in 1990 to 7,674 MT-C in 2000.

CO_2 emissions originating in the developed market economies will increase from 2,957 MT-C in 1990 to 3,476 MT-C in 2000, with a yearly average increase of 1.6 per cent. CO_2 emissions originating in the developing market economies sharply increase from 984 MT-C in 1990 to 1,555 MT-C in 2000, with a yearly average increase of 4.7 per cent. The planned market economies' generation of CO_2 will grow from 2,107 MT-C in 1990 to 2,550 MT-C in 2000, with an average yearly increase of 1.9 per cent. The main reason for the relatively low rate of increase in CO_2 emissions in the planned market economies as a whole is the low rate of economic growth in the former Soviet Union and Eastern Europe. By contrast, China's increase in CO_2 emissions is 4 per cent per year.

It is interesting to note that CO_2 emissions originating in Japan will increase at an average rate of only 1.58 per cent, showing a tendency to stabilize toward the year 2000. On the other hand, CO_2 emissions originating in the United States will, in this baseline scenario, increase at an annual average rate of 1.75 per cent, but without showing any tendency to decline toward the end of the decade. China, differently from Japan, does not show any tendency for the rate of CO_2 increase to decline. Even though the rate of increase of CO_2 emissions in China is relatively high, per capita emissions in 2000 are nevertheless only two-thirds of the world average, about one-third of the figure for Japan, about one-fifth the figure for Australia, and about one-eighth the figure for the United States. The per capita CO_2 emissions in China are, however, in 2000 about twice the average for the developing market economies.

100 per cent CO_2 emission tax scenario

Today there are many economists who advocate the need to apply a surtax, or so-called "carbon tax," to the consumption of fossil fuels in order to curb CO_2 emissions. However, it has been hard for them to know, for example, how large such a tax should be to stabilize global CO_2 emissions at the 1990 level toward the year 2000. This is why we have made simulations of a number of possible tax rates, ranging from just a few per cent to some 200 per cent.

By way of example, in our 100 per cent tax scenario, it is expected that most of the developed market economies will achieve, or nearly achieve, a target of reducing CO_2 emissions in 2000 to the 1990 level.

For example, in the developed market economies as a whole, this "rate of achievement" is 96 per cent, and is accompanied by a drop in the average (over the period 1991–2000) economic growth rate of 1.1 percentage points compared with the baseline projections. It is interesting to note that, according our model, in the United States the 100 per cent tax scenario is just enough to achieve the target, in which case the United States's average annual economic growth rate would decrease by 1.5 per cent.

In the developing market economies as a whole, the rate of achievement is 67 per cent, ranging from 79 per cent in the Latin American NIEs to 60 per cent in India. The average drop in economic growth rate for the developing market economies as a whole is 0.5 percentage points.

Among the planned market economies, the rate of achievement in China is 82 per cent, accompanied by a 2.2 per cent drop in economic growth rate. In the former Soviet Union and Eastern Europe the level of CO_2 emissions in 2000 is stabilized at a level slightly less than in 1990, accompanied by a 1.2 per cent drop in economic growth rate (see table 1).

Global cooperation alternative scenario A

According to scenario A, it is expected that the rate of world economic growth will decrease by an average annual 2 per cent during the decade 1991–2000, compared with the baseline projection. The decrease in the annual average growth rate of the developed market economies as a whole is 2.1 percentage points (in Japan 3.3, in the USA 2.2, and in the EC 1.7).

On the other hand, the rate of economic growth of the developing market economies as a whole will decrease by an average annual 1.6 per cent during the same period. It is of interest to note that the average decrease in growth rate for the Asian NIEs (Republic of Korea, Taiwan, Hong Kong, and Singapore) is 2.1 per cent, and for the Latin American NIEs (Brazil and Mexico) is 2.9 per cent. In the developing market economies of the Asia and Pacific Region as a whole, the decrease is 1.7 per cent (2.2 per cent in East Asia, 2.7 per cent in the ASEAN group, and 1.2 per cent in "Other Asia and Pacific"). In the Middle East, the decrease is 0.6 per cent, in Africa it is 0.8 per cent, while in Latin America and the Caribbean it is 2.3 percentage points.

It is worth noting that the annual average growth rate in the planned

Table 1 **Cut-back scenario simulations using the FUGI model: 100% carbon tax annual growth-rates of real GDP for the period, 1991–2000 (unit: %)**

		Deviations from the baseline 100% CO_2 emission tax				Rate of achievement
	Baseline	1991	1992	1993	1990–2000	(CO2 in 1990/2000)
World	2.9	–2.329	–4.134	–1.995	–1.129	89.5
Developed market economies	2.6	–3.411	–5.976	–2.333	–1.115	96.1
OECD	2.6	–3.426	–6.068	–2.368	–1.132	95.6
The Major Seven	2.7	–3.199	–5.838	–2.856	–1.156	97.0
Japan	3.9	–1.747	–2.454	–0.871	–0.220	68.3
USA	2.2	–4.197	–6.780	–2.603	–1.503	99.6
EC	2.6	–2.920	–6.535	–3.580	–1.233	93.6
Developing market economies	4.3	–0.596	–1.074	–0.812	–0.543	67.4
Oil-exporting countries	3.7	–0.039	–0.576	–0.970	–0.390	66.9
Non oil-exporting countries	4.6	–0.863	–1.310	–0.732	–0.611	67.6
NIES	4.9	–1.570	–2.407	–1.307	–1.060	66.5
Asian NIES	6.0	–4.912	–6.342	–0.721	–1.354	66.7
Latin America NIES	4.4	0.0	–0.550	–1.531	–0.905	79.2
Asia and Pacific	5.3	–1.614	–2.441	–0.701	–0.677	64.7
East Asia	5.9	–5.469	–7.140	–0.635	–1.398	67.1
ASEAN	6.0	–0.575	–1.949	–1.576	–0.849	64.9
Other Asia	4.3	0.0	0.036	–0.032	–0.058	63.3
Middle East	2.8	0.0	–0.367	–0.735	–0.229	71.1
Africa	3.6	0.0	0.327	–0.316	–0.113	65.2
Latin America and Caribbean	4.0	0.0	–0.445	–1.119	–0.672	71.8
Planned market economies	2.8	0.0	–0.452	–1.980	–1.740	95.3
Former Soviet Union and East Europe	1.0	0.0	–0.289	–1.400	–1.191	103.8
Former Soviet Union	1.0	0.0	–0.227	–1.166	–0.910	102.7
China and other Asian PMEs	4.6	0.0	–0.641	–2.613	–2.267	82.0

Source: Projections and simulations using the FUG1 model.

market economies as a whole will decrease by 2 per cent during the 1991–2000 period. It is expected that the average annual decrease in the USSR will be 0.9 per cent, while the decrease will be a much greater 2.9 percentage points in China. The major reason for this drastic fall in China' s growth rate is that country's relatively higher proportion of coal as an energy source (see table 2c).

Global cooperation alternative scenario B

In contrast to the simulation results of scenario A, the average annual growth rate of the world economy as a whole will rise – by 0.09 per cent – rather than fall, compared with the baseline projection for the decade 1991–2000.

In the developed market economies as a whole, the average annual growth rate increases by a similar 0.09 per cent (0.45 per cent in Japan, 0.01 per cent in the United States, and 0.02 per cent in the EC).

In the developing market economies as a whole, the average rise in growth rate during the same period is 0.04 per cent. The increase is 0.07 per cent in the Asian NIEs and 0.03 per cent in the Latin American NIEs. In the developing market economies of the Asia and Pacific Region, the average increase is 0.05 per cent (0.07 in East Asia, 0.09 in the ASEAN group, and 0.01 per cent in "Other Asia and Pacific"). The increase is 0.05 per cent in the Middle East, 0.01 per cent in Africa, and 0.02 per cent in Latin America and the Caribbean.

In the planned market economies as a whole, the average rise in growth rate during the same period is 0.12 per cent (0.04 per cent in the USSR, and 0.19 per cent in China) (see table 2d).

Global cooperation alternative scenario C

In scenario C, which is a sort of compromise between scenarios A and B, it is expected that the average annual growth rate of the world economy as a whole will decrease by 0.4 per cent compared with the baseline projection during the period 1991–2000.

In the developed market economies as a whole, the average decrease in the growth rate during the same period is 0.37 per cent (0.56 in Japan, 0.34 in the United States, and 0.25 in the EC).

In the developing market economies as a whole, the average decrease in the growth rate during the same period is 0.31 per cent. In the Asian NIEs the decrease is 0.41 per cent, while in the Latin American NIEs it is a considerably larger 0.64 per cent. In the developing market economies of the Asia and Pacific Region, the corresponding decrease is 0.32 per cent (0.45 in East Asia, 0.32 in the ASEAN group, and 0.23 in "Other Asia and Pacific"). The corresponding drop in growth rate is 0.08 per cent in the Middle East, 0.14 per cent in Africa, and 0.07 per cent in both Latin America and the Caribbean.

In the planned market economies as a whole, the average annual drop in growth rate during the decade 1991–2000 is 0.73 per cent (0.16 in the former Soviet Union and 1.23 in China) (see table 2e).

Table 2a **Cut-back scenario simulations using the FUGI model. Scenarios A, B and C: annual growth rates of real GDP for the period, 1991–2000 (unit: %)**

		Deviations from the baseline CO_2 cut-back scenario		
	Baseline	A	B	C
World	2.9	−1.978	0.089	−0.426
Developed market economies	2.6	−2.082	0.093	−0.370
OECD	2.6	−2.103	0.095	−0.374
The Major Seven	2.7	−2.281	0.102	−0.382
Japan	3.9	−3.233	0.447	−0.556
USA	2.2	−2.201	0.011	−0.341
EC	2.6	−1.682	0.019	−0.247
Developing market economies	4.3	−1.605	0.037	−0.312
Oil-exporting countries	3.7	−1.412	0.048	−0.265
Non oil-exporting Countries	4.6	−1.692	0.033	−0.333
NIES	4.9	−2.594	0.046	−0.557
Asian NIES	6.0	−2.044	0.070	−0.408
Latin America NIES	4.4	−2.903	0.032	−0.639
Asia and Pacific	5.9	−1.601	0.053	−0.295
East Asia	6.0	−2.183	0.070	−0.440
ASEAN	6.0	−1.638	0.087	−0.254
Other Asia	4.3	−1.179	0.013	−0.229
Middle East	2.8	−0.597	0.047	−0.072
Africa	3.6	−0.822	0.013	−0.137
Latin America and Caribbean	4.0	−2.329	0.024	−0.490
Planned market economies	2.8	−1.972	0.121	−0.727
Former Soviet Union and East Europe	1.0	−1.050	0.043	−0.197
Former Soviet Union	1.0	−0.896	0.038	−0.161
China and other Asian PMEs	4.6	−2.882	0.191	−1.232

Source: Projections and simulations using the FUGI model.

Table 2b **Baseline projections of world energy requirements and CO2 emissions: annual average increasing rates for the period, 1991–2000 (unit: %)**

	Total energy requirement	Fossil energy	(Coal)	Alternative energy	CO_2 emissions
World	2.6	2.3	2.5	4.3	2.3
Developed market economies	2.3	1.7	1.9	4.4	1.6
OECD	2.3	1.7	2.0	4.4	1.7
The Major Seven	2.1	1.7	1.7	4.1	1.6
Japan	2.5	1.8	2.5	5.3	1.6
USA	1.7	1.8	1.9	0.2	1.7
EC	3.2	1.7	1.9	6.2	1.7
Developing market economies	4.9	4.7	5.3	5.9	4.7
Oil-exporting countries	5.0	5.0	4.7	5.2	4.9
Non oil-exporting countries	4.9	4.6	5.3	6.0	4.6
NIES	5.6	5.5	6.3	6.1	5.5
Asian NIES	5.9	5.6	6.5	7.2	5.7
Latin America NIES	5.4	5.4	6.0	5.6	5.3
Asia and Pacific	5.4	5.3	5.6	6.2	5.3
East Asia	5.9	5.6	6.5	7.2	5.7
ASEAN	6.1	6.0	8.6	7.8	5.9
Other Asia	4.8	4.8	5.0	4.2	4.8
Middle East	3.7	3.6	3.3	4.8	3.6
Africa	4.7	4.7	4.8	4.6	4.6
Latin America and Caribbean	4.9	4.3	5.2	6.1	4.2
Planned market economies	1.8	1.8	2.3	1.8	1.9
Former Soviet Union and East Europe	0.9	0.9	0.2	1.3	0.8
Former Soviet Union	1.0	0.9	0.8	1.7	0.8
China and other Asian PMEs	3.9	3.9	4.0	4.4	3.9

Source: Projections and simulations using the FUGI model.

Impacts of global disarmament on the world economy

In order to assess possible impacts of global disarmament on the world economy during the period 1991–2000, we have introduced the following scenarios.

Table 2c **Alternative projections of world energy requirements and CO2 emissions: annual average increasing rates for the period, 1990–2000–scenario A (unit: %)**

	Total energy requirement	Fossil energy	(Coal)	Alternative energy	CO_2 emissions
World	0.9	0.8	0.9	1.4	0.8
Developed market economies	0.4	0.2	0.3	0.9	0.2
OECD	0.4	0.2	0.3	0.9	0.2
The Major Seven	0.2	0.1	0.1	0.3	0.1
Japan	0.4	0.3	0.4	1.0	0.3
USA	0.1	0.1	0.0	0.1	0.1
EC	0.8	0.5	0.5	1.4	0.5
Developing market economies	3.2	3.0	3.7	3.9	3.0
Oil-exporting countries	2.8	2.7	2.0	4.1	2.6
Non oil-exporting countries	3.3	3.2	3.8	3.9	3.2
NIES	2.6	2.4	3.6	3.3	2.5
Asian NIES	3.8	3.6	4.0	5.0	3.6
Latin America NIES	1.6	1.4	2.4	2.4	1.4
Asia and Pacific	3.8	3.7	3.9	4.3	3.7
East Asia	3.7	3.5	4.0	5.0	3.5
ASEAN	4.4	4.3	7.3	5.8	4.3
Other Asia	3.5	3.5	3.5	2.9	3.5
Middle East	3.0	3.0	3.5	3.9	2.9
Africa	3.7	3.7	3.8	3.8	3.6
Latin America and Caribbean	2.3	1.5	1.9	3.8	1.5
Planned market economies	0.5	0.5	0.7	0.2	0.5
Former Soviet Union and East Europe	0.0	0.0	−0.1	−0.2	0.0
Former Soviet Union	0.2	0.1	−0.0	0.1	0.1
China and other Asian PMEs	1.5	1.5	1.5	1.9	1.5

Source: Projections and simulations using the FUGI model.

Scenarios on arms reductions

It is assumed that most countries in the global society will freeze their military expenditures at 1990 levels starting from the end of the Gulf war in order to open the new era of arms reductions towards the year 2000. Utilizing human and financial resources freed from arms reductions the developed market economy countries are able to in-

Table 2d **Alternative projections of world energy requirements and CO2 emissions: annual average increasing rates for the period, 1990–2000–scenario B (unit: %)**

	Total energy requirement	Fossil energy	(Coal)	Alternative energy	CO_2 emissions
World	0.8	0.1	0.2	3.9	0.1
Developed market economies	0.4	–0.6	–0.7	3.8	–0.6
OECD	0.5	–0.5	–0.6	3.7	–0.6
The Major Seven	0.2	–0.6	–0.9	3.2	–0.7
Japan	1.3	–0.1	0.5	5.9	–0.3
USA	–0.5	–0.5	–0.6	0.2	–0.6
EC	1.3	–0.5	–1.0	4.8	–0.6
Developing market economies	3.1	2.4	3.0	6.0	2.4
Oil-exporting countries	2.9	2.7	2.5	5.2	2.7
Non oil-exporting countries	3.2	2.2	3.0	6.1	2.3
NIES	3.9	3.2	4.0	6.2	3.2
Asian NIES	4.0	3.4	4.2	7.3	3.4
Latin America NIES	3.7	3.1	3.6	5.6	3.0
Asia and Pacific	1.4	3.0	3.3	6.3	3.0
East Asia	4.1	3.4	4.2	7.3	3.4
ASEAN	4.0	3.7	6.2	7.8	3.6
Other Asia	2.6	2.5	2.6	4.4	2.5
Middle East	1.5	1.4	1.1	4.8	1.4
Africa	2.7	2.4	2.5	4.6	2.3
Latin America and Caribbean	3.5	2.0	2.9	6.1	1.9
Planned market economies	–0.1	–0.3	0.1	1.9	–0.3
Former Soviet Union and East Europe	–1.1	–1.3	–2.0	1.4	–1.4
Former Soviet Union	–1.0	–1.3	–2.3	1.6	–1.4
China and other Asian PMEs	1.9	1.8	1.8	4.6	1.8

Source: Projections and simulations using the FUGI model.

tensify civilian research and development expenditures towards the twenty-first century as well as fixed capital investment for improving their own quality of life. Except those countries suffering from serious government current budget deficits such as the United States, it is hypothesized that most of the developed market economies will be able to increase their ODA contributions to the developing world by

Table 2e **Alternative projections of world energy requirements and CO2 emissions: annual average increasing rates for the period, 1990–2000–scenario C (unit: %)**

	Total energy requirement	Fossil energy	(Coal)	Alternative energy	CO_2 emissions
World	0.7	0.1	−0.2	3.5	0.0
Developed market economies	0.4	−0.3	−0.8	3.2	−0.4
OECD	0.5	−0.3	−0.7	3.2	−0.4
The Major Seven	0.3	−0.3	−1.0	2.8	−0.4
Japan	0.8	−0.3	−0.2	4.6	−0.5
USA	−0.1	−0.2	−0.7	0.8	−0.3
EC	1.1	−0.5	−1.2	4.1	−0.6
Developing market economies	3.0	2.3	2.8	5.7	2.3
Oil-exporting countries	2.7	2.5	2.6	5.0	2.5
Non oil-exporting countries	3.1	2.2	2.8	5.8	2.2
NIES	3.4	2.7	3.5	5.6	2.8
Asian NIES	3.8	3.1	3.7	6.9	3.2
Latin America NIES	3.1	2.4	2.9	4.9	2.4
Asia and Pacific	3.3	3.0	3.0	5.9	2.9
East Asia	3.8	3.1	3.7	6.9	3.1
ASEAN	4.1	3.8	6.7	8.0	3.7
Other Asia	2.6	2.4	2.4	3.8	2.4
Middle East	1.8	1.7	2.1	4.6	1.7
Africa	2.7	2.4	2.4	4.4	2.4
Latin America and Caribbean	3.2	1.6	2.2	5.9	1.6
Planned market economies	−0.4	−0.6	−0.6	1.6	−0.6
Former Soviet Union and East Europe	−1.0	−1.2	−2.0	1.3	−1.4
Former Soviet Union	−0.9	−1.1	−2.2	1.3	−1.2
China and other Asian PMEs	0.8	0.6	0.6	3.2	0.6

Source: Projections and simulations using the FUGI model.

an amount equal to a half of the resources freed through cut-backs of military expenditures. On the other side, both developing market economies and planned market economies would be able to increase their gross domestic capital formation as well as expenditures on education and welfare, etc., for the purpose of improving their living standards using those resources freed through arms reductions.

Simulation results

Table 3 summarizes the impacts of the global military cut-back scenario on the economies of the interdependent world showing their deviations from the baseline. Among the simulation results, it is worth noting that the global economy will grow by an annual average 0.65 per cent faster than in the baseline scenario during the 1990s and that world trade in current prices will be enlarged by 532 billion (US dollars) in the year 2000 compared with the baseline.

The growth rates of the developed market economies as a group are slightly affected by the shock caused by the enactment of arms reduction policy during the immediate periods for conversion, 1991–1992. In the first half of the 1990s the growth rates of the developed market economies will be decreased by 0.14 per cent compared to those of the baseline and show a remarkable recovery in the latter half of the decade with growth rates achieving a level of 0.68 per cent over the baseline.

Although the economy of the United States will decline rather strongly from the arms reduction shock during the adjustment period for conversion (a decrease of 0.60 per cent over the period 1991–1995), it is expected that it will soon be revitalized through the combined effects of intensified civilian R&D, lowered interest rates, improved labour productivity and increased exports (an increase of 0.68 per cent over the period 1995–2000). As a result, the US real economic growth rate will increase by 0.04 per cent when averaged over the whole decade and its twin deficits will tend to definitely decrease during the 1990s.

On the other hand, although Japan's ratio of arms expenditures to GDP will remain less than 1 per cent, the Japanese economy will also benefit from global arms reductions through the expansion of the global economy and world trade. Its real GDP growth rate will increase by 0.95 per cent during the 1990s. Also, the EC economy as a whole will expand much faster than in the baseline scenario (an increase of 0.14 per cent in 1991–1995 and 0.37 per cent in 1995–2000).

It is important to note that the annual growth rate of the developing market economies as a whole will be accelerated by 1.04 per cent per year in the 1990s (0.53 in 1991–1995 and 1.55 in 1995–2000) through the multiple impacts of expanded world trade and financial flows coupled with their efforts at self-reliance.

In the Asia-Pacific region, average improvement of the economic growth rates is 1.14 percentage points over the baseline projections.

Table 3 **Arms reduction scenario simulations using the FUGI model: annual growth rates of real GDP for the period, 1991–2000 (unit: %)**

		Deviations from the baseline		
	Baseline 1991–2000	1991–1995	Arms reduction 1995–2000	1991–2000
World	2.9	0.075	1.231	0.651
Developed market economies	2.6	−0.135	0.677	0.269
OECD	2.6	−0.137	0.687	0.274
The Major Seven	2.7	−0.176	0.775	0.298
Japan	3.9	0.369	1.529	0.948
USA	2.2	−0.597	0.684	0.041
EC	2.6	0.140	0.367	0.254
Developing market economies	4.3	0.532	1.552	1.041
Oil-exporting countries	3.7	0.318	1.194	0.755
Non oil-exporting countries	4.6	0.626	1.694	1.158
NIES	4.9	0.303	1.473	0.886
Asian NIES	6.0	0.183	1.355	0.770
Latin America NIES	4.4	0.363	1.536	0.946
Asia and Pacific	5.3	0.613	1.662	1.137
East Asia	5.9	0.149	1.327	0.739
ASEAN	6.0	0.780	2.065	1.423
Other Asia	4.3	0.770	1.561	1.165
Middle East	2.8	0.264	1.360	0.811
Africa	3.6	0.153	0.453	0.303
Latin America and Caribbean	4.0	0.685	1.851	1.265
Planned market economies	2.8	0.365	2.577	1.467
Former Soviet Union and East Europe	1.0	0.668	2.820	1.739
Former Soviet Union	1.0	0.642	2.216	1.426
China and other Asian PMEs	4.6	−0.019	2.322	1.149

Source: Projections and simulations using the FUGI model.

Similarly, the Middle East shows a 0.81 percentage-point improvement, while Latin America and the Caribbean show a 1.27 percentage-point improvement over the baseline.

So far as the planned market economies are concerned, the real economic growth rates of the former Soviet Union and East European economies freed from much of the severe burden of arms expenditures will be able to recover soon after the adjustment period and increase by an average 1.74 per cent during the 1990s (0.67 in 1991–1995 and 2.82 in 1995–2000) compared with the baseline. China's economic growth is expected to improve by an average 1.15

per cent during the decade of the 1990s (−0.02 in 1990–1995 and 2.32 in 1995–2000).

FUGI global model for early warning of displaced persons

A new generation of the FUGI global model is designed to serve as a global early warning system for displaced persons. It covers (1) selected indicators and (2) a system for early warning monitoring designed to warn of situations threatening the large-scale generation of displaced persons.

Considering the various types of circumstance in which situations involving displaced persons occur, it would seem apt to classify these into four broad categories.

Selected indicators

The list of "selected indicators" was chosen in the course of consideration of what might be the most important indicators in regard to displaced persons that could be used to elucidate a system for a Global Early Warning System (GEWS). This most basic list consists of four major displaced persons categories, as follows:

I. Destruction in environment (ecologically displaced persons)
II. Failures in development (economically displaced persons)
III. Absence of peace and security (PS displaced persons)
IV. Violations of human rights (HR displaced persons)

Category I, destruction in environment, includes a number of sub-indicators: (1) natural disasters (flood and drought, etc.); (2) water pollution; (3) air pollution; (4) soil pollution; (5) erosion and loss of topsoil; (6) nuclear pollution; (7) ecological imbalance (as caused, for example, by deforestation).

Category II, failures in development, is very complex, and we have included in it 12 sub-indicators. It is in this field, however, that our research is most advanced. The 12 sub-indicators for this complex, development-oriented model are the following:

1. Poor economic growth.
2. Stagnant per-capita income and unequal income distribution.
3. Increased international per-capita income disparities: in our global model, average per-capita income in the developing countries as a whole is indexed as a "standard" from which international income disparities can be calculated. Thus the relative income level of a given developing country in international society – whether it is extremely poor or doing relatively well – can be seen.

4. Higher domestic prices in terms of consumer price index (CPI).
5. Increased unemployment rate and disguised urban-rural unemployment: the issue of "disguised unemployment" is a concept that has been applied in particular to rural areas, but it must also be seen as relevant to urban unemployment and the spread of urban slums.
6. Deficit in current balance of payments: in cases where there is a disappearance of export potential and a country must nevertheless rely on imports, an economic pattern is created that must rely on capital aid from other countries.
7. Depreciated currency exchange rate: current exchange rates in a certain sense reflect each country's economic strength. If the dollar is "strong," this may be seen to reflect a faith in the dollar, or in other words a strong faith in the United States economy. If a given country's economy is facing a crisis, its exchange rate is likely to depreciate rapidly.
8. Increased debt service ratio (indicator of external debt): "debt service ratio" is a technical term that indicates the percentage of a country's export earnings that are allocated as a combination of amortization of principal plus interest for the repayment of foreign debts. It can indicate situations of economic crisis and degree of "country risk," as seen from the point of view of international bankers. Countries that have borrowed too heavily must in any case repay their debts with foreign exchange earned from exports. But if the debt is too large in comparison with export potential, it cannot be repaid, and this leads to economic crisis.
9. Decreased capital inflow and increased capital outflow: this indicator is also used in bankers' discussions of "country risk." The important point here is that capital does not flow into countries that are considered to be extremely "risky." At the same time, it if often a noticeable fact that capital from risky countries "flees," so to speak, to foreign countries.
10. Decreased foreign exchange reserves: in heavily indebted countries, these are seen to be nearing depletion.
11. Food–population imbalance: if population and the possibilities for supplying food become greatly imbalanced, there will be famine and starvation.
12. Mass poverty and socio-economic disparities: this refers to situations in which the great majority of the people are very poor but certain wealthy classes lead a very elegant life in their midst.

If such socio-economic disparities should be seen to be increasing rapidly, the economic elements are present that make it likely that there will be widespread eruptions of political confrontation, which could possibly lead to civil war.

Category III, absence of peace and security, consists of six indicators, as follows:

1. Political conflicts and violence.
2. Absence of rule of law: this phrase is one used by Aga Khan and refers to situations where social order and the application of the rule of law to protect the population and facilitate social order are virtually lacking.
3. Growing ratios of military expenditures to GDP: under circumstances where civil war is thought likely to occur in the future, military expenditures would no doubt be further increased, even if this meant forcibly making great sacrifices in other areas.
4. Insurgency.
5. Internal war.
6. Danger that the above might lead to international warfare.

Category IV, violation of human rights, consists of seven indicators as follows:

1. Failure to meet "basic human existence needs": this refers to very severe situations that are equivalent to the denial of the right to live as a human being. These would include severe problems having to do with such things as public hygiene, housing, and nutrition (including, of course, situations of mass famine).
2. Ideological oppression and enforced exile for ideological reasons.
3. Ethnic discrimination and enforced exile for racial reasons.
4. Religious oppression and enforced exile for religious reasons.
5. Poor ratio of educational expenditures to GDP: this refers to educational factors as they affect human rights. It may be observed that countries where educational expenditures make up only a very small part of GDP generally do not do a very good job of protecting human rights. Since the education of human beings is fundamentally linked to respect for human rights, it is not surprising that in countries that begrudge educational expenditures one sees lack of respect for human rights and human life.
6. Absence of social security and welfare: a country that is suffering from hunger has basically no surplus resources to be devoted to matters of social security and welfare. In some countries, the money available for these purposes is inadequate as a result of excessive military expenditures.

7. Absence of respect for human life and cultural rights: this indicator, which includes the degree to which "cultural rights" are neglected, was inspired by Aga Khan. In the case of Thailand, this indicator does not register at all, meaning that Thailand is very stable in this regard. This presumably shows that in Thailand there is a high level of "love of country" and respect for traditional culture.

The above indicators are divided into those that are economically variable and can be precisely calculated, and, on the other hand, those that are very difficult to evaluate in the absence of special ratings produced through the judgments of experts.

Early warning monitoring

Large-scale occurrences of displaced persons usually have complex and interrelated causes. We have tried to look at these causes in a comprehensive way as involving the four above-mentioned categories.

Thus, as a countermeasure, we first of all prescribe economic development in the developing countries, carried out in such a way that there is no spread of environmental destruction. As ingredients in effecting this purpose, we must no doubt have both a sense of awareness on the part of all countries, and assistance from the developed countries to be provided in the spirit of the common responsibility of the human race.

The focus of development strategies must surely be directed to the consideration of how to eradicate poverty among the general mass of the population. What, then, might comprehensive policies for that purpose be? Emphasis must be given both to self-reliant efforts on the part of the country in question and also to economic and technological cooperation from the developed countries.

Using our Global Early Warning System for Displaced Persons (GEWS), we have investigated the risks of large-scale occurrences of displaced persons in 13 selected countries in Asia. Based on our findings, we have further studied the question of how to alert people to concrete dangers as early as possible and how to design countermeasures. Building upon this already developed early warning system for Asian countries, part of our work in the future can be expected to be that of extending the early warning system to make it applicable to all of the world's developing countries in all geographical regions. As pointed out earlier, a seventh-generation FUGI model is currently in the stage of research and development. This model classifies the world into approximately 180 countries and regional units, thus making it possible to treat almost all countries at the individual-country level. A prime characteristic of our global model is that it permits the study of how the individual-country models are mutually interdependent, and especially the study of how the economic policies of the most powerful countries affect the developing countries.

Our objective is to develop a truly comprehensive global modelling system that will have this type of development model at its core, supplemented by subsystems having to do with environment, peace, and security as well as human rights, and that will in this way permit the further development and global application of a global early warning system.

Through advances in the life sciences, we now know something about the "wisdom" possessed by individual cells. It is because each cell of a living organism possesses information concerning the whole that there is the possibility of mutual adjustments and cooperation. This ought to suggest the possibility of closer cooperation in our global society, given the possession by each country of global information.

We should hope that our research will not stop at the individual-country level but can, by providing from a global vantage-point information on issues affecting the potential appearance of displaced persons, throw new and brighter light on possibilities for global adjustments and cooperation in our living human society.

In this way, we look forward to the establishment of a global early warning system that can help eliminate the factors of instability which are represented in the appearance of displaced persons in our global society, especially in the developing regions, and that can at the same time help point to ways by which our human society can improve and become firmly grounded in a greater degree of genuine humanism.

Editors' note

Due to constraints of space, it was not possible to reproduce the FUGI model here. For further illustration of the FUGI model, refer to other published works by Akira Onishi.

References

Onishi, A. 1976. "Using a Multi-Nation Economic Model Projection of Economic Relations Between Japan and Developing Countries in Asia, 1975–1985." *Technological Forecasting and Social Change* 10.

—— 1980. "FUGI – Future of Global Independence in Input-Output Approaches in Global Modeling." In: Gerhart Bruckmann, ed. *Proceedings of the Fifth IIASA Symposium on Global Modeling*. Oxford, UK: Pergamon.
—— 1983a. "The FUGI Macroeconomic Model and World Trade to 1990." *Futures: The Journal of Forecasting and Planning* 15(2), April.
—— 1983b. "Project FUGI and the Future of ESCAP Developing Countries." In: B.G. Hickman, ed. *Global International Economic Models.* Amsterdam: North-Holland.
—— 1985. "North-South Interdependence: Projections of the World Economy, 1985–2000." *Journal of Policy Modeling* 8(2), July.
—— 1989. "Prospects for the World Economy and the Asian-Pacific Region." In: M. Shinihara and Fu-chen Lo, eds. *Global Adjustment and the Future of Asian-Pacific Economy*. IDE.
—— 1990. "Uses of Global Models: A New Generation FUGI Model for Projections and Policy Simulations of the World Economy." *International Political Science Review* 2(2), April.

Comments on chapter 10

1. Itsuo Kawamura

At the beginning of my comments on Professor Onishi's paper, I would like to emphasize his long and dedicated assistance to the work of the United Nations system in the area of long-term economic and social projections as shown in the list of publications cited in his present paper. I will be speaking mainly as a user of the results of model simulations, deferring to the other experts to make technical comments.

Professor Onishi's ambitious attempts at modelling could be compared to the new development in production technology in the manufacturing sector. We have seen the innovations in information-based production technology. The merging of design, manufacturing, and managerial functions has been termed the "factory of the future" – computer-integrated manufacturing (CIM). Professor Onishi seems to have achieved similar tasks in the field of modelling computer-integrated manufacturing (CIM). The key features of FUGI model 6.0 are integration and flexibility, which could yield enormous systemic gains in efficiency modelling efforts. It could accommodate any baseline forecasts derived from other modelling efforts and provide requested scenario results. It seems to contain some artificial intelligence so that the model can estimate parameters and run scenarios in conformity with the prescribed relevant range of probable values.

In order to give his model more transparency, the main request I have, however, is that Professor Onishi would provide us with more information on its workings; on the functional form of behaviour equations and the methods and results of the econometric parameter estimations. The following are a few preliminary comments and questions.

FUGI model 6.0

The new generation FUGI model 6.0 divides the world into 180 countries and country groupings. An individual country model (unit) consists of four major blocs: I, environment, II, development, III, peace and security, IV, human rights. Blocs (1), (3), and (4) are sub-blocs and have weak feedback relations among these blocs and with bloc II.

Bloc I (environment) consists of four sub-blocs: (1) eco-system, (2) population, (3) foods, (4) energy. Sub-bloc (2) (population) has strong relationships with sub-bloc (1) (labour and production) of bloc II (development) and determines the population by sexes. Sub-bloc (4) (energy) decides the demand for energy (crude oil, coal, and natural gas). However, there is no supply-side equation in this model. On the other hand, the price of crude oil is determined by mark-up method in the sub-bloc (4) (prices) of the bloc II (development) without regard to the demand. In this connection, it might be mentioned that, for example, an energy simulation model developed by Edmonds and Reilly (1983) can determine simultaneously the demand for supply and demand of fossil energy (crude oil, coal, and natural gas) by the use of their real prices and world trend of supply and demand conditions. Another example of the modelling efforts in this area is that of Amano (1989). In his energy model, crude oil price is determined by demand and supply relationships. We would like to know how the FUGI model deals with this problem. In the FUGI model, the imposition of CO_2 tax would shift the demand away from fossil fuel toward alternative fuel, but it cannot catch the feedback effects of the change in the supply induced by the change in the relative prices, which might further influence their prices.

Bloc II (development) consists of (1) labour and production; (2) expenditure on GDP at constant and current prices; (3) income distribution; (4) price; (5) money, interest rates, and financial assets; (6)

government finance; (7) international balance of payments; (8) international finance; (9) foreign exchange rate, and (10) development indicators.

Some comments are called for with respect to the modelling of each sub-bloc of the system. For instance, in sub-bloc (1), labour force, employment, and potential gross domestic product (GDPP) are determined. However, GDPP does not seem to be fully incorporated in the system. In other words, such a sequence in which GDP, which is determined in sub-bloc (2) (expenditure on GDP), along with GDPP determines the ratio of operations and further influences the determination of prices in sub-bloc (4) (prices) is not considered in the FUGI model.

In sub-bloc (2), short-term market interest rate (call rate) is used as one of the explanatory variables in the consumption function (2–1.1). It might be more appropriate to use long-term interest rate instead.

With respect to sub-bloc (4) (prices), it may be more appropriate to have separate equations for determining the prices of manufactured goods from the developed market economies and those of the primary commodities. WPI is basically determined by mark-up method on unit labour cost and import prices (PM). Prices of fossil fuels are determined by crude oil export price (PEO) and WPI. PEO is determined, in turn, by export prices of developed market economies (PES<AME>). PES<AME> is determined by WPI and its own lagged value. In fact, all the prices are influenced directly or indirectly by WPI.

For sub-bloc (5) which determines demand for money and interest rates, we have the following suggestion. Instead of using the Central Bank's official discount rate (IN) for the determination of money supply (MI), short-term market rate (call rate) should ordinarily be used. For the determination of Japanese government long-term bond yield (IB<JPN>), (IN) is used in the model. However, since IB<JPN> is a market yield, it can be explained by the time structure of short-term rates.

Simulation results

It is difficult to comment properly on the two simulation results in the report: one on CO_2 emission tax and the other on arms reduction, since we do not exactly know how these simulations have been performed and further there are no references to the process of propagation of the policy effects.

1. 100 per cent emission tax scenario

According to this scenario, the rate of achievement of the target of reducing CO_2 emissions in the year 2000 to the 1991 level is about 90 per cent, accompanied by a drop in the average (over the period 1991–2000) economic growth rate of 1.13 percentage points compared to the baseline. As for Japan, the rate of achievement is 86 per cent and the drop in growth rate is 0.22 of a percentage point from the baseline. By way of comparison, we may cite the simulation results in the Japan Economic Planning Agency's report (1991) which points out that in order to maintain the 1990 CO_2 level in Japan, if other things remain the same, the baseline GDP growth rate of 3.75 per cent for 1990–2000 has to be reduced by 2 per cent to 1.75 per cent. FUGI simulation results imply much less severe impacts of carbon taxes on the growth rate of the Japanese economy.

As we noted earlier, the imposition of carbon taxes induces the shift away from fossil fuels to alternative fuels due to the change in their relative prices. However, because of the absence of supply side in energy functions in the FUGI model, it fails to catch the effects of the change in the relative prices of various fuels on the supply structure of energy.

Another question arises on the use of carbon tax receipts. It is not clear how these receipts are allocated among various uses. Depending on the methods of disposition of the tax receipts (for instance, R&D, ODA, or reduction in other taxes), the overall impacts would be quite different.

2. Arms reduction scenario

It is assumed that most of the countries would freeze their military expenditure at the 1990 level and most of the developed market economies, except those suffering from serious government current budget deficits, would increase their ODA contributions to the developing countries by using 50 per cent of the resources freed through arms reduction.

As for the methodology for the simulation of arms reduction, it may be more relevant to consider the arms reduction race than the freeze of arms expenditure at a certain level. For the developing countries, reductions in military expenditures not only increase their investment in human and physical resources, but also may serve as one of the indicators for allocating ODA among the deserving developing countries by the donors.

Another issue in the arms reduction simulation is the treatment of armament exports. Global arms reduction may significantly affect the prospect of major arms exporters such as the USSR, China, and Brazil.

In the simulation of the FUGI model, the impact of arms reduction on the growth rates of GDP differs rather significantly between the USSR and the United States. In the case of the USSR, the growth rate is expected to improve by 1.74 per cent a year during the 1990s over the baseline (0.67 per cent in 1991–1995 and 2.82 per cent in 1995–2000), while the US economy suffers the shock of arms reduction during the adjustment period for conversion (0.60 per cent in 1991–1995). The United States is expected to realize early beneficial effects of the conversion (an increase of 0.68 per cent in 1995–2000). As a result, US growth will be increased by 0.04 per cent per year during the 1990s over the baseline.

What accounts for such big differences? The US economy experienced successful conversion of its production from civilian to military uses during World War II and from military to civilian uses after World War II. According to the American Department of Defense, more than 100 military bases in the United States have been converted to civilian uses during the period 1960–1988. In this process, about 93,000 government employees lost their jobs but 158,000 new employees were hired (Klein 1991). In view of these developments, it is rather difficult to understand the much better performance of the USSR and China than the US in their efforts to convert to a civilian economy.

References

Amano, Akihiro. 1989. Energy Price and Environment during the 1990s. Working Paper No. 8922. Kobe: Department of Management, Kobe University. In Japanese.

Edmonds, J.A. and J.M. Reilly. 1983. "Global Energy and CO_2 to the Year 2000." *The Energy Journal* 4.

Economic Planning Agency Year 2010 Committee. "Choices for 2010: Message-Earth and Human Beings." ESP, August. In Japanese.

Klein, L.R. "Nihon Keizai Shimbun." 1991. *Japan Economic Journal*, Kyushu ed., 17 October. In Japanese.

2. Wilhelm Krelle

The general philosophy behind the model

Professor Onishi has now presented the sixth version of his FUGI model. This model deals separately with 180 individual countries (or groups of countries) and consists of more than 100,000 equations. All countries are modelled more or less along the same lines. The core of the model is an econometric forecasting system for each country, which considers the real economy as well as its monetary and financial side. The economy is, of course, an open one so that capital and labour flows between countries. The exchange rates, the balance of payments, and accumulation of debts or assets are dealt with explicitly. The special feature of version 6.0 is the inclusion of modules on environment, population, food production, energy demand, peace and security, and human rights. Thus quite a number of latent variables enter the model.

In the introduction to his paper Professor Onishi discusses the philosophy behind the design of his model. He refers to his model as a "dynamic soft systems approach" which probably means that the model assumes causal chains for each variable and does not (or at least not in an important way) contain interdependent relations. This makes it possible to deal with a huge number of variables and equations without running into problems of the existence and uniqueness of a solution and into the problem of numerical stability. Professor Onishi is not afraid of complexity, and rightly so. But I doubt whether the analogy with the self-organizing capacity of human beings and the functioning of the human brain is really revealing.

I also doubt that world models can lead to international cooperation and "indicate how the global economy should best be run." As a rule there are conflicting interests between nations, at least in the short run. If all nations follow a wrong perception or ideology, the outcome will be worse compared to an uncoordinated search process where each nation tries another approach. But necessary global restrictions, e.g., in CO_2 emissions, might be an example where models of this kind could contribute to the willingness to reach an agreement by which all nations should curb their CO_2 emission, and to what extent. Here the problem of equity and efficiency emerges (see Welsch 1991a,b). But global models have their own rights as displaying the applications of most advanced econometrics, irrespective of their actual use in economic policy. Politicians and officers in administration must gain confidence in the model approach in order to use it as a basis for their decisions. In Germany there are now econometric models, which are used in some ministries, but as yet at an experimental stage. Thus we will have to wait some time until world models are fully accepted.

A model with more than 100,000 equations is not easy to comprehend. In the next section I shall give some comments on the model so far as I understand it. In the third section I shall comment on the results of the model for different scenarios.

Some remarks on the FUGI model

The following remarks are given with some hesitation: I have only the general outline of the model as it is presented in Professor Onishi's paper on the FUGI model where the functional form of the behaviour equations and the results of the econometric parameter estimations are not stated. I should like to start by expressing my admiration for Professor Onishi's huge effort to get a model like this running and to connect the ecological, social, and political side of a society with the economic side. This is a really big step forward. The following remarks are not so much a criticism of what he did but suggestions for improving his work.

1. The presentation of a model of this size is not an easy task. Professor Onishi makes every effort to make it understandable. But there are still some desiderata: some variables are not defined (see note 14 in the appendix below), in the list of variables the number of the equation determining this variable should be given. The type of functional form of a behaviour equation should be outlined (linear, log-linear,...) and some statistical measures (R^2, DW etc.) should be given. This would save a great deal of time and effort for the reader.

2. It is not clear whether this model is constructed for short- or long-term forecasts. Some equations make sense only if the model is run for a very long time (e.g. the accumulation of CO_2 in the atmosphere or the warming of the surface of the earth); others make sense only in the short or medium run (e.g. the export demand functions, the price functions, and the exchange rate functions).

3. A good test of the model would be to let it run for many periods. If there are some instabilities or if some variables that should stay positive become negative, we are warned against using the model for long runs and can get some hints as to what should be improved.

4. There are many non-directly measurable (latent) variables in

the ecological, social, and political modules of the model. They should be determined by filtering them out from a preferably large number of indicators. Several methods are available for this: factor analysis or principal components as the simplest approach, the PLS-method of Herman Wold, the LISREL-method of Jöreskog or the DYMIMIC-approach of Dennis Aigner and others. It seems to me that Professor Onishi identifies a latent variable with a specific indicator. In this case I have some reservations as to the interpretation of the variables.

5. It is sometimes not clear whether the many equations in the FUGI model are supply or demand equations or reduced forms. This should be clearly stated.

6. Almost all variables are endogenized. But there are political and economic control variables that are subject to political decisions and that influence the economic, social, and political development. As Professor Onishi points out in his introduction, the model is constructed to help to coordinate these decisions. For instance in Germany the prime rate is a decision variable of the Bundesbank, while the tax and expenditure rates are decision variables of the government. If the government changes, the tax policy will change. Thus I suggest introducing these control variables explicitly into the country models.

7. There are many advantages in dealing with all economies in more or less the same way. But there are also some drawbacks, for instance, some equations imply that the central bank finances the government debts. This is explicitly forbidden by law in Germany and in other countries. It is a German condition for establishing a common European currency that this regulation must be introduced in all European countries. Similarly, the discount rate is used by the Bundesbank as an instrument for keeping the demand of money in circulation within a predetermined corridor. There are larger differences between the countries than the model suggests.

8. The FUGI model as it stands now includes the environment, the development of population, food and energy production, peace and security, and human rights, but it leaves out a very important part of human culture, namely the "general philosophy," that is, the "Weltanschauung" and thus the general drive and general direction of thinking and acting that determine people's preference ordering and therefore their way of acting. One side of this is "entrepreneurship", i.e., the willingness to take risks and to organize an economic activity. The degree of entrepreneurship (or in other words: the de-

gree of economic activity) may be filtered out from a set of observable indicators such as the attitude towards work (there is a public poll in Germany which asks questions in this respect), the number of newly founded business firms, the daily working time, and so on. Similarly, an index of political preferences (more left wing or more right wing), and an index of social instability could be established. These variables surely touch the economic sphere. I have tried this approach (Krelle 1988). This yields an interdependent system: the economic side influences the way of thinking and this in turn influences the economic performance of a society. In the FUGI model all "soft" additions to the hard core of the economic model are heavily influenced by the economic side, but there is almost no reverse influence, for example, a national disaster does not reduce production, and SO_x or NO_x or other pollutants do not have an influence on population or production.

9. I have other remarks concerning several details of the model but shall delegate them to an appendix.

The FUGI model solution for different scenarios

Professor Onishi starts with a baseline scenario which supposes "business as usual." "As usual" means: as in the reference period which stops at 1989 or 1990 at best. But there has now been a change of regime: the former planned economies are in the process of being transformed to market economies. This will start a long transitional period where the whole economic and political structure will be different. We do not have observations on that, so we cannot use the usual econometric methods. Moreover, these economies are in a state of disequilibrium and our theory is not well developed in this field. I wonder how Professor Onishi takes care of this feature of the world economy.

The second scenario is based on the assumption of a 100 per cent CO_2 emission tax. It is assumed that the oil price will increase from \$17.9 per barrel in 1990 to \$40 in the year 2000. But in the model the oil price (PEO) is an endogenous variable. It is also not clear what the government will do with the additional tax income. It may repay debts or increase expenditure, and this will have quite different effects on the economy.

The next three scenarios A, B, and C comprise different methods of reducing CO_2 emission (taxes, reduction of the growth rate, more research and development expenditure, more technology transfer to developing countries, and more development aid). The paper does not say which nations should reduce their growth rates and to what extent. This raises the question of balancing equity versus efficiency in international CO_2 agreements (see Welsch 1991a,b). The international income distribution is largely influenced by this. Moreover the reduction of the growth rate may be effected by very different means, e.g., by reducing the working time or the efficiency or capital intensity of production, and so on. Some of these measures will induce unemployment. It is not clear which assumptions are actually made in scenario A.

In scenarios B and C the R&D expenditure is assumed to expand. But one may doubt whether this really will reduce the CO_2 emission substantially in the period 1990 to 2005, as Professor Onishi suggests. Scientific progress and innovation cannot be accelerated indefinitely by injecting more money. Scientific and technical progress is a search process which takes time and is always connected with uncertainty. In the FUGI model R&D expenditure stands proxy for technical progress. Thus the whole growth process will be accelerated by R&D expenditure, which is aimed at reducing the CO_2 emission. One may doubt whether this is a realistic scenario.

The simulation results of the FUGI model under these scenarios are given in tables 1 to 3. The 100 per cent CO_2 emission tax lowers the growth rate on average from 1990 to 2000 by more than 1 per cent. The USA, the EC, and the planned market economies are hit most whereas Japan is hardly affected at all. In the first years after the introduction of the emission tax, the negative effects are much more accentuated: in the developed market economies (with the exception of Japan) the decline is around 6 per cent. This would be a catastrophe for the world economy. One may doubt whether this really will take place. This effect is much larger than the impact of the oil price explosions in 1973 and 1978. Higher oil prices induce investment in energy-saving devices, and the government that gets the additional tax income will also spend it mostly on home produced goods and services. Thus the consequences of this scenario may be too pessimistic.

Scenario A (a 10 per cent CO_2 emission tax and a reduction of the growth rate so that the CO_2 emission is stabilized) yields even worse results: the average growth rate in the world (from 1991 to 2000) will fall by 2.6 per cent, and even Japan will not be spared. This shows that the reduction of growth rates to achieve a stabilization of the CO_2 emission cannot be the right method.

Scenario B stands out in its results: by increasing R&D expenditure and directing it to research on energy problems, the growth rate will increase in all countries. This of course is the best scenario, but is it realistic? By today's technological standards there exist substantial potentials in energy saving (by insulating building, in hot water production, in electrical appliances, in cars and aeroplanes). In Germany these savings are estimated to lie above 50 per cent of what is needed now (see Jochem 1991, p. 121). In the short period up to the year 2000 a reduction of CO_2 emission must largely be accomplished by existing knowledge. Research and development are long-term investments.

The results of scenario C lie somewhere in the middle between those of scenario A and B.

One may also wonder whether average growth rates give the right impression of the effects of energy-saving measures. Take for example a 100 per cent tax on CO_2 emissions in conjunction with a simple growth model with a production function depending on labour, the state of technology, capital, land, and an exhaustible energy resource called "crude oil." The equilibrium growth rate depends on the savings ratio, on the rate of technical progress and on the growth rate of labour input. Note that the savings ratio can now affect the growth rate, whereas in the normal neoclassical growth models without exhaustible resources the savings ratio has no influence on the growth rate. The price of the exhaustible resource (oil) rises by a rate which is equal to the interest rate (by the hotelling rule). The interest rate depends on the same parameters as the growth rate and is constant over time. The level of production is a function of the savings ratio, the growth rate, and the amount of input of the exhaustible resource. This input is smaller now because of the higher price. Thus the long-term (equilibrium) effect of the CO_2 emission tax is a decline of the equilibrium growth path, but the growth rate stays constant. If the FUGI model is stable in the sense that its growth path asymptotically settles down to the equilibrium growth path, then the deviations from the baseline solution with respect to the growth rate should go to zero. There seems to be such a tendency in the FUGI model. But it would be interesting to see whether this happens eventually. The short-term decline of growth rates which Professor Onishi obtains should then be interpreted as the transition path to the lower equilibrium growth path.

It is interesting to compare Professor Onishi's results with those of other world models, see Hoeller et al. (1991). The most quoted paper is that of Manne and Richels (1990); but others are also of considerable interest: Edmonds and Reilly (1983), Mintzer (1987), Nordhaus (1990), IEA (1990), Whalley and Wigle (1990), Edmonds and Barns (1990). All these models forecast a much smaller change in the growth rate of GDP as a consequence of CO_2 emission reduction (mostly between 0 and –0.2 per cent). Thus Professor Onishi's FUGI model is much more pessimistic with respect to the economic effects of CO_2 reduction than other world models, with the exception of scenario B, which is not considered in the other models.

In a second part of his paper Professor Onishi deals with the economic consequences of arms reduction. He assumes constancy of military expenditure until the year 2000. The amount of money saved in this way goes into research and development and into development aid. His results (table 3) are plausible: there is a short-term negative effect on the growth rates in the OECD-countries (with the exception of Japan) and a long-term positive effect.

In the last part of his paper Professor Onishi points out another use for the FUGI model, namely as an early warning device for forecasting the refugee streams on a world level. Professor Onishi distinguishes between four types of "displaced persons" according to the reason for their emigration (destruction of environment, failure of development, absence of peace and security, violation of human rights). I wonder whether one can really assign every refugee uniquely to one of these categories. Violation of human rights is usually due to the absence of peace and security, which in turn will be caused by a failure in development or destruction of the environment. The verbal presentation of this model gets further than the mathematical formulation. Thus I think this is more a sketch of future research. Basically it seems to me a promising approach, though I doubt whether this system can give more information to diplomats and government officers than they already have by studying newspapers or public polls. Many of the selected indicators apply for the majority of the poorest countries in the world as well as for some "problem regions" in semi-developed or industrialized countries. But whether a substantial outflow of people from these regions will take place (as for example the flight of young Albanians over the Adriatic Sea to Italy or of East Germans via Hungary and Austria to West Germany in the last days of the GDR) is almost unpredictable. There is a process of psychological infection and mass hysteria where a relatively small incident can have a snowball effect. One could perhaps estimate the change of probabilities for events like mass flights of people or (as

I would prefer) degrees of internal tension and economic distress, which may result in social and political unrest or civil war or mass flights of people from these regions. But to forecast these events seems to me nearly impossible.

Concluding remarks

Professor Onishi's FUGI model is one of the most ambitious world models. It stands out in that it also considers the ecological and political sides of social life. It gives reasonable results but, due to its size and complexity, is difficult to handle. It needs Professor Onishi to do it. My remarks are meant to encourage him to continue his work and perhaps to improve his model along the lines that I have suggested.

Appendix

Comments on some equations of the FUGI model

1. The main arguments are labour, capital, and the summed up R&D expenditure (which is taken to stand proxy for the state of technology). One would think that in a model which contains a rather extensive energy module, the input of energy would be considered as an additional argument in the production function. But instead of the amounts of energy used in production, the crude oil *price* appears in the particular equation. This is difficult to explain.

2. The R&D expenditure does not explain the state of technology. It is possible to import knowledge. Japan did so in the first 20 years after the war as well as Germany and they lived quite well by saving R&D expenditure and using imported knowledge. The high R&D expenditures of the planned economies did not give them a comparative advantage.

3. In many equations a flow variable on the left-hand side of the equation has been explained at least partly by a rate, e.g. the exchange rate or the interest rate. In the case of linear equations this seems to be misleading since the partial derivative with respect to this rate is a constant independent of the size of the other arguments in the function, and that means independent of the absolute size of the explained variable on the left-hand side of the equation. Thus an equal change, for example, of the interest rate would yield an absolutely equal change in private consumption independent of whether private consumption was large or small before the change.

4. The investment function seems to be somewhat heuristic. The prime rate appears with a 1-period lag as explaining variable whereas the lagged investment appears with 5 and 6 as well as 9 and 10 periods of delay. The supply of crude oil appears also as an explaining variable but not the wage rate. The price of crude oil has a negative influence on investment. This may be true for energy importing countries but is not true for energy exporting countries. The boom in the Arab countries stemmed from the price rise of crude oil. I would prefer an investment function which has some theoretical underpinning. Expectations of the future are perhaps more important than specific values in the past.

5. In most medium- and long-term models the rate of technical progress plays a crucial role. In the FUGI model the summed up R&D expenditure takes the place of the state of technology so that the rate of technical progress is almost identified with R&D expenditure. But there is a difference between input and output in the production of knowledge, and there is a difference between inventions (which may be stimulated by R&D expenditures) and innovations that do not necessarily follow from inventions. In Great Britain the university system is generally recognized to be a very good one. Judging from the number of Nobel prize winners many inventions are made in that country. Nevertheless, its economic performance is not the best.

6. Technical progress is closely related to the change of labour productivity. But in the FUGI model labour productivity is only explained by a definitional equation.

7. The wholesale price index in the FUGI model is explained by import prices, the wage rate, and money supply. This seems to be a reduced form. From the supply side not only import prices and wage rates determine the price but also the interest and tax rates. From the demand side the price index is determined not only by the money supply but also by the velocity of money and (inversely) by the real GDP. This equation seems to be incomplete.

8. It has already been stated in the text that behaviour equations for the central bank do not conform to the actual behaviour of the Bundesbank.

9. The exchange rate seems to be constructed in order to explain the medium- and long-term trend of this rate. To explain the short-term behaviour of the exchange rate one needs far more monetary variables and expectations of the future development of the explaining variables, e.g. the disparity between the growth rates of money supply in the different countries, the debtor or creditor position of the country, the rate of change of the rates of interest and expected rates of change of the foreign exchange rate itself should be taken into account.

I cannot see from the exchange rate equation whether the non-arbitrage conditions are satisfied. This should be checked.

10. In the equations for the ecosystem a lot of not directly measurable variables appear. I cannot see how they can be measured or estimated. There is no repercussion of "natural disaster" on population and production. I do not see how "starvation" (STARVATE) is explained. It is listed as an endogenous variable. It appears as an explaining variable in other equations.

11. The population model seems to be tailored to a society in transition from underdevelopment to a developed, industrialized society. In a fully developed market-type society the birth rate seems to follow its own laws, which are only remotely related to economic variables such as GDP per capita. For really underdeveloped countries the Malthusian theory (population expands until the minimum subsistence level is reached) still seems to be valid.

12. In the equations for oil, coal, and gas demand the real prices of the substitutive energies should also enter the demand function. I am surprised that the supply of alternative energies should have a sensible influence on the demand for the traditional energy carriers.

13. The peace and security variables as well as the variables for human rights are ultimately explained by economic variables, but they have no influence on the economic sphere so far as I can see. Almost all these variables are not directly measurable. It would be interesting to know how they are estimated.

References

Edmonds, J.A., and D.W. Barns. 1990. Estimating the Marginal Cost of Reducing Fossil Fuel CO_2 Emission. Mimeo, August.

Edmonds, J.A., and J.M. Reilly. 1983. "Global Energy and CO_2 to the Year 2000." *The Energy Journal* 4: 21–47.

Hoeller, P., A. Dean, and J. Nicolaisen. 1991. "Macroeconomic Implications of Reducing Greenhouse Gas Emissions: A Survey of Empirical Studies." *OECD Economic Studies* 16: 45–78, Spring.

IEA. 1990. Follow-up to Noordwijk Ministerial Conference on Atmospheric Pollution and Climate Change. IEA/SLT (90)2.

Jochem, E. 1991. "Reducing CO_2 Emissions – the West German Plan." In: Jim Skea, ed. *Energy Policy, Special Issue*. 19(2): 119–126, March.

Krelle, W. 1988. Latent Variables in Econometric Models. Discussion Paper B-104, SFB 303, Bonn, October.

Manne, A.S., and R.G. Richels. 1991. "Global CO_2 Emission – the Impact of Rising Energy Costs." *The Energy Journal* 12(1): 87–107.

Mintzer, I.M. 1987. A Matter of Degrees: The Potential for Controlling the Greenhouse Effect. World Resources Institute Research Report 5. Washington, D.C.

Nordhaus, W.D. 1990. A Survey of Estimates of the Cost of Reduction of Greenhouse Gas Emissions. Mimeo.

Welsch, H. 1991a. "Equity and Efficiency in International CO_2 Agreements." Institute of Energy Economics, University of Cologne. In: E. Hope, O. Noreng, S. Strom, eds. *European Energy Markets and Environmental Perspectives*. Oslo and London.

—— 1991b. Inequality Aspects of Alternative CO_2 Agreement Designs. Institute of Energy Economics, University of Cologne, August.

Whalley, J., and R. Wigle. 1990. The International Incidence of Carbon Taxes. Paper prepared for a Conference on Economic Policy Responses to Global Warming. Turin, September.

3. Fu-chen Lo

Over the last 15 years, the FUGI model has undergone an almost unbounded expansion of its scale. From 15 regional models in 1977, it covers some 180 countries and areas with a total member of over 100,000 equations in the current sixth generation model. The current FUGI model has also been expanded to incorporate various subsystems such as environmental conditions, human rights, peace and security, even early warning of displaced persons. To maintain such a huge data system alone would not be an easy task. Despite its scale and complexity, every time I have an opportunity to compare the baseline projections of the FUGI model with the results of other major world models, I have always been impressed by its reasonably well-behaved estimates. Professor Onishi claims that a highly sophisticated artificial intelligence (AI) capability has been embodied in his software system. To my own limitation, it may require others to review Professor Onishi's new innovation.

I would rather concentrate my comments on his simulations of the worldwide impacts of CO_2 cut-backs and arms reduction in the coming decade.

Arms reduction

Military expenditures absorbed, over the last two decades, about 5 per cent of the world GDP annually. The United States and the USSR accounted together for nearly one-half of the world's total military expenditure. The overall share of world military expenditure of industrial countries averaged 53 per cent of the world, and overall share of the Eastern European countries was 25 per cent in the last decade; the ratio of military expenditures to GDP averaged 9.2 per cent in this region. On average, developing countries spend 6 per cent of their combined GDP on the military.

The South's combined GDP is only 15 per cent that of the North's. Yet it buys 75 per cent of the arms traded every year. Over the last decade, the third world military spendings were rising annually at 7.5 per cent – three times faster than in the industrial countries over the last three decades. If it were frozen at its current level, as it was assumed in Professor Onishi's scenario, the annual savings of the South could be as much as $150 billion by the year 2000.

Table 1 **World military expenditure and GDP, 1972–1988**

	World military expenditure 1972–1988 (%)	Military expenditure as percentage of GDP 1972–1988
Industrial countries	52.7	3.8
Eastern Europe	25.4	9.2
Developing countries	22.0	5.9
Asia	8.1	6.3
Middle East	8.0	11.6
North Africa	1.8	9.6
Sub-Saharan Africa	1.5	3.7
Latin America and Caribbean	2.5	2.3
World (total)	100.0	4.9

Source: D.P. Hewitt (IMF 1991).

Professor Onishi assumed that except for the United States, the developed market economies would be able to increase their ODA contribution to the developing world by using a half of the resources freed from cut-backs of military expenditures. Table 3 in his paper shows an additional 0.65 per cent of the global economic growth can be expected from his arms reduction scenario. Trade will be expanded by a additional $532 billion by the year 2000.

Since G7 countries, particularly the United States, are major suppliers to the arms trade, we can expect a negative impact on their GDP growth rates in the initial period (1991–1995), the same as China (a third or fourth arms trader). But the USSR, which has been the world number one arms trader, shows a net increase of GDP (0.642 per cent in 1991). Is this an indication that we can expect a much faster structural transformation in USSR in comparison with other major arms producers? Military expenditures of both the USSR and the United States in the past two decades were 6.9 and 6.1 per cent of GDP, or a share of 26 per cent of the central government expenditures respectively (IMF Working Paper 1991).

According to The Human Development Report 1991 (UNDP, p. 81), it looks as though military spending could be reduced by 2–4 per cent a year during the 1990s, for the industrial countries, if the present understandings between the super powers come to fruition. This would translate into savings of $200–300 billion a year by the year 2000, and savings during the decade of as much as $2 trillion. In the third world, if military spending were frozen at its current level (as assumed by Professor Onishi), then another annual saving could be as much as $150 billion by the year 2000.

Global CO_2 cut-backs

In recent years, extensive studies on the greenhouse effect show that the accumulation of carbon dioxide (CO_2) and other greenhouse gases are expected to produce global warming and other significant climatic changes over the next century. In order to conduct a serious economic analysis, we are facing three major problems.

First, we are faced with very long-term effects, in the order of 250 years (Cline 1991). For instance, "the most aggressive action now being seriously considered – a freezing of global emissions at current level (Professor Onishi's scenario) would reduce very long-term global warming from a central estimate of 5° to 10°C by the year 2275." Taking into account the magnitude of potential technological change and the impact of the discount rate over such a distant horizon, it becomes meaningless to plan.

The second issue is the estimated cost of abatement. We can expect that the abatement-cost function could be a very stiff function. Based on US estimates, Nordhaus (Nordhaus 1991) argued that the long-run marginal cost of reducing GHG emissions is estimated to be $40 per ton for a 25 per cent reduction and $120 per ton for a 50 per cent reduction. The total global costs of these reductions are about $2 billion per year for a 10 per cent reduction, $31 billion for a 25 per cent reduction, and $191 billion (1 per cent of world GDP) per year for a 50 per cent reduction.

Thirdly, the greenhouse damage function (total benefit of GHG emission reduction) is even more difficult to estimate with certain scientific knowledge (such as the impact of changing crop yields, land lost to oceans, and so on) but in the long run, we must face the risk of unexpected side effects that could cause more damage than the value of having avoided carbon build-up.

Professor Onishi simply added a "carbon tax" to the consumption of fossil fuels in order to cut the CO_2 emissions. Under this assumption, he has applied a proportional roll-back policy regardless of per capita discharge of emission differences between the developed and developing countries. Considering the global environment as a limited public good to every world citizen, a progressive tax regime could be considered in order to differentiate the tax rates between the developed and developing economies. In anticipating a higher population growth and economic development of the third-world countries in the coming few decades, it is unlikely that they can afford high-cost energy for some time. It also implies that the third-world

Table 2 **Projection of energy consumption and carbon emission rates, 1989–2010**

	Share of energy consumption 1989	CO_2 emission (million tons) 1989	Growth rate 1989–2010	Accumulated percentage by 2010
Developed market economies	49.9	2,996	2.7	170
Planned economies	31.5	2,160	2.8	180
Developing market economies	18.5	1,166	3.5	210
World	100.0	6,322	2.9	180

Source: EPA Year 2010 Committee Report (1991).

countries will apply a higher discount rate for the possible future benefits from a global CO_2 abatement. As Cline argued, for each decade that passes without action, global mean temperatures are expected to rise by 0.3°C, so there is no time to postpone this issue without action. Since greenhouse gas is basically a stock accumulated since the industrial revolution, the question of who discharged first, who comes later, can be used to argue against a proportional rollback policy, or even a "tradable permits policy."

References

Hewitt, Daniel P. 1991. Military Expenditure: International Comparison of Trades. IMF Working Paper, May.

Roger, S., and S. Sen. 1990. *Military Expenditure: The Political Economy of National Security.* Oxford: Oxford University Press.

Cline, W.R. 1991. "Scientific Basis for the Greenhouse Effect." *The Economic Journal* 101, July.

Nordhaus, W.D. 1991. "To Slow or Not to Slow: The Economics of the Greenhouse Effect." *The Economic Journal* 101, July.

UNDP. 1991. *Human Development Report 1991.*

Economic Planning Agency (Japan). 1991. *EPA Year 2010 Committee Report.*

11

Macro-modelling: A panel discussion

1. Paul Armington

I want to expand briefly on what previous panellists have said regarding the strategy and method of global modelling. My remarks are organized around the following diagram. It is a picture of the future building of economic knowledge. It consists of four floors, stairways between them, and a high-speed elevator. There is no entrance or exit, since we all stay inside this building, living on one floor or another. Most of us stay on one floor most of the time; some like to go up and down a lot.

The logic of this building's structure is best explored by starting on the ground floor and working our way upward, until finally we reach the "Starlight Lounge." (I have not included the Penthouse, which is left to the reader's imagination.)

On the ground floor, we are dealing mostly with hard facts: technology (how to get from inputs to outputs) *plus* data *equals* input-output models. These were extensively represented in our sessions on the research in progress at Japan's MITI (Ministry of International Trade and Industry) and IDE (Institute of Development Economics) as well as in New York focused on the UN. On the second floor, workers who have invested intellectually in static optimization theory are taking IO information, adding equilibrium theory, and producing CGE (compatible general equilibrium) models. The paper by Professors Piggott and Whalley was an illustration of this genre. Trudging from there up the steps to the third level, we come to a large busy floor of folks who are adding the ingredient of time, thus to produce dynamic equilibrium models. (These models normally involve transitory disequilibrium as well, but equilibrium conditions define the main features of these models.) We spent most of the first day looking at what's cooking at this level. Finally, we must press upward to the Starlight Lounge, where the essential added ingredient is disequilibrium theory and where the researchers are thus turning out dynamic disequilibrium models. Here we have explored models of processes that may exhibit no turning points, at least in our lifetimes (like Dr. Pitcher's model of future greenhouse gas emissions); models of cycles that are predictable but too long for market forces to iron out (like Professor Dubovsky's Kondratiev waves); and models that could be stable or unstable in the long run depending on whether policy makers can take a "hint" from scenarios and do the right thing (as in the case of the FUGI model).

As we ascend from floor to floor, our knowledge *could*, in theory, accumulate without significant loss of information. The mathematics of differential equations and the computational tools available for handling them permit us to envisage a global model of dynamic disequilibrium that combines the main results of work occurring on all floors. The logical specification of such a model would define dynamic equilibrium (or steady state) as a mental construct but would leave open (for empirical testing) the stability properties of the model and hence of the "real world" (which itself can be conceived as a model of the universe of all possible worlds).

But practical research is constrained by limited resources: limits on data, money, hardware and software capacities, and on human ingenuity and perseverance. Given these constraints, we face trade-offs that force each of us to choose which floor we want to work on most of the time. This, in turn, leads to less communication and integration of global economic research than would be desirable and feasible under less severe resource constraints.

So, unless the movers and shakers of budgets bring forth the equivalent of a new Manhattan Project (which would not be an inappropriate response to Professor Leontief's finding that we humans are like mastodons faced with the problem of preventing our own extinction), researchers need to focus on flattening the trade-offs between research strategies. We need to make the staircases in our building less steep, and we need to learn how to use the elevator even more.

Several means for moving in this direction come to mind:

- Hold more meetings like this one, taking stock of models and methods.
- Bring together the inhabitants of different floors to focus on particular policy issues, to demonstrate the comparative advantages of different approaches.
- Develop "democratic" software systems to facilitate comparison of alternative frameworks. PC-based software for handling all manner of models, combined with improved long-distance electronic communications, opens up new opportunities for improved inter-system communications at low cost among researchers all over the world.
- Encourage modular development of systems, with interchangeable components (such as country IO modules or global modules focused on determining international prices of commodities or financial assets).
- Extend the common language of modelling by clarifying variable definitions, standardizing their names, and providing standard concordances among sets of variables, e.g., concordances between country IO dimensions and the SITC.
- Enlarge and focus the global effort to collect better, more pertinent data, starting at the ground floor of our building and also taking into account the requirements imposed by theory used on all the upper floors. I agree with Professor Leontief that inadequate data is the main bottleneck now to our progress – not theory or computing power or labour time.

To galvanize action by governments, our profession needs a clearer vision of how better data will be used to address real problems. To achieve credibility, this vision needs to comprehend all four floors of the building. So the profession needs credible spokesmen for the whole building. And, in terms of the resource envelope for this work, we need to start thinking in much larger terms than previously contemplated. Any programme to "save the mastodons from extinction" has to be large to be credible. But the quality of the programme has to match its size. To achieve this quality, we must combine, in roughly equal proportions: (a) sound theory grounded in mathematics, (b) scientific rules of evidence for estimation and validation, (c) artificial intelligence, and (d) humanistic understanding.

The United Nations University could help to lead this huge effort, through its own future building that is now in progress.

2. Clopper Almon

All researchers in international trade and development face a common problem: the high cost and restricted access to data that is collected by international organizations. I would like to make a concrete proposal for something the United Nations University could do at little or no cost which might be able to reduce drastically this "barrier to entry" into research on these topics.

Let me preface this suggestion with a brief account of what the Inforum group at the University of Maryland has been doing in data dissemination. For the United States, we have put most of the large, national databases into a standard, highly efficient format, namely, into data banks for our Public Domain G (PDG) regression, data handling, and graphics programme. In this format, most series can be represented with two bytes per data point. By comparison, the tapes or diskettes we use as sources typically require about 10 bytes per data point; a Lotus worksheet requires eight bytes per point. There are also programmes for updating large, historical banks from small banks of recent or revised data. In this efficient format, we put the data on Internet, where it is accessible at fairly high speed from around the world. (To access it, use Internet to attach to info.umd.edu, then login with "info." You then get a menu. You want to "View" the "EconData" directory.) Bodies of data already available in this way include the national income and product accounts, the flow of funds accounts, indices of industrial production, employment, hours, and earnings, employment by states and areas, state personal income accounts, foreign direct investment, producer price indices, consumer price indices, etc.

When we turn from data produced by the US government to that organized by international agencies, we encounter an ugly fact: these agencies regard data that they organize as their property. Despite requests, no international agency has given us permission to share any data obtained through it with any other academic user. It is my hope that UNU might be helpful in dealing with this situation.

There is already an organization dealing with the sharing of data among researchers, namely, the Interuniversity Consortium for Political and Social Research (ICPSR), whose offices are at the University of Michigan. Some 300 universities from around the world are members of the ICPSR, and the number is steadily growing. On request, ICPSR disseminates data on tape to member universities. At marginal cost, it will also – unless prohibited by the data provider – supply data to others. In order of diminishing success, it has tried to obtain data from the World Bank, the International Monetary Fund (IMF), the Organisation for Economic Cooperation and Development (OECD), and the United Nations.

The World Bank is the most cooperative. It sells to ICPSR tapes for its World Tables and World Debt Tables and allows them to be distributed to members but not to non-members. The Bank is also now concluding a CD-ROM with the printed version of these publications. We have put these data into G banks for easy use on personal computers. I have asked the bank for permission to put them on Internet, either in an open format or in an encrypted form where the Bank or the ICPSR would control the password. This request has been neither granted nor denied.

The IMF comes second in cooperation. It produces four major bodies of publicly available data: the International Financial Statistics, the Director of Trade Statistics, the Government Financial Statistics, and the Balance of Payments Statistics. The last three it makes available to ICPSR – for members only. Even this level of cooperation seems to be controversial within the IMF, and we are advised not to rock the boat. We have put the data into G banks, but can share them only with others who already possess tapes. The most used of the four publications, the International Financial Statistics, is no longer available through the ICPSR because the IMF is now selling these data on CD-ROM. A one-time purchase costs $150; a quarterly subscription by a department costs $300 a year; a monthly subscription by a library, $1,000 per year. While these prices are eminently reasonable in themselves, they are a lot more expensive than the free tapes used to be from the ICPSR. While the CD-ROM makes it possible to extract a few series conveniently enough, it is very slow and cumbersome for the large-scale extraction necessary to put all the data in another format that can be used for graphs, regression, or other manipulation.

Thus far, the OECD has been willing to talk with ICPSR, but has not come to any agreement. In my view, the OECD has gathered data at taxpayers' expense and should be looking for inexpensive ways to make it available to researchers. No such objective, however, seems to be directing OECD officials to whom either the ICPSR or myself have talked. Perhaps changes are on the way; but at the moment ICPSR has OECD data, and we have none that we can share, although we have a substantial amount.

However, the least cooperative organization of all is the United Nations. They have refused to talk to ICPSR. I have considered getting the tape of national accounts data, but was dissuaded by their staff. The UN maintains a great bank of bilateral data, but nothing obtained from it by one researcher may be shared with a researcher at another institution.

Altogether, these restrictions amount to a massive barrier to many potential researchers on entry into international economics, a barrier erected by the very organizations one would suppose should be trying to further such research.

All of these organizations, however, allow researchers at the same university to share the data acquired by that university. And that is where my recommendation comes in. I would like to suggest that UNU consider appointing Research Fellows in International Economics. They would be entitled, of course, to use data which had been acquired by UNU. The UNU could then attack first the problem of obtaining for itself the extensive United Nations data. Then it should set about acquiring the OECD, IMF, and World Bank data. The costs of these data might well be minimal, since an exchange for UN data might be arranged. Also, Fellows who wanted data not owned by UNU might have to provide UNU with the funds to purchase it. But the data could then be shared with all other UNU Fellows. Presumably, UNU would need to provide some sort of librarian services for these data banks. I would be happy to volunteer my own services and experience in organizing such data. If necessary, to cover the cost of operating the data bank, Fellows might be asked to pay a small annual fee. It could hardly be significant in comparison to the thousands of dollars that it now costs an institution to acquire the basic data for empirical research in international trade and development.

3. Syed Nawab Haider Naqvi

Some thoughts about macro modelling in the LCDs

I wish to start my comments by noting the somewhat obvious but very fundamental principle of modelling, including macroeconometric modelling: As we model "reality," without describing it in very great detail, we should not put such a structure on "reality" as might cause it too much violence. Instead, our structure should help us understand reality better by thinking about it systematically. Not only that: our models should also help us analyse alternative visions of this reality and select the one which approximates the "best" or the second best, if the relevant constraints on achieving the best must also be reckoned with. And we should not forget that at the centre of our efforts to understand reality is our desire to change it for the better. The focus of this change should be to improve the well-being of the people. This is what the pioneers in the field of macroeconometric model building – especially Tinbergen and Klein – have done; and this is exactly what we must do.

I can easily show that disregarding such a focus has led to the construction of models that are not very useful. But I will put the matter more positively in terms of an agenda for modelling in the context of the theme of the conference.

The questions that I put are: what does reality look like, especially in the LDCs; what economic structure would do this reality "too much" violence; and what would be an appropriate agenda for simulating reality? I should think that, stripped of all the secondary issues, the most pressing aspect of the reality that we must understand – and change – in the LDCs is the persistence of poverty, even though things are getting better there, except perhaps in Africa, where things are getting worse. A part of this poverty can be explained in terms of the lack of physical resources, especially capital and skilled labour, and insufficient technical progress. Also responsible for poverty are the inappropriate domestic policies that pay too little attention to the rate of economic growth of per capita income, to an unfair distribution of income and wealth, to the rate of unemployment, and macroeconomic imbalances, energy shortages, and the degradation of the environment. Then, there is an inhospitable world environment that penalizes the LDCs' exports, does not transfer enough resources to them, and is relatively insensitive to the mounting debt problem. These are just a few causes of the winter of our discontent; but these are of fundamental importance.

Hence, each of these aspects of the reality in the LDCs should be modelled. I wish to comment on only a few of them.

(i) Models that we do not need

It should be clear that we do not need the models that do too much violence to the reality in the LDCs and thus do not provide clues to the alternative ways of changing it for the better. Of course, we do not need a theory involving a high degree of abstraction from the real world; but such abstraction can be carried on only so far as we can still "see" some strategic aspects of the reality. The love for a beautiful theory cannot be sustained if it involves a disdain of "fact."

In this category of models with a disdain of facts fall those that assume that reality *in fact* looks like the textbook neoclassical version of it – where all markets clear so that there is no unemployment, and where all factors are paid according to their marginal products, satisfying the Euler equation, so that no exploitation of any kind exists. In such an efficiency-oriented world, governed exclusively by the rules of Pareto-optimality, no significant distributional issues can ever arise. Such a world is familiar to us as economists; but to insist that the real world actually behaves according to the neoclassical prescription would be an incredible statement for most economists – of course – with the exception of the rational-expectationists.

(ii) Models that we do need

(a) To begin our discussion, let me emphasize that notwithstanding the nihilism of Lucia and others, we do need macroeconometric models of the type built by Klein and his associates in order to conduct a systematic and structured discussion of the complex set of forces that is responsible for sustaining poverty, and of the ways and means to alleviate it. It should also be clear that such models should be large enough to comprehend the reality on the ground, and to provide enough elbow room for the interaction among the variables in response to specific poverty-alleviating policies. For instance, any fruitful poverty-alleviation programme must feature a reasonably high rate of economic growth while keeping the rate of inflation, budgetary deficits, and the imbalance in international payments within socially and economically acceptable limits; and it must also take into account the problems of indebtedness and energy shortages. But to keep such complexities in view we need a model of at least 100 equations or so encompassing the production-expenditure relationships, the inter-industry structure of inputs, the monetary-fiscal policy interactions, the labour market reactions, and the foreign-trade linkages. Of course, one can build very large models; but my own experience suggests that one can deal comfortably with most of the key issues facing a typical developing country even with a moderate-sized model. To get cross-country information on a comparable basis, these (national) models can be linked with Project LINK.

(b) Our macroeconomic models should also have a "human face." Specifically, this means that we need to feature distributional considerations in them; and that they must focus on the fact of large unemployment in the LDCs. Let me take up the unemployment issue first. The current insensivity to this issue can be illustrated by reference to the fact that macroeconometric models in the developed countries do not highlight the need to reduce unemployment. For instance, even though it estimates unemployment (endogenously), Project LINK does not generate scenarios corresponding to alternative unemployment-reducing policy shocks. Considering the big social and ethical issues that large unemployment rates raise in both the developed and the developing countries, this lack of concern for reducing unemployment can be explained only in terms of a metaphysical belief in the truth of theories that deny the existence of (involuntary) unemployment or consider it necessary for capital formation and productive efficiency.

As for the national models, the distributional issues in general, and the unemployment problem in particular, can be tackled in the context of an appropriately specified labour-market sub-model, which is then embedded in a bigger macroeconometric model. In this context, the distribution of income should be seen as a function, among other things, of demographic variables like the labour participation rates. We can get a hold on unemployment, disguised or open, not by estimating it directly, but by determining the values of variables like population, participation rates, labour migration, and labour demand (employment) sector. This will give us all the information that we need about the labour market. But apart from the problem of how to do it, the important point I wish to re-emphasize is that the unemployment problem and distributional issues are too important to be ignored by an adequate macroeconometric model, and the model that does not reckon with it is not very helpful in conceptualizing the reality in the LDCs.

(c) An important constraint in the feasible growth rate of the non-oil producing developing countries is the shortage of energy; and the big rise in the price of oil imports remains the single most important element of this constraint. Furthermore, the need for generating domestic resources also makes governments tax oil and oil products, which raises the *domestic* price of oil, and which has a definite inflationary impact on the economy. But estimating the inflationary potential of an increase in the price of oil requires a detailed knowledge of the inter-industry structure of input relations, such that a typical input/output table summarizes. Thus, to estimate the full impact of a given increase in the domestic prices of oil, it is essential to link an input/output structure to a fairly detailed macroeconometric model. Such a linkage will also bring the "supply side" considerations into the macroeconometric model, which are essentially demand-oriented – a point that Klein has amply emphasized (Klein 1978).[1]

(d) Another consequence of recognizing the reality properly is the inclusion of equations in the macro models regarding the indebtedness problem of the developing countries, which assumed explosive proportions with the ending of a long period of abundant capital flows in 1982. Since then capital flows from the developed to developing countries have become negative. On top of it, OECD protectionism has cost the developing countries an average of $55 billion per annum. An important step in understanding this phenomenon – and to do something constructive about it – would be for Project LINK to lead the way by generating scenarios corresponding to alternative trade regimes – less protectionist regimes as opposed to more protectionist regimes. In particular, the effects of rising OECD protectionism on the developing countries' exports should be analysed.

(e) I may also comment on how the environmental issues should be properly addressed in a typical macroeconometric model of the LDCs. Klein has suggested that to make allowance for environment pollution we redefine the GNP as NEW (Net Economic Welfare), which prescribes that investment in capital allows for the purchase of anti-pollution devices, together with the GNP-creating capital goods (Klein 1983, pp. 36–38).[2] Solving an equation system that features the NEW will produce a "clean" though *lower* GNP as compared to the "dirty" though higher GNP. I may submit, however, that in the developing countries we cannot afford a lower growth rate of the GNP, be it dirty or clean. The way out, I believe, is to view environmental improvement as leading to an increase in *human* capital as opposed to just physical capital; and as one that leads to an improvement in the *quality* of labour as compared to just an increase in the *quantity*. Solving a model that redefines the uses of capital and labour in this way may well lead to the NEW being actually *higher* than "dirty" GNP.

4. Kirit S. Parikh

Any modelling effort should be directed towards addressing some well-defined issues. I therefore begin by emphasizing issues that I consider to be important in the context of the global changes in the economic, environmental, and political spheres that we see taking place. I would then pose the question: What can modelling do to help usher in a better resolution of the problems created by global change?

The issues that I consider to be most important for the developing countries are: How do the LDCs find their place in the sun? Have the rich left any sunshine at all for others? Are the rich nations of the world willing to provide that place, let alone lend a helping hand?

The post-revolution Eastern Europe is making its own claim on the global resources for the reconstruction of its economies. The post-colonial developing countries now compete with Eastern Europe for aid in an environment where aid fatigue has already set in in many developed countries. Moreover, the global tendency towards market segmentation reflected in Europe 1992, a free trading block of North America, the ASEAN trade region, etc. is likely to make it difficult for developing countries even to help themselves. If these trading blocks lead to greater trade creation than trade diversion, the LDCs can gain. However, it is not clear what the outcome would be.

But the most serious constraint on the ability of developing countries to grow arises from the concern for the global environment. The global commons have a limited carrying capacity. Much of it has been exhausted and stressed by the industrial world. The limited carrying capabilities of the global commons cannot sustain even the current state of development of the global economy. New institutional arrangements are needed. A new social contract would have to be made among the nations of the world. Today the industrial countries talk about developing countries bearing a fair share of the costs of cleaning up the global environment. This would impose further constraints on the developing countries and slow down their economies. What is in fact required is that the developing countries get a fair share in the right to use the global commons, i.e., in the global environment's carrying capacity. The countries of the industrial world have brought the global commons to the present state through their profligate lifestyles and unsustainable consumption patterns. The amazing thing is that they do not even apologize but instead ask the

LDCs to share in the burden of cleaning up the mess they have created. The perceptions of this problem are so distorted by such talks of fair share that even well-meaning analysts have been brainwashed and say as some have said at the conference that the LDCs should be "bribed" to enter into global environmental agreements rather than say that the LDCs should be "compensated" for the burdens imposed on them.

Unfortunately, the LDCs have very few bargaining chips. They need the industrial world's capital, they need the developed countries' technology and they need and will continue to need the developed countries' markets. The only saving grace, however, is that without the cooperation of the LDCs and a cooperation that is willingly given, we will not be able to save the global commons. What is clearly required is a fair allocation of the carrying capacity of the earth. A fair allocation is one that is based on a per capita basis. However, in order not to provide an incentive for population growth, the allocation should be frozen to a population level of a past year. Such allocations, for example, can be in the form of emission quotas. Countries should be free to trade them. Tradable emission quotas would permit developing countries to set their own environmental priorities. They would then be able to spend their meagre resources on tackling problems of local pollution which affect their poor in rural and urban areas much more severely than global pollution. This would also encourage developing countries to select efficient technologies and processes to reduce their emissions. One should also point out that the desired ambient air quality can be attained and maintained at minimum costs through tradable emission quotas.

One can ask the question: What can the analysts and modellers do here to help? As I have argued above, we need to arrive at new social contracts and create new social institutions. These can emerge only after analysts show what alternative institutions and forms of social contracts mean for all: who gains, who loses, who benefits, who bears the burden, who adjusts, and by how much. A quantitative understanding of these questions is critical for informed dialogue, without which a just and acceptable outcome is impossible.

A second issue of great importance is the question of free trade and access to markets. While the benefits of free trade of commodities and the need for it have been studied and modelled and analysed in many ways in the past, factor mobility has not received as much academic attention. During the 1980s we have seen that capital flows have acquired an importance that is equal to if not more than that of trade. Unfortunately, mobility of labour is not as freely permitted as mobility of capital. Free movement of labour can be of tremendous benefit to mankind. This was shown by an analysis we had carried out with the help of the Basic Linked System of national policy models developed at IIASA, where some 34 applied general equilibrium models, which covered the world, were linked in a general equilibrium framework. Migration of some 300 million people over a period of 15 years (1985–2000) showed dramatic increases in the global GNP. The increase was more than 20 per cent of the GDP and exceeded US$1 trillion at 1970 prices at the end of 15 years. Of course, we recognize that migration on such a scale may cause much cultural stress. Cultural diversity should also be preserved as it may be as valuable as biodiversity. If we want to preserve such cultural diversity and avoid the tremendous social stress caused by migration and population growth, the best remedy that we all know is rapid economic growth in the developing countries. The developed countries that have put a fence around themselves to prevent the migrants from coming in are earning, in a sense, a rent of the fence and it is only just that they share a part of this rent with the poor whom they are keeping out.[3]

Once again the long-term issues of population growth and migration and the resulting tensions can be effectively dealt with through rapid economic growth requiring substantial transfer of resources in the poor countries. If such transfers are to take place in the current climate of aid fatigue, the analysts and the modellers have a role to play in informing the public and creating a climate of charity based on self-interest.

5. Shinichi Ichimura

Modelling and development economics

Modelling of the world economy requires special attention to the developing countries. In this connection, I would like to make a few remarks. First, modelling of developing economies does not suit simple model-building based on the time-series of macroeconomic statistics like the one for developed economies, not only due to the shortage of statistical data or their poor quality but also due to the structural changes that the national economies rapidly pass through.

The simple modelling based on time-series does not have the statistically required stability of the structures of equations and parameters. One needs a more careful device in modelling and the use of international cross-section analysis or CGE types of modelling, which can depict these potential changes in the future.

Secondly, for this purpose, we must try to improve the theoretical and empirical contents of *development economics* much more. Pure theory of general equilibrium or many other types of theoretical contributions in the last two decades or so popular in economic journals are usually not good enough for the analyses of the developing economies in the contemporary world. I would say that development economics is nothing but economics. Adam Smith, David Ricardo, J.S. Mill, Alfred Marshall, J.M. Keynes, and many other modern contributors to economics worked in the field of development economics. We must construct the theoretical bases for analysing the conditions of contemporary developing countries on the basis of careful observations of realistic conditions in many developing economies all over the world. I feel, though, that much effort of economists has been inappropriately devoted to too abstract theorizing with little relevance to real economic issues in developing countries in the world.

Thirdly, there is one serious consideration that we econometricians as professionals have to pay attention to – that is how to make available our own empirical research to other professionals. I have a few regrettable experiences in the use of statistical data and empirical findings that others have produced. Some people never make these available to others, and some take offence if others make use of their data or findings in the published results of estimated equations. This is very strange in comparison with cases of experimental physics. In many countries some businesses are making money by offering statistical data for very high prices. Academic scholars cannot afford to buy them, whereas our own empirical findings are usually offered free to them. We really need to establish a rule in these empirical fields among ourselves and between academic research workers. I am trying to establish a journal that can accept lengthy articles with data, so that academic scholars can have an advantage in empirical as well as theoretical publications. I hope that international organizations like the United Nations University will consider overcoming these difficulties and offer us better opportunities to contribute more in promoting world development.

Notes

1. Klein, Lawrence R., "The Supply Side," *American Economic Review* 68 (1978).
2. Klein, Lawrence R., *The Economics of Supply and Demand* (Basil Blackwell, Oxford, 1985).
3. See Fisher, Fohberg, Keyser, Parikh and Tims, *Hunger: Beyond the Reach of the Invisible Hand*. Research Report, RR-91-15, October (International Institute for Applied Systems Analysis (IIASA), 1991).

Contributors

Clopper Almon, Professor, Department of Economics, INFORUM, University of Maryland at College Park, USA

Paul S. Armington, Director, International Economic Department, The World Bank, USA

Yasuhiro Asami, Head, World Economic Model Group, Economic Planning Agency, Japan

Iwan Jaya Azis, Professor, Faculty of Economics, University of Indonesia

Dave Barns, Senior Research Scientist, Battelle, Pacific Northwest Laboratories, USA

Richard Baron, Visiting Scholar, Battelle, Pacific Northwest Laboratories, USA

Olav Bjerkholt, Assistant Director General and Head of Research Department, Central Bureau of Statistics of Norway

Ralph C. Bryant, Senior Fellow, The Brookings Institution, USA

Faye Duchin, Professor and Director, Institute for Economic Analysis, New York University, USA

J.A. Edmonds, Technical Leader, Economic Programme, Battelle, Pacific Northwest Laboratories, USA

Maurizio Grassini, Professor, Universita degli Studi di Firenze, Dipartimento di studi sullo stato, Italy

Bert G. Hickman, Professor, Department of Economics, Stanford University, USA

Shinichi Ichimura, Vice President, the Institute of International Relations, Osaka International University, Japan

Toshie Iwase, Special Researcher, World Economic Model Group, Economic Planning Agency, Japan

Akira Katayama, Researcher, World Economic Model Group, Economic Planning Agency, Japan

Itsuo Kawamura, Professor, Faculty of Economics, International Christian University, Japan

Lawrence R. Klein, Professor Emeritus, Department of Economics, University of Pennsylvania, USA

Wilhelm Krelle, Professor, Institut für Gesellschaftswirtschafts-Wissenschaften, University of Bonn, Germany

Masahiro Kuroda, Professor, Faculty of Economics, Keio University, Japan

Ikuo Kuroiwa, Economic Cooperation Department, Institute of Developing Economies, Japan

Wassily Leontief, Professor Emeritus, Institute for Economic Analysis, New York University, USA

Fu-chen Lo, Senior Academic Officer, the United Nations University, Japan

Yuangzheng Luo, Professor, the Beijing College of Economics, China

Valery L. Makarov, President, TSEMI, Russian Academy of Sciences, Russia

Akinori Marumo, Professor, Graduate School of International Relations, International University of Japan

Warwick J. McKibbin, Professor, Research School of Pacific Studies, The Australian National University, and Senior Fellow, the Brookings Institution, USA

Masahiro Mimura, Statistical Research Dept., Institute of Developing Economies (IDE), Japan

Chikashi Moriguchi, Professor and Director, Institute of Social and Economic Research, Osaka University, Japan

Atsuo Nakagawa, Researcher, World Economic Model Group, Economic Planning Agency, Japan

Jun Nakano, Assistant Head, World Economic Model Group, Economic Planning Agency, Japan

Nebojša Nakićenović, Project Leader, Environmentally Compatible Energy Strategies, IIASA, Austria

Syed Nawab Haider Naqvi, Professor and Director, the Pakistan Institute of Developing Economics

Koji Nishikimi, Development Studies Department, Institute of Developing Economies (IDE), Japan

Tsuyoshi Okawa, Researcher, World Economic Model Group, Economic Planning Agency, Japan

Akira Onishi, Vice President and Director, Institute for Systems Science, Soka University, Japan

Iwao Ozaki, Professor, Faculty of Economics, Keio University, Japan

Kirit S. Parikh, Director, the Indira Gandhi Institute of Development Research, India

John Piggott, Professor, Department of Economics, University of New South Wales, Australia

H.M. Pitcher, Staff Scientist and Technical Project Leader, SGM, Battelle, Pacific Northwest Laboratories, USA

Kenneth G. Ruffing, Assistant Director, The Projections and Perspective Studies Branch, DIESA, UN

Takao Sano, Councillor, Institute of Developing Economies (IDE), Japan

Masahiko Shimizu, Professor, Faculty of Economics, Keio University, Japan

Shuntaro Shishido, President, International University of Japan

Anatoly Smyshlyaev, Deputy Director, The Projections and Perspective Studies Branch, DIESA, UN

Byung-Nak Song, Professor, Department of Economics, Seoul National University, Korea

Guy V.G. Stevens, Senior Economist, Division of International Finance, Board of Governors of the Federal Reserve System, USA

Chiharu Tamamura, Senior Research Fellow, Statistical Research Department, Institute of Developing Economies (IDE), Japan

Norio Terashima, Researcher, World Economic Model Group, Economic Planning Agency, Japan

Toshihisa Toyoda, Professor, Faculty of Economics, Kobe University, Japan

Jean Waelbroeck, Professor, Free University of Brussels, Belgium

John Whalley, Professor, Department of Economics, Center for the Study of International Economic Relations, University of Western Ontario, Canada

Marshall A. Wise, Research Scientist, Battelle, Pacific Northwest Laboratories, USA

Erno Zalai, Chairman, Dept. of Policy Analysis and Modelling, Budapest University of Economic Science, Hungary